"Joseph Maddrey's book allows us to di
the painful journey, and the triumph of
You will be as lucky to meet Wes in these pages as I was in real life."

- Bruce Joel Rubin
(Screenwriter of *Deadly Friend, Ghost,* and *Jacob's Ladder*)

"The battle over the soul of Wes Craven goes to Joseph Maddrey, no
contest. His comprehensive exploration of Craven's career leaves no
nightmare unturned, offering up a humane portrait of a horror icon."

- Clay McLeod Chapman
(Author of *What Kind of Mother* and *Ghost Eaters*)

"An inspiration for indie filmmakers of every genre."

-Peter Filardi
(Screenwriter of *Flatliners* and *The Craft*)

"Those who think of Wes Craven mainly as the father of Freddy
will undoubtedly be surprised by this compelling portrait of a
complex, rarely satisfied artist, while hardcore Craven fans will
be delighted by new revelations and keen insight."

-Lisa Morton
(Bram Stoker Award-winning author and screenwriter)

"Wes Craven was a filmmaker of golden talents. His trove is sinister, vivid
of wit. Impeccably fraught. He was also charming, effortlessly astute;
observant as a spy. The gifted Joseph Maddrey has brilliantly captured the
magic of a filmic icon in his long overdue *The Soul of Wes Craven*."

- Richard Christian Matheson
(Author of *Created By* and *The Ritual of Illusion*)

Paperback Edition
ISBN-13: 979-8-9890130-2-9
Copyright © 2024 Joseph Maddrey

Cover Art ©2024 Bill Sienkiewicz
Cover Design by Alex Lodermeier

Published by Harker Press
http://HarkerPress.com
Book Design by Dustin McNeill

THE SOUL OF WES CRAVEN

BY JOSEPH MADDREY

EDITED BY
NATALIE TOMASZEWSKI

Wes Craven on the set of *Serpent and the Rainbow*. (Universal, 1987)

TABLE OF CONTENTS

FOREWORD

WITH A LITTLE HELP FROM HIS FRIENDS

"What do you see when you turn out the light?"

- The Beatles
("With a Little Help From My Friends")

On March 12, 2010, I had lunch with Wes Craven—the celebrated (and, in some circles, notorious) director of *Last House on the Left*, *The Hills Have Eyes*, *A Nightmare on Elm Street*, *The People Under the Stairs*, and the *Scream* trilogy—at the Chateau Marmont in Hollywood. A year earlier, I had requested an interview with him for a documentary I was making about the history of American horror films, but a series of delays prevented an on-camera interview and led to a more casual conversation. The 70-year-old filmmaker had just completed *My Soul to Take*, his first film as writer/director in more than a decade, and he was preparing to direct *Scream 4*, an attempt to revitalize his most successful franchise. It was a pivotal moment in Wes's life and career, and he seemed to be in a reflective mood. I seized the opportunity to talk about things other than horror movies. Or maybe it was Wes who steered the conversation.

Right away, he asked why I was interested in his work, which prompted me to do something that most interviewers don't do; I talked about myself. I said I'd grown up in a small town in Virginia, the son of a Methodist minister, and that the first formative event of my life was my mother's near-death when I was eight years old. After that, the specter of death was ever-present but rarely discussed in my family, except in the vaguely reassuring terms of a liberal Protestant church. (There was no fire-and-brimstone talk in my father's church; he was a New Testament guy.) Within a few years, I was looking for answers instead of consolations, and I gravitated toward philosophical literature and horror films. I explained to Wes that, in some ways, his films had comforted me because they didn't pull any punches when it came to acknowledging the reality of violence and death and existential fear.

Once I'd told my story, Wes told me his. He said his father had died when he was five years old and that he'd been raised in his mother's fundamentalist Baptist church. He talked about a childhood yearning for an authentic religious experience that never came, and his teenage discovery of modern literature. I mentioned that I had recently written a book on the modernist poet T.S. Eliot and Wes enthusiastically said he'd studied Eliot in grad school, with a teacher who had profoundly affected his life. Around that same time, Wes said, he became an ambitious writer, utilizing poetry and prose fiction to explore the biggest issues at the heart of his inner life. He wasn't afraid to ask hard questions and he wouldn't settle for easy answers. Because he wasn't allowed to watch movies in high school or college, cinema came later.

Wes's account was a thumbnail sketch of a complex and intense—and ongoing—journey, one that the filmmaker was still navigating. In 2010, he told me his latest film *My Soul to Take* was "in an abstract way" autobiographical. He said the story revolved around a teenager unaware of the details of his ancestry and uncertain of his identity. The screen story reflected Wes's own coming-of-age: the main character in *My Soul to Take* doesn't know much about his father, has been sheltered from the dark truths of the larger world, and has a mostly-inherited sense of self. Of course, because *My Soul to Take* was "a Wes Craven movie," this setup escalated into horrific violence. Wes described the film as "*Stand By Me* with knives."

In October 2010, when *My Soul to Take* finally came out in theaters, I discovered that the narrative hinged on a rather esoteric notion of self-discovery. The main character is one of seven teens, all born on the same night in the same small town, haunted by the same exurban legend. As the protagonist begins his own journey, the other six teens die at the hands of an unseen killer. In interviews, Wes explained that he saw the story as a complex metaphor of a hero's journey, in which the main character must lose as much as he gains before he can come into his own. The metaphor works but the film did not. After nearly four decades as a fan-certified Master of Horror, Wes's most personally revealing film bombed at the box office. Since then, *My Soul to Take* has been perceived as a footnote on his career instead of the culmination of his lifelong cinematic journey.

Prior to the film's release, Wes told me he thought *My Soul to Take* would stand apart from other recent genre films because he was asking hard questions instead of simply stringing together scare scenes. He thought it was a cutting-edge horror film because it dared to be so personal and idiosyncratic. He explained, "You have people like Thelonious Monk, John Coltrane, and Miles Davis, these pioneers who invented a whole new kind of music. In some ways, the younger generation of jazz musicians have better technique, but they're not inventing new music so much as they're playing better versions of what has come before. I think the danger of a young filmmaker who studies tons and tons of movies is that they become technically adept without putting as much of their soul into the movie."

In contrast, Wes had always put his own soul into the films he wrote and directed. Viewed chronologically, those films illustrate his own journey. Things lost. Things learned. Viewed comprehensively, alongside the largely unknown prose and poetry of the filmmaker's early years, the films comprise Wes Craven's spiritual biography.

After years of being characterized as Frightmaster, Professor of Horror, Sultan of Slash, Guru of Gore, Father of Freddy, King of Scream, etc., Wes said, "In Europe, people are much more willing to see the entire person behind the movie. And most American critics don't take horror seriously. It's easier to dismiss horror than to try to understand it."[1] This book is an attempt to see the entire person behind the movies, to understand the man who gave us some of our most enduring cinematic nightmares. Following Wes's untimely death from brain cancer in 2015, I gathered as much of his written work as I could find. I also interviewed over a hundred people who knew him at different times in his life. All of them played a significant role in Wes Craven's self-realization. And, much as they supported Wes in life, they have supported me in trying to bring his story into greater focus.

I could not have done this without the help of those friends, family members, colleagues and collaborators who spoke to me. I gratefully acknowledge them here: John G. Abbott, Alexandre Aja, Adam Alleca, Lee Aronsohn, David Arquette, Janis Balmer Avery, Cathlin Baker, Matthew Barr, Thomas Baum, Glenn Benest, Rowland V. Bennett, Bromley Bilton, Doris Bilton, Ted Bilton, Mary Blocksma (my editorial guru—*thank you, Mary!*), Giles Blunt, Dorothy Booth, Sara Bottfeld, Michael Bray, Carole Craven Buhrow, Michael C. Burton, David Cameron, Karen Marlowe Campbell, Bonnie Broecker Chapin, Steve Chapin, Bev Cherulnik, Doug Child, Douglas Claybourne, Donna Craven, Jessica Craven, Jonathan Craven, Mimi Meyer Craven, Judi Chaffee Culbertson, Sean S. Cunningham, William Darfler, Sarah Denby, Christine Polley Dickey, Gretchen Dutschke-Klotz, Andrea Eastman, Carl Ellsworth, Robert Englund, Rob Everett, Bill Eville, J.D. Feigelson, Carly Feingold, Jeffrey Fenner, Roy Frumkes, David S. Garnett, James Gilbert, Kathryn Randall Gilbert, Shep Gordon, Mark Haslett, Dick Helfrich, Frank "Fritz" Hemrich, Lance Henriksen, Richard Hine, Tom Holland, Jim Hopper, Paul Howard, John A. Huffman Jr., Max A. Keller, Delious "Tim" Kennedy, Cornelia Kiss, Jeannine Pittman Kott,

Introduction

William Kotzwinkle, Dylan Kuhn, Iya Labunka, David Ladd, Charlie Landino, Heather Langenkamp, Elliott Larson, Marty Bihlmeier Larson, John R. Leax, William E. Lindberg, Greg Livingstone, Peter Locke, Patrick Lussier, Kenneth Lyon, Jon Mack, Dan Maddalena, Marianne Maddalena, Donald Martin, Nicholas Mastandrea, Jon G. McGill, Tom McLoughlin, Chuck Minskoff, Nina Okerwall Morrison, Steve Niles, Sue Oestreich, Timothy O'Neill, Don Peake, Richard Potter, Lynne Buri Potts, Louise Burton Proteo, Tristine Rainer, David Reich, Stanley Rowin, Bruce Joel Rubin, Joe Ruddy, Clarice Rybicki, Ned Sadar, Paul Schneider, Bill Schopf, Judson Scruton, Corinne Sebrasky, Christopher Shinkman, Nick Simon, Jack Smith, David Snodgrass, Nancy Bryant Starr, Katherine Hobbie Storms, Harry Strachan, Madeline Sunshine, Nina Tarnawsky, Alix Taylor, Maryann Thompson, Michael E. Uslan, Calvin A. Veltman, Bruce Wagner, Jeanne Murray Walker, Ron Watson, David Werle, Janyth Williams, William C. Wood, and Cody Zwieg.

I am also grateful for the research assistance of Andrew Ade, Westminster College; Linda J. Alexander; Emily Banas, Wheaton Archives & Special Collections; William C. Barrow, Michael Schwartz Library, Cleveland State University; Renee Boronka, Cleveland Museum of Natural History; Jennifer Boyer, Montpelier Historical Society; Keith Call, Buswell Library, Wheaton College; Paul Carnahan, Montpelier Historical Society; Michael F. Cavotta, Collinwood Alumni Association; Suzanne Desrocher-Romero; Elijah Drenner; George Edson, Montpelier Historical Society; Robert Epstein, Fairfield University; Tim Ferrante; Rob Freese; Rob Galluzzo; Daniel Griffith, Ballyhoo Films; Jessica Guardado, William H. Hannon Library, Loyola Marymount University; Brian R. Hauser, Bucknell University; Louise Hilton, Margaret Herrick Library, Academy of Motion Picture Arts and Sciences; Tom Knost, Collinwood Alumni Association; Alex Lodermeier; Loryl MacDonald, Thomas Fisher Rare Book Library, University of Toronto; Genevieve Maxwell, Margaret Herrick Library, Academy of Motion Picture Arts and Sciences; Susan McCauley; Brian McQuery; Cristina Meisner, Harry Ransom Center, University of Texas at Austin; Luke Meyer, SeeThink Films; Mary E. Miller, New Tech Collinwood High School; Steven Morowitz; John Kenneth Muir; Kim Newman; James A. Perkins, Westminster College; Herbert Ragan, National Archives and Records Administration / William J. Clinton Presidential Library; Natalya

Rattan, Thomas Fisher Rare Book Library, University of Toronto; Alayna Rosenbaum; Benjamin Rubin, Hillman Library, University of Pittsburgh; Oren Shai; Amy B. Siskind; Amy Soden, Wheaton College; James Stimpert, Sheridan Libraries, Johns Hopkins University; Ashley West, The Rialto Report; Audrey Whitlock, Gordon-Conwell Theological Seminary; Morgan Yates; and Frank Zalar, Collinwood Alumni Association.

Finally, I acknowledge those fellow journalists, authors, and filmmakers whose interviews with Wes served as foundational research. They include Steve Biodrowski of *Cinefantastique, Fangoria,* and *Fear* magazines; Daniel Farrands and Andrew Kasch, directors of the documentary film *Never Sleep Again: The Elm Street Legacy*; Dennis Fischer of *Cinefantastique* and *Monsterland* magazines; Lawrence French of *Cinefantastique*; Lee Goldberg of *Fangoria*; Thommy Hutson, author of *Never Sleep Again: The Elm Street Legacy*; Alan Jones of *Shivers* and *Starburst* magazines; R.H. "Bob" Martin of *Fangoria*; Brian J. Robb, author of *Screams & Nightmares: The Films of Wes Craven;* Marc Shapiro of *Fangoria*; Ian Spelling of *Fangoria*; David A. Szulkin, author of *Wes Craven's Last House on the Left: The Making of a Cult Classic*; Stanley Wiater, author of *Dark Visions: Conversations with the Masters of the Horror Film*; and John Wooley, author of *Wes Craven: The Man and His Nightmares*. I am also grateful to Rachel Belofsky, whose work on a forthcoming documentary film about Wes has been inspiring

Apologies—and thanks—to anyone I may have neglected to mention here.

CHAPTER ONE

CRAVEN'S RAVIN'S
(1939 - 1958)

Ours is a world of words: Quiet we call
"Silence"—which is the merest word of all.
All Nature speaks, and ev'n ideal things
Flap shadowy sounds from visionary wings

– Edgar Allan Poe, "Al Aaraaf"

If this was a Wes Craven movie, it might start with a scene of a black bird flying out of a stormy gray sky and spiraling down toward a drab-looking American city of industry. At the bottom of the screen, "Cleveland, Ohio. 1939."

While I'm at it, let's set the moving image of that black bird, turning and turning in the widening gyre, to the tune of Béla Bartók's "Romanian Folk Dances," Suite 56, Part 3. I think Wes would have liked that. A simple, elegant beginning. Pure cinema.

But this is reality we're talking about.

Isn't it?

The historical facts are straightforward. Wesley Earl Craven was born in Cleveland on August 2, 1939. He was the youngest of three children—and perhaps an unexpected challenge for middle-aged parents Paul Eugene Craven, a factory worker, and Caroline Miller, a housewife. The couple had married in 1927 and welcomed their first son, Paul Jr. ("Jim" to family and friends), into the world just eight months before the start of the Great Depression. Five years later, they had a daughter, Carole. The family of four endured the hardships of the 1930s, but Paul and Caroline's marriage would not outlast the Second World War. According to relatives, the husband and father abandoned his family to live with another woman, although he and Caroline never formally divorced. A few months after V-Day, on July 31, 1945, 40-year-old Paul Craven Sr. collapsed suddenly at work due to a probable coronary thrombosis. He was buried on his younger son's sixth birthday, leaving Wes to grow up in the dark shadow of a father he barely knew.

That's one beginning. Here's another:

Wes's astrological birth chart shows the planet Saturn—father of Jupiter, the Roman sky god—squaring Pluto, the god of death and the underworld, and residing in the fourth house of the horoscope wheel. Astrologers and Jungians would interpret this as portending a turbulent childhood and a lifetime of intense conflict and deep exploration. But we don't need an astrological chart to tell us that.

At the moment of Wes Craven's birth, the civilized world was undergoing a violent transformation. On September 1, 1939, Germany invaded Poland. Two days later, France and England declared war on the Nazis. Two years later, the United States entered the global conflict between Allied Forces and Axis Powers, with the future of human civilization hanging in the balance. For Clevelanders, the war meant careful rationing, food shortages, and an influx of skilled and unskilled laborers into the city, which became a major munitions production hub. As an adult, Wes reflected on the events of that particular time and place as his emotional foundation, saying, "The first five years of my life had that tonality of World War II going on, and me realizing dimly as a child that the world was trying to kill itself."[1]

Wes vaguely remembered his father as "a frightening, big man, and angry," associating him mainly with loud arguments around the house.[2] On at least one occasion, Wes incurred his father's wrath for something that seemed, to the child, insignificant. He never forgot it. According to family lore, Paul Sr. had urged his wife to get an abortion at some point. Did he tell his family that he didn't want a third child? Could that be why his father always seemed so angry around him? Paul Sr. was gone before Wes could ask, leaving the boy to wonder if his father had loved him, what he was really like, and what happened when a person died.

It was not the boy's first encounter with sudden death. In a 2006 interview, Wes described a scene he'd witnessed one year prior: "The man next door [was] raking leaves on our front lawn. He fell over and died."[3] What must the five-year-old have thought when he learned that his father had suffered the same fate; that he had been stricken down and permanently silenced by an invisible, godlike force? Later, Wes said he and his brother dreaded their fortieth birthdays because they were afraid they'd die the same way. Wes might have felt like he was living in a fatalistic story about a family curse, something by Edgar Allan Poe or Nathaniel Hawthorne.

The future filmmaker also encountered death on the movie screen at the Telenews Theatre in Cleveland. He recalled footage of European "cities in flames, suicide bombers diving down smokestacks of exploding battleships, civilians weeping or fleeing."[4] These visions made a lasting impression on his tender mind: "Grownups can be very, very scary."[5]

Paul Eugene Craven and Caroline Miller Craven, 1932
(courtesy Donna Craven)

The Cravens: Paul Jr., Caroline, Carole and Wes, 1945
(courtesy Donna Craven)

When the war was over, American soldiers returned home with horror stories. Wes's maternal uncle Donald, who had served in the Navy from October 1943 to April 1946, described a landing barge attack, "bodies flying everywhere."[6] After that, Wes had recurring nightmares of war. In one, he saw a group of young men—including his older brother—leaving home for war, looking terrified. In the dream, he couldn't understand why they would submit themselves to such a horrible experience.[7]

Mercifully, not all of Wes Craven's childhood was so bleak. For the first eight or nine years of his life, he resided comfortably with his single mother and two older siblings in a three-story side-by-side on East 82nd Street in Cleveland's working-class Hough Avenue neighborhood. It was a friendly community of densely-packed houses with a lot of kids, where families supported each other and collectively rallied around the national war effort. The hub was the Hough Avenue Baptist Church, a few blocks north of the Craven family home. There, Wes's mother Caroline met her closest friend, Dorothy Bilton.

The Bilton family lived near the intersection of 77th Street and Superior, a few blocks west of the church. In some ways, they mirrored the Craven family. Like Paul and Caroline, Edward and Dorothy Bilton had three children. The oldest, Ted, was roughly the same age as Paul Jr., while the middle child Doris was the same age as Carole Craven. Ted recalls that in late 1938, the Cravens showed up at Hough Avenue Baptist and the two mothers bonded over the news that they were both pregnant. "Both of them were later in life," Ted explains, "so it was a rather ironic coincidence." Bromley Bilton was born on July 28th, five days before Wes. The two boys seemed destined to be friends.

A newly single mother, Caroline Craven had to find full-time work to support her family. She took a secretarial job with Baptist Mid-Missions, a global outreach project based in downtown Cleveland, and her friend Dorothy agreed to watch young Wes during the day. Doris Bilton, a teenager at the time, remembers seeing Bromley and Wes romp around the house and yard, discovering baseball, making trouble, and behaving like all-American boys. In those formative early days at the Bilton house, Wes also developed an interest in cinema, as he explained in a 1999 interview: "One of Eddie Bilton's big hobbies was 8mm photography. And also he would rent a movie from the local camera shop, which was the custom in those days, and I was completely enthralled by film."[8]

Bromley Bilton and Wes Craven, c. 1945
(courtesy Donna Craven)

Bromley Bilton recalls, "My dad would rent 8mm Mickey Mouse / Donald Duck types of cartoons. We would set up a screen in our driveway and my dad would bring out the projector and the neighbors would come and watch the films. It was kind of a drive-in movie type environment. We didn't think of it that way at the time, but that's kind of what it was. And it was a good ol' time." Ted Bilton adds, "Every time the family got together, Wes was waiting, kind of leaning over Dad's shoulder as he was running the projector. I wasn't particularly interested in film, even though I did get my own camera to take pictures. Wes was more interested than anybody in our family, so Dad ate that up."

Ironically, the church that brought the Bilton and Craven families together forbade its parishioners to watch movies, with the exception of mild Disney fare. The leadership of the Hough Avenue Baptist Church was committed to the principles of the General Association of Regular Baptists, established in 1932 as a bulwark against the perceived liberalism of mainstream Protestant churches in America. The GARBC Articles of Faith prescribed a belief in Biblical inerrancy and declared the 66-book Protestant canon the literal Word of God, while the GARBC Constitution asserted the organization's commitment to evangelism, missionary work, and "Biblical separation from worldliness, modernism and apostasy." For the people of Hough Avenue, "separation from worldliness" meant no drinking, no smoking, no dancing, no card-playing, and (almost) no movie-watching.

Wes Craven grew up in this forbidding atmosphere of strict fundamentalism. He remembered, "Our lives were very much circumscribed by the church. Our religion was very strict. The Bible was (I can still slip into their language) the holy creative word of God, was wholly inspired, and should be taken word for word. They took everything very literally according to their interpretation, believing in the six-day creation and in the five cardinal 'no, nos.'"[9] He also noted that the church regarded Hollywood films as the literal work of the devil.[10]

Bromley Bilton has similar memories of church rules, although he expresses mild amusement about where the lines of judgment were drawn: "We were not allowed to go to movies or dances. Cards were verboten. Couldn't do that. No gambling. But we had so many other things going on that I didn't know I was missing anything. The crazy thing, looking back, is that we were allowed to go roller skating. The church held a couple of [skating events]. They turned the lights down, had the crystal ball spinning around in the center of the room. It never dawned on me that that was an awful lot like dancing."

Despite the ban on dancing, the church maintained a strong music ministry. Ted Bilton remembers that summer services were held outside, so the church choir could be heard blocks away. "We didn't call it a concert," he stipulates. "It was a preaching service. Trolley buses would go by or people would walk by and hear a full-blown church service." Although Wes expressed an early interest in music and took classical guitar lessons at a music shop in Cleveland, he did not participate in the church's music ministry. He did, however, become an active member of the church's youth group. Older parishioners reportedly liked him because he was always making jokes. For a time, he was welcomed and felt supported by the religious community, and came to regard the church as his "second family."[11]

Dick Helfrich, a member of the youth group, recalls that Wes's mother and his mother—both members of Child Evangelism Fellowship—were very close, but that he and Wes didn't have much in common. "Our families got together for church picnics from time to time, and I was at the age where all I wanted to do was find the closest ballfield near the picnic area. But Wes never seemed to be much interested in that. He was more interested in wandering around in the woods and finding stuff."

Wes had become a nature lover—and particularly, a bird watcher—at a young age. His maternal grandfather gave him his first pair of birding binoculars, and Wes and his mother would sit in the backyard to "watch the purple martins and, in the evening, nighthawks come diving out of the sky with a screech and a swoop by, with an audible sound of wind through wings."[12] Cleveland was once known as "The Forest City," built around a pristine wilderness at the mouth of the Cuyahoga River. During the war years, however, the natural resources began to disappear. In his 1950 guide *Birds of the Cleveland Region*, Arthur B. Williams claimed that many of the region's native birds—including the Northern Raven— had already fled the industrialized city.

A few local organizations were fighting to preserve the city's natural beauty. In 1940, the Cleveland Museum of Natural History became home to The Kirtland Bird Club, which conducted springtime "Bird Walks" and annual "Christmas Bird Counts." One of Wes's early classmates remembers that elementary schoolchildren in Cleveland were bused to the Museum of Natural History in Wade Park on field trips. The Cravens lived relatively close to the museum and Wes might have gone on one such field trip, or might have explored the park on his own. Whatever the case, he forged strong emotional memories of the tree-lined neighborhoods and "wonderful parks" in his native city, and fondly remembered the environment of nearby Lake Erie. He told one interviewer that he grew up with an abiding "sense of water and a sense of trees," which later inspired a "sense of arboreal mystery and the subconsciousness of water" in his films (most notably, *Shocker* and *My Soul to Take*).[13]

Unfortunately, by the time he entered Addison Junior High School, Lake Erie had become too polluted and Wade Park too dangerous to explore. Natural beauty and arboreal mystery gave way to urban blight and haunted symbols of the inevitability of death and decay. Wes's experience during this time was not unlike that of T.S. Eliot, who grew up in a transitional neighborhood in St. Louis during the 1890s. Eliot utilized the bleak imagery of his childhood home—industrial smoke and fog; half-deserted streets; and poor, elderly women gathering firewood from vacant lots—in his earliest poetry. Eliot also drew inspiration from early memories of water, especially the Mississippi River in springtime and the New England coastline in summer. When the time came, Wes would do the same.

Wes attended Wade Park Elementary and Addison Junior High until 1948 when his family moved east to suburban Collinwood, where he briefly attended Nottingham School. Reflecting on his childhood neighborhoods, he said, "There was violence in the street a lot of the time, and most of the schools I went to were quite violent and confrontational."[14] Sudden demographic changes and subsequent race-related tensions in Cleveland might have been a factor in the family move from downtown Cleveland to Collinwood; the Hough neighborhood was predominantly white before the war but became mostly black in the decade and a half that followed. Wes witnessed a mass migration of ethnically-diverse immigrants into the city, leading to racial strife. One family member recalls, "When he was a kid, there were race riots in Cleveland. He told me about being in recess at school one day and this girl lifted up her skirt to show the other kids a huge knife she was planning to take downtown with her, to participate in race riots." Bromley Bilton notes that the infamous Hough Riots also took place in the blocks between his and Wes's childhood homes, in summer of 1966. In hindsight, Wes decried the "milieu of hatred and prejudice in the world I grew up in."[15]

Between 1948 and 1958, the Craven family moved several times throughout the greater Cleveland area. Wes recalled they were constantly "getting booted out by landlords who needed apartments for their children who were getting married."[16] As a result, he was constantly meeting new kids in new neighborhoods, and learning to adapt to different ways of thinking and behaving. "I think that's part of the reason why I became my own storyteller and learned how to think in extreme cases."[17]

In junior high, Wes was bullied by a kid named Freddy. Both boys had jobs delivering newspapers and they used to pick up their papers on the same street corner. The tense daily encounters gave Wes nightmares, including one in which the bully kicked a flattened tin can at him, which severed his Achilles tendon.[18] As an adult, he would incorporate both the bully and the wound into his films *A Nightmare on Elm Street* and *The Hills Have Eyes*.

Cleveland city records show that in 1951, Caroline Craven was employed as a secretary for the Christian Business Men's Committee and living with her children in an apartment building on East 176th Street in North Collinwood. Soon after, the four-suite apartment building was demolished to make way for Interstate 90 and the Cravens returned to the Hough neighborhood, where they briefly resided in an apartment on East 86th Street. There, Wes had an encounter that would inspire his most famous cinematic creation.

In interviews over the years, he remembered being awakened late one night by strange sounds—drunken muttering, stuttering footsteps, and "a scraping, rustling noise"—coming from somewhere outside his second-story bedroom window.[19] Curious, Wes got out of bed and went to the window to investigate. He looked down and saw an older man ambling down the sidewalk in front of the apartment building, with a distinctive "scraping step." The man wore a ragged overcoat, a "weird striped sweater," an old-fashioned felt hat, and dark boots.[20] He figured the guy must be a drunk.

Wes continued to watch as the man abruptly stopped walking and slowly tilted his gaze up toward the second-story window. The boy figured he was safely hidden in the darkness of his bedroom, but then the man sneered at him. Decades later, Wes remembered the feeling that there was something uncanny, perhaps even supernatural, about this stranger's awareness of him— almost as if "he somehow knew me."[21]

Instinctively, he backed away from the window and sat on the edge of his bed, stunned. He knew he couldn't be seen, but now he also couldn't see what the man was doing and he knew he would never be able to get back to sleep until he was certain the stranger was gone. He counted to a thousand, then cautiously returned to the window. The man wasn't standing where he had been standing before. Now he was standing directly below the window, still staring up. According to Wes, the man "thrust his head forward with a triumphant grin and an insane leer," taking obvious joy in the act of frightening a child.[22] Paralyzed, Wes watched as the man then shuffled toward the front of the apartment building, glancing back over his shoulder to promise he wasn't done yet. As the man disappeared around the corner, Wes regained control of his body—and raced to the entrance of his family's apartment.

There, he pressed his ear against the outer door and listened. He heard the front door of the apartment building swing open on creaky hinges, then heard the man "scrape into the foyer."[23] At that point, Wes ran to wake up his older brother, Paul, who promptly armed himself with a baseball bat and went out to confront the sadistic stranger. When he returned, Paul said no one was there—but the stranger continued to haunt Wes Craven, who eventually transformed the nightmare man into Freddy Krueger. "The essence of that man was that he enjoyed terrifying a child and enjoyed destroying the comfort of innocence. So that became Freddy."[24]

One of Wes's fellow horror writers has compared the experience of being a child with an overactive imagination to driving a powerful automobile before one has learned to steer. Exhilarating, perhaps, but also terrifying— because children cannot control their fears the way adults can. They live at the mercy of their imaginations. Those who can imagine the worst must learn to cope with the worst.

Every day after school, Wes found himself alone in a drab apartment in a somewhat dangerous neighborhood, with only his imagination for company. He later told a college friend that he was one of the first latchkey kids, and that he developed a ritualistic after-school routine to cope with being alone. When he arrived home, he would look under all the beds and check all the closets in the apartment, to make sure no one was hiding there, waiting to get him.

In 1953, Paul Craven Jr. stoked his brother's fears by taking him to a movie theater to see a forbidden sci-fi/horror film: George Pal's lavish adaptation of H.G. Wells's novel *The War of the Worlds*. The story, about a coordinated Martian invasion of Earth, haunted 14-year-old Wes. Fifty years later, he said he still vividly recalled the film's "goose-necked-lamp" aliens and the eerie sounds they made.[25] This might have been Wes Craven's first time watching a scary movie, although he also mentioned having seen the 1948 B-movie *The Creeper,* about a neurotic young woman haunted by dreams of a serial killer who slashes his victims with a mutant cat paw.[26] These cinematic experiences did not prompt Wes to seek out more scary movies, but they might have nudged him toward the work of authors like Edgar Allan Poe.

Wes became a bookworm during his teenage years, noting that he was "very fortunate to have a mother who took me to the library all the time."[27] Around the age of fourteen, he got a job as a page at the Cleveland Public Library's Main Branch, and subsequently read "everything" Poe ever wrote.[28] He also imbibed the library's collection of books about World War II, scuba diving, and UFOs, then developed a passion for the picaresque novels of Charles Dickens, the existential novels of Fyodor Dostoevsky (he cited *Crime and Punishment* as a major influence), and other 19th century classics, including Emily Brontë's supernatural romance *Wuthering Heights*.[29] These works, Wes said, transformed him into the "quirky kid who read books all the time, painted, wrote poetry."[30]

Early exposure to the Western Canon also made him an increasingly independent thinker. Bromley Bilton says he continued to spend time with Wes at bi-weekly church functions but gradually realized that they lived in completely different worlds. "When I moved out to Willoughby and he went to Collinwood, we kind of separated. He read a lot more than I did, I know that, but I don't know that we ever talked about that. Because, again, we only came together for church.

We double-dated a couple of times, but he did his thing at Collinwood High and I did my thing out in Willoughby."

By then, the congregation of the Hough Avenue Baptist Church had also fractured, following an unexplained sanctuary fire in the spring of 1953. Rumor says the fire began because workers were repairing a pipe organ and one of them left a cigarette burning there on Saturday evening. Whatever the cause, only the outer walls remained standing on Sunday morning. The Craven family remained loyal to the parish as it constructed a new sanctuary in suburban Cleveland Heights, near Collinwood. The relocation of the church was no doubt a factor in Caroline Craven's decision to move her children back to Collinwood in 1954.

The church remained an abiding influence on Wes, for good and ill. As an adult, he remembered how his religious upbringing had prompted him to focus his thoughts and energy on things other than the material reality of the everyday world—providing a foundation for his career as a serious storyteller.[31] Unfortunately, he also felt compelled to renounce his early love of the beauty in nature. In 2010, he explained, "There was a song we were taught to sing as children: *'This world is not my home; I'm just passing through. My treasures are laid up somewhere beyond the blue.'* And in sermons and everything else, [the message was] that everything that was not part of the church's belief was 'the world.' And that *you* were not part of 'the world'... which is a great way to drive somebody totally insane." The 1919 hymn continues: *"The angels beckon me from heaven's open door, and I can't feel at home in this world anymore."*

As he got older, Wes couldn't feel at home in the world or in the church. From an early age, he had been indoctrinated into a rigid set of religious beliefs, and his mother's association with Child Evangelism Fellowship—a group whose stated purpose was to evangelize boys and girls with the Gospel of the Lord Jesus Christ—was a strong inducement for him to proselytize. For years, he struggled to do so. He later told friends that he had routinely carried a red Bible with him to school; when people would ask him about it, he was supposed to explain that the book was red because "the Bible is meant to be read." Often, his face also turned red.

During his years at Collinwood High School, he was surrounded by Catholics. The Collinwood neighborhood had a large population of Italian immigrants, so there was nothing odd or uncommon about being devoutly religious in that environment. What *was* odd and uncommon—or so it seemed to Wes—was his own lack of heartfelt belief. In 2010, he told author John Wooley that he had begun to feel guilty because he didn't really believe in the dogmas he'd been taught. He said he struggled to evangelize because he'd never had a personal experience of being "saved" or "born again"—no moment of mystical intuition, or being filled with the Holy Spirit. As a result, he felt that he was cursed with "an irredeemable soul." At church revivals, "The pastor would say, 'I know there's somebody here [...] who still hasn't either truly, really given his or her soul to Christ, or has backslidden and needs to rededicate his or her life to Christ.' I can remember resisting that for years and years and years, and finally going forward, just feeling like my spirit was broken, like I had to do this. And still not feeling it."[32]

In a separate interview with me, he added, "I was totally guilt-ridden, because they said 'If you don't witness, you'll go to hell and it'll be on your ledger.' Once or twice a year, they would bring in preachers from the outside who were revivalists. That was a big thing with the Baptist church. With this general sense that the whole church has fallen asleep and is not doing what it should be doing, they'll bring in this person who'll wake you up and put you on fire again. And they would always talk about people who have gone through the motions of having given their heart to Jesus, but they haven't really. And [they said] if you do that, you're committing a sin against the Holy Spirit, and that's the one unforgivable sin. Of course, I immediately assumed I'd done the unforgivable. So now I'm really going to hell."

Wes stated that his "failure" to find Jesus led to "a very dark view of myself."[33] Throughout his high school years, he struggled to reconcile his coming-of-age with the teachings of the church. In a 2002 interview with fellow Wheaton alum Ron Watson, he said, "When I came into puberty and the issue of masturbation would come up, I would try to imagine Jesus on the cross when I started to feel like jerking off; and inevitably Jesus would do like a mutation into a woman with her arms open. And try as I might, that image would suddenly take over. So long Jesus, hello Molly, whoever she was. That sort of struggle to keep the wolves of the body at bay became an issue as soon as I became sexual. It could be a nightmare, because I was constantly feeling that I was the only one doing that sort of thing and that was proof that I was not a Christian."

In the same interview, he elaborated, "In one of the houses [where] we lived, I had the horrible misfortune of finding two things somebody had left in the attic. One was an encyclopedia from the early 20s on gynecological malfunctions and the other was—I have since learned—one of the classic anti-sexual books. One of the things it talked about was masturbation. It never used that term; it was called 'self-pollution.' It had a chapter on how it could cause blindness. Here's a kid who doesn't know diddle-squat about sex, has just started masturbating and wonders whether it's alright and he finds this book and it says you're going to go blind. I remember this text as if it were yesterday: 'You can tell them at school because they tend to be falling asleep at odd moments and can't concentrate on their studies.' Well, that was me. I was convinced that I was the only one doing it and that I was going to go blind and go insane."[34] One of Wes's family members recalls that Wes said his mother amplified the problem by frequently interrogating a closed bathroom door: "Wesley, are you doing something *evil* in there? Are you doing the *devil's work* in there?"

Fearful that he was in fact evil or insane, Wes sought an emotional outlet. In a 1980 interview with NPR's Terry Gross, he remembered an experience he had in a train switching yard, behind his house on Clarkstone Road. There, he tried to exorcise his personal demons by hunting rats with a mail-order bow-and-arrow set. For a year, he couldn't hit a moving target. Then, one day: "This little tiny animal let out this enormous scream that echoed over all the box cars in the stock yard, and chilled me to the bone. I realized that what I had been thinking and fantasizing was totally different from what I had actually done." It dawned on him that the creature was still alive and suffering from a wound he had inflicted, so now he had to put the rat out of its misery. That was an even more horrifying—and guilt-inducing—experience. "When it was done, I was totally drained. I was totally shocked—not only by what I had done for amusement, but how fiercely that thing struggled to stay alive. That moment never left me."[35]

Luckily, he found a healthier emotional outlet at Collinwood High. In February 1956, the name Wesley Craven appeared for the first time in the school newspaper, *The Collinwood Spotlight*. He was credited as a staff writer. Two months later, on a Friday the 13th, his by-line appeared on a short article titled "Watch Those Black Cats!!" A pithy history of superstition, it was an appropriate debut for a future horror filmmaker.

The young journalist's wit was on display again in the fall of '56, in an article about the Press Club's field trip to the physics lab at nearby Western Reserve University, where he had a shocking encounter with a Van de Graaff Generator. Wes explained, "If you are insulated from the ground and put your hand on the generator, your hair will stand on end. If you're not insulated from the ground, you disappear in a very tricky little puff of smoke." The article was accompanied by a photo of the reporter's "hair-raising experience" as poof—I mean, *proof*—of his daring.[36] (According to his friends, Wes could never resist a play on words and, apparently, neither can I.)

In early 1957, as he entered his senior year, Wes became the front-page editor of *The Spotlight* and launched a column entitled "Craven's Ravin's." The title acknowledged his love of birds (and perhaps Edgar Allan Poe?) as well as his self-deprecating sense of humor. The masthead on the column featured an illustration—presumably drawn by the author himself—of an anthropomorphized raven punting a C-shaped worm into the title block. The text was equally playful and predatory.

COLLINWOOD HIGH SCHOOL, CLEVELAND, OHIO

Years later, Wes said that coming of age as the youngest child in a "broken family" was probably what turned him into a writer: "I heard all the family stories and was sort of an observer, and the witness becomes the writer quite often."[37] Not coincidentally, the first ravin' facetiously maligned "some of the more outstanding people" in the columnist's (fictional) family tree.

Wes Craven, *The Collinwood Spotlight*, October 1956

Combining droll humor with a dash of horror, Wes described a 12-year-old cousin named Greenly, who suffered from a craving for wood. When the boy gobbled up the floor of a second-story bedroom closet, his mother accidentally fell to her death. (Oh, Dr. Freud, what big ears you have!) After that, Greenly ate his family out of house and home—"and garage."[38]

In subsequent installments of "Craven's Ravin's," Wes continued to write about "regrettably still-living relatives," including an Uncle Harold, who mysteriously disappeared as a result of his "time-killing hobby" of leaning out of windows; Great Grandfather Sandburg, who collected garbage and hate-mailed it to communist Russia; Grandma Snerdly, who helped Boy Scouts cross the road and donated concrete cookies to Girl Scouts; cousin Wolfgang, who had ten thumbs and was constantly being mistaken for an enthusiastic hitchhiker; and great-grandfather Henry Codahander, who invented the water faucet. Some Craven family members have suggested that Wes could have taken inspiration from real-life relatives, including a grandmother who made famously inedible cookies. Occasionally, the columnist's pets even warranted mention. In one installment, a sensitive oyster named Herman "fell madly and hopelessly in love with a castanet and died of complete physical exhaustion while trying to clap back at it."[39]

In another column, interspersed with the facetious family history, Wes presented an equally wry list of childhood fears. He declared his fear of drowning and delivered a grim public service announcement about the dangers of taking baths. He wrote, "On Saturday nights before I go out, I always scrape myself with a butter knife. It's just as effective and much safer (as long as you remember to use a dull butter knife)."[40] For overcoming a fear of rats, he advised, "Wear heavy leather gloves, carry a baseball bat or loaded revolver, keep your throat covered and memorize the telephone number of a doctor who can administer anti-rabies shots."[41] In one of the most imaginative installments of "Craven's Ravin's," the author ranted about a rare species called "doofuddies" that lived under the stage of the Collinwood High School auditorium. An early incarnation of *The People Under the Stairs*?

One likely source of inspiration for these darkly humorous exploits was Al Feldstein's *MAD* magazine, which Wes referenced in the sixth installment of his "ravin's." He also cited Roald Dahl's short story collection *Kiss Kiss* as a personal favorite. "Craven's Ravin's" was, like Dahl's stories and Wes himself, intelligently absurd, mordantly funny, and occasionally sad.

During his final semester of high school, Wes was chief editor of the *Spotlight* and an active member of his school's Radio English class, the Boosters club, the Junior Council on World Affairs, the Classbook Committee, and the Announcer's Club. Frank Hemrich, a fellow classmate in the Announcer's Club, remembers that he and Wes read the weekly news over the school's PA system. "He was very clear in his speech. He didn't mumble. If you missed what he said, it was your fault. His diction was very clear." Wes also served as an announcer in the Cedar Hill Baptist Church's radio ministry and, according to one family member, briefly contemplated pursuing a career in broadcasting.

The prospective broadcasting career might have been inspired by Ilona Sadar, a classmate who was voted "best vocalist" in the school's 1958 yearbook. According to her younger brother Ned, Ilona frequently sang at weddings and funerals; one year she sang the jazz standard "St. Louis Blues" at the public auditorium in Cleveland. Her siren song drew Wes Craven into a household and a family that became very important to him. Ned remembers, "When he and my sister were dating, it was common for them to spend time with me and my parents. We would always sit around the table, talking. My parents didn't lecture us; we just talked about what was happening to friends, what was happening with relatives, what was happening in the news. It was kind of a *Leave It to Beaver* family. We talked a lot about the virtues of saving and the importance of education. There was a lot of talk about self-reliance. My parents were very open to talking about anything, and Wes was always an active participant in the conversation." Being the youngest member of his family, and more of a silent observer than a participant, Wes was grateful to be treated as an adult.

Ned Sadar continues, "My other memories of Wes revolve around two things. Number one, we would occasionally sit around and play the guitar together. I was self-taught and I believe Wes was as well. Number two, we were both archery bow enthusiasts, so we would go out and do some shooting together. My mother's great aunt had some property out east of Cleveland and we'd go out there and shoot at nothing, or go out and try to find squirrels or rabbits." Unfortunately, Wes's mother interfered. In a 2002 interview, Wes recalled that he broke up with Ilona because his mother didn't want him to date a Catholic: "She was unacceptable because she worshipped idols."[42] But even after the breakup, according to Ned, Wes would still come around and spend time with the Sadar family on Friday and Saturday nights.

Outside of his home, Wes remained vocal. In December 1957, he emceed a dinner dance for his graduating class, during which he received a trophy in creative writing and an honor certificate in journalism. In the January '58 yearbook, Wes's peers prophesied that his head-in-the-clouds style of storytelling would earn him a bright future career as the "man in the moon." At that time, Wes planned to attend college for two years, before becoming a Naval Air Cadet and taking to the skies. His first "big dream" was to learn how to fly a plane. Above-average scores on the Ohio State Intelligence aptitude test and high placement in a national Merit Scholarship competition gained him admission to prestigious Wheaton College, an evangelical Christian school west of Chicago.[43]

Despite Wes's obvious literary talent, attending college was not a foregone conclusion. No one in his family had pursued a higher education degree—his mother came from a family of Ohio coal miners and his father from granite manufacturers and quarry workers in Vermont—but Carole Craven's boyfriend (and future husband) had attended Wheaton and recommended it as a "good Christian school."[44] Even so, Wes almost didn't apply to Wheaton—because his mother worried that Wheaton might be "too liberal."[45]

Wheaton College historian Paul M. Bechtel writes that in 1957—the year Wes applied for admission—the school required applicants to take the Scholastic Aptitude Test (SAT). Allegedly, the incoming freshman class of 1957 was the only group of students admitted to Wheaton *solely* on the basis of SAT scores. The institution's focus on academic performance worried some that Wheaton's professors were prioritizing intellectual rigor over a lifelong commitment to Christ.

Once Wes was accepted by Wheaton, however, Caroline took out a government loan to pay for his tuition. According to one family member, it took decades to repay it. Even when Wes became a famous Hollywood filmmaker, she refused to let him help. Whatever Caroline's misgivings about Wheaton College, she made a lifelong commitment—as a single, working parent—to her son's education. Reluctantly but resolutely, she sent him out into "the world" to find his path.

Wes couldn't help feeling that he had let his mother down. In the final installment of "Craven's Ravin's," a column he had inaugurated with a story about a boy inadvertently killing his mother, Wes offered this darkly humorous account of Christmas at the Craven house: "From my mother I got a clever little box containing cyanide, a very sharp letter-opener, and a swell length of rope that must be good for something. Mom said it was a do-it-yourself kit. But I can't figure out what she meant..."[46] Shortly after his mother's death in 2002, Wes said this in an interview with journalist Jason Zinoman: "[My mother] didn't understand me. She never tried to. I think something about the way my mother looked at me, behind her eyes was the sense that her son was crazy. The word 'crazy' came up all the time... For all her genuine love toward me, I never felt like she loved who I really was."[47]

For the first half of 1958, Wes remained at home and worked alongside his brother, splicing cables for the Ohio Bell Telephone Company. In September, he set out for the plains west of Chicago.

CHAPTER TWO

THE MISEDUCATION OF THOMAS SPARROW

(1958 - 1963)

"The question, for all those who cannot live without art and what it signifies, is merely to find out how, among the police forces of so many ideologies (how many churches, what solitude!), the strange liberty of creation is possible."

– Albert Camus, *"Create Dangerously" (1957)*

Founded in 1859, Wheaton College was conceived as an institution of higher education that would balance 19th century Christian evangelism with serious scholarship. Despite an early 20th century schism between religious fundamentalists (who believe the Bible is infallible and should be interpreted literally) and more liberal-minded evangelicals (who believe the Bible is a mix of history, myth, metaphor, and poetry), both the school's religious agenda and its commitment to high academic standards remained strong in the late 1950s and early 1960s. Wheaton alums who graduated during this time period have described their *alma mater* as "the most academic of the conservative colleges," "the Yale of Christian colleges," "the fundamentalist Harvard," and—more bluntly—"fundamentalism with brains." Poet and playwright Jeanne Murray Walker (Class of '66) sums up: "Wheaton was—and still is—a profoundly serious academic institution that defined itself as 'Evangelical,' which we were taught was not 'Fundamentalist.' Everyone took a Bible course, which was not a snap even though many of us had already memorized large swaths of the Bible. The course was conducted with the kind of academic rigor more typical of a good seminary, and spirituality at Wheaton was tempered by the formality of the Protestant religious tradition. It was not a fanatic cult, as were some of the Baptist churches a few of us had come from."

When Wes Craven arrived on campus in the fall of 1958, Wheaton's course catalog described the school as "an independent, Christian, coeducational college of liberal arts and sciences," formally nondenominational but "conservative in its religious, political, and economic views." The college platform emphasized a guiding belief in "the Scripture of the Old and the New Testaments as verbally inspired by God," and in Original Sin. The administrators prescribed strict standards of conduct for students as well as faculty, and instituted a mandatory pledge for all to abstain from the use of tobacco and alcohol, as well as dancing, gambling, joining secret societies, and attending theaters (movie or otherwise). The pledge did not outlaw radio or television but it encouraged Wheatonites to maintain "the spirit of this pledge" in their listening and viewing habits.[1]

The rules rattled some students while others took them for granted. Because Wes Craven came from a strict fundamentalist Baptist household, Wheaton probably seemed to him like a comparatively liberal environment—a place where he could let his mind, if not his body, run wild. In a 1995 interview, he broadly characterized his undergraduate years as the beginning of a "Candidian search," alluding to French philosopher Voltaire's satirical coming-of-age novel *Candide*.[2] The novel, which Wes once called "the greatest book I have ever read," depicts the disillusionment of a young man raised to believe that he lives in "the best of all possible worlds."[3] As an adult, Candide gradually learns that the world is in fact rife with violence, cruelty, and manipulation. Finding little evidence of a benevolent God at work, he ultimately renounces his childhood faith and resolves to "tend his own garden" and let the world take care of itself.

For many of Wes's contemporaries, life at Wheaton College was an equally transformative experience. Reverend John A. Huffman, president of Wheaton's Class of '62 and future pastor to President Richard Nixon, credits history professor Earl Cairn with introducing him to "the much larger world of historic intellectual life with many of the philosophical challenges one must face if one is to be an honest thinking Christian."[4] Huffman says his time at Wheaton allowed him to test and thereby strengthen his faith, instead of thoughtlessly adhering. Poet John "Jack" Leax, who attended Wheaton from 1961 until 1963, remembers that teachers like Kenneth Kantzer in the Bible Department and Art Holmes in the Philosophy Department helped students to expand their understanding of Christianity. In a 1959 essay, Kantzer asserted that "a true and living orthodoxy must never become static," and that a "living orthodoxy" must "rethink for its own generation the doctrines of revelation and inspiration." Although he stipulated that evangelical Christians are bound to the same "facts" as orthodox believers, he emphatically stated that "no Christian need ever fear the honest search for truth."[5] It was this philosophical tension between established dogma and earnest questioning that made Wheaton a unique and profoundly influential learning environment.

While some students found their faith reinforced by the philosophical tension, others perceived a contradiction between Wheaton's conservative platform and the professors' commitment to a liberal education. Leax remembers that many teachers at Wheaton "were trying to move to a stronger intellectual basis. And, of course, as you begin to move in that direction with probing, intelligent students, not everybody is going to come out the way you want them." Feeling torn between loyalty to established traditions and new habits of critical thinking, many students struggled. Jeanne Murray Walker reflects, "Chapel

Wes Craven, Collinwood High School yearbook, January 1958

Wes Craven (far right) with Wheaton College friends (Louis Hilderbrand, Graham Gilbert, Gary Roper, and John Abbott), c. 1958 (courtesy Donna Craven)

and the academic courses and everything else was charged with life-or-death intensity, because—well, because so many students were testing their faith and grappling with what they wanted to become."

Wes Craven strived to discover The Truth at Wheaton, no matter the cost. In a 2002 interview with fellow Wheaton alum Ron Watson, he explained, "I found myself being really intrigued by Christianity. We were reading Martin Buber and a lot of very interesting Christian thinkers and I started thinking about it in terms of concepts, and for a while there was a real identification with the faith. I think for the first time, I was in the presence of people who had real brains instead of appealing to emotional issues. It elevated it for me and I became really concerned with just intellectually finding Christianity and following it and defining it for myself."[6] In a 2010 interview with me, he added, "Being raised in the fundamentalist church—combined with my mother, who was very powerful in my life, and who was very much about keeping things hidden (like what my father was like, and the whole history of her relationship with him)—left me with a desperate desire to know the truth. College for me was trying to fill in the blanks of all the stuff that was kept from me because it wasn't savory or it didn't fit the belief system."

In the beginning, Wes sought relief from the intensity of life at Wheaton by exercising his outrageous sense of humor. One classmate remembers that Wes drew satirical cartoons for the school newspaper and signed them "Abe Snake." Apparently, these weren't published but were instead put up on a bulletin board or on the wall in the cafeteria. Wes's satirical humor was often directed at college administrators. The name "Abe Snake" came from a comedy routine by Stan Freberg, about a hard-drinking, gambling con man who runs for President on a promise to be "the best darn politician that money can buy." Turning Freberg's skit on its head, Wes targeted the president of Wheaton College, V. Raymond Edman, known on campus as "Prexy." Edman authored several books, including a compilation of twenty-one sermons in which each sermon riffed on a word beginning with the letter D. (Duty, Discipleship, Danger, Darkness, Disability, etc.) With material like that to spoof, Abe Snake was in heaven.

According to his freshman year dorm mates, Wes was equally mischievous with friends. Greg Livingstone (Class of '62) remembers, "One day I had a terrible drippy cold and Wes offered to give me some Contac pills. Latest thing, he said. I said, 'Wes, don't tell anybody, but I can't swallow pills.' Wes immediately started yelling for the other guys to join us. They held me down and crammed the Contac pills down my throat… and I've been able to swallow pills ever since!"

Another victim was Bill Lindberg (Class of '62), who remembers, "I met Wes in September of 1958. I had just arrived on campus and the first meal I ate at the dining commons was in the presence of Wes and eight or ten of his instant buddies." Bill was an easy target. Standing 6'5", he showed up for that first meal wearing a wool suit with a tie tack pinned to his lapel like some kind of achievement medal. "The guys had fun mocking me," he confesses, good-naturedly. Just wait.

Lindberg later became involved with a student ministry group that frequently traveled to Chicago to spread the gospel to inner-city kids. One day, he returned to Saint Hall dorm with a harrowing story. "I was paired with a senior who would meet with people, have Bible study, talk, get prayer requests, et cetera, so I was following her around. We knocked on this one door and a man let us in. We were really there to talk to his wife. He never said one word. He just sat there, real close to me, and stared at me. So I started to get a little worried."

Later that night, Lindberg remembers, he was summoned to the lounge, where there was a telephone. "I picked up the phone, and this gruff voice says, 'Are you Bill Lindberg?' I said yes. 'Were you in the city this afternoon?' I said yes. He says, 'I want to tell you, sir, you can never come back to my apartment, ever again. If I see you in Chicago—*ever*—I will shoot you with my shotgun and kill you.' Bang. Hangs up the phone. There were ten or twelve guys sitting around, so I told them what had happened, and they walked me back to my room, saying, 'Bill, you should call the assistant dean and tell him your life has been threatened.' The next morning, the assistant dean said, 'Bill, this is a serious matter. We have to figure out what's going on.' That scared me more than the guy in the city had!"

The situation continued to snowball. "It went from the assistant dean to the dean of students to the president of the college to the local authorities in Wheaton to the regional authorities in Illinois to the FBI. There was a prayer meeting on campus; 500 students came and prayed that I would not lose my life. Then the prayer request circulated to another hundred or two hundred churches across America. They were all having prayer meetings for this poor guy whose life had been threatened in Chicago. Finally, the president of Wheaton College said, 'Bill, you should not go back in [to Chicago] but if you insist on going, then we have to send an armed presence to protect you.' I'm thinking to myself, 'What a mess.'"

Re-enter Wes Craven. "The Saturday morning before I'm supposed to go back to Chicago, I hear a knock at my door and it's Wes. He said, 'Bill, come down the hall, I want to talk to you.' I went and saw all my new friends waiting for me. Wes said, 'Bill, we want to apologize. This whole thing is a hoax. I went across to Elliot Hall and I was the one that made that phone call to you. I'm so sorry.'

"I had to go back to the dean and confess it was a hoax. He wanted to know the names of everybody involved. 'The ring leader is going to be suspended.' But I wouldn't tell him. I knew that if I did, Wes would have been bounced out, because he was a thorn in the side of the administration. But I just loved Wes. I thought he was so unique and so entertaining. He was a force."

Since there is no official record of any reprimand, Wes must have kept a lower profile at Wheaton for the remainder of the school year. Bestselling author Judi Chaffee Culbertson (Class of '62), who met Wes as a freshman, remembers him as a relatively quiet person. "I didn't know him well as a freshman, and I don't think that he was very involved with other people," she says. "I do remember he had a girlfriend from high school who wrote letters to him. Her name was Ilona. I remember that because he thought it was funny that she could sign her letters to him 'Yours, Ilona,' and it sounded like 'Yours, alone.' I also remember being shocked that he was so unconcerned about grades. He would sleep through an exam and not even care."

In the fall of 1959, when he returned to Wheaton for his sophomore year, Wes lasted only a few weeks. He disappeared from campus due to a mysterious illness. His friend and future collaborator Bruce Wagner offers this account: "When Wes was a callow nineteen-year-old college boy, he got the measles. He was in the infirmary with a fever. In the middle of the night, getting up to pee, he couldn't feel his legs. Within a few hours, the kid was in ICU with paralysis of unknown etiology creeping up waist to belly, belly to nipple, nipple to sternum—a quicksand of flesh. In the morning, when the fever decamped, the paralysis remained."[7] In later years, Wes suggested the illness might have been transverse myelitis, a rare disorder caused by inflammation of the spinal cord, or possibly Guillain-Barré syndrome, a condition in which the body's immune system inexplicably attacks the nervous system. He never knew for sure.

Reflecting on his time in the hospital, Wes said, "I kind of put my head together about dying."[8] Such a simple, straightforward statement fails to convey the soul-crushing horror of a long-lingering, life-threatening experience; Wes didn't know if he would ever be able to live a normal life or if he would be confined permanently to a bed, physically dependent on a mother who thought he was crazy. Religion offered little comfort. One family member says he regarded his illness as a divine judgment—proof that he was "a bad person." He felt crazy, even suicidal.

The only relief was the support received from students and faculty members of Wheaton. Wes remembered, "People I didn't know came to visit, to pray for my recovery. To me, their thoughts and prayers represented the best side of Christianity. I'll never forget that side of Wheaton College. Never."[9] Among the classmates who visited Wes in the hospital was his future wife Bonnie Broecker Chapin (Class of '63). She recalls, "I was working at a lovely little hospital in Wheaton as a kind of nurse's aide or a candy striper, and Wes was a patient. I was shy and the older nurses thought it would be funny to have me assigned to his room. So I looked in on him. I saw his guitar and his mother sitting there. He was a young guy, maybe a year older than me, and I said, 'I cannot go give him a backrub.' I refused to do it." Although she saw him only a few times before he was discharged, Bonnie says the image of Wes and his mother made a lasting impression: "I just remember his mother's face. She looked so miserable. Here's her youngest son in the hospital. [I later learned] her husband had left many, many years ago. It seemed too much for her to handle—even though she did eventually live to a ripe old age."

Wes remained hospitalized for six months, unable to feel anything below his armpits. Eventually, he returned to Cleveland for the remainder of the 1959-1960 school year. While his Wheaton classmates celebrated the school's centennial anniversary—one alumnus remembers a raucous season of "food, foam, and fun"—Wes remained confined to bed in his mother's apartment on Coit Road. His niece Corinne, who was seven years old at the time, recalls visiting him there. "He never said too much but he would sit and strum his guitar. I sat next to him as he softly sang, 'My dog has fleas and dirty knees.' That made me laugh. That was Uncle Wes. He was always doing things to make us laugh." By early 1960, Wes had recovered enough to work alongside his brother again while awaiting his second chance at Wheaton.

The lingering physical effects of Wes's illness shattered his hopes of becoming a Naval Air Cadet. In 1992, he said, "Because of my physical impairments, I couldn't fly any longer." The setback must have seemed like further proof that he was cursed by God, but the long-term effect was to steer him away from the military and an impending war, toward the life of an artist.[10] When he returned to Wheaton for the 1960-1961 school year, he focused his studies on psychology and literature. "That year was when his mind really started flying with new ideas," says a filmmaking colleague. "After that, he knew he had to do something creative." Until then, Wes's writings had been mostly humorous; now, his work became more philosophical and ambitious.

Sociologist and linguist Calvin Veltman (Class of '63) remembers that he and Wes lived in adjoining rooms in a home on Scott Street, and that Wes instantly challenged the established rules of his new home: "It was only okay to stay up late if you were studying, so Wes found an old, empty, four-gallon wine jug to pee in. Once a week, he'd go downstairs and empty it in the toilet. That allowed him to stay up until 2 or 3 AM every night." Veltman guesses Wes spent many of his sleepless nights reading and writing—and perhaps avoiding nightmares. "He carried a pattern of fears and nightmares with him on a regular basis. It was part of who he was."

Wes began recording his dreams for "Personality Theory," one of four psychology classes he took at Wheaton (along with "Introduction to Abnormal and Clinical Psychology," "Problems in Psychology," and "Psychology of Adolescence.") "Personality Theory" was a senior-level course focused on the dream-related theories of Sigmund Freud and Carl Jung. Wes said he became "fascinated by Freud and Jung's exploration of dreams," so he started keeping a dream journal. "I was recalling four to five dreams a night. I would spend a lot of time during the day just writing them down. By the end of that semester I stopped, but I retained the facility to recall my dreams."[11] Over time, dreams became "as much a part of my reality as waking life."[12] They also became part of his writing.

Although Wes was obviously interested in psychology, he declared English literature as his major. The decision brought him into the orbit of English department head Clyde S. Kilby, who—like his colleagues Kenneth Kantzer and Art Holmes—was devoted to helping students find a *living* Christian tradition. Kilby had arrived at Wheaton College in 1935 with no allegiance to any particular Christian literary tradition—because, he said, in the fundamentalist atmosphere of Wheaton at that time, there was no literary tradition to speak of.[13] He noted that Wheaton founder Jonathan Blanchard regarded fiction as "a well-told lie" at best and a destroyer of "the ordinary effect of truth" at worst.[14] Kilby didn't agree, so in 1955 he created a junior-level course at Wheaton titled "Christian Philosophy of the Arts." The course posed a series of philosophical questions for aspiring Christian artists: "Should my belief in the fundamentals of the Christian faith make any difference in my attitude toward the arts? Have I as a Christian more, less, or exactly the same right to enjoy the arts as others who may not profess a Christian view? May a Christian devote his life to the creation or study of music, painting, literature, and the other arts? Are the arts dangerous to the spiritual life? Are they to be cultivated, to be shunned, or to be simply ignored?"[15]

In a personal account of his time at Wheaton, author and scholar Thomas Howard (Class of '57) shared a similar list of the questions that arose in Kilby's course: "Was I to understand that art was not, after all, an amusing pastime? Were paintings more than wallpaper? Was the artist interested in something other than lovely vignettes? Was there something being said here about the nature of human experience? What if a man were unhappily aware of ugliness and botch in the world? Was he bad for being angry or presenting it to us on a canvas? What demands did integrity make on an artist? Did they qualify his freedom to paint only loveliness? What constitutes sentimentalism? Was it a sin? What about the quest for form? How did this affect a man's iconography? If a painter were not concerned with photography, what was in his mind? What is implied in the great effort of all poetry and music and painting, to see and shape and articulate human experience? Is there more at stake in existence than what we busy ourselves with every day? What of the commonplace? Are we, in effect, blind? Do we fail to see terror and glory lying all about us? Is this what art is about?"[16]

In his attempt to answer these questions, Clyde Kilby took some cues from novelist and lay theologian C.S. Lewis. Like Lewis, Kilby argued that imagination was "a worthy avenue of spiritual witness" and that the power of literature resided in its use of metaphor.[17] Kilby criticized *overtly* Christian literature "in which the recitation of a cliché becomes the only language which is thought to be good theological specie," and offered a viewpoint that Wes Craven could probably appreciate for deeply personal reasons: "We have concluded too often that accepting Christ and 'accepting Christ' are identical, where the latter phrase means going to the front during an evangelistic campaign, getting on one's knees, saying certain words, standing up and shaking hands, and afterward giving one's testimony."[18] The literature professor urged his students to pursue the genuine over the superficial.

Wes came to the same conclusion on his own, partly due to the influence of Gabriel Vahanian's 1961 book *The Death of God: The Culture of Our Post-Christian Era*—which Wes told me he read "like you might read the *Communist Manifesto* if you were living with the general of a communist army." Vahanian argued that, for many people, mainstream American Christianity had become a "religiosity" instead of an authentic religion, a superficial routine instead of a serious process of questioning and contemplation. As a result, achieving an authentic belief in God required contemporary Americans to "rebel against Christianity."[19]

Clyde Kilby did not encourage his students to rebel against Christianity, but by championing certain types of art, he nudged them away from fundamentalist separatism. Rowland V. Bennett (Class of '62) recalls, "Kilby was suggesting to us—obliquely, very tactfully—that there were broader ways to interpret the faith. And he certainly emphasized metaphor. I can vividly remember him pointing his finger, to emphasize the importance of what he was saying. He wasn't pointing up or down but like when your mother says 'Now listen, darling, don't forget this.' Then he said, 'Metaphor. *Metaphor.*'"

Kilby explained, "To understand the function of metaphor is to use art for what it truly is, not a reproduction of nature and not a mere recombination of known elements, but a fruitful adventure into the very nature of being whereby the truth of things is as validly described and disclosed as in mathematical and scientific creation."[20] He concluded that the creation of great art was an analogue to God's creation. In one of his later essays, he reflected on the relationship in a passage about nature: "How can it be that with a God who created birds and the blue of the sky and who before the foundation of the world wrought out a salvation more romantic than Cinderella, with a Christ who encompasses the highest heaven and deepest hell, with the very hairs of our heads numbered, with God closer than hands and feet, Christians often turn out to have an unenviable corner on the unimaginative and the commonplace?"[21] To help the next generation of Christian artists avoid this, he advised his students to contemplate the natural world and their place in it—something Wes had been doing for years.

Wes probably also took inspiration from T.S. Eliot, first among the writers that were "discussed intensively" in upper-division courses.[22] English

WHEATON COLLEGE   WINTER, 1962
WHEATON, ILL.   VOL. 17, NO. 2

INK WASH

THOMAS SPARROW

KODON

1

Wes Craven in *The Tower*, Wheaton College yearbook, 1962

professor Robert Warburton, for example, taught a sophomore level course placing Eliot at the end of a centuries-long tradition of "major writers" that included Chaucer, Shakespeare, Milton, Swift, Wordsworth, and Tennyson. Wes's friend and fellow English major Judson Scruton (Class of '62) remembers that in 1960 or 1961, the school sponsored "a big panel discussion" on Eliot's masterpiece, *Four Quartets*. "I was on the panel," he says, "Wes was there and encouraging of the panel." If so, Wes was likely aware of Eliot's theory of poetic metaphor, embodied in his description of an "objective correlative" as "a set of objects, a situation, a chain of events which shall be the formula of [a] *particular* emotion."[23] For many members of the Silent Generation, Eliot's objective correlative was *the* definition of poetry. When he started writing poetry, Wes may have been emulating Eliot.

In the fall of 1960, Wes and Jud joined an extracurricular club known as the Poet's Corner, along with Robert Siegel, Gretchen Klotz, Judi Chaffee, and Mary Blocksma. "We used to meet late in the afternoons in a classroom," remembers Judi. "There were maybe seven or eight of us. We had all submitted poems and we passed around these purple mimeographed sheets and discussed the poems." Gretchen Klotz—who describes her fellow club members as "seeking people, most of whom were believers but still asking questions because they didn't know all the answers"—specifies that they weren't writing "despairing beatnik poetry" but poetry "about finding a spark that might be from God, along with some romantic love that was earthly or heavenly. There was a lot of searching but, on the whole, not in darkness."[24]

Nearly every member of the group would go on to become a published writer. Even in such distinguished company, Scruton says, Wes stood out. "If you had to say who had the artistic temperament and who was most likely to succeed at being a successful artist in some form, you probably would have said Wes. There were some very bright, interesting people in that group, but he had that askance view that saw behind or under things. You could see him processing things behind his eyes. If a professor called on him for a particular answer to something, he could appear stunned because he was three worlds away, but he was a very intelligent human being."

Four of Wes's earliest poems, signed "W.E. Craven," were distributed privately among the group members, the byline suggesting a reverence for T.S. Eliot. One of the poem titles, "Leaves of Crabgrass," acknowledge debts to Walt Whitman and Allen Ginsberg. And then there's the self-evident "Written while reading Kerouac, Huxley, and Scruton, listening to Brubeck, Bartók, Ahmad Jamal, and thinking about my indigestion." Wes's dark musings in a sonnet titled "Nightlight" illustrate Eliot's theory of the objective correlative and support Scruton's memory of Wes as "a quiet, thoughtful guy" with a "macabre underside." Scruton also remembers his friend as a very good classical guitar player, which enhanced Wes's reputation among the female members of the Poet's Corner. "I don't remember that he had any particularly strong relations to the girls in the group, but they were attracted to him. He was quite handsome as a young man."

Poet Lynne Buri Potts (Class of '61) says she was not an official member of the Poet's Corner because she was "intimidated by these people who seemed to know they were writers." She was lured into the mix by her friend Robert Siegel but stayed mostly on the fringes of the group, admiring and questioning. When she met Wes Craven, she fell for him instantly. "I don't know when we started dating," she says, "but I know when I 'discovered' him. Wes didn't pick me out. I 'discovered' him by reading his poems in the *Kodon*."

Kodon was Wheaton's student-run literary magazine, and it was there that W.E. Craven made his debut in the fall of 1960, with a poem titled "Skid Row Nocturne." Echoing the cultured malaise of the *fin de siècle* poets from England and France, "Skid Row Nocturne" combines images of urban blight and ethereal moonlight with a stagnating air of ennui. The poet might have been summoning objective correlatives from his own Cleveland childhood. Potts reflects, "He didn't tell me a lot but I knew they were poor. I knew his mother was single. I knew she was sort of a fanatic Christian. And I knew they had rats in their houses."

In the spring semester of 1961, W.E. Craven published two more poems in *Kodon*. The first was a fragmented nocturne titled "Three Poems on Memory... All for the Price of One," in which nature imagery and musical metaphor convey the tormented restlessness of an insomniac. At the heart of the poem is an "infuriatingly untouched" addressee who "slashes" the poet's mind and leaves him bleeding.[25] A shorter poem titled "Vespers" also employed nature imagery and addressed an absent lover—but with less chagrin. The second poem might have been part of an ongoing series, because a completely different poem titled "Vespers"—this one, a somber ode to a bird's missing mate— was published in the November 1961 issue of California's *Westways* magazine.

Why was the young poet writing so consistently about night and loneliness and forlorn lovers? Lynne suggests that "we were both troubled at the time. I was certainly a mess and he was too, although I appeared to be more socially adapted. I was attracted to Wes because he was eccentric and different. And complicated. Which I found really quite seductive. But he was so fraught in those days with his own questioning and insecurities. We never just had fun together."

Wes may have still been recovering, physically and mentally, from his near-death experience and long-term paralysis. Later in life, he admitted to a friend that "residual effects" lingered for some time, including the need to "pee every thirty minutes, literally, or I would wet my pants," an embarrassing condition he kept to himself during his time at Wheaton.[26] His poetry seems to have been his main outlet for his anxieties.

When Lynne graduated from Wheaton College in the spring of 1961, she moved to New York to attend grad school and the couple continued their romance via written correspondence. "He wrote me a lot of letters," she remembers, "and he always included a little drawing of a bird with the return address. He signed them 'Thomas Sparrow.'" The new moniker was a marked contrast to the mischievous raven who served as Wes's high school mascot.

During the 1961-1962 school year, Wes published one poem and three illustrations in *Kodon* under the new pseudonym. Friend and fellow *Kodon* contributor Mary Blocksma (Class of '63) recalls, "He always wrote under that name. And he wrote beautiful stuff. I loved his writing and I loved his art. He used to draw little cartoons on my notebook in class, to entertain me. He was so talented. So smart. And lonely. Because who could ever know who he really was? He had many friends, but he was complicated." Lynne agrees, "I used to think, I'm not really getting who this man is. I really didn't understand what he was deeply like. I just knew he was kind of neurotic."

Wes may have tried to provide some insight into his psyche when he gave Lynne a copy of Domenico Gnoli's 1961 book *Orestes, or the Art of Smiling*. Gnoli's story is about a young prince who suffers from a "melancholic nature," "unstable moods," "a heavy heart, and a sulking soul."[27] The prince's only true love is for birds, so when all the birds in his kingdom die or fly away—with the exception of his mother's all-knowing parrot, Lucien—Orestes embarks on a quest to find a new source of happiness. Lucien slyly pairs the prince with a poor girl named Violante, who has been in love with the prince since they were young children. When Orestes sees her smile, he too smiles helplessly for the first time... but his quest is far from over. Lucien imprisons Orestes and explains that he must "win" Violante by tunneling out of his prison. Feeling confident and hopeful, Orestes accepts the challenge and the story abruptly ends.

Wes apparently regarded storytelling as his own method of tunneling out of a psychic prison, perhaps proving himself worthy of love. In the fall of 1961, W.E. Craven, poet of endless night, gave way to Wesley Earl Craven, philosophical storyteller. In *Kodon*, he published a "short and sincere" tale called "Onward, Christian Soldiers," about an ROTC cadet participating in Field Day maneuvers at an unnamed college. While going through the motions, cadet Sam Erickson worries that he is becoming "a member of a mob, a non-thinking lump of blank-brained ectoplasm," so he resolves to stage a mental "revolt"—

following the example of René Descartes, Søren Kierkegaard, Carl Jung, Karl Marx, Arnold Toynbee, Bertrand Russell, and Adolf Hitler—before nervously falling back in line. At the end of the story, despite his cowardice, the would-be hero quietly resolves not to surrender "all of his individuality."[28]

The story might have been inspired by personal experience. In the 1958-1959 school year, every male student in their freshman or sophomore year at Wheaton had to take basic Military Science. Unless Wes declared himself a conscientious objector—which seems unlikely if he wanted to be a Naval Air Cadet—he must have participated in ROTC drills. After his illness, however, he was undoubtedly excused from the program. Banished to the life of the mind.

In the Winter 1961 issue of *Kodon*, Wes published another revealing short story, "The Day Harry Won," about a man whose brain declares war on his body. In the story, Harry disciplines his disobedient body by attacking his rumbling belly with a tumbler full of cool water. When his belly regurgitates the peace offering, Harry exacts revenge on his gut by drinking a fatal dose of poison. The tone of the story is playfully comedic until the shocking ending. One wonders if and how this story might have stemmed from the author's personal experience. When he was paralyzed from the chest down, did Wes feel that his body had betrayed him? Did he contemplate suicide—if not a revenge against his body, then perhaps against God? The story offers only questions.

Judson Scruton recalls another macabre story Wes wrote around the same time, about a tunnel full of rats. "I don't think that's ever been published," he says, "but it showed that he was heading toward horror in a fast way. He was a sensitive soul, really. But I think part of that [soul] was a very dark, subterranean world that he tried to exorcise." Judi Chaffee Culbertson remembers an equally dark poem that Wes published at Wheaton under a pseudonym. "A Birth," a short riff on the Biblical story of Jonah and the Whale, appeared in the fall '61 issue of *Kodon* and was credited to an anonymous resident of "Sunny Acres, a mental hospital in Ohio."[29] Judi says this poem made her wonder if Wes had seen a psychiatrist during his convalescence in Cleveland. Sunny Acres was the name of a sanatorium that existed on the outskirts of the city around that time. Originally built as a hospital for tuberculosis patients, it was later transformed into a facility for the care of the chronically-ill.[30] According to one

Cleveland historian, the staff offered various programs to help patients stave off "boredom and possible depression," including Art Studio, which encouraged self-expression through painting, drawing, reading, and writing.[31] At Wheaton, Wes found a similar outlet for his deepest, darkest thoughts—creative writing and a group of talented friends that cared enough about art, and about him, to support his work.

By the spring of '62, the *Kodon* group had solidified around a few key players. Judi Chaffee Culbertson, chief editor of the literary magazine during the 1961-1962 school year, says, "The office was on the second floor of the Student Union building and we used to lock the door and have parties. We'd put on 'The Twist' and drink rum and Coke, or cheap wine." Gretchen Dutschke-Klotz (Class of '62) remembers things differently: "We didn't do anything in that room that was against the pledge we'd all taken. Unless one would consider learning The Twist as disobeying the dance rule. I think we felt uncertain on that one." To her, the *Kodon* office was "a safe place" because "the door could be locked and the *Kodon* people could be who they were: rebels." She clarifies, "Not only rebels against the fundamentalism of Wheaton College and of our own backgrounds, but against a society which we did not want to conform to. Against the middle class, conservative values of our families."

Wes has denied that he ever thought of himself as a rebel. In 2010, he told me, "Brando had that famous moment [in *The Wild One*] where someone asked 'What are you rebelling against?' and he answered, 'What have you got?' I think that's a rebel. I'm not a rebel. I was raised a fundamentalist. How much of a rebel can I be? I'm an outsider." After hearing Wes's distinction, Gretchen elaborates, "We were outsiders from American culture, but I'd say we were also outsiders from Wheaton fundi culture. I believe most of us were still believing Christians at that time, but we did not agree with the fundamentalist narrowness. I don't know where Wes fit in on the believing or not believing scale. I don't remember any specific conversations. I just remember that we had fun in that office."

Under the leadership of Judi Chaffee, the *Kodon* staff certainly had a productive year. In March 1962, they inaugurated a three-day Fine Arts Festival on campus. Judi remembers inviting National Book Award winner Nelson Algren as well as Pulitzer Prize winning poet Gwendolyn Brooks to attend. She convinced the latter to serve as a celebrity judge for poetry submissions to the spring issue of *Kodon*. Wes Craven won awards in three out of four categories. His short story "The Weapon" earned first place for prose fiction; his one-act play "The Hitchhiker" second place for drama; and "Three Poems on Memory" second place for poetry.

"The Weapon" was about a cave dweller named Org. At the outset, Org witnesses his estranged brother Shag killing a lizard with a sling-shot and then promptly recalls that, earlier in the day, he'd been hit on the head by a stone. Suddenly, suspicion occludes Org's normally sunny disposition— filling him with fear, resentment, and anger toward his brother, which quickly morphs into intense hatred. Org goes home to his scornful wife Cragthynthia and begins plotting revenge against Shag for the imagined slight. Later, he spends the night scheming and conspiring with his pet bird. Finally, with Cragthynthia's help, Org builds a catapult and launches a humiliating assault on his brother's home.

Halfway through the story, Org contemplates the possibility that he's being ridiculous. He thinks maybe he should make peace with his brother instead of attacking him—but then his dark thoughts rise up again, and he renews his campaign against Shag. Feeling righteous and eager to show off his superior wit and strength, he loads a catapult with leftover food. Before he can launch it, however, Org is bombarded with the remains of two dead buffalos, which Shag has launched at him using a much bigger catapult. "The Weapon" concludes on this note about the absurdity of war.

Wes's play "The Hitchhiker" was not published in the spring issue of *Kodon*, but it was supposedly performed on campus during the Fine Arts Festival, sometime between March 28 and 30. In his semi-fictional memoir *The Bishop, the Hunchback, and the Lunatic*, Wheaton alum Philip McIlnay ('60 – '62) writes that he had "the male lead in a campus-wide production" of a certain famous horror filmmaker's play "about knights and ladies of the Medieval Period."[32] (McIlnay also wryly notes that, as far as his kids were concerned, his appearance in a play written by the creator of *A Nightmare on Elm Street* was their father's greatest claim to fame.)

The Summer 1962 issue of *Kodon* featured Wes's short poem "See and Tell" and a short story called "Death Mask, Three-Quarter View." The poem poses the question "What is death?" and answers with a series of impressionistic fragments about a funeral that is surreal in its mundanity. Was the author remembering a specific funeral? Or perhaps imagining his own?

"Death Mask, Three-Quarter View" also uses short vignettes to tell an impressionistic story while presenting a psychological portrait of the author. The first fragment is a narrative about a man named Adam, who returns home to his wife after being pursued through the woods by a mysterious white wolf. As the wife wonders aloud what happened, Adam struggles to convey the intensity of his experience. The third-person narrator explains that Adam regards the white wolf as "an old enemy whose ways are part of myself." At the end of the story, he hears the creature howling outside and senses an "awful gravity" pulling him back into the woods to confront a seemingly grim fate.

In the second fragment, a preacher named Samuel B. Hopkins inspects the wreckage of an "aged airship" surrounded by a mob of rural farmers. Seeking to dominate the mob, Hopkins revs the powerful engine of the "ancient" plane. When he does, a propeller rips through the bodies of several members of the mob. The survivors respond by assaulting the preacher and destroying the machine. The author ends this fragment with a poetic suggestion that the plane resembles "a fallen bird eaten by mice and shrews, an angel beset by clutching demons steaming on the cylinder heads of sad, sad death."

The third and final fragment is set in a small apartment, where an old woman and her young son anticipate the arrival of an eviction notice. The pair have a brief conversation about recently-evicted neighbors, prompting the boy to visit their empty apartments. Through the open doorway of one apartment, he sees a vast forest beneath dark, oppressive clouds. He ventures inside and discovers a cabin in the woods, then he hears the howl of a wolf and hastily flees to a different apartment. Inside the second apartment, he sees "flat fields of cultivated soil" and "a great tangle of bodies and metal." The sight of a huge funeral procession—presumably related to the violent death of Samuel B. Hopkins—scares him so much that he returns home to his mother.

At the end of the three-part story, the boy declines to tell his mother what he has seen in the other apartments, or to ask her any questions about the meaning of what he saw there. The omniscient storyteller explains that the boy does not want answers, explanations, or endings, because "endings are always bad."[33] The implication is that this "death mask" remains unfinished. Instead of conveying meaning, "Death Mask, Three-Quarter View" conveys only a vague and mysterious dread of the unknown, along with a sense of melancholy—and solitary—resignation. The house, with its doorways to other worlds, may represent a fearful and fragmented psyche.

"Death Mask, Three-Quarter View" was the last work of fiction that Wes Craven published at Wheaton, but it was not his final word. Allegedly, he wrote—or rewrote—all the copy for the 1962 yearbook, going above and beyond his credited role as literary editor. Jeanne Murray Walker remembers, "He holed up in *The Tower* office, where he wrote day and night for a couple of weeks. Friends brought him food. This became a much-mythologized story about Wes, because it was the best yearbook anyone had ever read." Another classmate concurs, "When the 1962 yearbook came out in the spring of my freshman year, I started leafing through it and realized I had to read it cover to cover. It was that good. The copy sang." In one particularly philosophical passage, the voice of *The Tower* equates Wheaton College's student body to a collective soul: "The particles of lives form together, are caught in one light and resolve to the shape of a year. To the people who pass through it, a year is symbolic of a universe within… a mind, a soul, a will growing through alternative events and exerting its selective pull."[34] The author goes on to rhapsodize about the four seasons; the birth, death, and rebirth of nature as it mirrors the comings and goings, triumphs and losses, of his fellow Wheatonites.

Wes's contributions to the yearbook led to a perception that he was a big man on campus. During his senior year, he made an even bigger impression as editor of *Kodon*. Judi Chaffee Culbertson recommended Wes to be her successor but says she later regretted the decision. "I knew he was a good writer. I didn't think he'd be a great editor. Mary Blocksma should have been the *Kodon* editor after me. But I recommended him to the Pub[lications] Board and he was chosen. Then, of course, he ran the ship into the ground."

Controversy surrounding the Fall 1962 issue of *Kodon* began with a party at Wes's house—and a musical collaboration between Wes and his friend Nancy Bryant (Class of '63). She remembers, "Some students lived in private homes, and Wes lived with a bunch of lit majors. They had a house party and

I got invited and they put on a performance of *Waiting for Godot*, which was a real education for me because I hadn't thought much about plays and that sort of thing. Then somebody asked Wes to play guitar, so he got his guitar and started playing. And I started singing. We did Joan Baez. He had all her picks and licks down, and I could sing all of her songs. She and I had basically the same range. Somebody took a picture of us and it was used as the cover for *Kodon*." The right half of the photo, featuring the singer flanked by onlookers, appeared on the front cover; the other half, featuring Wes Craven, head lowered, sitting in shadow with his guitar, appeared on the back. John Leax, a *Kodon* staff member and contributor that fall, remembers the image prompted an instant negative reaction. "The photo was taken without any particular lighting, so it was rather a dark, moody kind of cover. And right off, the response from the administration was that this was a sign of despair and so on."

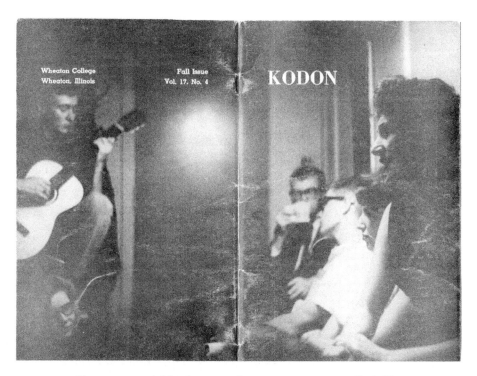

The controversial *Kodon* cover featuring Wes Craven (far left)
and Nancy Bryant (far right),

Wes Craven broods in *The Tower*, Wheaton College yearbook, 1963

Wes Craven seems to have anticipated a critical reaction—and not just to the cover art. In an introductory editorial, he issued a preemptive strike: "It may be thought that this magazine fails its responsibility as a 'Christian Publication' to represent the joy and love of Christ. Such sentiments are admirable, but also puerile and terribly vitiating if distorted." He asserted that his first and most important job as the editor of *Kodon* was to be honest, and that the stories published in the magazine would reflect "the agony and ecstasy of human awareness" without any moral filtering.[35]

According to Wes, two pieces in the Fall '62 issue caused problems: "A New Home," Marty Bihlmeier's story about an unwed mother, and "The Other Side of the Wall" by Carolyn Burry, about a white woman in a relationship with a black man.[36] Apparently, premarital sex and race relations were taboo subjects at Wheaton. At the time, the institution's most visible attempt to engage with the burgeoning Civil Rights Movement was a weekly "Colored Sunday School" program on the South Side of Chicago. Judi Chaffee Culbertson participated. "We used to go in by bus to the projects every Sunday," she remembers. "We'd take a bag lunch and supposedly convert the black people that we visited. For me, it was an experience. It was a world I hadn't seen yet and I was eager for new experiences, so I did it my freshman and sophomore years. But it wasn't considered a socially conscious kind of thing. It was an evangelical thing. You were supposed to convert the little children." Career educator Bill Schopf (Class of '63), who also participated, does not recall race relations as an issue at Wheaton. "They just tried to ignore that subject."

According to other classmates, Carolyn Burry participated in the Colored Sunday School and met her future husband—a black man—through the program, prompting her parents to pull her out of school and blame Wheaton College for her "corruption."

Whatever the root cause of the *Kodon* flap—whether it was the "brooding" cover photo, the editor's preemptive strike, the sensitive subject matter of two stories, or (one alum suggests) a single swear word—all of the issue's contributors became objects of scrutiny. Mary Blocksma says, "We were suspect to the people [in power]. We were often accused of using metaphors to hide our terrible thoughts." In early November, Blocksma wrote and directed an original play titled "Song of Ourselves," which was performed in Edman

Chapel for Parents' Day. The cast included Wes Craven and Nancy Bryant, who performed several folk songs. According to the playwright, it was a "silly damn skit," hastily written because the administration wouldn't allow her to put on a Shakespeare play. "They were suspicious of Shakespeare—although we had a Shakespeare course that was taught by our dear Dr. [Beatrice] Batson—but that was the atmosphere at Wheaton." (According to Batson, Wes Craven was "a fine, serious-minded student" who excelled in Shakespeare and drama.[37])

John Leax was dumbfounded by the reaction to *Kodon*. "I had recently transferred to Wheaton from Wilmington College, which is a Quaker College in Ohio. I went from being one of the most conservative people on campus to suddenly becoming one of the more liberal people on campus, without changing anything. When I contributed to the literary magazine, I had no idea that this magazine would be at odds with anything or anybody. It just seemed to me to be a literary endeavor in keeping with what I had experienced at Wilmington. But suddenly, there was this outrage." As a result, Leax was forced to reassess his own sense of self: "Branded an outsider, I became an outsider. The other phrase I would use for it is 'marginal': That's the term that Thomas Merton uses for the artist and the monk. *The marginal.*"

Jeanne Murray Walker was a freshman when she contributed a poem to the Fall 1962 issue, and she too remembers the *Kodon* controversy as a point of entry for rebels and outsiders. "When I arrived on campus from Lincoln, Nebraska, I was a geek and an accomplished violinist who was beginning to understand that my future did not lie with the violin. I took a creative writing course, won the *Atlantic Monthly* competition in both fiction and poetry, and fell in with the *Kodon* crowd, in the office where Wes sat at the editor's desk. I remember Wes reading some of the poems I gave him with amused horror, which he probably tried to hide. He certainly gave me trenchant advice on how to revise them. On the other hand, he was a deeply gentle guy and I don't remember him hurting anyone—even to get a critical point across. He didn't argue. He just had very good taste at a young age and I was interested in learning from him. He didn't seem to be maudlin and self-indulgent like the rest of us. I think he was probably incredibly smart and aware of the norms of good writing. From reading good literary work, he had picked up the manners and control of people who were older." Two years later, Walker would take up Wes's mantle as the editor of *Kodon*. "I certainly did end up joining the group of student radicals at Wheaton," she says. "Because I was committed to a free student press. Anything else seemed to be a weird pretension."

On November 29, 1962, Wes publicly defended his editorship of *Kodon* in an essay for the school newspaper, addressing a reader's accusation that the stories in the magazine had a "naturalistic whine."[38] At the time, literary Naturalism—popularized by late 19th century authors like Frank Norris, Stephen Crane, and Theodore Dreiser—was frowned upon by many of the authority figures at Wheaton, including the college president. In an essay on "Christian Ethics," V. Raymond Edman echoed theologian Carl Henry's argument that Naturalism exerts a negative effect on human thought and behavior, inculcating "a complacency toward moral evil" by implying that human life is shaped by environment and circumstances, thereby positing a world devoid of supernatural influences.[39]

Wes did not defend literary Naturalism but argued that it was unfair to label Bihlmeier's and Burry's stories Naturalistic, because (he said) the characters in their stories have too much agency to fit within the tradition of literary Naturalism. He wrote, "The characters in last *Kodon*'s fiction, although influenced appreciably by their environment, were not at its mercy. They had become entangled in the web of their own moral decisions just as much as they had been trapped by circumstance." He went on to contextualize the stories as existential narratives, suggesting that the authors were not trying to mislead or corrupt readers but to help them empathize with people from different backgrounds and lifestyles—which, he added, "is the first step towards the practice of love." Craven concluded his essay with the assertion that, under his watch, *Kodon* would continue to illustrate "the value of Christianity in the presence of shadow as well as light."[40] His statement echoes—no doubt, intentionally—one of V. Raymond Edman's favorite aphorisms: "Never doubt in the dark what God has told you in the light."[41]

It was a sturdy defense, but not sturdy enough. A December 13, 1962 article in the school newspaper reported that Wheaton College's Publications Board had formally asked Craven to review his editorial criteria for *Kodon*. Board member and college dean Richard Gross opined that the magazine under Craven's editorship did not reflect the true "posture" of the institution.[42] A former student board member accurately remembers, "The college's point of view was that they funded the college publications and saw them as an extension of the college, so they felt like they had a say in what went into them. Wes obviously felt like it should have been totally his decision. He was not about to compromise."

As of December 13, Wes had not been officially censured, so he oversaw one more issue of *Kodon*. The Winter 1962 issue featured many of the same writers and artists that had appeared in the previous issue, although Marty Bihlmeier and Carolyn Burry were noticeably absent. Most of the pieces in the new issue were relatively innocuous, with the exception of Michael Burton's short story "A Search for Consistency" and an introductory editorial by Wes. Burton (Class of '65) says, "I doubt there was any story published at Wheaton that had more potential to stir things up than mine. It was a Camus-inspired cry against the absurd, 'without appeal' (as Camus wrote) to any established frame of meaning or religious / philosophical ideas. Somehow it slipped through." Burton and Wes discussed the implications of the story before it was published, so Wes must have realized its subversive potential.

In fairness, Albert Camus's brand of existentialism was not verboten at Wheaton; Camus was taught in upper-level English courses. In the fall of 1963, his novel *The Plague* would be named as the college's "Book of the Semester." A few years after that, English department head Clyde Kilby championed Camus's novel *The Rebel* in a published essay, summarizing its theme as follows: "There are two possible attitudes, say, in prayer. One is Your-will-be-done-amen. The other is to tell God what is wrong in the world, saying in effect, 'This thing, my Father, is an injustice based upon my conception of the world as Your own child—something I myself see that You must also see and adjust." Kilby concluded, "The sort of Christian who prays, Thy-will-be-done-amen, says in effect that this is the best of all possible worlds."[43] Wes Craven, like Voltaire and Camus, believed otherwise.

In his editorial "To the Woman Who Came to My Office and Wept," an emboldened Wes explicitly challenged the status quo at Wheaton College. He pointed to a schism on campus between those who believed that Christian literature should be overtly Christian, wholesome, and optimistic; and those who believed that art, "if well-conceived and wrought," would supply "its own merit and dignity."[44] Echoing the words of Clyde Kilby, he criticized a culture of religiosity that values tired clichés over challenging metaphors and concluded that "too many of us Christians are afraid of the dark. We feel we have the answer to everything in Christianity. This is not so. We have contact with the *One* who does have these answers, but this does not justify making ourselves minor deities with perfect knowledge, 'happy happy happy all the day,' never doubting God, or questioning the miseries of life, or living narrowly, stupidly or even squalidly ourselves." Wes professed his own belief in the cathartic power of literature that boldly acknowledges darkness. No doubt realizing that he was making his last stand at Wheaton, he added, on behalf of his fellow literary rebels, "We are not rebelling against Christianity, but against make-believe; we are not trying to shock, but awaken."[45]

Wes's declaration is echoed by the opening paragraph of Beatrice Batson's 1968 book *A Reader's Guide to Religious Literature*. The longtime Wheaton College professor of English wrote, "It is often stated that the primary purpose of the imaginative writer is not to convert but reveal. And rather than working within the confines of a particular sector of political, moral or religious beliefs, he can escape all categories of limitation by exploring the deeper dimensions of man. One can, I believe, accept this statement and still use the term 'religious' literature." In her own survey of "religious literature" from the Middle Ages to the Twentieth Century, Batson excluded what she called "religious Polyanna."[46]

Although some contemporary Wheaton professors might have agreed with Wes's perspective, his editorial awakened a sleeping giant. After editing his second issue of *Kodon*, he was "denounced" from the pulpit by college president V. Raymond Edman in a chapel service. According to Wes, Edman "announced I had been derelict in my duty as editor" and promptly shut down the literary magazine for the remainder of the 1962-1963 school year.[47] The controversy almost ended Wes's college days as well. He claimed, "I was asked and almost urged to leave [Wheaton College]. I felt deeply at the time that it was necessary to try to make art relevant to what's going on in the world. It seem[ed] they want[ed] to turn off the source of information and denounce reality."[48] After *Kodon* was discontinued, he faded into the background for the rest of his time at Wheaton.

Some of his fellow literary rebels, however, would not be silenced. In late October 1962, Calvin Veltman launched a column for the school newspaper about a personal crisis of faith. The series of articles, which ran until January 1963, denounced exclusivity and isolationism as well as unthinking conservatism and unthinking liberalism, indoctrination, and bigotry. Veltman still remembers the response he received from some of his fundamentalist peers. "When I was sitting in my office, they came in and they said, 'Could we speak with you, sir? We'd like to let you know that we're praying for you.' I said, "Well, thank you.' They said, 'Well, we didn't mean it that way... We're praying for your soul. You're a lost soul.' I thought my initial response was good enough, so I said, again, 'Thank you very much.'" Veltman's last essay was titled "Farewell to Fundamentalism."

Phil McIlnay took things even further. In the fall of 1961, McIlnay launched an off-campus publication titled *Brave Son*, with the purpose of providing Wheatonites "an opportunity for written expression of their position on various issues." According to Paul Bechtel, "The articles [in *Brave Son*] were, like those in the controversial issues of *Kodon*, quite critical of the college and of contemporary Christian culture."[49] Veltman reflects, "We were living in the time of the Civil Rights and anti-poverty movements. In our view, [the fundamentalist] view of Jesus, Christianity, and politics was just too simplistic and did not show any empathy whatsoever for the poor and needy. Lining up with the religious right just seemed wrong. We were not repudiating Christianity, after all. It was supposed to be a university, not a Xinjiang indoctrination center, but you wouldn't have known that when they started censoring stuff."

Brave Son was discontinued in the spring of 1963, and several of its staff members were reportedly threatened with expulsion. Veltman says, "I had to apologize to the President and the Board for having suggested that Jesus was more likely a liberal than a John Birch conservative. It was one of those 'I'm sorry if someone was offended' apologies, without apologizing for my position, but it satisfied them." Because he was willing to apologize—and to shave his beard—Veltman was allowed to graduate. McIlnay, who responded by creating another controversial magazine (*Critique*) in March 1963, was not. In his semi-fictional memoir, McIlnay wrote, "I was dismissed from the College in 1963 over a disagreement regarding a Free Press. I, like Milton, was for it. The College President, like Stalin, was against it. I lost, of course." The official reason for his expulsion (according to McIlnay) was acting "outside the pattern of the college and in violation of the spirit of the institution," and, unofficially, Edman's belief that the editor of *Brave Son* and *Critique* was a "cancer on the student body which needs to be removed."[50] Veltman says, "The idea was to graduate the seniors and throw the others out."

Wes Craven retreated to subtle pledge-breaking during his final semester. He remembered, "I hitchhiked to another town and saw *To Kill a Mockingbird*, and that was my first film. It was wonderful. It really put the lie to the whole notion that films were inherently evil."[51] Around the same time, he began experimenting with filmmaking. In a 1997 interview, Wheaton professor Robert Warburton claimed Wes "hauled me up to empty rooms in the tower of old Blanchard Hall where they were making mood films, experimenting with scene, color and atmosphere."[52] One of the film projects was an adaptation of Fyodor Dostoevsky's *Crime and Punishment*.

Wes also routinely escaped to Old Town Chicago, where he and Nancy Bryant played live music at a popular club on Wells Street. Bill Schopf remembers, "Nancy had a contract there and Wes accompanied her on the guitar. A couple of times, he sang with her—and the owner of the nightclub got irritated because he didn't want Wes singing. He wanted Nancy singing because Nancy had this great voice. I don't know if the Wheaton people were aware that they were doing that. I have a feeling they were, at the time, kind of backing off—because they had to know that a bunch of us were snapping the pledge right and left, and they probably didn't want to kick us all out of school two months before graduation. So things were kind of loosening up a bit."

Bryant remembers her last few months at Wheaton as the calm after the storm: "Once I met Wes and started hanging out in Old Town with musicians, I paid very little attention to what was going on on campus. My mind was elsewhere. I was thinking about gigs and singing and that kind of stuff. Wes and I played several gigs together. We even traveled to Racine, Wisconsin. I guess if the college had found out about that, we might have been expelled." For her—and for Wes—it was worth the risk. "Wes was a very good musician, and I think his guitar was extremely important for him in his life. When things got heavy duty, he had his music to go to. And I've always been grateful to Wes for what we did together, because the feedback we got really gave me a lot of confidence."

Song of Ourselves: Nancy Bryant and Wes Craven in *The Tower*,
Wheaton College yearbook, 1963

In March 1963, Wes Craven wrote his final missive in a Wheaton publication—a sarcastic newspaper editorial calling for the immediate eradication of indistinct but "ineluctable problems" that "fly o'er our cringing heads, great ugly birds of perplexity, filling our ears with the conflict of their wings."[53] No doubt the editorial was ravin' Craven's belated response to the *Kodon* and *Brave Son* censors—but it was a half-hearted jab. He didn't want to fight; he wanted to move on.

One week later, however, he received a hearty defense from a literary celebrity who visited campus. In a March 15 lecture at Wheaton, Pulitzer Prize-winning poet W.H. Auden hailed the "very excellent [Winter 1962] editorial by Mr. Craven," and asserted, "There is no such thing, or can be, as a Christian art any more than there can be a Christian science or a Christian diet. There can only be a spirit in which art or science are conducted."[54] Wes took the message to heart and later told a friend that Auden's defense of him was one of the happiest moments of his life.[55] Even so, it didn't change things at Wheaton. During the next two years, Michael Burton and Jeanne Murray would continue to push the boundaries as the next editors of *Kodon*. A renewed student interest in the magazine was Wes's legacy at Wheaton.

Ultimately, Wes became so jaded about Wheaton College that he didn't care if he graduated. Nancy Bryant says, "There was this big project in one of his lit classes. You had to make a scroll and chart the history of literature on it. You had to transfer a big pile of 3 x 5 notecards onto this big long chart. It was a big part of your final grade, so if he didn't get it done, he wasn't going to pass. And if he didn't pass, he wasn't going to graduate. Everybody was up in arms about this, but Wes was not as upset about it as everyone else was. Wes gave out a bunch of cards, and some of us girls were filling in blanks because we had to make sure Wes didn't fail. And at the bottom of the scroll, Wes wrote his name with a really beautiful flourish. *Wesley Earl Craven*."

Even after clearing that hurdle, Wes had to go to summer school. In the summer of 1963, he enrolled in six courses—three literature classes, a psychology class, a Bible class, and a history of music. Around the same time, he broke up with his long-distance girlfriend Lynne and began dating his future wife Bonnie Broecker. She remembers, "I graduated in June and then I had to go to summer school and take Zoology so I could go to nursing school. And Wes had to take something in order to graduate, so we were on campus together and I bumped into him. He rode out to my house on his bicycle and that was the beginning of our romance."

That summer, Wes also applied to graduate school. On the advice of Clyde Kilby—and encouraged by his future brother-in-law Wallace S. Broecker—he submitted some writing samples to Elliott Coleman, founder and director of the Johns Hopkins University Writing Seminars in Baltimore. Wes remembered, "I wrote him a letter and said I was interested in checking out his program. He said, 'Come whenever you want.' So I hitchhiked to Baltimore after finishing at Wheaton. I had no money, no great plans. But Elliott was kind enough to find me a student loan and gave me a job as an assistant."[56] In the fall, he began a new chapter.

Bonnie Broecker and Wes Craven, Wheaton College graduation, August 1963
(courtesy Donna Craven)

CHAPTER THREE

THE INNER JOURNEY OF NOAH SONGSTI
(1963 - 1969)

"To go against the order of society is always to risk plunging into anomy. To go against the order of society as religiously legitimated, however, is to make a compact with the primeval forces of darkness."

– Peter L. Berger, *The Sacred Canopy* (1967)

In 1946, Elliott Coleman—an ordained Episcopal deacon turned poet and publisher—established a new type of creative writing program at Johns Hopkins University. According to fellow professor Richard Mackey, "Elliott never lectured. He never taught. He simply let people learn." Louis D. Rubin, one of the first graduates of the now-famous Writing Seminars, adds, "Elliott doesn't have to teach very well; all he has to do is be Elliott Coleman. That is to say, to be a man that young men and woman who want to write can show their things to, can respect the fact that he's interested in them, and just derive some pride and satisfaction in writing by that man's interest and that man's example."[1] In 1973, Coleman himself explained, "Perhaps the theme at Hopkins has been Criticism as an Act of Love, in praise or blame, but always praise first: to try to find the genius of the writer and then encourage it."[2]

Judson Scruton says he first became aware of Elliott Coleman when the poet gave a lecture at Wheaton College in 1962. The subject of the lecture was "the meaning of metaphor"—a topic that undoubtedly piqued the interest of English Department head Clyde Kilby. After the lecture, Kilby recommended two of his students—Scruton and Robert Siegel—to join Coleman's one-year Writing Seminars program. Both did well enough for Coleman to keep recruiting students from Wheaton. In the spring of 1963, Kilby recommended Mary Blocksma, Bill Schopf, and Wes Craven.

That fall, all three Wheaton alums arrived in Baltimore as incoming students at Johns Hopkins University. Wes and Bill lived in adjoining apartments on 33rd Street. While there, they studied every major novelist of the 19th and early 20th centuries, as well as major works of philosophy and Theatre of the Absurd.[3] Schopf elaborates, "The initial reading list was all Proust and Joyce: *Remembrance of Things Past, Ulysses, Finnegan's Wake*. I tried to read everything and loved *Dubliners* and *Portrait of the Artist*. We also read Thomas Mann: *Death in Venice* and *The Magic Mountain*. I think the second semester was Mann and Dostoevsky. At one point, we also had to translate a poem from the German into English and I had a poem by Herman Hesse. I can't remember everything but I know they were hefty reading lists. There was no test or anything. It was just, 'We want you to read this, we expect you to read this, and then we'll talk about it.'" In interviews, Wes cited many of the same authors (including Mann and Dostoevsky, Bertolt Brecht and Samuel Beckett) as personal favorites; he also named James Joyce's *Dubliners* one of the ten books that exerted the greatest impact on him.[4]

Wes and Elliott Coleman had an instant rapport, maybe owing to a mutual interest in tragic themes. Coleman reportedly gravitated toward works of art that expressed "the agony and cost of artistic creation, the conflict between faith and disbelief, the impossibility of love, the edge between insight and madness, and the role of metaphysics versus (or alongside) that of the natural order." Wes had expressed many of the same interests in his Wheaton-era writings. Coleman also occasionally regaled his students with personal stories about "the crazy Colemans hidden in his family closet, well-known writers he didn't care for, and campus issues in need of after-hours expostulation."[5] Wes could preach on those topics as well.

In a 2010 interview with me, Wes said he and Elliott Coleman "talked about religion a lot. And his feeling was that most of what people who say they're Christians say is bullshit." In a more diplomatic mood, he said Coleman helped him to face the future instead of dwelling on the past, explaining, "Coming out of fundamentalism into 'the world' as they call it—which is as good a term as any—can be wrenching, because you can't leave it without one part of your brain that's been inculcated with this stuff for fifteen, twenty years [saying,] 'You are backsliding, you're working with the devil,' all these horrible things […] and if somebody can help you feel OK about it, that's a really important person."[6] Ultimately, Elliott Coleman helped Wes develop a humanistic philosophy, and reinforced his understanding of the purpose of art—to awaken.[7]

In his 1965 essay "The Meaning of Metaphor," Coleman writes that literature can never be a substitute for religion, any more than religion can be a substitute for literature. "It is wrong to use the terms of religion in our poems and stories in a complacent or sentimental way, when what is needed is to find out what we really are, what we really think and feel, and then to meet the great metaphors of religion head-on."[8] During the 1963-1964 year at Johns Hopkins, Wes Craven was trying to figure out what he really believed. Bill Schopf, who was also transitioning away from fundamentalism, remembers it as an anxious time. "In a way, Wes was kind of my mentor through that. I think sometimes he got frustrated with me because I didn't bail out of it sooner. He could be extremely mentoring and kind of therapeutic in a friendship, or he could be brutally sarcastic and sometimes just outright mean. I remember one time—and I'm not sure why he did this, but it was typically Wes—he convinced me to drink a full bottle of gin. I had never been drunk before. In retrospect, I could have died. There was that side to him. There was kind of a war going on inside him."

In the spring of 1964, Wes externalized the war by writing his first novel, *Noah's Ark: The Journals of a Madman*. Many years later, in a conversation with author John Wooley, he remembered the book by describing the setting of his story (St. Michael's Cemetery near LaGuardia Airport) and the three main characters. He explained that 13-year-old Noah Songsti, his dwarfish younger brother, and a "semi-feral" friend turn out to be elements of a single, "mildly schizophrenic" kid, and that the novel was about the "reintegration" of that character through a "journey of wisdom."[9]

```
            NOAH'S ARK
    The Journals of a Madman

           (a novel)

               by

       Wesley Earl Craven


    An essay submitted to the Faculty
    of Philosophy of The Johns Hopkins
    University in conformity with the
    requirements for the degree of
           Master of Arts

        Baltimore, Maryland
               1964
```

Noah's journey begins when he witnesses a car plummet from a bridge near his home in the cemetery. The identity of the driver is a mystery that prompts Noah to examine his own identity. He locks himself in a tower overlooking the cemetery and resolves to sort out the details of his relationships with various family members—as well as his beliefs about God—before reentering the world. The author explicitly states in the text of the novel that Noah's search is an extended metaphor, an analogue to the Biblical tale of Noah and the Ark, with the ark representing the writer's mind, and the "living creatures in the ark" representing the writer's "impressions and memories."[10]

Wes undoubtedly took some inspiration from Elliott Coleman, who believed that every person is a "walking metaphor." In his 1965 essay "The Meaning of Metaphor," Coleman explains, "There is no name, except yours, for what you really are; and that is only an approximation. And then, you are not static; you are becoming something; and so your real name is always changing."[11] T.S. Eliot once wrote that trying on different poetic voices while searching for one's own voice is the secret to transforming a young poet "from a bundle of second-hand sentiments into a person."[12] Wes, who had already adopted a series of literary personas, understood this statement implicitly, and *Noah's Ark* seems to be an effort at disentanglement. His "true self," Elliott Coleman theorized, would appear in "an intense (even if relaxed) metaphorical state," as the writer's "awareness of inner depths becomes acute, almost unbearable." In such moments, the writer's act of literary creation becomes an act of self-creation.[13]

If the reader interprets *Noah's Ark* as a straightforward metaphor (which will reduce the power of the story but make it easier to analyze), Wes's novel seems to be about multiple personality disorder. Noah shares a literal headspace with his precocious brother Raphael, a physically stunted but smart and sensitive Other, and his feral friend Cobbitt, a bold and blasphemous foil. The author tells us that Noah and Raphael share the same father, a respectable but not very interesting man named George. Cobbitt, on the other hand, appears to be the son of George's sadistic brother Jason, who might or might not have been murdered by George in an attempt to hide the facts of Noah's true heritage.

The novelist weaves a tangled web, dropping occasional clues to Noah's genealogical mystery within a compelling but haphazard narrative that reads like a stream-of-consciousness confession. The surface story revolves around the Dickensian innocent, naïve to the secrets and the darkness of the world, which might be how Wes Craven viewed his younger (pre-Candidian) self. In contrast to Noah, Raphael represents a complex worldview that is rooted in book learning—but Raphael's stunted appearance makes him insecure and inclined toward pessimism, so he mostly keeps his opinions to himself. Ultimately, Raphael is little more than a voice inside Noah's head, suggesting to the innocent that his family is a metaphorical death-trap: "The only way this family is connected is by the hooks everyone has set into each other. Hooks to hold each other down, or ourselves up, or hooks that have been there from birth. We're like a bunch of wretched prisoners of some war we don't even care about, chained together and hating each other even more than the chains that hold us together, and we snap at each other if we get too near, and the chains cut us and yank us back if we try to get away."[14]

The third character, Cobbitt, offers liberation. According to Noah, Cobbitt walks "a funambulist's balance between earnest irony and unmitigated blasphemy."[15] He is a sincere devil's advocate, constantly pushing Noah out of his comfort zone, forcing him to acknowledge things he doesn't want to acknowledge, to experience things that horrify him. It is probably not a coincidence that Cobbitt's name looks like a condensed version of "Coleman, Elliott." Despite his misgivings, Noah confesses that he needs Cobbitt. "I was nearly out of my mind until I found him," he says. Cobbitt responds to Noah's confession of near-madness by declaring that God is the true madman.[16] He helps Noah to escape his imprisonment inside the "ark" by forcing him to confront his true identity as Jason's son. Once Noah does that, he is able to shed—or perhaps absorb?—his alternate personalities, to go from being a bundle of second-hand sentiments to a true self.

In later sections of the novel, Noah feverishly recollects a series of formative experiences and nightmares—including one that was obviously based on Wes's personal experiences. In the scene, Noah hunts rats in a train yard with a bow and arrow, egged on by a neighborhood bully named Jaggard. Noah subsequently dreams that Jason (eventually revealed to be his real dad) is waiting for him in the back of a church with a fishing knife in hand. One major aspect of Noah's journey, it seems, is to escape the shadow of a violent, perhaps insane father.

Afterward, Noah is hunted by a mysterious white wolf—presumably the same mythical creature that stalked a character named Adam in Wes's earlier short story "Death Mask, Three-Quarter View." In *Noah's Ark*, the author connects the two works by specifying that Noah's grandfather was named Adam. As in the Old Testament, the sins of the father haunt the younger generation. Noah ultimately escapes the wolf, but he then becomes mortally sick and takes refuge inside a flooded crypt.

There, Cobbitt nurses Noah back to health, feeding him chicken soup from a fleshless skull. When Noah regains his strength, he follows the sound of "churchy" music out of the crypt, through dark woods, and into a long subterranean drain pipe.[17] When he reemerges from the other end—as if meeting the challenge posed at the end of *Orestes, or the Art of Smiling*—Noah perceives that he has been transformed. Wes-as-Noah concludes, "I felt the beginning of wisdom, and a compassion for everybody that came into me and was covered with my ignorance, my weakness, my stupidity."[18]

With the phrase "the beginning of wisdom," the novelist invokes a passage from the Old Testament Book of Proverbs: "The fear of the Lord is the beginning of wisdom, and the knowledge of the Holy is understanding." Instead of concluding with fear and knowledge, however, Wes Craven ends his / Noah's journey with New Testament love and humility. He expresses gratitude for the outer and inner voices that have possessed him, thereby creating a new self. Noah's trinity finally becomes One through love—because, as Elliott Coleman wrote, "Every metaphor well applied is a work of love."[19]

Did 21-year-old Wes Craven feel that he too had emerged, awake and transformed, from the darkness of his early youth? In a postscript to his unpublished novel, he describes *Noah's Ark* as a work of fiction but also suggests that he no longer perceives much of a difference between fiction and nonfiction, reality and dreams. "For you see," he writes, "there is nothing to know[,] only everything to believe [and] I simply believe that my years in the tower have shown me that believing is the supreme act of creation, and doubt the first act of destruction."[20] It is a remarkably affirmative ending to his story-so-far.

One year later, adopting a bit of aesthetic distance from the project, he reflected on the conclusion of the novel in a private letter to a friend, speculating about Noah's reemergence from the tunnel minus Cobbitt and Raphael: "I frankly don't know exactly which it was, (old Noah never said and I didn't ask), but either Cobbitt and Raphael got lost, or eaten by the white wolf, or perhaps… perhaps they never existed at all except in Noah's mind." Cagily suggesting that an author can hardly know more about his characters than the characters can know about their author, Wes deflected: "Besides, don't we all, at one time or another, come crawling out of the tunnel all alone, even though we could swear there were others with us?"

In June 1964, Wes submitted the novel as his Writing Seminars thesis and subsequently received a Master of Arts degree from Johns Hopkins University. Elliott Coleman opined that *Noah's Ark* showed great potential for the novelist to become a filmmaker—because the novel was "so visual." Wes later said he was "crushed" by that evaluation—because he didn't want to be a filmmaker; he wanted to be an author.[21] He spent the next several years submitting *Noah's Ark* to publishers, while also writing and submitting new short stories. One particularly macabre tale written during this time period is titled "The Doctor." Probably written in the spring of 1964, it revolves around a man whose psychiatrist has convinced him that his brain is infested with spiders, and the only cure is violent removal of the nest using a long silver hook. Noah had emerged from his long dark tunnel, but Noah's creator remained very aware of the darkness.

In the spring of '64, Wes moved into a house on Rossiter Avenue in Baltimore, where his friend Judson Scruton was living with a new wife and baby daughter. The newlyweds quickly became alarmed by their houseguest's erratic behavior. Scruton remembers, "Sometimes when Wes was out late and my wife had gone to bed, Wes would pry open a window and climb in, rather than ring the doorbell and wake us. It scared her considerably. Wes would also do things like—in middle of the night—get flashlights and go down to the basement and see if he could find insects to yell at. I mean, he was strange. He had an attraction toward the macabre and the bizarre. I forgave him all that because I really liked him and I appreciated the guitar-playing, sensitive person that I knew from literature courses and from the literary magazine. But he was certainly strange."

Around that time, Wes took a trip to New York City, where Bonnie Broecker was attending nursing school, to look for a job. Scruton says, "We drove up from Baltimore to see her. She was a really great, sweet girl. But, my oh my, she could have a temper with Wesley Earl. They were two very volatile personalities. The fights they had were legendary. They'd break up, they'd get together, they'd break up, they'd get together." One conflict revolved around whether or not to get married—which, for a couple of ex-fundamentalists, was a prerequisite to sex. The couple's passion was real but so was their hovering around a life-altering decision.

Bonnie remembers, "Wes kept breaking up with me. He was in a program at Johns Hopkins and his mentor, Elliott Coleman, said to Wes, 'You're making a big mistake getting married. You have this talent, you should just go with it. Getting married is going to be a distraction.' So Wes broke up with me. Of course, I was devastated. But we got back together and Wes invited me down to Baltimore and we stayed with Jud Scruton, who I didn't really know at the time. We were there for several days and Jud said, 'You guys should just get married.' I think that's the reason we got married. We eloped without really giving it a whole lot of thought."

Scruton drove the couple to a rustic shack deep in the Maryland countryside for their honeymoon, then returned a few days later to pick them up. "They didn't have a lot of money," he remembers, "so they were trying to find some place where they could go and just be themselves. But they picked this weekend when it was close to a hundred degrees, and [a destination] out in the middle of nowhere. They didn't bring that much water or food or anything. They wanted to be left there and picked up two or three days later. When I came back, they were furiously scratching insect bites and loudly lamenting their experience."

Bonnie remembers things differently: "We had our honeymoon in somebody's cabin. It was very, very rustic but it was nice. There was nothing else around, just the cabin. I'm sure we didn't have a telephone or anything. There was no electricity. We had to light kerosene lamps. We cooked our food in a very rudimentary way—but everything tasted great. We had a very nice time. And I remember the woman who owned the cabin was impressed because Wes had very carefully cleaned all of the kerosene lamps before we left. That's the kind of person he was."

Bonnie took a leave of absence from the nursing program at Columbia University and permanently relocated to Baltimore. Later that summer, Wes wrote to a friend about his tense, lazy lifestyle, "I don't have anything to do and me and my wife are always bitching at each other and I sleep all the time in the mornings, even into the afternoons, waking up thick headed and bleary eyed from long, dark dreams that haunt me all the rest of the afternoon and blur the line between waking and dreaming so much (I know how this sounds, but it happens to be the truth) that I don't know the difference sometimes, and I do horrible shocking things that one usually only does in dreams, and I guess I should find [a] psychiatrist again." Soon after, Bonnie learned she was pregnant and the father-to-be found a job selling rare coins at Hutzler's department store downtown.

The couple's future seemed desperately uncertain until an unexpected job offer shook Wes out of his malaise. He remembered, "I had routinely put my name in a file at a teaching placement bureau, and September had come and gone and I hadn't gotten a job. So it looked like I was gonna be a rare coin salesman for some undiscernible length of time."[22] Just as he had resigned himself to that fate, he received a call from an administrator at Westminster College, a private liberal arts school in rural New Wilmington, Pennsylvania. The caller explained that a member of the English Department faculty had died and the school needed an immediate replacement.

Wes and Bonnie moved into a two-story Victorian house near Borough Park, which they shared with another faculty couple. At a time when most faculty members had dogs, Wes had a cat—and when other professors would take their dogs for an evening stroll, Wes would take his cat for a "drag." (As to why Wes was a cat person, he once suggested that creativity is like a cat: "If you stare at it, it won't come. Look away."[23]) A colleague remembers Wes as an amateur hunter, explaining, "Wes and I spent a fair amount of time bow-hunting woodchucks… with very little damage to the local woodchuck population. In the process of this, I discovered that Wes was made very nervous by cows. He really didn't want to get anywhere near them."

One thing Wes apparently wasn't afraid of was losing his job. A former college administrator remembers that the president of Westminster College was "death on drinking" and forbade faculty members to consume alcohol on campus, adding, "Those of us who enjoyed an adult beverage every now and then were not sure whether it would be more harmful for us to see students in

Professor Wes Craven, Westminster College yearbook, 1965

local bars… or for the students to see us." Predictably, some faculty members rebelled against the ban. Wes and his housemates would sit on the front porch of their old Victorian house at night, drinking gin, vodka or bourbon out of tea cups. They hid the empty bottles in a window seat until visiting friends could retrieve them and safely dispose of them off campus. On one occasion, Wes and one of his inebriated fellow professors took their defiance further. A colleague remembers, "They got loaded and were caught by a security guard conducting mock baptisms in the college lake." Somehow, Wes managed to keep his job. That time.

In the classroom, Wes assigned William Strunk & E.B. White's *The Elements of Style* as one of the main texts. His recommended reading list included *Green Mansions* by W.H. Hudson; *Heart of Darkness* by Joseph Conrad; *The Brothers Karamazov* and *Crime and Punishment* by Fyodor Dostoevsky; *Doctor Zhivago* by Boris Pasternak; *The Bridge on the Drina* by Ivo Andrić; *Dubliners* and *A Portrait of the Artist as a Young Man* by James Joyce; *The Catcher in the Rye* and *Franny and Zooey* by J.D. Salinger; *The Fall, The Stranger, and The Plague* by Albert Camus; *Selected Short Stories* and *The Trial* by Franz Kafka; *Pincher Martin* by William Golding; *Perelandra* by C.S. Lewis; *Catch-22* by Joseph Heller; *Native Son* by Richard Wright; *The Age of Reason* and *Nausea* by Jean-Paul Sartre; *A Death in the Family* by James Agee; *Darkness at Noon* by Arthur Koestler; *The Diary of Anne Frank*; and *Tin Drum* by Günter Grass.

Katherine Hobbie Storms (Class of '68) says Wes's assignment of *The Trial* "changed the way I looked at literature, at the whole concept of literature," and prompted her to become an English major. It is tempting to assume the professor put a very personal spin on his discussions of Kafka, a novelist known for bizarre and surreal depictions of modern life. Years later, Wes would cite Kafka's novel *The Castle* as one of the ten most influential books he ever read.[24] He also said, "I think about Kafka all the time. His prose is so wonderful in its ability to render the drudgery, and the horror, of the ordinary: The awful things waiting to happen. It reminds me a lot of my own films."[25]

Kathryn Randall Gilbert (Class of '68) recalls some additional titles on Wes's recommended reading list: Lincoln Barnett's *The Universe and Dr. Einstein*, Hermann Bondi's *The Universe at Large*, I. Bernard Cohen's *The Birth of a New Physics*, James A. Coleman's *Relativity for the Layman*, George Gamow's *Gravity*,

Professor Wes Craven, Clarkson College yearbook, 1966

Calvin S. Hall's *A Primer of Freudian Psychology*, Erich Heller's *The Disinherited Mind: Essays in Modern German Literature and Thought*, Patrick M. Hurley's *How Old is the Earth?*, Julian Huxley's *Religion without Revelation* and *Evolution in Action*, Peter Medawar's *The Future of Man*, Bertrand Russell's *Our Knowledge of the External World*, Irving Stone's *The Agony and the Ecstasy: A Novel of Michelangelo*, and Victor F. Weisskopf's *Knowledge and Wonder: The Natural World as Man Knows It*. Obviously, Wes wanted to teach his students more than style and grammar. Gilbert adds, "His creative assignments included one that gave you options to eat a flower and write about it… or go to the one and only stoplight in downtown New Wilmington and put your ear to the road and tell a passerby that you could hear something coming, and write about the experience."

Former students remember that Wes would come to class—invariably late—and sit cross-legged on top of his desk as he regaled his audience. Jon "Gib" McGill (Class of '68) says he was an unconventional lecturer: "He would casually say something like, 'Well, what would anybody like to talk about today?' Usually the discourse would go off on a tangent having nothing to do with the assigned reading. I remember feeling disappointed in class because there was no way to prepare oneself for such random discussions. I should have paid more attention because some of the questions on our tests would refer to them."

According to another student, Wes's weirdly compelling class came to be known as "Craven 101." Janyth Williams (Class of '65) says, "Even though he was only four years older than I, Mr. Craven embodied my mental image of Washington Irving's Ichabod Crane. His brooding and gaunt classroom persona was somewhat unsettling, especially in the post-Camelot 1960s at that extremely conservative Presbyterian college. (We girls had early curfews and we were not permitted to wear slacks or shorts on campus.) No one ever cut Mr. Craven's classes, though, because he began every session with random and often unnerving observations about the absurdities of life—some of them narrowing down to our campus, our general lack of creativity, and the dull lives we students were all destined to lead. I wish I had written his stories down. The only actual story I recall was in mid-October 1964, when Mr. Craven came in and announced that his 'center of being' was in his left shoulder. He explained that *common* people are centered in their hearts or their brains, but he was centered in his left shoulder. He said he had to be very careful because if someone shot him there he would die instantly… and then he continued with quite a vivid elaboration on that concept. Back then, most of us Westminster students were naïve about marijuana and other drugs, so we just assumed he was a gifted visionary… which he obviously was, whatever the source."

One of Wes's most outrageous stories was memorialized in the freshman comp class's final exam. Kathy Gilbert explains, "He gave us a fanciful short story of his about a guy who had a worm bore through his head… and we had to punctuate, paragraph, capitalize and otherwise edit and correct." Another final exam fragment—a gonzo dialogue between an unidentified first-person narrator and a blowtorch-wielding, cigar-chomping anarchist—purported to be part of a novel-in-progress titled *The Life and Times of Sidney Smerdley*. The anarchist (possibly the novel's title character) grouses about New York City and reminisces about several colorful characters, including an Old Aunt Floozy, a nephew named Grundy Flack, a cousin Stanley who invented penicillin, and one Senator Snark. The six-page story fragment ends with the bombing of Rockefeller Center.

Things also got weird for students in Wes's American Theater / Modern Drama class. David Werle (Class of '67) says he convinced his teacher to coordinate an in-class reading of Samuel Beckett's absurdist play *Waiting for Godot*, and later bonded with Wes over music: "He noodled around with the guitar and the mandolin, so I suggested we put together a jug band because you don't have to have terrific skills to have a lot of fun." The jug band's sessions turned into "beer parties," which were verboten on Westminster's dry campus. "One evening, after a rehearsal, we were talking about how the college was almost oppressive. At that time, the Vietnam War was being rebelled against everywhere in the country, but there was nothing at all happening in New Wilmington, Pennsylvania. So we decided on the spot that we should march on something—and we decided to march on the lake. We started at one end of the lake and marched through chest-high water. At the end of the march, we were covered in grass and roots and mud and crud. I remember walking slowly back to Wes's house, where he crawled up in the sink and just sat there and drip-dried. Poor Bonnie came in and just looked at us and said, 'Oh, Wes.'"

After several close calls, Wes finally had a run-in with an authority figure that ended his time at Westminster. By the time James A. Perkins started teaching English at the college in 1973, the tale of Wes's firing had become local legend. He says, "The head of the English department was a stickler for folks starting class on time. Wes was not really capable of getting places on time. One day, when Wes had an eight o'clock class in Thompson-Clark Hall, the department was waiting outside his classroom for Wes to appear. Somehow, Wes realized that and went up the fire escape, through a window and into his class. Seeing him walk out at the end of the hour, the department head was amazed and enraged." Another colleague details the moment when young Ichabod Crane's luck finally ran out: "The department head told him that if he was late one more time, he was through. Shortly after this, Wes was charging into the building and up the steps, late again. At the same time, the department head was coming down the steps. Wes stopped, looked at him and said, 'Well, you got me.' It turned out the department head didn't know he had a class then. But that did it." Wes remained employed by the college in June 1965, when he judged a poetry workshop contest and presented awards to the contest winners at a ceremony in Hoyt Center. He did not return to Westminster in the fall.

In March 1965, Bonnie gave birth to their son Jonathan and the new father realized he could not afford to remain unemployed. He was reluctant to take another teaching job but understood the benefits of the profession: cheap prices at the college gas pump, summer vacation, and an intellectually-stimulating work environment.[26] With a bit of luck, Wes quickly found another teaching gig—in the Humanities department at Clarkson College, a tech school in upstate New York. The Craven family promptly settled in the sleepy town of Potsdam and Wes started teaching English to engineering students. He later told an interviewer for the London-based tabloid *The Daily Express*, "I was the course they had to get through with proper grades so they didn't get drafted."

Wes Craven as Ichabod Crane, Clarkson College yearbook, 1968

It was 1965 and the times they were a-changin'. Although the atmosphere at Clarkson was mostly conservative, a "Cultural Committee" sponsored eclectic programs on campus, including a lecture-demonstration on modern jazz (featuring a live performance by Thelonious Monk) and a cutting-edge "Cinema as an Art" series. Film screenings in 1965 and 1966 included works by director Federico Fellini (*La Dolce Vita, 8 ½*, and *Variety Lights*), François Truffaut (*The 400 Blows* and *Shoot the Piano Player*), Luis Buñuel (*Viridiana* and *The Exterminating Angel*), and Michelangelo Antonioni (*L'Avventura*). Many times over the course of his life, Wes acknowledged the deep and abiding influence those films and filmmakers had on him.

Wes said his interest in European cinema was stimulated by articles about *cinema verité* in publications like *Evergreen Magazine*.[27] In fact, a film critic for the Clarkson school newspaper prefaced a March 1966 screening of Luis Buñuel's film *The Exterminating Angel* with an allusion to a contemporary *Evergreen* essay. In the source essay, Buñuel suggested that cinema was "invented to express the life of the subconscious, the roots of which penetrate poetry so deeply."[28] Did this insight push Wes to begin examining cinema as a psychologically-revealing— potentially Kafkaesque—art form? Years later, he said he was drawn to "the way directors like Buñuel would go in and out of a dream state. […] It was a niche that was very interesting to me, and somewhat unexploited."[29]

Cinema wasn't the only subject Wes studied intently during his first year at Clarkson. In the fall of 1965, a group of students petitioned for a course in contemporary pop culture that "would span the period from 1900 to 1965, and cover the literature, art, and music of that era."[30] The following school year, the proposal morphed into a set of extracurricular presentations known as "The Free University of Potsdam." Wes almost certainly participated in the experiment, which kicked off with "a study and discussion of the role of the 20th century man in a changing world which is 'blessed' with revolutions, healthy neurosis, and the fear of total destruction, while being cursed with The Bomb, slow moving hypocritical structures and their lazy liberal antitheses." Seminars were held every Wednesday night in rented rooms at 35 Market Street," as "teacher and student, education and action" came together to survey Modern Theater (Ibsen, Shaw, O'Neill, Beckett, Ionesco, Baldwin, Albee), Cybernetics, Communism, and "The Computer Revolution."[31]

Not surprisingly, there was some pushback from the Clarkson administration to the idea of teachers and students mingling as peers—but there was also plenty of praise. In a November 1966 article, Paul Jensen hailed the program in the school newspaper: "It's the purpose of a teacher to educate his students by allowing them to use their thinking processes in order to be able to make decisions which will be facing them throughout their life. By 'spoon-feeding' students his own thoughts and prejudices on a subject, and expecting the students to reiterate them on an hour exam, the Prof. is actually guilty of indoctrinating his pupils rather than developing their logic and mental processes. The Prof. is also hurting himself by continuing throughout life with a closed mind to anything which may come in opposition to his views."[32] It is easy to imagine that Wes Craven embraced this criticism and championed a new approach.

Around the same time, a group of Humanities professors at Clarkson began teaching an evening course on 20th century literature. The reading list included D.H. Lawrence's *Sons and Lovers*, Boris Pasternak's *Doctor Zhivago*, Joyce Carey's *Mister Johnson*, Friedrich Dürrenmatt's *The Physicists*, Joseph Heller's *Catch-22*, Marvin Gettleman's *Vietnam: History, Documents, and Opinions on a Major World Crisis*, David Solomon's anthology *LSD: The Consciousness Expanding Drug*, and *The Best American Short Stories of 1966*.[33] According to the local Potsdam newspaper, Wes led the discussion of *Catch-22* in Clarkson's Snell Hall on January 9, 1967.[34] He later named Heller's novel as one of the most influential books in his life. No doubt he was equally intrigued by David Soloman's anthology of essays about the mind-bending new drug LSD. It boasted an introduction by Timothy Leary, who later appeared in two of Craven's films (*Shocker* and *Night Visions*)—both times as a spiritual advisor.

In his introductory essay "How to Change Behavior," Leary wrote that those who have a "visionary experience of some sort" are subsequently able to recognize the "game structure" of Western society, while "the rest of us spend our time struggling with roles and rules and goals and concepts of games." He concluded that "the most efficient way to cut through the game structure of Western life" is the use of consciousness-expanding drugs.[35] Leary's message, articulated more fully in his 1964 book *The Psychedelic Experience: A Manual Based on the Tibetan Book of the Dead*, resonated with a generation of disillusioned young Americans and rebels against religiosity. Wes probably heard the call in 1967 but he didn't disappear down that rabbit hole right away.

Other contemporary experiences had a more immediate influence. In December 1966, Wes played the role of Joseph Garcin in the Clarkson Drama Club's performance of Jean-Paul Sartre's hellbound play *No Exit*. Garcin is a murdered journalist, proud of his reputation for telling the truth no matter the cost, but haunted by a final act of cowardice, and (he says) damned for the cruel habit of psychologically tormenting his wife. Sartre's play was performed alongside Edward Albee's *The Sandbox*, which was directed by Wes's friend David Cameron (Class of '68), on December 14th and 15th. Steve Chapin (Class of '69) remembers composing some original music for the production with a clarinet and an electric bass guitar. According to a review in the local Potsdam newspaper, the result was "terse, electrifying drama."[36]

The brief run was followed by a raucous after-party. The Clarkson school newspaper itemized the damage: "one chemistry professor's private lab and office, entered, and used for a barbecue pit, filling it with smoke; lavatory walls smeared with paints and strewn with trash; the area littered with liquor bottles; and ES 128 left in shambles." The dismayed journalist inquired, "Who was in charge here? Where was the advisor?"[37] The official Drama Club faculty advisor was Psychology professor Stuart Fischoff—a future media psychologist who would, in the 1990s and early 2000s, write about the influence of horror films and video games on impressionable young viewers—but professor Wes Craven may have shouldered some blame.

That same month, Clarkson grad students Jerry Carlin and Boyd Kimball opened a student-oriented coffee house at 36 ½ Market Street. The Pendulum became the new home of the Free University of Potsdam and a center of activity for the town's growing counterculture. Clarkson journalist Jon Welch wrote, "Any night for the Pendulum, there is always something happening. It could be impromptu folk singing discussions, poetry readings or anything that crosses the mind of the people that happen to be there."[38] Ken Lyon (Class of '69) adds, "That place was a real life-saver for many of us, an alternative to Potsdam no-culture. There was no alcohol, but we served spaghetti, sandwiches, and a variety of drink concoctions. I worked in the kitchen and waited tables, which were telephone cable spools covered in burlap. Steve Chapin and his band played there at least once. I believe Wes went there occasionally for poetry readings."

On select evenings, Wes frequented the local movie theater, where he saw Michelangelo Antonioni's *Blow-Up* for the first time in April 1967. The film marked a turning point in his life: "The oblique, non-linear, suggestive ambiance, the incredible control of color (Antonioni painted whole streets in accord with his needs), the shocking (for that time) sexuality, and the impenetrable complexity of its mystery absolutely beguiled me."[39] It seems this film, more than any other, drew Wes to his future career in filmmaking. Afterward, he purchased a Revere C-103 16mm movie camera in a New York City pawn shop and started experimenting.[40]

He was also becoming more vocal about his political leanings. Professor Craven's name appeared in the Potsdam *Courier-Freeman* newspaper for the first time in February 1966, when he signed his name to a joint opinion letter about the recent appearance of Trần Văn Dĩnh, a Washington correspondent for the *Saigon Post*, at Clarkson College. The letter concluded, "We must offer the people of South Viet Nam more than they are offered by North Vietnam. We are not doing this at the moment, and military activity is not the way to do it."[41] Anti-war sentiment had been building on campus since Wes arrived, culminating in a Viet Nam Symposium at the Free University of Potsdam in March 1967 and an open letter from Clarkson faculty members to President Lyndon Johnson. The signees, including Wesley Earl Craven, urged President Johnson to "recognize the right of the Vietnamese people to self-determination and national reunification" and "to use the billions saved from a mistaken war effort to begin a war against the real enemies of all mankind: racial prejudice, greed, ignorance, poverty and the psychology that makes wars possible."[42] Although he was one name among many, Wes was taking a public stand using his real name—something he hadn't done since being "denounced" at Wheaton College. He subsequently participated in a public Vietnam forum on campus, as a steering member of the Northern New York Committee for Alternatives in Vietnam.

When the spring 1967 semester ended, Wes asked his wife Bonnie to accompany him on a cross-country road trip to Haight-Ashbury, the epicenter of hippie culture in San Francisco, California. Although he was a bit old to be a hippie (he was nearly thirty), Wes was still working out what he believed and what he wanted to do with his life. Bonnie remembers, "We went across the country and back again on a motorcycle. Wes really wanted to go, and these friends of ours offered to take care of Jonathan. To this day, I feel guilty about that. It was kind of a nice trip but I missed Jonathan so much. On the way, I found out I was pregnant with Jessica."

Wes later told a friend that one of the happiest moments of his life was when he and Bonnie left Chicago and "headed further west than I or anyone in my family had ever been."[43] After years of doing what he thought he was supposed to do, he felt like a pioneer in new territory. In Sheridan, Wyoming, he and Bonnie made a brief stop to visit Wes's college friend Bill Schopf, who remembers, "I was home that summer to see my parents. The phone rings and it's Wes and he's on a motorcycle with Bonnie, touring the country. So they bop by my house on this motorcycle. My mother was horrified. She was so conservative, and here's this long-haired guy and this woman on a motorcycle. 'My God, these hippies!' That was the last time I ever saw Wes."

From there, the couple headed to California. Along the way, they were waylaid by a group of rednecks in the Nevada desert—an encounter that would stay with Wes for years. Bonnie recalls, "It was Sunday afternoon and we were in a town that was really quiet. I would get really sleepy in the afternoons because I was pregnant, so I laid down in the grass and took a nap. I woke up to some hooping and hollering and [saw] Wes had been lassoed by these guys in a truck. Wes had a beard at the time and they said they were gonna take him out to the desert and cut his balls off or something like that. He was screaming, 'I'm a college professor and this is my wife!' I looked normal, so they let him go. But it was very scary." Years later, Wes told the story to journalist Jason Zinoman, who summed up: "Wes noticed an arrow zip by his ear and a group of three young men in a pickup truck approached, threatening, eyeing his long hair. 'We don't like hippies,' one shouted. Wes said if they touched him, he would sue. One member of the ragged gang responded that if they wanted to kill him, they could throw his body in the salt mines and no one would ever find it."[44] Only the presence of his beautiful wife saved him.

The couple resumed their journey and made it to Haight-Ashbury. "We did stay in San Francisco a little bit," Bonnie says. "I remember I only had summer clothes and it was chilly. Wes went to a Be-In or some kind of demonstration and I stayed back at the hotel." If Wes had any significant experiences in the Haight, he didn't talk about them publicly. One can only hazard guesses based on the accounts of others who were there.

Earlier that year, Golden Gate Park hosted the first Human Be-In—a peaceful gathering of more than twenty thousand people, including Timothy Leary, Richard Alpert (Ram Dass), Allen Ginsberg, and rock groups like Jefferson Airplane and The Grateful Dead. Ginsberg described it as "a gathering together of younger people aware of the planetary fate that we are all sitting in the middle of, imbued with a new consciousness, and desiring of a new kind of society involving prayer, music, and spiritual life together rather than competition, acquisition, and war."[45] The event inspired similar love-ins in New York and Los Angeles over the following months. It also inspired tens of thousands of hippies to make the pilgrimage to Haight-Ashbury. By late summer, when Wes and Bonnie arrived, the neighborhood was overrun.

In a memoir, Pattie Boyd describes an August 1967 visit to Haight-Ashbury with her then-husband George Harrison: "We were expecting Haight-Ashbury to be special, a creative and artistic place, filled with Beautiful People, but it was horrible—full of ghastly drop-outs, bums and spotty youths, all out of their brains."[46] In his own memoir, Harrison adds, "It certainly showed me what was really happening in the drug culture. It wasn't what I'd thought—spiritual awakenings and being artistic—it was like alcoholism, like any addiction."[47] Two months later, on October 6, hundreds of people in Haight-Ashbury staged a mock funeral for "hippie" culture, which had suffered a quick, painful death due to overexposure. By then, Wes and Bonnie were back in New York, preparing for the arrival of their second child.

Wes began leaning toward a more bohemian lifestyle, reportedly treating his family "like it was a kind of accident."[48] At one point, he left Bonnie and Jonathan for three days to live in an abandoned farmhouse with no running water. Bonnie admits that during this time, Wes could be downright cruel: "One time, he was out with Jonathan doing something—Jonathan was two years old—and Wes called and disguised his voice and said, 'There's been a bad accident...' And I completely freaked out. Then he laughed and said, 'Oh no, it's just Wes.' He had that sense of humor. He liked to scare people. And he was very good at it. So, in some ways, you couldn't quite trust him. You didn't know when that side of him was going to pop out."

Wes's career plans were equally mercurial. Before his cross-country journey, a neighbor said he had been "committed to education as a national project."

When he returned to Clarkson College in the fall, "he was different. He wanted to be an author—and he'd caught the 'movie bug.'"[49] So far, Wes had rarely been published outside of school newspapers and magazines. He'd submitted *Noah's Ark* to Doubleday and Dial Press, but had been rejected by both. He'd also submitted short stories to various magazines, including *The Transatlantic Review*, which in 1968 and 1969 published John Updike, J.G. Ballard, Anthony Burgess, Joyce Carol Oates, and Craven's future screenwriting collaborator Thomas Baum, but not Wes Craven.

Bonnie remembers reading her husband's short stories and thinking "they were so well written but the endings always had some really weird twist to them. You'd get kind of invested in the character of the story and then the ending would be a weird twist that would take you off somewhere else. That was just his style, although I didn't realize it at the time. I remember saying to him, 'You keep getting all these rejection notices with positive feedback, so maybe you should change the endings? Be not quite so weird.' Of course, he didn't change anything. He did his own thing. He was very sure of what he was doing. He'd put his rejection notices up on the wall. He was proud of them, so he plastered them on the wall behind his desk and kept going."

In the fall of 1967, Wes undertook a new writing project with Wheaton friend Judi Chaffee Culbertson, who had recently published *Games Christians Play: An Irreverent Guide to Religion without Tears*, a "goodbye song to the whole evangelical scene" that sold "phenomenally well"—over 50,000 copies. When it came time to write a followup, she proposed a "round-robin writing project" with her co-author Patti Bard and Wes—which they dubbed *Jefferson Airplane I.*

The unpublished 119-page manuscript consists entirely of letters exchanged between the three authors. The first letter, written by Patti (under the pseudonym Andrea), alluded to Wes's terrifying encounter with the "hippie brigade" in Nevada. The third letter, written by Wes, offered a hazy account of that experience but focused mainly on a novel he'd been trying to write. He claimed he had been struggling for some time to craft a "fully modern, fully free" followup to *Noah's Ark*. The experience in Nevada had ruined it.

In a subsequent letter, written in March 1968, following the birth of his daughter Jessica, Wes wondered why Patti and Judi were using fake names ("Are we hiding out from the fuzz?"). Apparently, he was no longer inclined to hide behind pseudonyms. Instead, he wanted to attach his name to the most audacious literary scenarios he could dream up, indulging himself in imaginative wordplays ("Up your LSD, he said acidly") and train-of-consciousness rants. His inhibitions turned all the way down, he declared, "Life speaks best to me with fingers and breasts, with the inside of things, with the heat of its pleasure and the volume turned all the way up, manic guitars and pagan drums." Desperate to feel liberated, he followed his stream of thought into outrageous and often surreal oblivions.

Around the same time, every Thursday at 9pm, Wes co-hosted a late-night radio show called "The Jazz Scene" on the local station WTSC-FM with Clarkson undergrad Dave Reich (Class of '69), who remembers, "I had been doing a jazz show for a couple of years when Wes approached me between classes. Wes wasn't much older than us students. And he had a certain air of cool and sophistication about him. He said, 'You know, I've been listening to your show on the radio. And I wonder… would you let me co-host?' I thought, 'He's a really cool guy, that might be fun.' So we did a two-hour show once a week."

Beginning on February 1st, the duo charted a musical journey through the "Seasons of Love." Wes brainstormed playlists for variations on the following themes: "Seeking" (February 1), "First Love" (February 6), "Passion" (February 15), "Joy" (February 22), "Fear" (February 29), "Anger" (March 7), "Betrayal" (March 14), "The Break-Up" (March 21), "The Blues" (March 28), "Drunkenness" (April 4), "Reunion" (April 19), "Parting, War & Death" (May 8), "Together Again" (May 9), and "A Lifetime…." (May 16). Reich says, "We'd meet up at the radio station a little bit before we went on air. Sometimes Wes would bring some records with cuts that he wanted to play. We would go through the station's music library and pick stuff out, then we would kind of wing it. And we'd talk about the music between every few cuts. Every time that mic went on, I was nervous—but Wes seemed so at ease. He had a really sharp sense of humor. Often, his wit went right over my head. I didn't know how to respond because I didn't catch a lot of his jokes. But it was fun. We had a good time together."

That same semester, Wes shot his first movie. On February 23rd, the Clarkson Drama Club formalized plans to shoot a student film—using Wes's new 16mm camera. The resulting film would spawn a series of local legends.

Clarkson historian Bradford Broughton claimed it was made by members of the Theta Chi fraternity, and shot inside their frat house on Elm Street, and that the frat house was once a funeral parlor.[50] This is a fabrication that began circulating on campus sometime after the release of *A Nightmare on Elm Street* (1984). The reality is that the Drama Club made three different films in the spring of 1968—two short films, plus a live-action 40-minute feature titled *Pandora Experimentia*. Ken Lyon, co-director of *Pandora*, says Wes was minimally involved with the short films but he was a key collaborator on the feature, serving as the film's cinematographer.

Lyon says he and co-writer John Heneage envisioned *Pandora* as a spoof of the popular TV series *Mission: Impossible*. The film was comprised of approximately twenty sequences, each revolving around characters searching for Pandora's box. Many of the sequences were pure farce. Lyon explains, "John thought it would be great to have someone cross the street but they've got a red light and they're frustrated. Finally, the light turns green and they cross the street—and get hit by a train. I remember John laughing hysterically over that. Another scene was set in the local jail. And another scene involved us throwing a dummy off a radio tower."

Brian Hauser, who organized a *Pandora Experimentia* reunion in 2015, describes how the radio tower scene directly inspired the jail scene: "While he was up there, Ken saw a police car approaching [...] The officer was initially convinced that someone had jumped from the tower, and was relieved if not entirely happy to find out that the trespassers were just making a movie."[51] The crew members were taken to the local jail, where police allowed them to shoot an impromptu scene behind bars. The production team also talked their way into the local bank and filmed a fake robbery using a stack of real hundred-dollar bills. Eventually, it seems, the entire town of Potsdam got in on the experiment. Lyon remembers that the odyssey concluded with a visual non-sequitur: "We had a scene out in a field with this big box that was just flats from an earlier Drama Club production, painted with flowers. Inside were twelve or fifteen girls in bikinis. When the flats fell down, all the girls ran out."

Reflecting on the project decades later, Lyon says the post-production process was equally ridiculous: "We had all this film, so John made a connection at St. Lawrence University in Canton, which was ten miles away. He got

Top: Ken Lyon and Wes Craven making *Pandora Experimentia*, 1968
Bottom: The crew of *Pandora Experimentia* (left to right): Wes Craven,
Ken Lyon, John Heneage (standing) and Ken Wood, 1968
(Photos courtesy Ken Lyon)

permission to use their film lab and we went down one evening when they had no classes and John and I edited the film. It was all hot-spliced. John did all the splicing, working with the equipment and gluing it together. I picked out the frames. We had film strips hanging from cords all across the room, and I'd say, 'Put this one here, that one there.'" When it came time to add audio, "We spent a night in a barn with two turntables and tape recorders—I mean, a tape recorder and a reel to reel—and we selected audio clips. The film didn't have any dialogue in it. It was all music. Maybe thirty tracks total. And the audio was played separately. When we showed the film, we had to keep the picture and the audio in sync." The music cues included Ennio Morricone's theme from *The Good, The Bad, and The Ugly* and Dave Brubeck's "Unsquare Dance."[52]

On May 8, 1968, the Clarkson school newspaper reported that "the Potsdam Underground" had completed its cinematic experiment, and urged students and townies alike to attend the upcoming screenings on Friday and Saturday night—luring locals with the promise (or was it a threat?) that "you might be one of the cast."[53] "I remember a food fight, with a bowl of spaghetti ending up on my head," remembers one cast member. "Dr. Stuart Fischoff played a fairly large role in the production. He starred in the film with a patch over his eye. He was riding a snowmobile in part of it." Another alum says the film's premiere was a big deal for the entire town of Potsdam: "The idea of a movie made by students, without movie-studio type equipment and whatever other industrial-strength resources I assumed were needed, was new and exciting. I was impressed by the quality of it, even though the content was a little light—involving a lot of cars driving around and people moving between cars and buildings."

All things considered, *Pandora Experimentia* was a hit—and a boon for its cinematographer, who started making narrative films at home. Wes's then-wife Bonnie remembers, "He made a short film starring me, believe it or not. It was filmed in our house and it was called *The Café*. To us, it was absolutely hilarious. Wes also filmed something with some friends who lived across the street. I remember a scene where Jonathan was eating spaghetti and he had spaghetti falling out of his mouth." For Wes, it was the beginning of a new career—and the end of his career in higher education. "At the end of that [school] year, my department chairman came to me and he said, 'You know, it's time for you to get serious. You're not working on your PhD, you haven't published anything, and you're running around with this stupid camera, acting like an idiot. It's time you became a serious Humanities professor.' And I quit."[54]

In a letter for *Jefferson Airplane I*, Wes told his friends that he had quit his cozy teaching job and denounced academia because he thought it was "certified castration." In the same letter, he reflected on his life as a husband and father, and speculated about his own father, an ever-present ghost. "There was a place in time when he spoke and smoked and joked with my mother about things, I suppose; although all I remember was once when he asked—Do you hear me? And then again, *Do you hear me?* Until I answered yes, for fear of his anger; But the crime, and the hand that would make me regret it, are both cut away now [...] Now he is a few old photographs, a grainy bicep flexed in black and gray and a strange face beneath a balding brow, and a fuck you if you don't like it sort of grin, the kind that would win the women, as it did, and embitter the wife, as it also did, and haunt the son, as it does." Did Wes worry that he too was a bad husband and a bad father destined for an early death?

In 1968, Wes Craven was 29 years old, well on his way to his imagined death at age 40, and feeling destined to "turn in his life in somewhat bitterly." In the spring, he expressed a dreamy restlessness and told his *Jefferson Airplane* correspondents that he no longer cared about getting published; all he wanted was to exchange honest and sincere words with true friends. Perhaps a sense of loneliness prompted him to pursue filmmaking—a collaborative art—over solitary prose writing.

In the summer, he struck out for New York City to look for a first job in the film industry. He tried to exploit a connection to documentary filmmaker Richard Leacock—a relative of former student Steve Chapin—but, as he wrote in *Jefferson Airplane I*, Leacock had been "very nice and concerned" but hadn't offered him a job. After that, "I went the rounds, crossing off names, writing down new ones then crossing those off. And everywhere I went they wanted to know what experience I'd had, who I'd worked for. And when I would say I was a college teacher for four years and had just made one school-grown movie (plus a TV political and a commissioned cycle scramble), they would look at me like, My Gawd, who *is* this nut?" Wes decided he really must be crazy—"or very very naïve"—to try to land a job in an industry where it seemed that even the janitor had "a Master's from NYU in cinema."

The Cravens: Bonnie, Jessica, Jonathan and Wes, c. 1968
(courtesy Marty Larson)

Back in Potsdam, he played the role of irresponsible wild man to the hilt. Family friend David Cameron says, "I remember in particular a family picnic day that summer at a nearby quarry swimming hole. Wes spent most of the swimming time diving from the highest cliff point. He was very focused and separate from the rest of us who were paddling with Bonnie and Jonathan in the shallow end. He didn't challenge me to high-dive with him; just did his thing. On leaving the site, we all piled into their station wagon. Wes turned onto an abandoned rail-line—the tracks and rails had all been removed—and began driving along that, gradually accelerating until Bonnie started nervously saying his name. Looking ahead, I could see, as could Bonnie, that there was a gap in the trail where a small bridge had been removed. Wes was grinning and continued to accelerate, with Bonnie saying, 'You wouldn't!' But of course he *did*. The gap wasn't much longer than the station wagon, which dropped like a stone into the shallow ditch rather than cinematically leaping across. Thankfully, no one was hurt—although this was before seat belts—but everyone was in shock. Except Wes, who was laughing hysterically. Once Bonnie saw that everyone was unharmed, she smacked Wes on the shoulder, then broke into tears that ended in a laugh and a familiar wry smile that said 'this is what living with this guy is like.' Then she opened the door and said, 'I'll be back.' We were in farm country and Bonnie knew all she needed to do was find a farmer. Sure enough, about half an hour and a bag of leftover picnic Oreos later, Bonnie came riding back on the rear of a huge farm tractor. The farmer looked the situation over, gave Wes a witheringly disgusted look and proceeded to hook a chain to the car bumper, then got back on the tractor and gently tugged the car up out of the ditch. He unhooked, waved off Bonnie's offer of cash, and drove away. The ride back to town was kind of quiet."

At the end of the summer, Wes remained jobless. Unable to reclaim his position at Clarkson, he began calling local public high schools and landed a job as an English teacher at Madrid-Waddington High School, twenty miles north of Potsdam. The Craven family moved into the village of Norwood, where Wes felt a million miles away from the life he wanted to be living. At night, he continued to write short stories. In a 2010 interview with me, he remembered, "We lived in a house that had been converted. At one time, it had been a two-story house, and now it was separated into upstairs and downstairs. And there was a stairwell that had been converted into a closet. The stairs went up to a ceiling and then stopped. There was no place to have a studio, so I went in there and made a desk that dropped down, so I could sit on the stairs and drop down the desk. And I had a sign on the door: 'This way lies madness.'"

In the cold light of day, the self-professed madman cut his hippie hair, trimmed his beard, and led a respectable life. At Madrid-Waddington High, he taught English and served as an advisor to the sophomore class leaders. According to *The Massena Observer*, he also supported a local Boy Scout Troop, going with them on a canoe trip to Saranac Lake and Fish Creek State Park in late August.[55] Behind this façade, wild ideas were brewing.

Madrid-Waddington alum Joe Ruddy thinks Wes's experience at the school might have inspired one of his future films: "The high school was built during the civil defense period—it opened in the fall of '62—so it was built with a bomb shelter, complete with bottled water and canned food on pallets and a very extensive labyrinth underneath the school. By 1968, there was a room for teachers—at least, teachers who smoked—next to the entrance to the bomb shelter. Basically, it was an underground boiler room. A boiler room that was exceedingly similar to Freddy's boiler room in *A Nightmare on Elm Street*. For those of us who knew the boiler room at Madrid-Waddington, the imagery [in the film] was striking."

Did Wes imagine that the school's labyrinth might have a monstrous caretaker? At the very least, he felt at odds with the authority figures there. Around Thanksgiving 1968, he wrote to Judi Chaffee Culbertson and Patti Bard about a handbook of rules passed out to students by a tyrannical school principal he called "Miss Snark." Even worse, he wrote, was the handbook of rules given to the teachers.

Around that time, Wes wrote a prose piece titled "The Bogg Report," a satire of administrative and bureaucratic procedures at a small high school. (Abe Snake rises again!) "It was one of those things that nobody would want to get caught holding," remembers fellow English teacher Jack Smith. "The teacher's room was in the basement, and one time we heard the principal on her way downstairs. She was about five-feet-nothing and she always wore high heels that you could hear clicking down the hallway. And somebody had a copy of 'The Bogg Report.' We wanted to make sure she didn't see it. We were all… if not in terror, at least in awe of her."

In *Jefferson Airplane I*, Wes described the outlets that helped him survive the "tyranny" of his daily life: visiting old friends, watching movies, reading *Gargantua* by Rabelais, diving off cliffs into icy clear water in the Adirondacks, and floating in a canoe at night under a "Van Gogh sky, getting my bearings." In the same letter, he said he'd tried LSD a few times but casually dismissed the results: "It was blah blah blah and I saw blah blah and now know blah blah."

A subsequent LSD trip must have made a bigger impression on him. In 2010, he told me, "If you trip, you suddenly realize that reality itself is a lie. It can be taken apart, and suddenly you are just looking at the molecules. Then you realize that there is this long history of drug-induced glimpses outside the whole structure of reality, into seeing something that's the bigger picture. That's when I started to think that God is much bigger than our concepts. If God is infinite, then we're incapable of conceiving what any God could be. We make up these versions that are the most sophisticated versions we can think of, but the truth is still beyond us. At that point, I had a new awareness of [God as] just consciousness and the planet and nature. That's what's sacred. That's where the miracles are." Timothy Leary couldn't have said it better. In 1969, however, Wes remained pithy and dismissive.

On March 16, 1969, between 11pm and 1am, Wes played guitar on a live Blues radio show called "Corners of Your Mind," alongside his former student Steve Chapin and friend Paul Sears. Chapin recalls, "We played music over joints, listened to Procol Harum, The Band, Hendrix, etc., raging against the 'Nam War." Soon after that, Wes wrote his last letter in *Jefferson Airplane I*. It was a sprawling collection of symbol-laden fragments summing up his life and the state of American culture in the wake of the Tet Offensive, the My Lai Massacre, the assassinations of Martin Luther King Jr. and Robert Kennedy, the rise of Richard Nixon, Apollo 8, and the moon landing. A disorienting leap into the heart of darkness.

Wes summed up his post-college experience as "a five-year drift away" from the indelible truths of his early life, saying, "Vietnam had a lot to do with it. And drugs, maybe. And just a sense of getting out into the world of other people that would look at you like 'Are you crazy?' From the point of just not believing that what we had been told was true—and certainly through the whole Vietnam era—it just seemed like one lie after another was being revealed. At a certain point, I think the entire culture felt like everything had been a lie. Everything you'd been told about the government, about America trying to do good in the world; everything you'd been told about sex; everything they told you about religion—it was all one big fabrication. Everything kind of fell apart. And sometimes in a rather joyous and raucous way. Woodstock and demonstrations, burning down Banks of America and all that stuff. We were abandoning everything. Rock and roll was very anarchistic. It was just like, 'Let's throw everything out and see what's real.'"

Writing to a friend, thirty-year-old Wes shared news of the fatal heart attack of a Wheaton College friend at the age of twenty-seven. He then declared his own youth dead, if not yet buried. "My mind's life has been an ass-backwards advance from unshakeable conviction to rapturous confusion," he wrote, apparently convinced that his own life was over. Two looming questions—"Are you crazy?" and "What's real?"—prompted him to continue his Candidian journey into the unknown. His co-writer Judi remembers, "He said he wanted to be the first crazy person that didn't die young. He was very invested in that."

The Soul of Wes Craven

CHAPTER FOUR

PRIMAL SCREAM

(1969 - 1972)

"No form of art goes beyond ordinary consciousness as film does, straight to our emotions, deep into the twilight room of the soul."

\- Ingmar Bergman,
The Magic Lantern: An Autobiography (1987)

In 1969, the office building at 56 West 45th Street in midtown Manhattan was a major hub for the burgeoning documentary film industry. The ninth and tenth floors belonged to Richard Leacock and D.A. Pennebaker, *cinéma vérité* pioneers whose work minimized traditional voiceover narration, sit-down interviews, and directorial interaction, instead using camera movement and picture-logic to give viewers a sense of "being there." The 1967 documentary *Don't Look Back*, a portrait of Bob Dylan, brought the filmmakers mainstream success and prompted them to expand their production company. By the time Leacock-Pennebaker released *Monterey Pop* in December 1968, other documentarians were in orbit around them and the place was buzzing with activity. The previous year, Wes Craven had failed to land a job with the duo, but when he returned to 56 West 45th Street in the summer of '69, he caught a break.

Wes remembered, "Steve Chapin told me that he had a brother Harry who was a film editor in New York. Steve said that if I wanted to, I could look up his brother, and Harry would talk to me about possibly giving me a job, and if not, he could teach me something about film."[1] Harry Chapin had recently found success with his Oscar-winning documentary *Legendary Champions* (1968), after which he "cashed in his Academy Award credentials" for a job directing and editing two thirty-minute IBM industrials under the auspices of Leacock-Pennebaker alum Jim Lipscomb.[2] At the time, Lipscomb was busy planning the documentary feature *Blue Water, White Death* (1971), about an expedition to study Great White sharks off the coast of South Africa, so Chapin inherited creative control over the IBM films. He was ensconced in an editing suite rented from Lipscomb's business associate Roland Condon when Wes Craven connected with him.

Luckily for Wes, Harry Chapin was amenable. "I sat with him for about a week, just watching him cut. He explained to me why he was cutting, pacing, and a great deal of things which stuck with me." At the end of the week, a teenage messenger was fired from the post-production house and Chapin asked Wes if he knew any kids that might want the job. Realizing he needed get his foot in the door however he could, Wes volunteered. "I was 30 years old, had a Master's Degree in Philosophy, two kids, and took the job as a messenger! That's how I got into film!"[3]

Soon after, the Craven family relocated from upstate New York to Brooklyn. Bonnie remembers, "We looked all over New York for an apartment we could afford. Needless to say, that was very difficult. It turned out that an apartment came up in the building that Steve [Chapin] lived in, and also his mother lived in. So we got this apartment on Hicks Street in Brooklyn Heights." Jonathan Craven, who spent the formative years of his early life there, adds, "It was a nice neighborhood but all the neighborhoods in New York were sort of crumbling at the time. We slid into this rent-controlled apartment, in a building with a lot of units, and paid very little rent. Mom got a job working in a preschool and dad wasn't making much money yet, so there was very little money."

Dave Werle remembers visiting his former professor in Brooklyn Heights. "One amazing evening, we went to The Bitter End [a nightclub on Bleecker Street] to see Harry Chapin's band. They were playing in high company: Randy Newman performed first, then David Steinberg did a set, then Harry and his group. And Joel Grey was in the audience. It was an amazing night." Werle also recalls that Wes was beginning to develop his "techniques" as a fright-master during this period: "One night, I was leaving the apartment in Brooklyn Heights. We had gotten stoned and then I had to leave to go home because I had to work the next day. And the building had a touchy elevator. I left, got on the elevator—stupidly. It went about half a floor, then stopped, and everything went dark. And I *know* Wes was playing me. Because he gave me just enough time to start pounding on the door before the elevator started going again."

Wes could be just as scary behind the wheel: "If you ever rode in the car with him, it was a horror. I mean, if somebody pulled out, it was too bad for them. He just barreled right on. Didn't think twice about it. Wouldn't veer out of the lane. But he knew the timing, so he just missed every time. For me, it was a subtle glimpse of his ability to bring you to the edge. It's the sort of thing you can't teach someone to do; he just had that skill. I'm not even sure it was something he really *wanted* to do, but he did it and he did it better than most."

On West 45th Street, Wes worked hard to learn the movie business and to prove that he was capable of being more than a messenger. Working closely with Harry Chapin, he wrote story treatments and did some "rough editing"—probably syncing up dailies.[4] Once he had proven himself, he was promoted to the role of supervisor for Roland Condon's post-production house. For ten months, Wes continued to learn from other documentary filmmakers in the building, including Michael Wadleigh, who edited *Woodstock* (1969) there; Albert and David Maysles, who were working on

Gimme Shelter (1970); and Pulitzer Prize winning novelist Norman Mailer, who was finishing his third film *Maidstone* (1970).

Wes might have seen himself in Mailer, a literary rebel of the World War II generation, who gleefully played the role of "philosophical psychopath." Mailer was so committed to *cinéma vérité* that he hired D.A. Pennebaker to shoot his first film, *Wild 90* (1968), with no script, no retakes, and no concern for continuity.[5] *Maidstone* had a screenplay, but it was written only after the film was shot and edited. Mailer insisted that his unconventional creative process was necessary to capture "the hard side of the real," and that *Maidstone* "inhabited that place where the film was supposed to live—that halfway station between the psychological and the real which helped to explain the real."[6] Wes privately regarded *Maidstone* as a failure but was nevertheless enthusiastic about Mailer's storytelling techniques and goals.[7]

During his first year in New York, Wes was not yet seriously contemplating a future as a director. "I never heard him say he wanted to make a film," Bonnie says. "But I do remember he said he was depressed [because] he wanted to have his picture on the cover of *TIME* magazine by the time he was thirty. Which really surprised me. I didn't think he'd had that kind of ambition." At a time when "don't trust anyone over thirty" was a counterculture mantra, Wes may have worried that his moment had passed. Although he'd been able to quickly work his way up to post-production supervisor at Roland Condon, he lost his momentum even more quickly. He accidentally spliced a film together in the wrong sequence, and was fired.

Suddenly out of work and with a family to support, Wes took a job as a cab driver. "He was pretty loose about it," says Dave Werle. "I remember Harry Chapin pulling out a counterfeit twenty-dollar bill and Wes grabbed it and said, 'I'll pass it to somebody in the taxi at night. They won't even know.' It was a horrible counterfeit. It looked like a Disney drawing. But it was so dark in those cabs, Wes said, you could hand people anything." In a bit of karmic payback, Wes got robbed twice at gunpoint while driving graveyard shifts.

For months, Wes was certain he'd blown it. He'd abandoned a respectable—if unfulfilling—career as a college professor, then crashed and burned on the fringes of the New York film industry. He'd become a disappointment to his mother and siblings, and an embarrassment to his wife and children. He decided to start over, alone. In a 1993 letter to a friend, Wes cited irreconcilable differences as the reason for his separation from Bonnie, explaining that he wanted to be crazy and she wanted to be sane. He granted the sane parent full custody of their children, but simultaneously absorbed a mantle of tremendous guilt that would stay with him for decades to come.

While his family learned to function without him, Wes apparently followed Timothy Leary's advice to tune in, turn on, and drop out. He moved into an East Village artist commune where, according to Ken Lyon, he was "doing the hippie thing and trying to survive." Wes candidly told one interviewer that this time in his life was entirely about "dropping out, doing drugs, getting into filmmaking."[8]

When he wasn't moonlighting as a cab driver, Wes polished prose for a "porno novelist." Ken Lyon remembers, "I went with him once to pick up a novel from a guy who was holed up in a hotel on 86th Street on the East Side near the park. This guy was sitting in bed in his underwear with a typewriter in his lap. He had been sitting there for three days. He kept all his food in dresser drawers—mayonnaise and bread and bologna—and he was delighted to read us this *ménage à trois* scene he had written, where all the characters were entangled and you couldn't figure out who was doing what. Wes and I were sitting there, like, *what the fuck are you talking about?* Then we took a bus across town to my parents' house on the Upper West Side and had dinner with my parents."

Finally, another young filmmaker at 54 West 45th Street presented Wes Craven with a second chance. Wes said, "I heard about this job at an office in the same building where I had been working before. It turned out to be Sean [Cunningham]'s office. He and a guy named Roger Murphy were making a small feature called *Together*, and they hired me to sync up dailies."[9] Cunningham had recently struck paydirt with a grindhouse documentary titled *The Art of Marriage* (1970), which the filmmaker describes as a "white coater." He explains that film distributors and exhibitors at that time "allowed you to get away with showing hardcore XXX-rated movies as long as they were under the guise of freedom of speech. You billed it as an 'educational' or 'medical' movie. At the beginning, someone would come out in a white coat and say, 'We're now going to show you marriage practices in Denmark and these are the ways you can improve your marital bliss.' And then for the next 80 minutes you saw people fucking like crazy."[10] *The Art of Marriage* was produced on a budget of $3,500 and ultimately grossed more than $100,000 in New York theaters, so Cunningham decided to make a more polished "white coater" that could play in suburban theaters for an even bigger audience.

Principal photography on *Together* took place in the early summer of 1970. In December, Cunningham test screened the first cut but the screening didn't go well, so he decided to shoot some additional scenes. Lyon recalls, "Wes called me because I had a car. He said, 'We're doing this film up in Westport. Can you come and drive us out there?' It was me and Wes and, I think, the cinematographer. Wes was doing sound. We went to this really nice estate up in Westport. It had a swimming pool and there was this eighteen-year-old girl who was doing a nude diving scene in it. At that time, she went by the name Evelyn Lang. That was the name she used in [the Barbara Streisand film] *The Owl and the Pussycat*. Her real name was Marilyn Ann Briggs. A few years later, she became known as Marilyn Chambers."

According to *The Marilyn Chambers Online Archive*, the future porn star had grown up with Sean Cunningham and was, at the time she appeared in

The future Marilyn Chambers in *Together* (Hallmark Releasing, 1971)

Together, dating Sean's brother. Chambers recalled, "Sean told me he wanted to make a documentary with real people. It was about ESP and that whole genre of films about awareness. Not free sex, but love, peace, couples feeling comfortable in their relationship—blah, blah, blah. I didn't even get a billing."[11] Not long after she took the plunge in *Together*, Marilyn moved to San Francisco and appeared in the hardcore sex film *Behind the Green Door* (1972), which became one of the most successful adult films of all time. Cunningham shrewdly re-released *Together* and gave "Marilyn Chambers" top billing.

In early 1971, however, *Together* was in limbo. Although Sean had only hired him to sync up the dailies, Wes was soon helping to re-conceive the film. In his new credited role as assistant editor, he was mentored by the "brilliant" but "irascible" cinematographer Roger Murphy, who had previously shot and edited *Monterey Pop*.[12] "Between Harry Chapin and Roger Murphy, I learned in very quick time, from the point of view of two very bright men, how to cut material."[13]

Wes also got some writing and directing experience on *Together*. After scripting some new scenes, he got behind the camera during a two-day shoot in Puerto Rico. By the time the two filmmakers returned to the edit suite in New York, they had forged a strong friendship and professional partnership. Cunningham remembers, "We wound up getting locked into that building [54 West 45th Street] I don't know how many weekends. They used to lock up the building at 8:00 on Friday and not open it till Monday morning, so you'd be in there for the weekend. You'd buy all the potato chips and soda that you could imagine, and just stay in there and work and work and work."[14] Cunningham adds that, while remaking *Together* with his friend, "I finally learned how film works—that it is a visceral experience, a non-rational thing."[15]

Like Wes, Sean Cunningham was a well-educated, literary thinker with a Master's Degree in Drama from Stanford University. He began his career as a stage manager at the Oregon Shakespeare Festival and at New York's City Center Theater. Eventually, he decided theater was a "bad investment" and created a film production company instead.[16] His first two films were far from Shakespeare, but they served their purpose: "Wes and I didn't have the luxury of entering the film business to follow a muse. I was trying to make a living to support my family and so was Wes."[17] *Together* started making money for the filmmakers on August 8, 1971.

During the film's initial theatrical run, Dave Reich, who had co-hosted a radio show with Wes at Clarkson, recognized one of Wes Craven's contributions to the film. "One time Wes and I were in the studio on the show and we were playing a cut—I can't remember what it was, but Wes was looking at the album cover and it showed a picture of a woman's body. You didn't see her face. You could just see the top of her arm and a little bit of the side of her breast. I remember he was fixated on it. He said, 'I just love this... This is the sexiest part of a woman's body.' I'm looking at it and thinking, *Okaaay. I mean, I can think of other parts I'd rather see,* you know? But whatever. A couple of years later, I'm at the movies with my wife, and there was this one shot where the camera lingers on that part of a woman's body. I said to my wife, 'You know, I had a professor who used to fixate on that part of a woman's body.' At the end of the movie, they're running the credits and it said 'Directed by Wes Craven.' I thought: Well, all right, I guess he's making movies in Hollywood." To be clear: Wes was only credited as an assistant producer on *Together*, and he hadn't made it to Hollywood yet... but it was a start.

In the summer of 1971, Wes also worked as an editor for Peter Locke, a fellow filmmaker who would become a lifelong friend and collaborator, on Locke's directorial debut. The counterculture comedy *You've Got to Walk It Like You Talk It or You'll Lose That Beat* was about a twenty-something New Yorker named Carter Fields who quits his job as a Wall Street stockbroker to pursue a more meaningful life. The sometimes-satirical, sometimes-crude odyssey through 1968 Manhattan featured a group of outrageous hippies, a men's room cabaret singer (played by Locke's future wife Liz Torres), and a gang of thieving girl scouts.

When *You've Got to Walk It* was released in September 1971, Norman Mailer publicly touted it as "a funny, witty, hysterical, cool and crazy job." Critics were less enthusiastic, many of them comparing it unfavorably to director Robert Downey's films *Chafed Elbows* (1966) and *Putney Swope* (1969). Downey was also an actor in Locke's film so the comparison was perhaps inevitable. Despite plenty of talent—and an original soundtrack by the future Steely Dan duo—*You've Got to Walk It* was a slow launch.

Sean Cunningham's second effort made a bigger impact. Following the success of *Together*, he began raising money for an "action melodrama" titled *Crime of the Century*—to be written and directed by his pal Wes Craven.[18] The financiers, operating as Hallmark Releasing Corporation, had successfully distributed the German import *Mark of the Devil* by promoting it as "the most horrifying film ever made." Now they needed a film that was more horrifying. Wes recalled, "[Sean] literally said, 'I have these guys who will give us $90,000 to make a movie—but they want it to be scary.' My response was, 'I don't know anything about scary movies.' Sean said, 'You were raised as a fundamentalist. Just pull all of the skeletons out of your closet.'" Over Labor Day weekend 1971, Wes began writing *Sex Crime of the Century*—which later became *Night of Vengeance*, then *Krug and Company*, and finally *Last House on the Left*.

The making of *Last House* has become legendary. Most of the stories—and the truths behind them—are conveyed in David A. Szulkin's exhaustively researched book *Wes Craven's Last House on the Left: The Making of a Cult Classic,* or on Arrow Video's 2018 four-disc limited edition of the film. In these studies, much is made of Wes's claim that he modeled his screen story on Ingmar Bergman's 1960 arthouse film *The Virgin Spring.* Speaking to Szulkin, Wes explained, "I had seen *The Virgin Spring* about a year before I wrote *Last House* and I loved the turnaround of the story. I thought it made for an incredible modern fable, as well as an ancient one. But it wasn't as if I sat down and went scene for scene… the Bergman movie stuck in my mind, and that was about the extent of it."[19] Both films depict the rape and murder of an innocent girl and the revenge exacted by her parents, but the differences between the two screen stories reveal stark differences between the filmmakers and their visions.

For Ingmar Bergman, *The Virgin Spring* was the continuation of a cinematic exploration of lifelong obsessions. The director had been making films since the mid-1940s but his work had become increasingly personal—and confessional—since 1957's *The Seventh Seal.* In his autobiography, Bergman described that film as one of the last manifestations of his dwindling childhood faith in God. By the time he directed *The Virgin Spring*, his beliefs had morphed into something more complicated. "The God concept had long ago begun to crack, and it remained more as a decoration than anything else. What really interested me was the actual, horrible story of the girl and her rapists, and the subsequent revenge."[20]

Bergman told his story into two distinct parts. The first part develops two young female characters. Karin is innocent and naïve and full of life. Her adopted stepsister Ingeri is pregnant out of wedlock and envious of Karin's close relationship with their parents. On the way to church, the two girls fight and get separated. Subsequently, Karin encounters three vagabond brothers, one of whom violently rapes her. Ingeri witnesses the attack but does nothing to help. The rapist ultimately beats Karin to death and steals her clothes.

The second half of the film follows the three brothers as they unknowingly take refuge in the home of Karin's parents, Töre and Märeta. The youngest brother becomes sick with guilt, then terrified that supernatural forces might steal his life as quickly and easily as his brother stole Karin's. The rapist brother unknowingly offers Karin's dress to her mother as a gift, prompting Ingeri to tell the dead girl's parents what she witnessed. Töre exacts his revenge, killing the two older brothers, while Märeta watches silently, intervening only to plead for the youngest brother's life. Töre kills the third brother anyway.

The Virgin Spring concludes with a scene in which Ingeri leads Karin's parents to the exact spot where their daughter was killed. When they discover the dead girl's body, Töre falls to his knees and asks God how He could have allowed this to happen. The only reply is silence—a cinematic moment suggesting God is either nonexistent or indifferent. Nonetheless, Töre asks for God's forgiveness and vows to build a church on the spot where his daughter was killed. In that moment, an underground spring opens up nearby. In the 1963 documentary *Ingmar Bergman Makes a Movie*, the filmmaker explains the ending: "I let God answer in the form of a ballad, as the spring begins to flow. For me that was a timid way of closing in on the issue, and setting forth my own views on the reality of God."[21]

Last House on the Left tells essentially the same story but with very different details, tone and emphasis. The shooting script, titled *Night of Vengeance*, introduces Mari Collinwood on her 17th birthday as she masturbates in the bathroom of her childhood home in suburban Connecticut. (At some point during production, the surname was changed to Collingwood.) Meanwhile, middle-class parents John and Estelle bemoan their little princess's decision to spend the night at a rock concert in New York City. The script identifies the band as Bloodlust but also makes reference to a chicken-dismemberment rumor, which suggests the writer was actually thinking of ex-fundamentalist shock rocker Alice Cooper, who supposedly bit the head off of a live chicken at a 1969 show.

Fair-haired Mari leaves the house with her wild and worldly friend Phyllis Stone, who tells a story about a depressing recent reunion with her deadbeat dad, then proposes that they try to "make it" with the band at the concert. A brief interlude visualizes their "semi-rape" by "dope-crazed musician priests." Mari responds with a gentler, more romantic fantasy, which morphs into an orgy sequence. Hot and bothered, the girls turn on the radio for distraction—and hear ominous snippets of news about a recent prison break.

When they arrive in the city, they try to buy some marijuana from a stranger, only to get kidnapped and tormented by the escaped criminals, a Manson-like family of psychopaths including sadistic thug Krug Stillo, his deviant friend Weasel, animalistic girlfriend Sadie, and hapless son Junior. The psychos take the teenagers into the woods near Mari's house, where Krug orders Phyllis to urinate on herself, forces the two girls to make out while their captors watch, then brutally rapes Mari. Phyllis runs for help but the criminals chase and murder her, then shoot Mari.

Meanwhile, Mari's parents report her missing to a pair of bumbling lawmen (Sheriff Boone and Deputy Snark), who overlook clues that might have saved the girls. Their ineptitude becomes comedically absurd as the story progresses, a distinctly Craven-ish snub to authority. Badly wounded Mari is finally forced to save herself; she manages to crawl back home, where her parents find her in the backyard at night and learn what has happened. Before she can say anything more, Mari dies in their arms.

As in *The Virgin Spring*, the killers eventually take refuge in the home of Mari's parents. As soon as they realize who their guests are, the parents plan revenge. Estelle seduces Weasel and bites off his penis, then stabs Sadie to death. In the earliest draft of the script, John Collinwood uses kung fu to kill Krug. Later, Wes changed the scene to a scalpel fight—because "the character was a doctor, and I thought it would be very interesting to have a doctor who would know every little vulnerable point in the body, and could make these insidious little cuts that would leave somebody bleeding to death."[22] Finally, Wes decided to replace the scalpel with a chainsaw, taking his inspiration from a movie poster he saw in Times Square—possibly for the 1968 film *Dark of the Sun*.

Top: Krug (David Hess) attacks Mari (Sandra Peabody) while Sadie (Jeramie Rain) and Weasel (Fred Lincoln) look on, in *Last House on the Left*
Bottom: The execution of Mari (Sandra Peabody) in *Last House on the Left* (Hallmark Releasing, 1972)

In contrast with the film, in which Junior dies by father-assisted suicide, the youngest member of the criminal "family" survives the shooting script—because Mari, in her final moments, begged her parents to spare his life. With this note, Wes Craven's story would have retained a sense of mercy. The shooting script also retains Bergman's ambiguous ending; the proposed final image is a shot of Phyllis's mutilated hand flashing a V—but it's unclear if the V symbolizes victory or if it's meant to be a peace sign. In contrast, the film concluded with a frozen image of the mild-mannered, middle class parents drenched in blood, appearing dazed and forlorn. A folk song on the soundtrack delivers a nihilistic message: "The road leads to nowhere."

In later years, Wes said he conceived *Last House on the Left* as a protest against the U.S. government's obfuscation of Vietnam War atrocities and a criticism of modern American culture's treatment of violence. Sean Cunningham remembers they conceived *Last House* as a response to a spaghetti western that left them disgusted by the unreality of most cinematic deaths. The western film, he explained, "didn't have anything to do with people dying and the real horror of people dying."[23] In contrast, Wes and Sean resolved to show the naked, ugly truth. The latter told *Creem* magazine in 1974, "Philosophically, the movie is anti-violence. But instead of having some milquetoast going around saying 'geez, violence is terrible,' it's like, okay, you guys like violence, here's some real violence for you. How do you like it *now*?"[24] In 1981, Wes elaborated, "[*Last House on the Left*] blew away all the clichés of violence. Before that, [onscreen] violence had been neat and tidy; I made it painful and protracted and shocking and very human. And I made the people who were doing the killing very human."[25]

Wes said he was shocked to find, during the making of the film, that he could empathize with the killers. "All sides of me were coming in at the same time, but there were sides of me I never knew existed, did not recognize, or ever want to see revealed. I think that was the key to it."[26] In fact, his initial script was much more horrific than the finished film. Phyllis's death scene originally called for Sadie to gouge out the young girl's eyes, cut out her tongue, carve off her breasts, and mutilate her vagina. The script also indicated that Krug and Weasel would have sex with the dead girl's corpse. Reflecting on these details, Wes said, "A lot of it was based on things that I was reading that were going on in Vietnam—you know, cutting off the ears and carving the unit name into the dead Cong's chest."[27] The film did not go that far, but it still went further than most horror films of the day. Wes didn't realize at the time how outrageous he was being, because he had almost no knowledge of horror cinema.

Wes saw his first modern horror film—George Romero's *Night of the Living Dead*—at a late-night show in Greenwich Village, probably in 1970 or 1971. Initially, he didn't want to go. "As far as I was concerned [horror films] were something I had not seen much of and were probably pretty dumb. And instead, in the first three minutes, I found myself—along with everybody else in the audience—screaming and laughing and jumping and cringing. And realized that a scary movie could be a lot of fun and stylishly made and even have some sort of political underlying statement that made you think a little bit."[28] Romero's film was unflinchingly violent as well as subversive. Critics interpreted its bleak ending—in which the black hero gets gunned down by a redneck posse—as a sly commentary on the death of American idealism.

Wes wanted to make a similar statement while having just as much fun with the medium. Recognizing Romero's use of the *cinéma vérité* techniques popularized by Leacock and Pennebaker, he decided to stage his own horror film as a documentary. He hired documentary cameraman Victor Hurwitz to visually capture each scene as if it was a real event unfolding in front of him. The director explained, "There would be no cut from beginning to end, and we shot it from three basic angles. And moved on."[29] Wes also opted to shoot *Last House* on Super 16mm film, using several different film stocks to give specific scenes—most notably, the murder of Phyllis—a dark and grainy look. For him, the aesthetic was reminiscent of the Telenews war footage he'd seen as a child.

Firsthand accounts of the production indicate that the director was open to improvisation within scripted scenes, frequently encouraging his actors to indulge the emotional effects of certain experiences rather than slavishly delivering the written dialogue. His goal, like Norman Mailer's, was to capture the hard reality of a fictional event, and the existential horror of the particular time in American history. His approach generated some very unpleasant moments during filming, especially for the young women playing Mari and Phyllis. The first draft script includes explicit descriptions of a variety of sex acts. Later, Wes admitted that the cast had talked him out of staging and shooting a hardcore rape sequence.[30] While simulating a rape and murder, however, some of the actors pushed the limits of usual role-playing. With the unflinching eye of a documentarian, Hurwitz captured the primal actions and reactions on film.

In what has become one of the most notorious and most celebrated scenes in *Last House on the Left*, the actors portraying the murderers show feelings of revulsion and remorse for "going too far." Years later, Wes described the pivotal sequence as follows: "The killing of Phyllis is very sexual in feeling, and ended with her being stabbed not only by the men but by the woman repeatedly. Then she fell to the ground and Sadie bent down and pulled out a loop of her intestines. They looked at it and that's where it all stopped. That's when they realized what they had done. It was as if they had been playing with a doll, or a prisoner they thought was a doll, and it had broken and come apart and they did not know how to put it back together again."[31] The humanizing reaction was apparently not scripted; the filmmakers simply captured the authentic moment as it happened. In final analysis, the scene expresses what the film is supposed to be about: disgust and mourning for the loss of humanity.

Last House on the Left emerged as a darkly revealing snapshot of America in 1971, showing how hippie idealism had given way to violence and darkness. Wes had started making a list of modern-day tragedies in his final letter in *Jefferson Airplane I*. Since then, the list had grown to include the Manson Family murders and the deadly Altamont Free Concert (documented in *Gimme Shelter*), the Kent State Massacre (not far from Wes Craven's hometown), the untimely deaths of Jimi Hendrix, Janis Joplin, and Jim Morrison, and the ongoing escalation of the war in Vietnam. The dreams of the Love Generation had become nightmares. Rock and roll had turned angry; drug use no longer connoted freedom, only death; and free love was becoming marketable sleaze. The notion of American exceptionalism had also been shattered by the war in south Asia. Wes said, "Because of the war, I felt no hope. *Last House* was a howl of anger and pain."[32]

He described a cathartic experience while making the film: "Certainly one of the things that the horror genre does at its best is express that rage that Kurtz expressed at the end of the river [in Joseph Conrad's novel *Heart of Darkness*], a sort of primal scream, and it's done by people who are in one way or another outside the usual mainstream of art who figure they have nothing to lose. When I did *Last House*, I was in this situation."[33] Wes's "primal scream" released years of private suffering and repressed anger. "The way I was raised—which was basically as a law-abiding, Bible-following person—a lot of the rage and wildness is kept out from your conscious mind. Finally, when I had gone through a divorce and left teaching, abandoning everything everyone was pleased that I was doing, and somebody said just make something wild and crazy, suddenly all this came out of me very easily."[34] And later: "I'm sure there is a certain amount of anger and even rage in being raised in a way that says half of the great sources of inspiration and joy in life are sins and you burn in hell forever. I'm sure that had done a lot of psychic damage."[35]

In his 1970 book *The Primal Scream: Primal Therapy, The Cure for Neurosis*, pop psychologist Arthur Janov encouraged the Me Generation to release "the pressure of holding the real self back" through outbursts of concentrated emotion. Such unfettered self-expression, Janov claimed, could prevent children from becoming neurotic and help adults escape repression and overcome feelings of resentment: "The Primal view of rage is that it is a rage against someone trying to crush the life out of you. We have to remember that neurotic parents are unconsciously killing their children, in a sense; they are killing off the real selves of their offspring; psychophysical death is a real process where life is being squeezed out of them. The result is the anger: 'I hate you for not letting me live.' To be anything else but yourself is to be dead." The goal of Primal Therapy was to break down a person's socially-reinforced defense system—their resistance to expressing emotion, particularly anger—"in order to release the real, defenseless self." Janov promised, "Make anger real, and it will disappear."[36] *Last House on the Left* was Wes Craven's primal scream therapy.

The director continued to dig deep to find the details for his first film. Among the late additions to the screen story was a dream sequence in which Mari's parents punish one of the criminals by performing rudimentary dental surgery on him. Wes said the idea came from a roommate who was a PhD candidate in anthropology: "She told me that two of the most powerful male fears are of having your teeth broken off and of the *vagina dentalis*, the fear that the vagina is going to eat you, taking away your manhood. So Weasel's nightmare and his death actually touch on two basic fears."[37] The director believed certain fears are part of Jungian psychology's collective unconscious—a repository of ancestral memories and experiences that is accessible in dreams—and he wanted to reach viewers on that subconscious level.

Other decisions made during the nine months Wes spent editing *Last House* suggest he wanted the film to have a mythological quality. He told author David Szulkin about a dense weave of sound effects—nearly thirty separate tracks—added to the sequence revolving around the murder of Phyllis. Sixteen of those tracks featured bird calls—most notably, a whip-poor-will. The resulting cacophony can be interpreted as an allusion to the ancient Greek myth of Philomela. As told in Ovid's *Metamorphoses* (which Wes read as a teenager) and referenced in T.S. Eliot's poem *The Waste Land* (which Wes studied at Johns Hopkins), Philomela's tragedy begins with her being kidnapped and brutally raped by her brother-in-law Tereus. To conceal the rape from his wife Procne, Tereus cuts out Philomela's tongue. Later, when Procne learns what has happened, she and her sister exact revenge on Tereus, feeding him his own dead son. In the end, the gods transform the three tormentors into songbirds. The possibility of an intended connection between the rape of Philomela and the rape of *Last House*'s Phyllis is pure speculation, but Wes certainly shared Ovid and Eliot's magpie intelligence.

If he was making literary allusions, he didn't expect his viewers to notice. In fact, Wes said that while he was making *Last House on the Left*, he never expected anyone to pay much attention to the film.[38] After delivering the director's cut, he put the film in his rearview and went to work on his next project, Peter Locke's *It Happened in Hollywood*. A zany sketch comedy featuring hardcore sex, *Hollywood* revolves around a horny girl-next-door named Felicity Split, who wants to make it big in Tinseltown. She screws everyone—from the talent agent to the makeup girl—on her way to a breakout role in a big-budget, pornographic adaptation of the Biblical story of Samson and Delilah.

The film's most inventive sequence features Felicity masturbating while talking on the phone to a casting director, who is simultaneously getting a blowjob from another actress. When the casting director ejaculates, his semen magically travels through the phone and lands on Felicity's body. It might be one of the most memorable "money shots" in the history of adult cinema—and it might have inspired one of the most memorable scenes in *A Nightmare on Elm Street*. In Wes's 1984 horror film, shape-shifting serial killer Freddy Krueger slips

the film's heroine some tongue through a phone handset. The casting director in *Hollywood* does what Freddy can only dream of in an R-rated horror movie.

Critic Jim Holliday cited the Marx Brothers film *A Night at the Opera* and Shakespeare's *A Comedy of Errors* as inspirations for Locke's second film, but the more likely inspiration was Gerard Damiano's film *Deep Throat*. When it premiered at the World Theater in New York on June 12, 1972, *Deep Throat* brought hardcore sex into mainstream American cinema, launching an era of filmmaking that one *New York Times* columnist famously dubbed "porno chic." Two of *Deep Throat*'s boosters were Al Goldstein and Jim Buckley, co-publishers of the shamelessly sleazy tabloid *Screw*. After witnessing the success of *Deep Throat*, they decided to get into the film business. In the fall of 1972, Buckley served as Peter Locke's co-producer on *It Happened in Hollywood*, and Goldstein played a "High Priest" in the film's climactic set piece. Goldstein later claimed that Wes Craven directed the film, but the credits clearly identify him as the assistant director and editor.[39] Wes also made a brief onscreen appearance as one of the "King's Litter Bearers," paying homage to Locke's King.

Today, the production details of *It Happened in Hollywood* are known only to those who made the film. Neither Wes Craven nor Peter Locke deigned to talk about the project in later years—although they had no misgivings about attaching their names to it in 1973. (The closing credits include a long roster of ridiculous pseudonyms like Tammy Twat, Buster Hyman, Flo Zeasily, and Alan Spitz, but Wes and Peter both used their, ahem, Christian names.) The gleefully irreverent tone of the film suggests they were proud to shatter taboos at a time when shattering taboos was particularly lucrative. *Deep Throat* star Harry Reems, who played Felicity Split's boyfriend in *Hollywood*, said that he and his filmmaking peers thought of themselves as "pioneers."[40]

The success of subsequent X-rated films like *Behind the Green Door* (released in August 1972) and *The Devil in Miss Jones* (February 1973) heightened the gold rush. For that brief moment in time, adult cinema was a golden ticket and a lot of young, ambitious filmmakers got in on the action. In the 2005 documentary film *Inside Deep Throat*, Wes explained, "Frankly, in one way or another, everybody was connected to that business because it was just—psychologically, socially—it was *happening*." (For the record, Wes later clarified that he did *not* work on the film *Deep Throat*: "We might have been in a nearby studio, but that's about it."[41])

Unfortunately, Wes's big break led to a big backlash. Surprisingly, the backlash had nothing to do with what had happened in *Hollywood*.

After multiple test screenings, *Last House on the Left* opened at a pair of theaters in Hartford, Connecticut, on August 23, 1972. Wes was in California when he heard from Sean Cunningham that the film was generating a lot of attention. At first, Wes thought he might get recognized as an up-and-coming filmmaker. Instead, critics lambasted his directorial debut. Some viewers did more than criticize; they rioted. Wes remembered, "We immediately got reports that there were protests, there were fistfights, and in theaters people tried to get at the projectionists to destroy the print. Projectionists themselves were cutting up the prints."[42] When the filmmaker saw the results on an audience, he became frightened. "It was scary. And then everybody's reaction to us—especially me, since I had written and directed it—was 'You are a perverse, horrible, twisted person.'"

Wes's family members were especially shocked and dismayed. His ex-wife Bonnie remembers, "When that came out, I was already going out with [future husband] Tom [Chapin]. We went to see the movie with Tom's college roommate and his brother Harry. When we came out of there, it was like, *Oh my God, what was that we just saw?* I think we had to go to 42nd Street to see it—and it was horrifying." Wes said several of his housemates had a similar reaction: "I was living on the Lower East Side in a group apartment, and it was a very rich amalgamation of people—academics and hipsters and dope dealers and musicians—and they all went to see my movie when it came out, and almost all of them were appalled. I had people who would no longer leave their children alone with me."[43]

Despite an overtly crass marketing campaign, the film's distributor publicly defended their product as a work of art. A September 8 op-ed in the *Hartford Courant* insisted that *Last House* "does not justify violence, nor does it glorify the degenerates who perpetuate the violence." A subsequent ad went further, claiming, "The movie makes a plea for an end to all the senseless violence and inhuman cruelty that has become so much a part of the times in which we live. WE DON'T THINK ANY MOVIE CAN GO *TOO FAR* IN MAKING THIS MESSAGE HEARD AND FELT!" It was the horror movie equivalent of defending a sex film as an educational documentary. The expectation that

viewers would perceive the anti-violence message was undoubtedly naïve. For many years, that artistic statement fell on mostly deaf ears.

One of the few exceptions was *Chicago Sun-Times* critic Roger Ebert, who in an October 26 review wrote that Wes Craven's debut film "covers the same philosophical territory as Sam Peckinpah's *Straw Dogs* (1971), and is more hard-nosed about it."[44] In 1972, Peckinpah had defended his own film, saying, "You can't make violence real to audiences today without rubbing their noses in it. We watch our wars and see men die, really die, every day on television, but it doesn't seem real. We don't believe those are real people dying on that screen. We've been anesthetized by the media. What I do is show people what it's really like—not by showing it as it is so much as by heightening it, stylizing it."[45] Ebert's review pointed out that Craven's film is more philosophically sincere than Peckinpah's—because *Last House* does not stylize or romanticize violence the way Peckinpah does; Craven approaches his subject with a cold, unflinching documentarian's gaze.

Wes received some additional encouragement from future filmmaker Roy Frumkes, who saw *Last House on the Left* in late 1972 and promptly wrote the director a fan letter. Frumkes remembers, "I got Wes's name off the credits, and the name of the production company, and I sent him a blind letter. I said, 'I could tell this was your first film but I thought you did a great job.'" If Wes was surprised to receive a fan letter, Frumkes was even more surprised by his response. "Two weeks later, a box—a large box, big enough to put a TV in—arrived in the mail. Inside was a note from Wes saying, 'If you like it so much, you can have it. My crew at the screening, they spit on me. I feel like I've contributed bad vibes to the world. So here's everything. All the scripts. All the outtakes.'" Frumkes later befriended Wes and encouraged him to continue making films. For many years, he was one of the only people that did.

In early 1973, when *It Happened in Hollywood* was released, Wes managed to gain a foothold in one corner of the film industry—but his career route was already looking precarious. *Deep Throat* and its imitators had been playing for months to capacity crowds in New York theaters, leading to a showdown between theater owners and city attorneys over the legal definition of obscenity. In March, a New York judge declared *Deep Throat* "indisputably and irredeemably" obscene, "a Sodom and Gomorrah gone wild before the fire."[46] Screenings of the film were banned locally, even as it made its way to theaters in smaller cities around the country. More court cases followed, with one jurisdiction after another making their own determinations about what constituted obscenity. On June 21, the U.S. Supreme Court intervened, declaring that only a work "utterly without any redeeming social value" was legally obscene. This vague litmus test would be applied to all adult films. Subsequent films by Sean Cunningham, Peter Locke, and Wes Craven acknowledged the changing landscape.

In February 1972, *Variety* magazine reported that Cunningham's follow-ups to *Last House on the Left* would be *Strictly for the Money*, "a comedy about a young filmmaker" directed by William Markle, and *Frog*, "a black-oriented actioneer" written and directed by Preston Webster.[47] *Strictly for the Money* apparently morphed into a porn mockumentary titled *Loops*, which was released in August 1973. In a post on the Internet Movie Database, filmmaker Shaun Costello explains, "In 1972 porno was all the rage, and we thought that a documentary, or docudrama, about the making of XXX rated films might just be successful at the box office. The actors who participated in the shooting of the loops were myself, Harry Reems, Fred Lincoln, Lucy Grantham, Sargeant Tina, and several Gypsies. The footage turned out to be hilarious, but it needed another element in order to hold an audience's interest for feature length. I wrote a story about a filmmaker who was making porno on the side, unbeknownst to Mrs. Filmmaker. We hired an actress / belly dancer named Cathy Joyce to play my wife, and shot the script I had written. We intercut the new dramatized scenes of the filmmaker and his wife with the original documentary footage of the making of porno loops, and the result was a feature length docudrama, or docu-comedy, called *Loops*."

An August 1973 review in *The Independent Film Journal* named Wes Craven as co-editor of *Loops*, and summed up: "What the film says is that porno films are made with little money, smaller casts and even smaller imaginations. And it's that complete lack of imagination or real interest that eventually gives this film a focal point and some depth." The reviewer describes the fictional filmmakers as "sidetracked, somewhat pathetic and, when the chips are down, both cynical and ashamed of what they're doing," and concludes that *Loops* is "a usefully realistic study of what turns out to be a dingy way to make a living."[48] Apparently, however, audiences weren't interested in a realistic study of porno. The film opened to mixed reviews and dismal box office. After that, *Loops* essentially vanished.

Cunningham moved on to the softcore sex comedy *The Full Moon Murders*, a.k.a., *The Case of the Smiling Stiffs*, about a couple of horny *Dragnet*-style detectives on the trail of a female vampire who doesn't go for the jugular. Meanwhile, Wes returned to his typewriter. When he received his first royalty checks for *Last House on the Left*, he was living in poverty. Once the film was picked up by national distributor Samuel Z. Arkoff, however, his fortunes changed. Wes remembered "going to the Bank of New York and walking in there with a $50,000 check, because I didn't know what to do with this [and the banker said,] 'We'll start you with an account, sir. We'll get you an American Express card. We're just gonna set you up.'"[49] He decided to use his newfound fortune to finance a long stint of spec screenwriting, hoping to redeem and rebrand himself as a mainstream filmmaker.

Wes said, "I wrote at least seven scripts—comedies, love stories, a story about a divorced father trying to pursue a relationship with his kids, a story [based on Anthony Herbert's book *Soldier*] about an American war hero that was court-martialed for reporting American atrocities in Vietnam."[50] He quickly learned that nobody wanted to finance a mainstream movie from the director of *Last House on the Left*. There was reportedly some discussion about making a *Last House on the Left Part 2* or *Son of Last House*, but neither the writer/director nor the producer wanted to do that. The idea lingered until 1985, when the original film's financiers hired Danny Steinmann (fresh off the success of *Friday the 13th: A New Beginning*) to write and direct a sequel—but, according to Steinmann, the project was shut down by Wes Craven.[51]

Wes claimed that the only directing offer he received between 1972 and 1974 was from the producers of *Let's Scare Jessica to Death*, a mind-bending Gothic horror film about a seemingly delusional woman who encounters vampires in a rural Connecticut town.[52] A film like *Let's Scare Jessica to Death*, emphasizing atmosphere and psychological horror over violence and gore, might have been a good fit for Wes. Determined to avoid the horror genre, however, Wes returned to the world of adult cinema and accepted an offer from Peter Locke to produce what would become the strangest entry in his filmography.

CHAPTER FIVE

THE ECSTATIC BLASPHEMY OF ABE SNAKE
(1972 - 1977)

"The question is whether pornographic films indicate that we are a sick society, enjoying a Roman decadence that presages the barbarian at the gates and the plunge of Western civilization into the abyss of blood and darkness, or whether they prove that we are becoming a more tolerant, permissive society."

- Kenneth Turan and Stephen F. Zito,
Sinema: American Pornographic Films and the People Who Make Them (1974)

On February 21, 1973, *Variety* magazine profiled a new hardcore sex film titled *The Devil in Miss Jones*, describing it as "a bizarre melodrama" about a middle-aged virgin who commits suicide and then faces moral judgment in the afterlife.[1] Entertainment industry trades didn't normally give much attention to adult cinema, but this film was different—an ambitious existential narrative about repression and morality.

Actress Georgina Spelvin says she took the title role without thinking much about the taboo nature of the material: "The fact that there was hardcore sex involved was incidental as far as I was concerned. [...] I had made myself believe that I was an actress. I was showing true life as it really was—including actual sex as it really happened—instead of the phony stuff that you got from Hollywood."[2] In the afterlife, Miss Jones repents by indulging in all the carnal sins she avoided in life. At the conclusion of this modern-day Eve's dance with the devil, a heavenly moral arbiter condemns her anyway. In the final scene, the film depicts Hell as a small, gray room inhabited by a middle-aged man with no interest in sex. Ironically, the role was played by Gerard Damiano, the film's director.

Variety observed that the ending of *The Devil in Miss Jones* took the message of Jean-Paul Sartre's play *No Exit* ("hell is other people") to its "logical and surprisingly moralistic extreme," suggesting that Damiano's new film had elevated adult cinema to an "art form."[3] A few months later, *Chicago Sun-Times* film critic Roger Ebert compared *Miss Jones* to celebrated contemporary art films like Ingmar Bergman's *Cries and Whispers* (1972) and Bernardo Bertolucci's *Last Tango in Paris* (1973), unambiguously declaring that it had given artistic validation to the entire "genre" of sex movies.[4] Reviews like this helped to make Damiano's work a mainstream hit, as well as one of the ten most profitable films of 1973, heralding the golden age of adult cinema and drawing many talented filmmakers to the form.

Damiano later said that the only reason he made porn was because it was, at the time, "the only thing that would sell, the only media an independent filmmaker could work in."[5] He had conceived his previous film *Deep Throat* as a comedic counterpoint to dour arthouse films, then imagined *The Devil in Miss Jones* as a counterpoint to *Deep Throat*. Uninterested in repeating himself, he followed up by exploiting the popularity of another maligned film genre. *Miss Jones* gave way to *Legacy of Satan* (1974), an erotic knockoff of *The Exorcist*, and the hardcore psychological thriller *Memories within Miss Aggie* (1974). The former played on a double bill with *The Texas Chainsaw Massacre*. The latter paid homage to *Psycho*, granddaddy of the modern horror film.

Naturally, Damiano wasn't the only contemporary filmmaker to recognize the commercial possibilities of combining sex and horror. Wes Craven had contemplated the combination when he made *Last House on the Left* but ultimately backed away from the notion of shooting a hardcore rape scene for his film. A few years later, he was suffering from critical and personal backlash over the crudity of that film while Damiano and other directors of hardcore sex films were being celebrated in the mainstream press. Perhaps responding to a perceived injustice, he decided to write and direct his own hardcore sex film—and make it even bolder than *Last House*.

The Fireworks Woman premiered at the D.C. Playhouse in New York and the Art Cinema theater in Boston in September 1975. A contemporary review in *The Boston Phoenix* attributed the film to director Peter Locke and producer Sean Cunningham but made no mention of Wes Craven. Within a month, *The Fireworks Woman* was playing at multiple theaters in Los Angeles—but the commercial reception was modest at best. The film quickly disappeared, along with the true identity of its writer/director. Seven years later, a truncated VHS release of the film featured a roster of pseudonyms, crediting "Abe Snake" as writer/director (and actor), Carmen Rodriguez as producer, and Hørst Badörties as co-writer and director of photography. Abe Snake is, obviously, Wheaton College's most notorious satirist. Carmen Rodriguez seems to be a pseudonym for Peter Locke and/or Sean Cunningham. Hørst Badörties was a pseudonym for Roger Murphy, who received co-writing credit (with Wes Craven) on the film's 1974 script.

One of the stars of *The Fireworks Woman* remembers the cinematographer as a "heavy-set guy, large and teddy bearish," which might explain the pseudonym. Horse Bardoties is the name of the protagonist of William Kotzwinkle's 1974 counterculture novel *The Fan Man*—an obese, skeevy hoarder singularly devoted to recruiting 15-year-old girls for his church choir. Kotzwinkle later contributed to the screen story for *A Nightmare on Elm Street 4*, but says he never met Wes Craven nor had anything to do with *The Fireworks Woman*. Perhaps Craven was simply a fan of *The Fan Man* and decided to pay homage to the novel? If so, he modified the main character's name slightly. The word *"horst"* refers to a bird

of prey's nest, lending additional credence to the theory that the lifelong birder selected this pseudonym for Abe Snake's cohort.

In the early 2000s, Wes Craven was publicly identified as Abe Snake, the writer/director of *The Fireworks Woman*, by journalists Bill Landis and Michelle Clifford, in their grindhouse cinema fanzine *Sleazoid Express*. A decade later, when interviewer Simon Abrams asked the filmmaker about the rumor, Wes sheepishly admitted, "I might have directed that one. But apart from that one, I didn't make any others. But I might have directed that one."[6] The brief exchange suggests that he *might* have been willing to talk about the film, under the right circumstances. A few years later, Ashley West, host of *The Rialto Report* podcast, had a preliminary, off-the-record conversation with the director about his work in adult cinema. In 2017, West recalled, "Although he might not have said this as explicitly as I'm making it out, he did view his experience in the adult era as being one of freedom, where he could literally do whatever he wanted and see how it came out, and play around with ideas. Which he could never do when he was making the bigshot movies that made a name for him. And he was happy to talk about it as well. He was kind of on the verge of coming totally clean and talking about it."[7] Unfortunately, Wes passed away soon after.

Whatever his misgivings, Wes was consistently candid about the challenges he faced as a young independent filmmaker in the mid-70s. Claiming that *Last House on the Left* was regarded by industry insiders as a fluke rather than a calling card, he said, "Many people who knew me never thought I could be [a director], because I was very quiet and wasn't the sort of person who would bark orders and scream on the set. A lot of the people in the business think that is what a director should do. So I had to learn a lot of skills."[8] When Peter Locke arranged financing for another film written and directed by his friend, Wes seized the opportunity to make a film over which he could have creative control. He hoped he could make something that would transcend its origins. Roy Frumkes recalls, "He said his intention was to dignify porn. He had sent the script to Norman Mailer, and Mailer liked it, so he was very happy with that."

Today, the initial 61-page draft of the script, titled *The Fireworks Man* and dated 1974, resides in Mailer's collected papers at the Harry Ransom Center in Austin, Texas. At the outset of the script, title character Nicholas Burns drives into the coastal town of Eastport on the 4th of July and gives an innocent young girl a cherry bomb—with which she proceeds to blow herself up. The script then refocuses on Angela, a 15-year-old girl recovering from the traumatic deaths of both parents in a car crash. Her brother Peter, a 22-year-old priest in training, consoles her until their intimacy leads to an illicit sex act. After that, Peter seeks refuge in the arms of the Catholic church while Angela mourns the loss of her lover. She flees Eastport on a small boat but can't escape thoughts of Peter, which manifest as a literal sea storm that tears her clothes off. She returns to land at Eden Harbor, where she meets a friendly young couple but loses her boat. Nicholas Burns finds the boat and invites the trio to join him in a Bacchanalian picnic.

The script specifies that Burns serves *Lacryma Christi* wine, a mythic vintage made from Christ's tears after Satan's fall from heaven. After a bit of drunken revelry, he departs the scene and the three revelers fall helplessly into a *ménage à trois*. A mysterious black dog, the hellhound of European folklore, follows the trio to Peter's church, where Angela makes a desperate attempt to reconcile with her brother. He urges her to repress and deny her feelings for him, which he describes as a "monstrous self-indulgence." Angela returns home and tries to heed his advice, but she can't control her sexual desires. She visits a doctor for help, but he proclaims her—and her desires—"normal, normal, normal." On her way home, she is raped by a sadistic (seemingly possessed) fisherman named Fred. Angela blames herself. Peter does nothing to console her, instead urging her to devote herself to serving others—which ultimately leads to a perverse tryst with a pair of his parishioners. Understandably disillusioned, Angela urges him to leave the church for her. He refuses.

In the final act, Peter goes home and self-flagellates. After Angela comes to him in a horrifying dream, he confesses to his Monsignor about the illicit affair with his sister. The Monsignor opines that Peter has done nothing wrong and advises him that some things are "meant to be left to God." Meanwhile, Angela reconnects with Nicholas Burns, Eastport's perverted Pied Piper, who gives her much the same advice—and makes her a Faustian offer. Burns says he can give her what she wants, in exchange for an unspecified price to be paid later. Angela accepts his offer and orchestrates a bold and bawdy declaration of independence. After nightfall, half of the members of Peter's congregation arrive at her beach house to participate in an orgy. While orchestrating his own fireworks display, Burns lures Peter to Angela's house. Peter leads her away, effectively claiming her as his own. The couple flees Eastport on Angela's boat as Peter's Monsignor narrates their fate. Three days later, we're told, the boat washed up on a nearby shore, but Peter and Angela's bodies were never found—presumably having been claimed (along with their souls) by Nicholas Burns.

Events in Wes's personal life might have provided some inspiration for the screen story. Sometime after the release of—and vitriolic response to—*Last House on the Left*, Wes went into therapy. According to a female friend who knew him at that time, he was suffering from painful emotions related to his fundamentalist upbringing and the recent separation from his wife and children. Wes recalled, "She said, 'I have a friend who's in therapy with somebody that she really likes. Maybe you should go down and have a talk.'"[9] The friend referred him to a therapist associated with the New York-based Sullivan Institute for Research in Psychoanalysis.

The Sullivan Institute was created in the late 1950s by Jane Pearce, a junior colleague of celebrated psychologist Harry Stack Sullivan, and her husband Saul Newton, a charismatic but un-credentialed practitioner of psychotherapy. A decade later, the couple established an experimental commune of therapists and patients on New York's Upper West Side. They lived according to therapeutic practices outlined in Pearce and Sullivan's 1963 book *The Conditions of Human Growth*, which hypothesizes that an individual's personality is largely formed by early interactions with parents, and that negative feedback from anxious parents creates personalities that gravitate toward socially-validated behavior while avoiding any sort of risky behavior. The authors imply that *all* parents are anxious parents and that modern-day America is heavily populated by psychologically-handicapped adults.

The stated goal of Sullivanian therapy was to overcome inherited psychological handicaps through creative stimulation and interpersonal experimentation, which would then help patients to radically reevaluate all of their relationships and to break away from stultifying social norms such as monogamous romantic relationships and "nuclear" family structures. The authors write, "The turning point for successful therapy occurs when the patient makes the discovery that experience is more important than the avoidance of anxiety and that love and truth are more important than prestige and security."[10] For many young, anti-establishment New Yorkers who heeded Timothy Leary's call to "tune in, turn on, and drop out," Sullivanian therapy probably seemed like a way to re-engage with society on equally radical terms.

By 1972, the communal experiment had become popular—especially among young artists, writers, and musicians—and the group leaders decided to expand the group. According to former members, Newton and Pearce inaugurated a "lay therapist" training program, authorizing select members—"people with little formal education who had not yet been 'fucked up' by the system"—to conduct introductory therapy sessions with new patients.[11] The trainees would gather personal information and report back to the leadership on each patient's qualifications for membership in the group. Amy B. Siskind, author of *The Sullivanian Institute / Fourth Wall Community*, stipulates, "Not all patients of psychotherapists were invited to join the community—only those who were thought to be potential assets in the sense that they would be able to pay for their therapy and would not require institutionalization or a great deal of care and attention." Once a patient was approved, the process of "identity transformation" began.[12]

According to Siskind, the first task was a thorough review of a patient's personal history, beginning with their earliest memories and focusing on "familial and emotional life"—especially a patient's relationship with their mother.[13] Former group member Artie Honan says his therapist told him, "If you're not with other people, you're with your mother." He interpreted that to mean "my mother had created my view of the world during my early years. If I was alone, I was stuck with her thoughts and attitudes. But by being with other people, I was exposed to other influences."[14] Another former group member, Alice Graves, adds, "A main tenet of our therapy is that our mothers hated us and withheld love."[15] Sullivanian therapists generally let fathers off the hook, theorizing that a father's influence was usually less oppressive and therefore less damaging than a mother's—although Pearce and Newton stipulated, "If he is very angry, the father, or any older person living in the household, can have a somewhat disproportionate influence."[16]

In a 2002 interview, Wes Craven said, "One of the big struggles of my life was to come to terms with my mother. There was a period after I went to New York where I wouldn't call her more than once a year because every time I would call her she said, *Do you have a coat to wear? Do you have money? Do you have an apartment? I hope you're not on the street.* I'd done well, but she didn't know how to relax. Thank God, at a certain point, after a certain amount of therapy and living, you realize you just have to let that go. You're not going to get that from mom and you give her whatever love you can and just skirt all those issues that are upsetting to her and become your own parent; become that ideal parent that you would want; just become that yourself."[17] In a 2014 interview with *The Fourth Wall* documentary filmmaker Luke Meyer, Wes said the focus on a mother's influence was a novel feature of Sullivanian therapy that drew him in.

Wes's resolution to re-parent himself probably coincided with the beginning of what Amy Siskind refers to as the novice stage of Sullivanian therapy, in which a community of patients became "the good mother" for each individual patient. In this stage, Siskind writes, "the patient was introduced to the Sullivanian community and became a member. The introduction could happen in a variety of ways; the patient could join a summer house with other Sullivanians, a women's or men's group, or be invited to a party by the therapist, or by another patient in the waiting room."[18]

Michael Bray remembers accompanying Wes on a canoe trip in the fall of 1974, when Bray was living in a communal apartment on the Upper West Side. "There were six of us guys who lived in the so-called penthouse. Wes had an apartment two or three floors below. Somebody said he was in therapy, so we invited him to go with us on a canoe trip down the Delaware River." The newcomer, he adds, was a "mild-mannered, gentle, affable fellow," but the canoe trip was a nightmare. "We launched around Dingmans Ferry or someplace like that, and evidently it was not quite the right place. One of my roommates and I were in one of the canoes and we managed to get ourselves in an eel run, and right in the middle of the eel run was a big rock. The canoe turned horizontally and rolled over into the river, so all our stuff—and us—were going down the river for the rest of the eel run. We ended up on an island, where we stayed overnight, and there was a huge rainstorm. There was thunder and lightning and we were staying in tents. We joked about it later, in Wes's absence. We said, 'That was a Freddy Krueger experience. It must have been Wes Craven who created this nightmare on the Delaware.'" Ironically, the experience seems to have been a more affirmative one for Wes; he later told a friend that the ill-fated canoe trip was one of the happiest moments in his life—because he "discovered I could do almost anything I had to, and that I really wanted very much to live."[19]

Wes Craven in March 1973 (courtesy Mary Blocksma)

Wes told filmmaker Luke Meyer that he also participated in the Sullivanian group's summer excursions to the coastal community of Amagansett, where the house parties were legendary. Siskind reports that one party "had over 100 people, half of whom were in the pool at the same time! The 'wildness' consisted of heavy drinking, couples (and larger groups at times) departing for various bedrooms to have sex, dancing, which was often done in circles, loud rock music, jumping, splashing, and other games in the pool."[20] Alice Graves remembers an even more raucous "orgy party" in the summer of '75, which she likens to a scene from Fellini's film *Satyricon*: "The house is filled to the rafters with drunk naked people chasing each other around with squirt bottles of Johnson & Johnson's baby oil."[21] When interviewed about the "Amagansett experience" in 2014, Wes said he felt that the group's discouragement of monogamy seemed shallow, "phobic of intimacy," and completely void of romance—which might explain the final scene in *The Fireworks Woman*, in which Peter rescues Angela from an orgy party.[22]

As Wes became more integrated into the group, he seems to have reached what Amy Siskind identifies as the third stage of the therapeutic process, in which full-fledged "participants" were expected to adhere to strict guidelines about how to raise their children, thereby escaping the vicious cycle of producing emotionally crippled adults. She writes, "Full-time child care was hired for all children of group members, based partially on the belief that no parent should have to take care of their child on a full-time basis, and partially on the notion that mothers usually behaved in an envious and hateful manner toward their children."[23] A good parent, according to the group leaders, was one who "provided for his or her children with good care, education, clothing, and enough money to buy or do anything they wished," but who spent "as little time with them as possible."[24] Former group member Jon Mack adds, "In a few cases, parents actually signed over their parent rights to be adopted by another. Some parents fought back."[25]

By his own account, Wes wasn't initially thinking about the influence that Sullivanian therapy would have on his children because he hadn't encountered many other young parents in the group. Eventually, however, some members of the group encouraged him to fight for custody of his children Jonathan and Jessica, presumably so they could be separated from their mother and integrated into the group experiment. Wes said he was told that "we have lawyers, we have people who are part of the group who can help you get that done. And that was where I started to say, 'There's no way that's gonna happen, No way.'"[26]

At this point, he realized he had unwittingly joined a group that was as fanatical and controlling as the fundamentalist community he'd grown up in. Despite his reluctance to leave a creative community of friends, he refused to put his children into a situation where they would be forced to live according to someone else's beliefs and practices. As a result, Wes was ostracized from the group. "One of the people, a spokesman for the group, said, 'You've got to get out. You're endangering us. You're endangering yourself, if you can't get on the program. You have to get out. Now.' So I literally left. Went out and sat down on the stairs of the brownstone, and just wept."[27]

Family members say Wes felt duped and betrayed, and that his ostracism was doubly painful because it reminded him of an experience he'd had at Wheaton College. After the *Kodon* flap, he was reportedly encouraged to see a specific therapist who reinforced the evangelical dogmas of Wheaton College. Now, for the second time in his life, Wes found himself in a cultish "feedback loop." And for the second time, the experience left him without a support system. Adding to the ill will, Sullivanian group leaders purportedly spread a series of misleading rumors about why Wes had been shunned. Michael Bray says he was told that Wes got kicked out of the group because he was working in adult cinema. Another former member heard that Wes was making films financed by the mob.

It was around this time, probably in the late spring or summer of 1974, that Wes directed *The Fireworks Woman*. The project was set up through an office in the building at 56 West 45th Street—a telephone number on the title page of the script is identical to the number on the title page of Wes's 1971 draft of *Last House on the Left*—and co-writer Roger Murphy solicited Norman Mailer's feedback on the script via a letter from "Lobster Enterprises," the same production entity that made *Last House*. Apparently, there was some initial talk about casting Mailer in the role of the Monsignor, and Rip Torn (who had appeared in Mailer's films *Beyond the Law* and *Maidstone*) as Nicholas Burns. In the end, Roger Murphy played the Monsignor and Wes Craven played Burns.

Wes Craven as Nicholas Burns in *The Fireworks Woman*
(Lobster Enterprises, 1975)

Murphy told Mailer that the film's budget was approximately $50,000, and that the filmmakers planned to shoot in and around the town of Westport, Connecticut, where Sean Cunningham had a house and where *Last House on the Left* had been shot a few years earlier. Editing began in the summer of 1974 (one of Wes's Wheaton friends recalls visiting Wes in his edit bay that summer, and hearing audio of a man crooning the name "Angela" in coital bliss) and the film was released theatrically the following summer. Although the original theatrical cut seems to be lost to the ages, VCA Labs released a 78-minute edit on VHS in the early 1980s. Many years later, Italian distributor Opium Visions released an 80-minute cut, titled *La Cugina del Prete* (*The Cousin of the Priest*) on DVD.

Today, a 73-minute cut of *The Fireworks Woman* circulates on the Internet. This shortest, most easily-accessible version begins with a ritualistic dance sequence, set to tribal drum music by future Emmy-winning composer Jacques Urbont. At the center of the dance is a tall man clad entirely in black. A top hat, a cape, and a sardonic smile complete the ensemble of young Wes

Craven in the pivotal role of Nicholas Burns. His arrival in the (now unnamed) coastal New England town sets the story in motion and casts an ominous shadow over the events to come.

The devilish huckster uses the celebratory spectacle of the holiday to liberate and entrap his quarry, beginning with two innocent young children. Although they do not appear in the 73-minute cut of *The Fireworks Woman*, Jonathan Craven remembers that he and his sister Jessica filmed an introductory scene in which they encountered Nicholas Burns on the beach. In the shorter version, their voices can be heard in an abstract montage sequence. Jonathan asks, "Hey, are you that guy who's going to shoot off them fireworks tonight?" Wes answers, "That's me, Nicholas Burns, at your service." Jessica follows up, "Can you give us something for the Fourth of July?" "Like what?" the fire-monger teases. The truncated film answers the question with the sound of an explosion and an image of a fiery hole on the beach, suggesting that Nicholas Burns has turned the kids themselves into fireworks.

As the film progresses, Burns appears more manipulative than violent. Like the title character in Hermann Hesse's novel *Demian*, he functions as the fulcrum of the narrative, the tempter who pushes the other characters out of their comfort zones. But Burns is not interested particularly in the souls of children. He wants to corrupt faith more than he wants to destroy innocence, and he uses Angela's "fireworks woman" to achieve his goal. The title role was played by Sarah Nicholson, a versatile actress who contemporaneously appeared in the mainstream films *Three Days of the Condor, Deadly Hero,* and *The Stepford Wives*, and played Patty Hearst in the TV movie *Patty* (all 1975). Before making *The Fireworks Woman*, Nicholson had also appeared in a few adult films for director Joseph W. Sarno, and she would go on to star in the X-rated psychological thriller *Sometime Sweet Susan* (1975). In 1976, the actress optimistically hoped that adult cinema would help "illuminate a lot of the fears and ridiculous ideas the American people have about sex."[28] Instead, her association with that side of the entertainment industry crippled her mainstream acting career. Reflecting on her association with "pornography" today, she says, "I hate that term. I don't view it as that. I just never identified with it or thought of it as that. And that's probably what allowed me to do certain things and not even think about it on camera."

As for her work with Wes Craven, Nicholson says she knew right away that the film would be more ambitious than other sex films. She recalls, "*The Fireworks Woman* had a real script. I remember there was a purple ribbon. It was all bound and embossed and all that stuff."[29] The physical description matches the manuscript that resides in the Norman Mailer collection. The 73-minute cut of the film, however, is in many ways different from that script.

As her part of the story begins, Angela recalls—via voiceover narration (not included in the original script) and vivid flashbacks—her illicit tryst with her brother Peter, who has gone on to become a Catholic priest. She says she understands why Peter ended the affair, but admits she can't stop fantasizing about him. "In dreams begin responsibilities," she intones, although she desperately wants to ignore her responsibilities to societal norms and restore her dream-life with Peter. The film depicts Angela's vivid recollections of her time with Peter as heavenly interludes, photographed in white light through gauzy camera filters that soften every edge. In contrast to the primal music featured in Nicholas Burns's introductory scenes, these hardcore sex scenes feature more soulful music: a beatific folk song called "Rainy Afternoon" and Johann Pachelbel's "Canon in D," a perennial favorite for churchy weddings. The combination of lighting and music suggests that Angela and Peter have a spiritual relationship as well as a sexual attraction.

With Nicholas Burns looking on, Angela goes to Peter's church and pleads for him to love her. Peter coolly responds, "If you want to avoid a precipice, then stay away from the edge. And above all, repress selfish desire." He advises Angela to forget him and "submerge" herself in "serving others," then passes her off to one of his parishioners as a maid. Elizabeth Walters, a wealthy middle-aged woman, invites her male friend Roger to join her and the new maid behind closed doors. Angela, perhaps a bit too eager to "serve," plays the role of submissive. According to contemporary reviews of the theatrical cut of *The Fireworks Woman*, this sequence originally included a moment in which Elizabeth forces Angela to urinate into her hands, essentially repeating a similar scene in *Last House on the Left*. That beat does not appear in the 73-minute cut but Roger observes that Angela has "soiled" her "pretty white dress," shortly before he cuts it off of her.

In the next scene, Roger goes to Peter's church and seems to taunt the priest with a vivid description of the sexual encounter, noting that Angela screamed Peter's name while she was suffering in ecstasy. Soon after, Angela visits Peter again and asks, "Why aren't you affected by me, like the others?" Despite an obvious physical attraction to her, Peter continues to repress his desire and adhere to his responsibility to "others." Angela protests that the others—meaning his parishioners—are vicious hypocrites, but Peter refuses to hear her and instead orders her to leave town.

Afterward, Angela prays to God "for the first time in many years" but receives no "answer from on high." Dismayed by God's silence, she obeys an inner voice that prompts her to get on a small sailboat and flee her home. At sea, Angela gets hopelessly drunk, drops anchor and drifts for three days, all the while dreaming of Peter. Voiceover narration (not present in the original script) frames her semi-conscious experience as a kind of mystical journey: "I tried to feel myself as part of the boat, grounded to something, but the tendency seemed to be for me to be swept away by memories and fantasies of Peter. […] Consciousness seemed to grow lighter and lighter until I simply floated away from my body. I became part of the sun, and for a while I had nothing with which to feel pain." At the end of her reverie, Angela experiences a vision of Peter hanging on the cross-shaped mast of the sailboat. As she writhes in pain on the deck below, he mocks her with laughter. The implication is that, for Angela, God has become a cruel prankster. Wes might have drawn some inspiration from his own torturous experience as a teenager, when he was wracked with guilt over his sexual impulses. *So long Jesus, hello Molly.*

Eventually, a seafaring young couple, Derek and Celeste, rescue Angela from her misery. Somewhat inexplicably, she becomes like a mythic Siren, seducing them both. The trio returns to land and indulges in a Bacchanalian picnic hosted by Nicholas Burns, who hand-feeds Angela bread and wine in a mockery of holy communion. In the 73-minute cut of the film, it is not clear when or how the trio met Burns; his sudden, unexplained appearance adds mystery to the narrative. After another sexual interlude, Celeste visits her parish priest—Peter, of course—and confesses, "There was just something about her. She had some sort of power. I don't usually do things like this." Celeste neglects to mention Nicholas Burns, leaving the viewer to wonder if he really exists.

A subsequent scene finds Angela wandering in a nearby harbor as Burns looks on. A pair of dock workers notice her too and become bewitched.

Eric Edwards as Peter in *The Fireworks Woman* (Lobster Enterprises, 1975)

One (identified as Fred in the script) tells his friend to remember that he has a "nice wife and four kids" at home, then he clubs the friend over the head with a dead fish (!) and proceeds to rape Angela. For added shock value, the theatrical cut of the film allegedly featured some extra footage with the fish. A 1975 review in *The Boston Phoenix* (perhaps planted by the filmmakers themselves?) reported, "Forty minutes into the action you'll find Locke [the film's supposed director] showing you rape with a deadly fish. To explain this particular scene would take so long you might just as well see the film, which contains a big-mouthed fish destined to be the Linda Lovelace of the future."[30] In a 1976 interview, Sarah Nicholson recalled, "It was a scene that even scared the crew. At one point, I was on my back on the ice and just happened to look up and see the sound crew in the loft; they had the most terrified look on their faces, and porno crews have seen everything."[31]

For the few critics who saw *The Fireworks Woman* in its original theatrical release, the "fish scene" became a cause célèbre. UCLA sociology professor Delos H. Kelly cited it in his 1979 book *Deviant Behavior* as incontrovertible evidence of a disgusting "attitudinal revolution" in 1970s America.[32] Striking a very different tone, adult cinema historian Jim Holliday practically raved about the excesses of *The Fireworks Woman*, writing that the film "had just about everything, including a nun's rape, a fish used as a dildo, urination, fisting, a nude six-year-old kid walking the beach, etc."[33] It seems Holliday exaggerated several details in order to make his point that the Golden Age of Porn was all about breaking taboos, and to support his contention that it broke too many. At some point, either the distributors or the filmmakers of *The Fireworks Woman* came to the same conclusion and decided to remove several minutes of footage from the film.

After this horrific encounter with the dock worker, Angela returns home in a semi-stuporous state. She tries to mentally escape into heavenly fantasies of Peter but soon becomes frustrated and begins spinning around an empty room like a whirling dervish in a purification ritual. (The script makes that exact comparison.) The filmmaker interrupts the dance with flashbacks to Angela's various encounters with a sneering rapist, a bloody fish head, and a cracking whip. Finally, the poor woman retreats to the shower and turns the water to scalding hot, wincing in pain as she endures her self-inflicted punishment, then collapses naked on the bedroom floor. Seemingly delusional, she is roused by a male voice calling her name from the beach outside her bedroom window. She looks out and sees no one there, then turns back to find Peter in the room with her. Her fantasy realized at last, she makes passionate love to him—until a cutaway shot reveals that the encounter has taken place only in her imagination; Peter isn't there. Defeated, she masturbates furiously and desperately to the haunting dirge "Now You're All Alone"—the same folk song that accompanied Mari's rape and murder in *Last House on the Left*. Her fantasy turns darker as Peter reappears and penetrates her anally.

With nothing left to lose, Angela visits Peter one last time. Again, he rejects her, declaring their love "forbidden" and warning that "the soul can be tortured forever" if a person gives in to temptation. Angela pleads her case: "It's not my soul—it's my *heart*. Can't you see that?" He can't. For a while, the film's narrative focus shifts to Peter. We follow him as he goes home, reads an ironic Bible verse ("Thou hast ravished my heart, my sister, my bride"), and whips himself with a belt. Falling asleep, he dreams of Angela tending to his wounds... and then some. He wakes up screaming in protest. The following day, he confesses to his monsignor that he suffers just as much when he's awake.

Eric Edwards, a classically-trained stage actor who would go on to become one of the most famous male stars in adult cinema, says he is grateful to have been cast in *The Fireworks Woman* as Peter. He remembers his character "had this battle going on inside, between being a priest and being in love with my sister, so there was a real acting challenge there. Which I didn't get very often. Having been trained at the American Academy of Dramatic Arts, I welcomed it.... although, whenever I had to delve into character, I found it difficult to concentrate on the physical aspect of what had to be happening. What I had to do was kind of break character and concentrate on 'getting it up' and all that. Which is kind of an odd thing to say, but it's a fact." As for working with Wes Craven, he remembers, "I was trained for the stage and I didn't want to overact on film, so I had to be brought down quite a bit. And he guided me in that area."

In the film's final act, Nicholas Burns brings the star-crossed lovers together by offering Angela a mysterious contract. "There is something you want," he explains. "And you can have it. There are no mysteries that can't be untied, no fight that can't be won. But it'll cost you. Know what I mean?" In a parallel scene, Peter's monsignor offers the same advice: "Leave it to God. There are no mysteries He can't unravel. No fights He cannot win. No matter who the adversary might be." In addition to giving the same speech, the two spiritual advisors each offer to share a smoke with their supplicants, behaving like shamans in a sacred ceremony. Angela heeds the voice of her tempter and embraces her source of power (such as it is); she plans an orgy and invites Peter's parishioners, hoping to lure Peter in the process.

The final set piece is a who's who of mid-1970s porn stars, a celebrity "Amagansett experience." The cast members gleefully intertwine on a living room floor while Angela oversees the proceedings like a proud brothel madam. According to one contemporary review of the film, the rapist fisherman and his wide-mouthed bass made a repeat appearance in the original cut, but that's not the case in the shorter version of the film. Meanwhile, Nicholas Burns phones Peter—using a cartoonish old lady voice—to tell him what's happening. The filmmaker then juxtaposes the ongoing orgy sequence with footage of exploding fireworks, coaxing the all-American celebration to its climax. When the orgy participants turn their attention to Angela, Peter interrupts and claims her as his own. His parishioners back off reverently as the priest drapes a coat around Angela's naked body and he gently leads her out of the house.

The couple walk down to the docks and sail off into the sunset, accompanied by one final bit of voiceover narration, in which Peter explains his decision: "I just can't leave it to God any longer. I've been doing that my whole life. Now it's time I took responsibility for myself." The implication is that Peter has liberated himself from the repressive influence of the church, choosing instead to tend his own garden. What's less clear is whether or not Peter has damned himself in the process. When asked for a moral reading of his character's decision, actor Eric Edwards responds, "I think that 'damned' is probably a good word to use, simply because I knew in my heart that I couldn't continue this. And yet, in dreams, perhaps it could be. But I don't know exactly. You never really know what the director or the writer is really trying to convey." One wonders if the director himself could have—or would have—offered a more definitive answer.

In the final shot of the film, the monsignor rushes to the coastline and sees the boat drifting away. Realizing that the conflict has ended, he makes a sign of the cross in mid-air, then turns and morphs into smiling Nicholas Burns. The transformation seems to be Craven's rejoinder to the metaphysical questions raised in his story; the revelation that the holy man and the mischievous liberator are one and the same conveys a final rejection of the dichotomy of good and evil, God and the Devil, suggesting instead (albeit vaguely) a non-dualistic philosophy. It is also significant that the filmmaker himself physically embodies the role of the mischievous liberator instead of the supposed holy man. As Nicholas Burns (and Abe Snake), Wes acknowledges that he has become exactly what his childhood church warned him about—a "Hollywood" filmmaker doing "the work of the devil." Without a doubt, making this film was a defiant act of personal rebellion, illustrating the filmmaker's decision to leave organized religion and societal norms behind him, and to take personal responsibility for the outcomes of that decision, whatever they might be.

In light of Wes's other work (especially *Last House on the Left*), *The Fireworks Woman* can be read as a social protest document, a rebellion against "traditional"—which is to say, puritanical—American values. Wes once told interviewer Stanley Wiater that because of his "very restrictive background," he "never wanted to have anybody saying 'You can only go that far.'"[34] He had been excoriated for "going too far" with *Last House on the Left*, but he went even further with his second film, releasing a primal scream of wanton lust from the monstrously self-indulgent Id of the Me Decade. *The Fireworks Woman* could only have been made—and perhaps only taken seriously—in that particular time and place, by a storyteller bold enough to put his subconscious dreams on film and ambitious enough to suggest that a hardcore sex film could reveal an important message about modern society and organized religion's stunting of human potential.

It may not have taken long, however, for Abe Snake to regret making such a grandiose statement. In later years, although Wes suggested that *Last House on the Left* broke too many taboos, he was always willing to discuss the film as a product of its time and place, an honest document of anti-war rage and a personal, primal scream. On the other hand, he never discussed *The Fireworks Woman* publicly, which suggests he regarded the latter as a more problematic film than *Last House*. In a late 1980s interview, he said, "I don't think that the great, sort of libertarian opening of the floodgates of morality in the Seventies has done the next generation a great amount of good. I think there was some sort of balance that had to be attained. The pendulum had to swing back the other way."[35] Perhaps reflecting on his second film as a more ignominious reflection of a mercifully bygone era, he added, "One of the ways to establish your freedom is to go to the extreme like I did in New York in the 70s. You just completely experience everything you possibly can that's outlawed. You waste a lot of time, in some ways."[36]

By December 1974, Wes was starting over. He had left the Sullivanian group and was living alone in a loft in Lower Manhattan, where he tried to re-forge a bond with his son and daughter. Years later, in a letter to his friend Mary Blocksma, he described an attempt to reclaim the holiday season for divorced dads by inventing his own post-Christmas celebration: "Saint Walrus Day." Wes wrote, "It seems that there are a large group of walruses, led by a certain Wally Walrus, that have banded together to visit the houses of divorced fathers whenever it is that their kids finally make it from their other homes to get their presents and give their hugs." The walruses left behind "distinctive puddles of water," carefully hidden presents, and a series of riddles that subtly revealed the locations of the presents. Jonathan Craven remembers the experiment as one of Wes's "crowning achievements as a parent."

It may have been around this time that Wes wrote his spec script about "a divorced father trying to pursue a relationship with his kids." He and Sean Cunningham also developed a few other off-brand ideas, including a satire of beauty contests titled *American Beauty* and an adult-oriented re-telling of the Brothers Grimm fairy tale "Hansel and Gretel." Reflecting on the former project, Cunningham says, "'This was a time when we weren't trying to sell to studios, so it was like, 'What do you think people might want to go see?' And that was Wes saying, 'Maybe we could figure out a way to shoot in a Las Vegas casino. It would be fun to make a movie with beautiful women in Las Vegas.'" As for the latter: "It's back to that thing of, 'What do people want to see?' Well, maybe a fairy tale. Fairy tales are always popular."[37] By 1976, Wes had written a 91-page feature film script for *Hansel and Gretel*, a remarkably faithful adaptation of the original source story with minor idiosyncratic embellishments.

At the outset of the script, kindly dad Zachary — who makes his living "selling wood" — has fallen on hard times and can no longer financially support his family of four. (Five, if you include the family pet, "Flying Dog.") His second wife Cybele suggests abandoning her two stepchildren in the woods, ostensibly for the children's own good. Browbeaten and drunk, Zachary reluctantly agrees. His son Hansel, hearing the conversation from an adjoining room, concocts his own plan; the next day, when the parents lead him and his sister into the woods, Hansel leaves a trail of shiny rocks behind them. Back at home, Cybele contemplates eating the dog. Zachary's rediscovery of his first wife's wedding ring—which he promptly pawns—saves the dog's life and feeds the kids when they come home.

Cybele doesn't give up. After Hansel has a nightmare in which Cybele sweeps Flying Dog off a cliff, the evil stepmother takes the children back out into the woods and leaves them for dead. Zachary is too busy dreaming of his dead wife to notice. This time, Hansel and Gretel plan to find their way home by following a trail of breadcrumbs, but the crows eat the breadcrumbs first. After a harrowing attempt to cross a river during a storm, they take refuge in a cave and, deep within the cave, find a gateway to an enchanted forest and a gingerbread house. The owner, an old woman, invites them in and puts them to bed. The following morning, a talking raven lures the boy into a rabbit cage and the old woman, an evil witch who eats children for breakfast (literally), turns Gretel into her servant. Gretel tries valiantly to rescue her brother, with no luck. Back at home, Zachary grows a spine and throws his cold-blooded wife out of the house, then goes looking for his children. The ever-faithful Flying Dog leads him to the mysterious cave.

In the third act, Hansel and Gretel conspire to trick the old, nearly-blind witch by using a chicken bone to convince her that Hansel is too bony to eat. The plan works for a while, but Cybele eventually catches on and orders Gretel to get into the cooking pot. Gretel convinces the old witch to climb into her own oven—to demonstrate how it's done—and then roasts her like a Thanksgiving turkey. Gretel then frees Hansel from his cage and the siblings flee the gingerbread house, which promptly disappears as the witch dies screaming. Afterward, they scour the enchanted forest for mythic treasures, then head for the cave-tunnel that will bring them home. When they re-enter the "real" world, their father and Flying Dog are waiting. And they live happily ever after.

Unfortunately, the *Hansel and Gretel* script didn't sell and Wes continued to make a very modest living "selling wood." The adult film industry was still going strong, but those involved were beginning to find themselves in legal peril. In July 1974, actor Harry Reems faced formal obscenity charges, for which he would be tried and found guilty in April 1976. For the purveyors of "porno chic," it was the end of an era. In the years to come, actors and filmmakers who had cut their teeth on pornography would try to expunge those credits from their resumés and distance themselves from the increasingly marginalized form. In the meantime, some of porn's proud pioneers started pulling their punches.

In the summer of 1975, Peter Locke's third film *Kitty Can't Help It* (a.k.a. *California Drive-In Girls*) was released, featuring the editorial stylings of one Wes "Hot Tracks" Craven. According to an article in *Variety* magazine, Locke and co-producer Jim Buckley opted to produce the film as an R-rated softcore sex comedy "because of the current legal climate" surrounding hardcore pornography.[38] Nevertheless, *Kitty* was designed to shock and dismay.

The screen story follows a female teenager who gets caught sleeping with her boss, promptly loses her job, and decides to move in with a girlfriend and start a new life. Kitty's domineering, racist mother drives her to a new apartment in a new neighborhood teeming with hippies and perverts, and quips, "Close your eyes and you can see Charles Manson." The film takes an absurdly comic detour through the sex lives of Kitty's new friends and neighbors— including, most notably, a guy who gets his rocks off by having his girlfriend smash banana cream pies into his backside—as it works its way back to Kitty, who has landed a new job. She quickly learns that her boss is a rapist, but a stranger named BJ rescues her and ferries her to safety in the Mojave Desert. Their ensuing sexcapade is interrupted by an angry iguana that bites BJ's tongue. Kitty reluctantly returns home and goes out with her roommate's boyfriend, who wins her heart by taking her to see a gore-porn flick called *Dr. Demento's Chamber of Lust*. Kitty has sex with him, gets attacked by her rapist boss again, and becomes embroiled in an elaborate car chase sequence—the obligatory climax for any 1970's drive-in movie. Despite its firm commitment to sex, violence, and comic absurdity, *Kitty Can't Help It* didn't make much of an impression at the box office. It was recycled on VHS a few years later, under the innocuous title *The Carhops*.

The Fireworks Woman, released a few months after *Kitty Can't Help It*, in the fall of 1975, met a similar fate—which may have been a relief to its writer/director. Despite lofty ambitions, Wes was unhappy with the theatrical version of his second film. His friend Roy Frumkes remembers visiting Wes in the edit bay soon after he completed the theatrical cut. According to Frumkes, "He was sitting there, just saying, 'Ugly people doing ugly things.' And he would say it over and over again." He was especially unhappy with "the way the porn scenes had to be extended" to please the film's financiers. Sometime later, Frumkes suggested that Wes should edit a private "director's cut," to realize his original vision. "To be clear," he says, "I was involved after the sound mix, after the answer prints, after everything. I said to him, 'Let's do a re-edit, like we did with *Last House*.' I had pushed him to re-edit *Last House on the Left*, which he did, and then I pushed him to re-edit this thing, which he did. I just felt like he owed it to himself to cut out some of the stuff that he hated. So the re-edited version—wherever the hell it is—is about an hour long. And it made him happy. The scenes were still effective."

Wes maintained his alliance with Peter Locke, who returned to making hardcore sex films, alongside *Flesh Gordon* producer/director Howard Ziehm. In his 2018 autobiography, Ziehm claims that Wes wrote the script for at least one of their collaborations, elaborating, "Wes had done some comedy writing for Peter's new wife, Liz Torres [a comedian with a cabaret act in Las Vegas], and he suggested we let him do the dialogue. I was fine with that but still wanted to keep the structure of the story under my control and quickly put together an outline that detailed the sex acts and set ups that I wanted to use, and sent it to Peter so Wes could get started."[39] The result was *Sweet Cakes*, an anthology film featuring four distinct segments.

In the opening segment, Wes appears as a photographer flirting with oversexed twins during a photo shoot. Ziehm remembers, "Wes agreed to take the role of the photographer, which did not require nudity or sex. Because the girls find the photographer to be attractive, they play coy and disrupt the flow of the session. But he is all business and they return home frustrated with no other option but to relieve their pent-up passion by making love to each other."[40] The resulting film was successful enough to inspire several more Ziehm and Locke collaborations, including an erotic spoof of Rod Serling's *Night Gallery* TV series, titled *Hot Cookies* (1977). Although it might sound like a natural fit for frightmaster Wes Craven, there is no evidence he was involved with that project.

Soon after, Wes decided to get out of the adult entertainment industry for good. In 2015, *The Rialto Report* unearthed a signed appearance release—dated October 28, 1975—indicating that Wes agreed to appear onscreen in director Radley Metzger's film *The Opening of Misty Beethoven* (1976), a hardcore parody of George Bernard Shaw's play *Pygmalion* that one critic has dubbed "the crown jewel" of the Golden Age of Porn.[41] Wes might have recognized a kindred spirit in Metzger, who began his career editing American trailers for European art films like Antonioni's *L'Avventura*, Truffaut's *Jules and Jim*, and Bergman's *Through a Glass Darkly*. For reasons unknown, he decided not to appear in Metzger's film. Instead, he moved to southern California.

Aside from having concerns about the long-term viability of a career in the beleaguered adult film industry, Wes might have been eager to put some distance between himself and the suddenly-controversial Sullivanian group. In

December 1975, an article published in *New York* magazine indicated that the group's activities had turned even darker since he left. "Totalitarian Therapy on the Upper West Side" highlighted "rumors of kidnapping children of members who were trying to sever ties with the group, of purges, of institutionalized paranoia, of venomous hostility to anyone who threatened to breach the circle of secrecy surrounding the group."[42] One family member says it was the publication of this article that finally forced Wes to acknowledge that he'd spent a year of his life on the fringes of a dangerous cult—and to examine his own apparent susceptibility to indoctrination.

Less than two years later, his friend Tristine Rainer asked him to make a thoughtful assessment of his life so far. In response, Wes compiled a short, pithy spiritual autobiography titled "Beliefs I have discarded, or believe I have." Rainer published the list (without explicitly identifying Wes as the author) in her book *The New Diary*, noting that it represented the author's recognition of a cyclical pattern of belief and disillusionment in his life. The list read as follows:

1. Mama loves me. Daddy will always be there.

2. Jesus loves me, this I know, for the Bible tells me so.

3. Christ died for my sins.

4. Mama loves me. Daddy will come back soon.

5. God is an American white male.

6. The Lone Ranger really lives.

7. You'd better not shout, you'd better not cry, you'd better not pout, I'm telling you why…

8. I'm an angel. I'm going to live forever.

9. If I do this, I'll go blind.

10. If I do this, I'll go insane.

11. If I keep doing this, I'll die of a heart attack, like my father.

12. If I go to college, I'll be smarter than anybody else.

13. If I learn to play the guitar, I'll have my pick of the girls.

14. If I study trigonometry, I'll be able to be a pilot.

15. This paralysis was God's judgment on me.

16. This paralysis ruined my body forever.

17. If I stay up all night, I'll write a good poem.

18. I'll die before thirty.

19. If we bomb the Vietcong in Hanoi, they'll quit.

20. If I march down south, blacks will love me.

21. We are a generation of vipers.

22. God is dead.

23. If I get married, I'll be happy.

24. I'll be able to realize everything in my son that I haven't realized in myself.

25. The Beatles are perfect.

26. If I swallow this pill, I'll be enlightened.

27. If I smoke this number, I'll be hip.

28. If I snort this stuff, I'll write a great script.

29. All cops are pigs.

30. We've got to get back to the garden, I believe we can.

31. If I get divorced, my mother will be crushed.

32. If I get divorced, I'll be punished.

33. This therapy will restore me.

34. All belief is sleep, the lowest form of consciousness.

35. If I make a hundred thousand on this film, I'll never have to worry about money again.

36. If I take this consciousness-raising training, I'll be high.

37. This whole spiritual trip is just Fundamentalism in drag.

38. I'm an outsider.

39. This anger will never go away.[43]

Wes's life-changing move to California, leaving his children in the care of their mother and stepfather, begs some important questions. Did Wes feel that he was protecting his children by distancing himself from them? Did he perhaps internalize the Sullivanian's group's judgment of him as an unfit parent and, for that reason, decide to minimize his influence on his children's lives? Or maybe he felt he had to move away from New York for the sake of his own sanity? Family members say that the move to California was simply a career move and a financial decision ("If I make a hundred thousand on this film..."). For reasons known only to Wes, he chose to make a new beginning far away from his family. Although it would cause regrettable stress in his relationships with his children—who could not help feeling that their father had prioritized his career over them—the move solidified his commitment to filmmaking and drew him back to the horror genre.

In a 1982 interview, Wes summed up the years between *Last House on the Left* and *The Hills Have Eyes* as follows: "I wrote Liz Torres's cabaret comedy act two times. I edited a lot of films, edited trailers. Wrote a lot of scripts for pay."[44] Carefully avoiding any mention of his work in the adult film industry, he also neglected to mention *Tales That'll Tear Your Heart Out*, a transitional film that foreshadowed his future.

The uncompleted anthology horror film was conceived by Wes's friend Roy Frumkes, who recalls, "I was teaching at SUNY Purchase and I thought, 'Well, I've got this job teaching production, so maybe I should do an anthology film in 16mm. And hire people that are on the east coast—good filmmakers who aren't getting much work—and give them all 1%, and have students working as grips, etc. So it happened. Sort of." The filmmaking recruits included DeWitt Bodeen, screenwriter of the classic RKO horror films *Cat People* (1942) and *The Seventh Victim* (1943); Ernest Tidyman, Oscar-winning screenwriter of *The French Connection* (1971) and *Shaft* (1971); Chuck Hirsch, producer of Brian De Palma's early films *Greetings* (1968) and *Hi, Mom!* (1970); cartoonist Al Kilgore, a regular contributor to the *Bullwinkle* comic strip; and Wes, who reportedly planned to use his pseudonym "Abe Snake" on the film.

Frumkes remembers, "The [wraparound] story starts off in a graveyard that's being exhumed to put up an apartment building, and all of the corpses indignantly get up to go home and finish what they were doing when they died.

Roy Frumkes and Wes Craven on the set of *Deadly Blessing*, 1981
(courtesy Roy Frumkes)

That was the idea I gave to all the filmmakers. Wes wanted to do a western. He said, 'Let's get David Hess [who played Krug in *Last House on the Left*] for the villain.' And the woman that played the lead, Victoria Alexander, was an old, old friend of mine. She's a hooker in this old western bar. In her first scene with Hess, he comes onto her. He grabs her and kisses her, and she bites his lip—for real. And he hauled off and belted her. Knocked her down. And they both loved it! I started to step in and she signaled me, 'No, this is good.'"

"We shot it all up in Westchester and I was a zombie in it. I was the corpse of a cowboy who died defending the honor of a prostitute. At one point, we went to Times Square, unloaded our equipment, had me in the makeup. Nobody bothered us! We were there for hours. It was so much fun. I remember Wes was clowning around. He would lie on the ground and he would use his legs as the clapper board." In a more serious moment, Frumkes adds, Craven was so committed to getting a particular shot that he literally went out on a limb:

"There was a stream and he wanted a shot from up above it. A tree was hanging over the stream and his director of photography wouldn't climb it, so Wes said, 'Okay.' He took the camera and he climbed up the tree himself. I thought, *That's commitment,* you know?"

Wes finished shooting and editing his segment of the film, but was never able to finalize the sound elements. Years later, some silent excerpts appeared on Arrow Video's Blu-Ray release of *Last House on the Left*, connecting the lost anthology film to Wes Craven's legacy as a horror filmmaker. In hindsight, it seems likely that the director's experience on *Tales* convinced him that it was okay to return to horror. By the fall of 1976, he and Peter Locke were on the edge of California's Mojave Desert, making *The Hills Have Eyes*.

CHAPTER SIX

CALIFORNIA DREAMING

(1977 - 1982)

"Film comes nearest to religion as the movie houses are empty,
it speaks across all the lonely traverses of the mind, it is at its
most beautiful in precisely those places it is least concrete, least theatrical,
most other-worldly, most ghostly, most lingering unto death..."

- Norman Mailer, "A Course in Filmmaking" (1971)

According to producer Peter Locke, *The Hills Have Eyes* began with a conversation he and Wes Craven had in 1974: "Wes had a bit of a hit with *Last House on the Left*, but nobody had asked him to do another movie. So I said to him, 'Listen, man, I don't know anything about terror movies, but you made money with one. Let's go!'"[1] At the time, Wes was hesitant to make another horror film; *Last House* had branded him a monster and caused him plenty of heartache. Still, as he explained to me in a 2010 interview, he wanted to keep making movies and he recognized that horror might be his niche: "Once you do one, people don't say, 'Oh okay, let's give him a comedy to do.' So, in a way, you get kind of stuck in that ghetto, and then it's like, 'Do I stop making films because I hate it? Or do I just not make them and not think about it?' Or do I say 'For whatever reason, I'm in a position where I can make films out of these [subjects], so what can be put into them and what have other people put into them'? And then you get to something really, really interesting that has to do with fairy tales and mythology and the dark side and all sorts of fascinating things. And you try to figure out what the hell you're doing without getting too intellectual about it."

Locke remembers that Wes went to the New York Public Library to research possible subjects for the new film. "We were on 56 West 45th Street and the library's on 42nd Street, so he'd go to the library after work. He was a late-night guy. And he figured out a couple of stories. One of them was the one that became our movie, which was based on the Sawney Bean family in Scotland. The other one was about another mass murderer. I can't remember the guy's name—but it was so horrible that we just didn't do it. Crazy fucking guy. He did awful, awful things to himself after he murdered people. He'd stick pins in his genitals. It was just insane. But we chose the one we chose, then he went off and wrote this Ancient Mariner thing."[2]

Locke's description suggests that Wes Craven's second horror film was almost based on the crimes of New York serial killer Albert Fish, who was executed in 1936 for the murder and alleged cannibalization of ten-year-old Grace Budd. Although the filmmakers rejected that story as too horrible, their inspiration for *The Hills Have Eyes* was equally gruesome. According to 18th century sources, Sawney Bean was an exile who bred a family of savages in the wilderness along the Scottish coast. The feral family survived by robbing and murdering travelers who wandered too close to their hunting grounds, then eating them. When human remains started turning up on nearby shores, Britain's King James sent spies to the region to hunt down the people responsible. A would-be victim led the King's army to the family's hideout, and bloodhounds cornered the Bean clan in a vast sea cave, where they were eating the dried and pickled remains of their latest victims. Soldiers rounded up the cannibals and took them to Edinburgh, to be tortured and executed in a public square. The men were dismembered; the women were burned alive.

For Wes Craven, whose first horror film had been inspired by the savagery of supposedly civilized Americans, the Sawney Bean story echoed a similar theme. He explained, "In that nut of a story was everything I thought about civilization. Because on the one hand you have this wildness that can just run rampant and prey upon the civilization. But then the civilization, when they catch up with them, is completely uncivilized itself. And has its own macabre wildness to it. I just took that and translated it into the 20th century."[3] Locke's description of *The Hills Have Eyes* as an "Ancient Mariner thing," suggests that Wes also drew inspiration from Samuel Taylor Coleridge's epic poem "The Rime of the Ancient Mariner," about a sailor who casually murders an innocent albatross and thereby inherits a divine curse. As part of his punishment, he must tell his story to everyone he encounters.

In the first draft of *The Hills Have Eyes*, titled *Blood Relations: The Sun Wars*, Wes includes a passage in which one character comments on a turkey buzzard circling above the desert. Unlike a "sea bird" reassuring sailors that they're close to land, he explains, a buzzard signifies no hope. This may have been Wes's oblique way of suggesting that his characters are cursed—and/or that the filmmaker himself felt like the Ancient Mariner, condemned to repeat his grim ballad about a conflict between two equally savage families.

The Hills Have Eyes took additional inspiration from Greco-Roman mythology, Jean Cocteau's fantasy film *Beauty and the Beast*, John Steinbeck's Depression-era novel *The Grapes of Wrath*, George Orwell's dystopian novel *1984*, John Wayne, and *The Texas Chainsaw Massacre*. Also, dreams. Wes had cultivated techniques for remembering and recording his dreams while he was a student at Wheaton, and eventually realized he could prompt dreams that corresponded with his work.[4] He said this happened for the first time while he was writing *The Hills Have Eyes*. He dreamed his screen story as a tale of two families: one defiantly savage, one ostensibly civilized. In the dream, the black-and-white dichotomy of the two families bled into a messy vision of moral ambiguity, with one member of the cannibal family becoming humane while several members of the civilized family become monstrous. In the script, Craven highlighted his theme by adding a pair of dogs to the story; one named Beauty, one Beast. Beauty doesn't last long.

The setting for the screen story was suggested by Peter Locke, who in the mid-70s was spending a lot of time on the road between Los Angeles and Las Vegas, where his wife was working. The savvy producer suggested to Wes that the Mojave Desert would make a good filming location because it didn't require film permits. At some point, the two friends went on a scouting trip to the desert area surrounding Victorville, which might have reminded Wes of his near-death encounter with a "hippie brigade" in Nevada—and the feeling of being supremely vulnerable in a vast, hostile environment. In our 2010 interview, he reflected, "The horror cliché of 'you're in the middle of nowhere, you're out in the boondocks and your phone isn't working'… It all boils down to the point where all the pertinences of human power—cars, guns, telephones—are removed. You increasingly end up alone in the middle of nowhere, which is exactly humanity's state. Because we're on this tiny blue speck in the middle of a universe that we have not found any other trace of life in. Well, that's a pretty… 'profound' does not even cover it. I mean, if you're on the Titanic, there's a moment when you realize you're in the middle of this immense ocean that can swallow you in a moment. That, I think, is one of the essential feelings of the human condition."

In addition to finding the perfect environment for such a horror story, Wes found that the desert gave him an exhilarating sense of creative freedom and opportunity. Locke remembers, "Wes was very adventuresome for locations. He didn't care about the difficulty of the locations. He was like a mountain goat. He used to run up the sides of the mountains and he'd be the first one up there, saying, 'I like this. Can we shoot here?' He wasn't worried about if you could get the camera up or anything. He just thought, 'Let's get the best thing we can—and everybody else should figure out their job, how to get their gear up—and let's go!'"[5]

Perhaps because he was new to the storied Great American West, the writer/director recognized he was on fertile ground for making a new myth—

or, to be more accurate, a new anti-myth. He developed *The Hills Have Eyes* as a distinctly American story, highlighting the historic conflict between the civilized East and the wild, wild West. Just as he and Peter Locke fled the concrete jungle of New York City for the libertarian frontier of southern California, so he imagined the civilized family in *Hills* fleeing the polluted, overcrowded city for a more idyllic life in the natural paradise of the southwest. Wes described his vision of America's past and future as follows: "The original draft had the family leaving New York in 1984, ten years in the future. [...] New York was uninhabitable and you had to have a passport to travel between states because they had become so territorial."[6] He elaborated, "Everyone's trying to get to the Sun Belt, so this family has decided to sneak across through the backroads, through the hills to get to California, the promised land. Like *The Grapes of Wrath* in 1984."[7]

Wes's fictional family's westward migration reflected not only America's 19th century expansion but also contemporary culture. In the 1970s, the country's main business model had shifted away from locally-owned companies and toward national conglomerates, away from the manufacturing industry, toward the service economy. As a result, "new wave" California culture was thriving while New York City was overrun with crime and teetering on the edge of bankruptcy. It's no accident that John Carpenter conceived his film *Escape from New York* around the same time Wes Craven wrote *The Hills Have Eyes*. Carpenter envisioned New York as a national prison run by criminals. Wes—who had been robbed twice at gunpoint while driving a cab in New York—had been one of the prisoners.

In his book *Shock Value*, Jason Zinoman quotes a letter Wes wrote to a college friend from the city in May 1970, expressing disgust with the sordid environment around him. He groused, "According to the news, the carbon monoxide level yesterday passed the unhealthy mark and simply left the edge of the graph. The noise is incredible now. The windows of all the subways are thrown open for air and the screaming of the steel wheels is a knife to the ears. Outside there is a continuous clot of traffic, construction and demolition everywhere with hundreds of drills and jackhammers going like hell all the time."[8]

Although Wes wanted to flee the oppressive city for wide-open vistas and clear skies, emptiness and silence, *The Hills Have Eyes* suggests there was an equally dark world waiting for him in the Mojave Desert. In the first draft script, the Carter family's escape from New York leads not to paradise but to an even more dog-eat-dog world. The filmmakers eventually dropped the futuristic *Escape from New York* prologue, but Wes retained his vision of *Hills* as a modern-day western film that refutes the notion of Manifest Destiny. Unlike the conquering heroes of countless Hollywood westerns, his pioneers go west only to be eaten alive.

Wes claimed that he partly based the film's "civilized" family on some of his own relatives and family friends from Cleveland. In 2003, he specified that the patriarch and matriarch of the Carter clan were inspired by members of his mother's church. The real Bob Carter, he said, "was head of security at Case Western Reserve University in Cleveland, and many of the lines of this character came directly from this man, my remembrance of things he said around the dinner table when I was a little kid."[9] Big Bob emerges as a kind of John Wayne caricature: bombastic, gun-toting, casually racist, and supremely confident that he can control the world and the people around him. Early in the script, he proudly identifies himself as a veteran cop who has spent a lifetime dodging bullets fired at him by "niggers" and Puerto Ricans. He is as callous—but not as complicated or compelling—as Ethan Edwards, the Indian-hater played by John Wayne in *The Searchers*. When the family camper breaks down in the desert, Big Bob gives his son a pistol and advises him not to shoot until he sees "the whites of their eyes," then heads off into the wilderness to save the day. But Wes Craven's film is not a John Wayne vehicle and Big Bob does not save the day.

Wes said that Ethel Carter, the matriarch who impotently advises Big Bob to mind his tongue and who refuses to acknowledge that her family is in real danger, was based on his mother. In a 2010 interview with me, he explained, "When the mother has been shot and she's dying, she looks around and says, 'This trailer's such a mess. It's so hard to keep a small space neat.' That's something my mother said about her tiny little cottage." Wes said he was fascinated by the idea that "somebody can have that so embedded in them that even as they're dying they're fussing about 'things aren't neat' and 'what will people think?' Which was one of my mother's favorite statements: '*What will people think?*'" In *The Hills Have Eyes*, Ethel Carter continues to deny reality until it bites her.

Bob and Ethel's three children—Doug, Bobby and Brenda—follow their parents' self-defeating behavior up to a point. Wes points out that when Bobby, the younger son, finds Beauty dead in the hills, he initially neglects to tell anyone. "This is how my family was," Wes says. "Tons of secrets and nobody would divulge what was going on, and therefore everybody was half-crazed."[10] The filmmaker recognized that such behavior wasn't unique to his family. In an interview with critic Robin Wood, he added, "As I got older, I began to see that as a nation we were doing the same thing," denying our biggest problems.[11] His responsibility as a storyteller, he decided, was to reveal inconvenient truths. A few years after he made *Hills*, Wes reflected on the policy of cultural imperialism embodied in the Vietnam War, and concluded that the old American myth of Manifest Destiny was a lie. Like *Last House on the Left*, *The Hills Have Eyes* became a protest document.

Although he knew he would be, in some ways, repeating himself, Wes didn't want to make another *Last House on the Left*. In 2010, he told me, "I feel like you have a right [as an artist] to do anything once, but to repeat it just because it might sell... I think that would be almost inexcusable." He wanted to make a more sophisticated, metaphorical horror film, and drew some inspiration from the recent work of his peer Tobe Hooper. *The Texas Chainsaw Massacre*, Hooper's iconic debut film, was every bit as harrowing as Craven's first film, but the former film was subtler. Instead of focusing a documentarian's gaze on depictions of violence and gore—and refusing to cut away—Hooper used carefully-crafted suspense to frame his horrors. In one infamous sequence, *Chainsaw*'s villain Leatherface hangs a screaming teenager on a meat hook; the filmmaker shows the hook, the woman being carried toward the hook, and the woman's reaction to being penetrated by the hook, but avoids a shot of the hook actually entering the woman's flesh, thereby forcing the audience to imagine the worst. From observing sequences like this, Craven realized that a horror film could exert more power over an audience by exercising restraint; the horror lies not in the imagery itself but in the emotional content of the scene.

Gravitating toward a new visual style, Wes took a more experimental approach to his storytelling—at least, on the page. The *Hills* script includes an impressionistic—if not surrealistic—sequence in which the filmmaker delves into the dreaming mind of one of his characters. Mid-way through the story, teenager Brenda Carter falls asleep and has a dream in which her father delivers a verbal warning she can't hear. Afterward, in a series of loosely connected images, the dream reveals the innermost yearnings of Brenda's older brother Doug, his wife Lynne, and their infant child (named Shanti in this draft) for physical intimacy, love, and security. Eventually, Brenda's dream morphs into a prophetic nightmare of Shanti being abducted by an unseen assailant. At the same time, in the waking world, Doug and Lynne make love the Wes Craven way ("deep in the innermost lobes of their brains, neurons from ancestral wet dreams stream down into their passion like a meteor shower") while Bobby listens to Mozart's Jupiter Symphony on headphones. As each of the characters tries to escape reality in their own ways, the hill-dwelling savages sneak up on them, taking advantage of the general lack of self-awareness.

It is easy to imagine such an ambitious dream sequence as part of a film by Bergman or Buñuel—or a psychological horror film in the vein of *Rosemary's Baby* or *The Exorcist*—but the produced version of *The Hills Have Eyes* is a more straightforward narrative with naturalistic visuals. The scripted scene exists, however, as evidence that Wes was gravitating toward the "expanded reality" horror films he would make in the 1980s. He obviously conceived Brenda's discarded dream as a supernatural (divine?) message tragically ignored, but in the final film—as in *Last House on the Left*—God remains silent.

Another metaphorically-loaded detail that failed to make the final cut of *The Hills Have Eyes* is Wes's name for the youngest Carter family member. Although the film identifies the baby as Katy, the script gives her the more significant name of Shanti, a Sanskrit word for inner peace. In perhaps the most harrowing sequence in the story, two members of the hill-dwelling family (Mars and Pluto) rape Brenda, mortally wound Ethel and Lynne, and abduct Shanti. In the script, Doug runs after the savages, screaming his abducted child's name into the night. Presumably, the screenwriter appreciated the irony of having a character screaming "peace" at the top of his lungs, not to mention the fact that the civilized characters go on to rescue "peace" by waging war.

Surprisingly, the abduction of Shanti was not the *coup de grâce* of the original script's pivotal sequence. Wes described his expanded vision of Doug entering the darkness: "In the script, he's calling out the name of his abducted baby and the camera pulls back and up, until he's quite small. Until we can see the lights of the trailer and the bonfire and even beyond, to the burning tree [where Big Bob was crucified and burned alive]. They all recede into the distance until they disappear against the black arc of an unlit planet moving among the stars."[12] Ambitious? You bet. But Wes had, after all, set out to make a modern myth—something larger than life but relatable to real experience. For him, *The Hills Have Eyes* was a personal story with cosmic significance. In our 2010 interview, he explained, "I was very much trying to touch on a feeling that I totally understand. On one hand, there's a sense of awe at the beauty and the wonder of the world. On the other hand, how small and fragile we are. How minuscule. I try to go for things that I really feel myself, or have understood myself. That's why that whole family was based on my mother and my mother's friends. I just felt like: *I know that world.*"

In the script, the surviving members of the Carter family plan their next move by trying to understand their attackers. *Do the hill-dwellers belong to some forgotten primitive tribe? Are they escaped convicts? Escaped mental patients? Part of a violent cult like the Manson Family? A Special Forces team gone wild like the soldiers who carried out the My Lai Massacre? Mutants created by nuclear testing in the Mojave Desert?* (In later years, Wes said the hill-dwellers were never meant to be mutants—but he contemplated the possibility in his script.) The screenwriter offers no concrete answer but, in an un-filmed scene, the cannibal family enacts a kind of primitive ritual—described as "a surrealistic circus / tribal / throwback to a collective subconscious atavistic wet dream nightmare"—circling the charred remains of Big Bob while Shanti lies on a raised altar, getting doused with chicken blood.

The names of the family members serve as another clue. Papa Jupiter leads the pack. His sons are Mercury, Mars, and Pluto (who, in the original script, is only thirteen years old). Here again, Wes has taken some cues from classical mythology. In the Greco-Roman tradition, Jupiter is the king of the gods; Mercury is his swift-footed messenger; Mars is the god of war; and Pluto is the ruler of the underworld. The use of mythological names might have been inspired by *The Texas Chainsaw Massacre*, which features an early scene where a character muses on the cosmic significance of planetary alignments, concluding that Saturn (father of Jupiter and Pluto) is "malefic." Did Wes perhaps think of his film as a rebellious next-generation *Texas Chainsaw Massacre*?

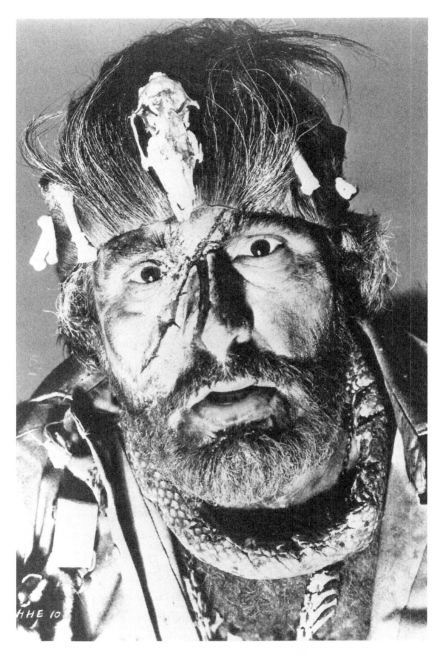

James Whitworth as Papa Jupiter in *The Hills Have Eyes*
(Blood Relations, 1977)

Michael Berryman as Pluto and Susan Lanier as Brenda Carter in
The Hills Have Eyes (Blood Relations, 1977)

In *The Hills Have Eyes*, Jupiter and his unnamed wife also have a daughter named Ruby. The non-canonical name indicates her status as an outsider within the family, which leads to her to betrayal of Jupiter and rescue of the Carter family child.

In the final act of the script, Doug dresses up as one of the hill-dwellers and infiltrates the ritualistic ceremony, while Bobby and Brenda lay a trap for Papa Jupiter, using techniques Wes learned from an Army Special Forces training manual. In another twist that didn't make it into the film, Bobby uses a C-B radio to contact the U.S. Army, then listens as Army commanders (code name: "Zeus") decide not to get involved. That decision—and the code name Zeus, the Greek equivalent of the Roman god Jupiter—suggests there's not much difference between the cannibals and the Army. The surviving members of the Carter family go on to prove that there's not much difference between the cannibals and themselves. Doug, Bobby, and Brenda become cutthroat warriors, while Ruby saves Doug's baby. When the battle is over, Doug inducts Ruby into the family, saying, "She saved Shanti. She's one of us. And we're one of her." There is no longer a meaningful distinction between "us" and "them," civilization and savagery. The script ends on this ambiguous note, with a shot of an Army helicopter touching down nearby, generating a huge dust storm that forces the protagonists "to cover their eyes and look away."

By comparison, the film ends on a simpler note. Although the filmmakers shot a "happy ending" in which the newly blended family embraces in a group hug, Wes ultimately decided to end on a shot of Doug pummeling Mars to death, his face frozen in rage. This final image, tinted blood-red, essentially reproduces the final image of *Last House on the Left* instead of positing a new beginning. Despite his decision to end on such a bleak note, when the filmmaker spoke about his films in later years, he focused on the more hopeful aspect of both stories. In 1985, he pointed out that *Last House on the Left* and *The Hills Have Eyes* each feature "characters who offer the possibility of change," adding that "change is one thing I have a basic faith in."[13] Elsewhere, he explained, "If you can change yourself in the most significant way, you can change the society or the world you live in. That's why I'm interested in Ruby [in *Hills*] and Junior [in *Last House*]."[14] For Wes, these supporting characters represent hope for the future.

The filming of *The Hills Have Eyes* took place in the fall of 1976 in the hills north of Apple Valley, California. The harsh desert environment— brutally hot during the day and brutally cold at night—and minimal production resources pit amateur filmmakers Locke and Craven against a more seasoned crew from the Roger Corman school of filmmaking. A storied encounter with a deadly Mojave Green pit viper didn't help the mood. Years later, actor Michael Berryman (who plays Pluto in the film) remembered that the rattlesnake was brought to set by a supposed "snake expert" found in a local bar. During the next day's shoot, the expert's pet got away from him. Berryman writes, "We were all sitting along the banks of a dry riverbed when I noticed that people were jumping up and running away from something. [...] Sure enough, the snake was on the loose! As people yelled out, the snake's owner could be seen running as fast as he could towards his pet. Before he could get to his reptile, one of our actors picked this snake up and went to hand it to Wes Craven! We were all in a state of disbelief and shock."[15] Luckily, no one was bitten—a huge relief since, the actor adds, the crew had no anti-venom on hand.

Despite all the hardships and narrowly-averted disasters, Wes won over the cast and crew with his enthusiasm and dedication to making a film that would transcend its origins and its budget. *The Hills Have Eyes* reflects particularly well on cinematographer Eric Saarinen, art director Robert A. Burns (who had previously dressed sets on *The Texas Chainsaw Massacre*), and actors Dee Wallace and Michael Berryman, who went on to become horror genre icons. By the time the shoot ended, Wes said he felt like the cast and crew had become a real family. He recalled "driving home from the last day of shooting and getting back to my apartment [in Los Angeles], and I felt like I was coming down from this incredible high. My family was gone. I got so depressed that I was crying."[16]

When the film was released in the summer of 1977, Wes was understandably nervous about how people would respond—not only to the film itself but to him as its creator. It had been five years since the backlash over *Last House on the Left*, and he was—in some ways—doubling down on his primal scream. An opening crawl in an early draft of the script, lampooning the documentary-style opening of *The Texas Chainsaw Massacre*, suggests that he wrestled privately with the fact of his notoriety as a sick, twisted filmmaker, and tried to adopt a public sense of humor about it. It reads:

In 1973, following the release of *Last House on the Left*, the writer/director of that film was committed for psychiatric observation. He was treated extensively with drugs, group therapies, electroshock programs and a final lobotomy. Despite these efforts at reform, Craven killed his nurse [...] and escaped to the Mojave Desert. At the end of 1,000 days of meditation he was taken up by a jet-black saucer and trained in Secondary Media Infiltration and parametaphysical survival on the Planet Jupiter. Upon his graduation he was returned to the planet Earth at Exeter. This film is his first since his return...

In reality, of course, Wes didn't kill anyone—but he did leave Sullivanian therapy behind and escape to the Mojave Desert, where he (and his film crew) came under the influence of Papa Jupe while making an outrageously violent film that some critics would denounce as the work of a madman. Wes might have drawn some additional inspiration for the crawl from William Sargant's 1957 book *The Battle for the Mind: The Mechanics of Indoctrination, Brainwashing and Thought Control*, which he once listed as one of ten books that had exerted the greatest influence on him. [17] The fourth chapter of Sargant's book is a study of psychoanalysis, shock treatments, and lobotomy as modern tools for curing neurosis. As to why the aliens returned the filmmaker to Earth "at Exeter"—and which Exeter the writer might be referring to—we can only guess. Wes might have been inspired by John Grant Fuller's 1966 book *Incident at Exeter: The Story of Unidentified Flying Objects Over America*, but a definitive explanation is probably lost to the ages, just as Wes's tone-altering disclaimer was lost from the film.

In contrast with the mostly hostile reception to *Last House on the Left* (and *The Fireworks Woman*), Wes received a fair amount of critical praise for *The Hills Have Eyes*, beginning with a review in *The Hollywood Reporter* by Roy Frumkes, who lauded his friend's talent for "tension, emotional and physical violence, editing and sound." [18] *Hills* also performed well in U.S. theaters—at least, until it was eclipsed by the nationwide release of *Smokey and the Bandit*. It went on to even greater success in Europe, where it won the Critics Award at the 1977 Sitges Film Festival in Spain and the Best Picture Award at the 1978 London Film Festival. The accolades pushed the filmmaker toward several new opportunities, and a chance to break out of exploitation cinema. Wes reflected that the greatest outcome of *The Hills Have Eyes* was that people started recognizing him as a professional filmmaker.[19] Now he could set his sights on Hollywood.

On August 6, 1977, Wes wrote a letter to his 9-year-old daughter Jessica, touting his new home in Los Angeles. He began, "There's not much really wrong with L.A. Just an occasional drought, earthquake, Smog attack, and now and then a devastating brush fire." He told her about his next-door neighbor, an actress who had recently appeared alongside Donna Summer in a new film, and said he was dating a novelist who was "properly horrified" by *The Hills Have Eyes*. He then regaled Jessica, who was homesick at summer camp, with a more imaginative anecdote—the purportedly autobiographical tale of a gold prospector in the Yukon, accompanied by his faithful hound dog Yellow Sam. He wrote, "Now, I don't know, Jessica, if you've ever been naked as a jaybird in Alaska in April, fifty miles up what was supposed to be the rushing Barefoot River, covered with soapsuds and ready to rinse, bubbles in your eyes and the black flies settling down like soot on your birthday case, but if you have, you can imagine how mad we were." After an outrageous account of a near-death experience that literally cost him a fortune, Wes grudgingly closed the letter, saying he needed to get to work on a new script.

Around that time, he began working on a screenplay titled *Deep in the Heart* for producer Peter Locke. The new screen story revolved around an ex-cop named Will Walker, who settles on a horse ranch in the Texas Panhandle with his wife Mary and 8-year-old son Buddy. Soon after they arrive in their new home, Will thwarts a bank robbery and helps to incarcerate a sadistic criminal named Sam Rappar. Three years later, Rappar and two accomplices escape from prison, kidnap a female reporter, and go on a killing spree. Following a shootout with Texas State Troopers, they hijack a small plane and head for Will Walker's ranch to get revenge. Rappar's brother Berriman—an homage to Michael Berryman?—poses as a telephone repairman in order to help the escapees fulfill their goal. Unfortunately for them, all three members of Will Walker's family prove to be tougher than the criminals.

The basic plot is reminiscent of *Last House on the Left* or Sam Peckinpah's *Straw Dogs*, but the more-than-capable hero at the center of the

story would fit comfortably in a contemporary drive-in action film like *Walking Tall* or *Death Wish*. The variation on a familiar theme suggests that the writer and producer were eager to break away from horror while holding onto their drive-in / grindhouse audience. In a November 1977 interview, Wes explained, "The violence in *Hills* is what you could call rough. On our next [film], we'd like to go more toward Hitchcock without getting artsy-craftsy to the point where we'd lose our market."[20] *Deep in the Heart* features some distinctly Craven-esque touches, including an elaborate finale with booby traps and a surprising bit of gallows humor from Will's 8-year-old son as he faces immanent death. Wes copyrighted a 2nd draft of the script, titled *The Last Battle*, in February 1978, but the film didn't get made.

Wes and both of his producing partners, Sean Cunningham and Peter Locke, continued to look for opportunities to do a new kind of film. In the summer of 1977, Cunningham caught a break. He remembered, "Someone asked me, 'Can you make one of those *Bad News Bears* movies?' I said, 'Sure, no problem.' He said, 'Yeah, but can you make it *now*?' So three weeks later, we were shooting this picture called *Here Come the Tigers*."[21] The job offer followed the release of *The Bad News Bears in Breaking Training*, the second of three films featuring Walter Matthau as the cantankerous coach of a rowdy kids' baseball team. Cunningham promptly rounded up his own team of merry misfits—including future *Friday the 13th* screenwriter Victor Miller, editor Steve Miner (who had begun his career as an assistant editor on *Last House on the Left*), composer Harry Manfredini, and child actor Ari Lehman—to make a film about a second string of Little League losers-turned-champions. Wes got in on the action too, working as a gaffer on the film and performing a bit of slapstick comedy onscreen. The film appeared in theaters one month before *The Bad News Bears Go to Japan*, and it must have been a success for Cunningham because he quickly reassembled the team to make *Manny's Orphans* (1978).

As Cunningham and his new crew continued down this path as independent filmmakers, Wes received an offer to direct his first union project for a major television network. Max A. Keller, a former Los Angeles attorney, had recently ventured into the film business under the banner of Inter Planetary Pictures, and one of the first properties he set out to develop was an adaptation of Lois Duncan's young-adult novel *Summer of Fear*. Keller says, "I co-wrote the script with Glenn Benest and I had a commitment from NBC. [They said] if we could bring in Linda Blair, they would produce the movie." Blair was primarily known for her portrayal of Regan MacNeil in *The Exorcist* (1973) but she had also made a few TV movies about wayward teenagers. *Summer of Fear* would cast her against type, as a bubbly girl next door whose cousin might or might not be a witch. As soon as Blair said yes, Keller started searching for a director.

NBC executive Charles Hairston suggested pairing the star of *The Exorcist* with the director of *The Hills Have Eyes*. Keller remembers, "Charlie had seen *The Hills Have Eyes* and he said, 'This guy would be a great director.' I said, 'Fine, let's try to bring him in.' So we got in touch with Wes's agent and said, 'Subject to NBC approval, we'll pick him.' But it turned out that Charlie didn't have the ultimate decision-making power. We had to go to Charlie's boss, Josh Kane. He said, 'I've got to see the movie.'" Keller promptly invited Hairston and Kane to his house in Los Angeles for dinner and a private screening of a Wes Craven film. Oddly, he did not select *The Hills Have Eyes*.

"Charlie had seen *Hills*," Keller explains, "but it was *Last House* that I had access to and that's what they wanted to see." The producer took the NBC execs to the screening room in his guest house and put on a VHS tape of Craven's infamous first film. He remembers, "As I'm in the room with Josh, watching the movie, I'm cringing. I'm going, *oh my god, never in a million years is NBC going to approve Wes to direct the movie. Never in a million years.* But we finish the movie... It's quiet... Josh comes into the house... We start to have our dinner... And he says, 'Whoa. He really knows how to keep you on the edge of your seat. We'll approve him. We'll do it. Let him take the shot.'"

According to an article in a 1982 issue of *Fangoria*, Wes Craven did a major rewrite on Keller and Benest's *Summer of Fear* script. The director said that what he liked most about the story was "the paranoid angle," so that's what he tried to amplify.[22] He also said he took some inspiration from the films of Roman Polanski—particularly, *Repulsion* (1965), *Rosemary's Baby* (1968) and *The Tenant* (1976).[23] Each of those films revolve around a character that begins to question their sanity, luring them—and the viewer—into a world of nightmarish uncertainty. Wes welcomed the opportunity to make a psychological thriller instead of a savage horror film, and the decision changed his career trajectory.

Summer of Fear became Wes Craven's entrée into the Director's Guild and gave him his first experience of shooting on 35mm film (both *Last House* and *Hills* had been shot in 16mm), using camera dollies, working with a union crew, and directing name stars. According to Max Keller, Wes adapted well—except for one particular incident when he demonstrated some insensitivity to union rules. The producer says, "We had a line producer that we hired to keep the film on track. His name was Bill Finnegan. One day I got a call saying, 'You gotta come to the set immediately. Bill and Wes are going at it.' What happened was: if it's 6:00 and you're supposed to finish filming [for the day], and you don't, it's very expensive. You go into overtime. Because everyone was union, because it was NBC, it was very very expensive to go into overtime and shoot for another hour. Thousands and thousands of dollars. So Bill Finnegan pulled the plug and said, 'That's it. We're finished for the day.' And Wes was furious. Just furious. Wes was usually very, very mild mannered—he didn't raise his voice very much at all—so for him to act pissed off like that, he really was."

"The next day, at lunch time, I brought them both to a fancy restaurant. I think Micheline, my wife and co-producer, was with us. We said, 'Wes, you understand it was going to cost us a lot of money...' He said, 'Yeah, I understand, but this was a scene that needed to happen. I just needed another twenty minutes...' And on and on. I said, 'Bill, do you think you could arrange, in the next day or two of shooting, to put another hour into the schedule so that Wes can do what he wants to do?' He said, 'Yeah, we'll figure it out.' That's what happened."

The scene in question was part of a dream sequence where the film's villainous witch appears in a doorway, bathed in red light and spectral fog. Arguably the most indelible imagery in the film, it would appear on cover art for multiple VHS and DVD releases of the film. Wes knew what he was fighting for.

On Halloween night 1978, *Summer of Fear* debuted as NBC's Movie of the Week, under the new title *Stranger in Our House*. It was a ratings success, bolstering Wes's reputation as an up-and-coming filmmaker. Among those who took notice was Italian producer Alessandro Fracassi, who ran the production company Racing Pictures S.R.L. According to Wes, Fracassi commissioned two scripts from him. The first was based on a ripped-from-the-headlines story about the November 1978 Jonestown Massacre in Guyana, recounted in

Marshall Kilduff's book *The Suicide Cult*. A February 28, 1979 notice in *Variety* magazine reported that Wes had signed on to write and direct the film, which would be shot in Colombia and San Francisco.

The second script Fracassi commissioned was *Marimba*, an original story about a group of Americans who stumble into the middle of a drug war in Colombia. At the outset of Wes's script, the main character seems to be Kent, a college kid taking flying lessons from an old Marine named Duke Ferguson. Brash and naïve, Kent offers to fly sorority girl Connie Willard to Colombia to pick up a shipment of marijuana (so Connie's sorority can sell it and give the money to poor people in Vietnam—right, right). Kent and Connie soon find themselves in at the mercy of drug lords. At this point, the writer kills off his main character (Hitchcock-style) and the drug lord quips to Connie, "I be your boyfriend now." The narrative then refocuses on Duke, who flies in to rescue her.

According to a September 1979 article in *The Hollywood Reporter*, the filmmakers planned to shoot *Marimba* in Rome; New York; Bogota, Colombia; and Miami, beginning in December. Wes said he went on three different scouting trips to Colombia, and he almost didn't survive one of those trips—not because he was attacked by drug lords but because he had an unreliable pilot. Jonathan Craven remembers that Wes observed "technicians at the airport in Medellín studying an 'owner's manual' while trying to fix something on the plane before takeoff." At that point, he was convinced he'd never make it home.

The experience inspired Wes to take flying lessons when he returned to Los Angeles. On May 1, 1980, he wrote to his daughter Jessica that he and Sean Cunningham—who was in town trying to sell his new movie *Friday the 13th*—went on "one of those $10 sample flights they give you at the flying school to hook people into taking flying lessons." Hovering high above the coast of Malibu and the wilderness of Topanga Canyon, Wes got hooked. A month later, in another letter to Jessica, he described his first solo flight: "I was surprised by how calm I was ... I guess at those moments when you just have to do something, then you can just dip into your special secret supply of 'can-do' and do it, just 'cause the alternatives are so icky." It was the fulfillment of one of his earliest dreams, to become a pilot.

For better or worse, *Marimba* never got off the ground. Wes went to Rome in June. Principal photography was scheduled to begin there in August—with actors Tim McIntire, Dirk Benedict, Chris Mitchum, and Monique van de Ven heading up the cast—but the financing fell through before the first frame was shot. The basic idea for the film continued to morph over the following years, until it was realized (sort of) by *Cannibal Holocaust* director Ruggero Deodato as *Inferno in Diretta* (1986), released in the United States as *Cut and Run*. Deodato's film retains none of the characters or dialogue from Craven's *Marimba* script but it does feature actor Michael Berryman, who played Pluto in *The Hills Have Eyes*.

In limbo between film projects, Wes contemplated whether or not to buy a house in Venice Beach, California. According to a letter he wrote to his daughter, his live-in girlfriend had her eye on an old Victorian house in the neighborhood. The couple needed more space for their growing stable of pets, which included two dogs and a cat nicknamed "the Roach"—a moniker "earned for her growing habit of living in all the cracks, crevices and holes in the house, and running into these whenever anyone comes into the room. She especially favors the hidden passageways under the stairs." Before he could buy the house, Wes needed to find another paying job. Years later, he recalled, "I quickly latched onto the first thing I could and it turned out to be *Swamp Thing*."[24]

The new project was a film adaptation of the DC comic book created in 1972 by writer Len Wein and artist Bernie Wrightson. The series was discontinued in 1976, but Michael Uslan, a young attorney-turned-movie producer, thought the existing storyline would be a solid foundation for a low budget horror film. According to the memoir *The Boy Who Loved Batman*, Uslan and his business partner Benjamin Melniker approached United Artists about co-financing the film, and the studio execs agreed on one condition: they wanted Wes Craven to write and direct. UA had recently made a big profit off of foreign sales of *The Hills Have Eyes* and the execs were eager to have another Wes Craven title to sell. Next, Uslan approached the president of Avco-Embassy Pictures, who agreed to put up the second half of the film's budget because he too was a Wes fan.

Uslan remembers it didn't take long to bring the writer/director into the fold. "We arranged a lunch for the four of us—me, Ben, Wes, and Wes's agent

Marvin Moss—at Musso and Frank's. Wes and I sat on one side; Ben and Marvin on the other. I began pitching to Wes, and Wes and I instantly connected. From the opening sentences, we just connected. We were establishing a creative link and a friendship at the same time, and we were really getting into the creative aspects of this project. Meanwhile, on the other side of the table, Ben and Marvin see we're hitting it off, so they start negotiating the deal. Next thing I know, these two guys are speaking Yiddish to each other. I have no idea what they said, but all of the sudden, they go, 'That works.' Ben takes a napkin, a paper napkin, takes out a pen, and starts to draw up a deal memo on the napkin—which I still have somewhere. He and Marvin pass it back and forth, make some changes, and suddenly we have deal memos. They draw signature lines and Marvin says to Wes, 'You good with this?' Wes says yeah. Marvin goes, 'Alright, then sign it.' Then Ben says, 'Michael, you sign this one.' And we were off to the races."

Although Wes wasn't familiar with the *Swamp Thing* comics, he was immediately intrigued by the story of "a monster who had a human being inside." He saw the story as a "Beauty and the Beast" analog through which he could "explore how a human being feels about his darker side or his ugly side being exposed, and whether or not someone can love that." In one interview, he explained why the theme appealed to him personally as a horror filmmaker: "It's like when people look at Wes Craven the filmmaker, and say, 'How can you make those terribly violent films?' It's like I'm Swamp Thing."[25]

By October 1980, Wes had reworked the story to emphasize this theme, turning one supporting character from a man to a woman (Cable) so he could "add a romantic element and work the story more on a Beauty and the Beast level."[26] He then fused several villainous characters from the comics into a super-villain named Arcane, and used that new character to hit the theme from another angle. He explained, "You have a beast that you know inside is a handsome prince, but you see him as a toad. [...] On the other hand, you have [actor] Louis Jourdan's character Arcane, who is someone who looks very nice on the outside, but when you see his true self, it's monstrous and ugly."[27] Producer Michael Uslan says Wes had an ingenious idea for how to develop the hero-villain dichotomy over the course of the screen story: "He said, 'The formula that transforms [Dr. Alec Holland into Swamp Thing], what it does is it makes you more of what you already are. It takes your true nature—whether

Beauty and the Beast: Adrienne Barbeau (as Cable) and Dick Durock in *Swamp Thing* (United Artists, 1982)

you're a good guy or a bad guy, moral or immoral—and it makes you more of what you are. Somebody who is evil becomes monstrous and somebody like Dr. Holland becomes even more of a force for good.'"

Wes also invented a completely new character to provide comic relief and give younger audiences someone to identify with. The character was a wizened old man in the first draft, but the writer decided to transform him into a wise-cracking African-American boy named Jude. He had finally found an opportunity to make a fairy tale for young audiences. Uslan says, "We set out to make a 1950s monster movie. The concept, as we used to joke, was we wanted to do a movie where the young people in the audience would cheer for the hero, boo at the villain, and run to get popcorn when the hero kisses the girl."

While the *Swamp Thing* producers set up their project based on Wes's script, producer Max Keller hired Wes to rewrite a script he owned. *Deadly Blessing*, an original screenplay by Glenn Benest and Matthew Barr, had been in development hell for some time. According to Barr, "We finished the first draft in 1977, and it spent about four years going through various Hollywood studios."[28] The script ultimately landed at Inter Planetary Productions after a chance encounter between Benest and Max Keller's secretary. Benest says, "Max read it, he optioned it, and we tried for about two years to sell it. We had interest at a number of different places but never enough for them to say, 'We'll make it.'" Hoping to push the project toward a green light, Keller hired Wes, who finished his revised draft on May 29, 1979.

Wes's draft begins with the horrific death of Jim Schmidt, a farmer raised in a rural Texas community of Hittites (a fictional religious sect conceived as an extreme version of the Amish) but later ostracized for marrying an outsider. After finding her husband impaled on farm equipment, Jim's widow Martha accuses the Hittites of murdering him, but the leader of the religious sect insists that Jim's death was the work of "the Incubus," a supernatural devil. Whatever the case, the horror is only beginning. Barr explains, "The Hittites as we portrayed them were very repressive on all levels—sexually repressive, very paternalistic, and harsh. And so in a way we were kind of positing that the horror was coming out of that repression or in answer to that repression."[29] Benest adds, "It's about secrets that people push down and won't allow to come to the surface. And the more you repress something, the more you suppress the truth, the stronger it gets. Until finally it gets so powerful that it comes out in the horrific ways."[30]

Wes obviously knew about repression and religious indoctrination, and he attempted to bring a bit more authenticity to the story. In one interview, he dismissed the original script as a formulaic hodgepodge, "Charlie's Angels in Stephen King territory," suggesting the previous writers had simply cobbled together scenes from other horror films.[31] He decided to hone the central mystery by eliminating red herrings, particularly "scenes casting suspicion on the girls from out of town [Martha's friends], and many more scenes with the Hittites creating more Hittite suspects."[32] He then replaced the discarded details with completely new scenes, adding some Hitchcockian suspense and a touch of fantasy, and turning Deadly Blessing into a subtler and more subconscious horror film.

In one of the new scenes, Martha's friend Lana—who has come to console her newly widowed friend—sees a "homunculus spider" hovering on the ceiling above her bed, which inspires a "really creepy nightmare right out of Bergman." In the dream, she explains to Martha, Death (the white-faced Death of Bergman's *The Seventh Seal*?) called on her at home, whispering her name, then firing a cannon at her front door. Martha's level-headed friend Vicky dismisses the dream with a bit of pop psychology: "You can choose to look at the shadows, or you can choose to look at the light."

Vicky, choosing to look only at the light, goes for an early morning jog—and runs into Jim's brother John. He's cute, so she promptly invites him to the movies. As a member of the Hittite community, John is forbidden to see movies because "movies are considered sinful," so he politely declines. Nevertheless, the damage is done. John's close encounter of the female kind incurs the wrath of his father, who banishes him from the Hittite community. Meanwhile, Lana continues to dream of Death, and her dream practically comes true when a mentally-ill woman from a neighboring farm tries to kill her. Wes's scripted ending reveals that the troubled young woman is the one who actually killed Martha's husband. The ending ultimately vindicates the Hittites, reducing the repressive cult to a red herring.

Sharon Stone as Lana and Maren Jensen as Martha in *Deadly Blessing*
(PolyGram, 1981)

In early 1980, a new production company called PolyGram Entertainment took interest in the revised script. Benest remembers, "Jon Peters and Peter Guber had taken over this new production company, and they needed product all of the sudden. They basically had four or five movies that they immediately put into production because they wanted product. So we got really lucky, because we were there at the right time and they were ready to go." Wes took on the role of director of film, which was budgeted at $2.5 million (significantly higher than all of his previous films), but not without some misgivings. He later said the film wasn't "intrinsic" to him, the way his previous films had been.[33] Despite an inclination to distance himself from the project, he made it his own, relishing the opportunity to make a film that was "a little more cinematic and less forensic" than previous horror films, a chance to "do something more artistic."[34] Most notably, he crafted a few indelible set pieces that link *Deadly Blessing* to his future work.

In the film, Lana's encounter with the homunculus spider is more than an anecdote; the encounter becomes a vaguely erotic dream sequence, in which the spider falls from the ceiling into Lana's open mouth while an unseen devil holds her head and whispers seductively into her ear. Another completely new scene, in which Martha encounters a live snake in her bathtub, was also inspired by a dream. Wes told me, "I dreamed [the scene that's in the final film]. I woke up in the morning, went to the set and said, 'Get me a snake.' And I basically shot the setup until some guy came in with a cottonmouth."

Snake imagery was nothing new in Wes's work. Ruby used a Mojave Green rattlesnake as a weapon in *The Hills Have Eyes;* the villainous Ferret uses a water moccasin in *Swamp Thing;* and a boa constrictor appears in the Samson and Delilah sequence in *It Happened in Hollywood* (but perhaps we shouldn't blame "Abe Snake" for that one). It is easy to speculate about why snake imagery would figure so prominently into the dreams and mythology of someone raised as a Christian fundamentalist. Although the snake in *Deadly Blessing* is carefully placed by one of the Hittites, the scene seems like a vague suggestion that "devilish" supernatural forces are at work.

As in Wes's script, the final film absolves the Hittites of responsibility for Jim's death—but the film goes one step further, confirming the community leader's theory that "the Incubus" was involved. In a new coda, Martha receives a visit from the ghost of her dead husband. Before he can warn her that the Incubus is real, the devil rips through the floorboards and pulls Martha down into Hell. According to the writers and the producer, the new scene was requested by the financiers. Glenn Benest remembers, "The whole point of the screenplay was that there is no supernatural demon or whatever. It's all people. And yet the ending is a supernatural thing that happens. And it totally ruined what the story was about. The way that happened was the studio said they wanted something like *Carrie*, and they talked Wes into doing a new ending, and they tacked on this ending."

In contemporary interviews, Wes took full responsibility for the tacked-on coda: "It became quite apparent early on that having an ending with the girls just saying goodbye to each other wouldn't be enough. To my astonishment, the producers gave in to my demand for the new ending despite it being off-the-wall to say the least."[35] Years later, he insisted the ending was "forced by the studio."[36] Whatever the case, Wes didn't dwell on it. He quickly turned his attention to *Swamp Thing*.

The shoot for *Deadly Blessing* had been no picnic; hardships included a virulent flu season that plagued the cast and crew, unpredictable weather ("from rain to sleet... 70 degrees one day to 28 the next"), and a series of on-set accidents, including one that put the film's biggest star, Ernest Borgnine, in the hospital.[37] The filming of *Swamp Thing* in the wilderness near Charleston, South Carolina, was even worse. In addition to the obvious challenges posed by traipsing around in acidic swamp water filled with deadly wildlife, the film was hampered by an unrealistic special effects budget and unhappy financiers who, in the midst of filming, demanded extensive cuts to the third act of the script.[38] Producer Michael Uslan says, "What neither of us really appreciated at that time was that if you're going to be doing a movie that includes the roughest, toughest locations, the worst weather, child actors, animals on set, special effects, stunts, special makeup, we really should have had a bigger budget. Bottom line, we had $1.9 million to make the movie; we should have had $19 million. But what did I know? It was my first time producing, so it was learn as you go."

Uslan adds that a real-life romance probably helped the director cope with the chaos. He remembers how Wes met his future wife on a cross-country flight to South Carolina: "Wes had boasted to her who he was. She wasn't particularly impressed. So he told her (God help us… it's a Hollywood cliché!) he would make her a star and that she could play a small role in our movie."[39] The flight attendant was 24-year-old Mimi Meyer, an Indiana native who also taught ballet. She remembers, "I was working back in B zone or C zone and Wes and Michael were in first class. I kept running back and forth grabbing things from first class and, on one of my trips back, Wes stopped me and said these exact words: 'You are the most beautiful woman I have ever seen,' and 'Will you come be in my movie?' I just said, 'That's nice. Thank you very much, but no.'" A week later, Meyer learned that the filmmaker wasn't going to take "no" for an answer; she received a Western Union telegram from Uslan, begging her to reconsider. "It said, 'My director can't eat. Stop. He can't sleep. Stop. He meant what he said. Stop. Please come and do the movie. Stop. It will change your life. Stop.'" The decision certainly did change her life. On July 25, 1982, she became Mrs. Wes Craven.

In the meantime, onscreen, she became Arcane's secretary. Mimi says, "I was the Girl Friday to the bad guy, played by Louis Jourdan. And I was a huge Louis Jourdan fan. *Gigi* is one of my favorite movies. In the script, his big act before he drinks the potion and turns into a monster is to kiss me, lay one on me. I was so excited. But when the time came, he said no, he wasn't going to do that. The reason he gave is because everybody knew Wes and I were together. They knew it from minute one. I flew down, spent one day on set, everyone was calling Wes 'sir,' and they ended up calling me 'Mrs. Sir.' Louis Jourdan said he didn't feel comfortable kissing the director's girlfriend. He was much older than me, and I looked like I was about twelve years old. I think he thought it would be inappropriate. But I was so bummed. *So* bummed."

In her autobiography *There Are Worse Things I Could Do*, actress Adrienne Barbeau remembers the production had big problems, including an incompetent assistant director, unsafe stunts, ill-fitting costumes, and a cocaine-addled crew. Although she declared it "the worst experience I've had since I was go-go dancing under black lights at Uncle Joe's Tavern by the Newark bus stop," she had nothing but kind things to say about the director: "Wes is very laid-back. His strength lies in getting the performance he wants from the actors. Reggie Batts, the fourteen-year-old who plays Jude, has never acted before and Wes works with him in an easy, non-defensive way. It's fun for me to watch the character I'm playing, Lt. Cable, take shape in a way I hadn't expected, thanks to his direction. I trust him."[40]

Ultimately, Wes regarded *Swamp Thing* as a professional turning point. "This film has many warm, humane moments," he reflected, "and in my other films, I had always wanted to make everything more human. This is simply a much happier film."[41] He also described *Swamp Thing* as part of his *oeuvre*, and "reflective of changes I've gone through in my life."[42] The title character seems to speak for the filmmaker when he suggests that the only way to get *out* of the swamp is by going *through* it. Wes had taken that same journey and found himself in a better place, delivering an offbeat romance while wooing his future wife.

Unfortunately, *Swamp Thing* was widely perceived as a failure at the box office. According to Wes, it was his first film that didn't immediately recoup its cost.[43] In Hollywood, as the saying goes, a filmmaker is only as good as his latest film, which put Wes in the position of having to build momentum for his next project. According to a March 1981 article in *The Hollywood Reporter*, he was thinking of writing and directing a new film adaptation of Edgar Allan Poe's short story "The Pit and the Pendulum."[44] A few months later, he was attached to a United Artists "epic" titled *Blinding Flash*.[45] Eventually, however, he would turn his attention to an original idea—one that would define his career, as well as the horror genre, for years to come.

The Soul of Wes Craven

CHAPTER SEVEN

THE DEATH AND AFTERLIFE OF FREDDY KRUEGER

(1982 - 1985)

"Craven's joke, if you can call it that, is that in the world of Nightmare
everybody is asleep when they are supposed to be awake.
It's only when you fall asleep that you see life for what it is."

- Mark Edmundson, *Nightmare on Main Street* (1997)

In 2014, one year before his death, Wes Craven said he knew what his legacy would be. He told an interviewer that his tombstone would inevitably identify him as "the Father of Freddy Krueger." Jokes aside, he accepted the fact that *A Nightmare on Elm Street* was the "most significant" and the "most personal" film he had ever made.[1] It was the first film he wrote entirely for himself, his first true spec script written on faith in his own abilities. It embodied his life philosophy in a subtle way and exerted a not-so-subtle influence on all of his future. In 2010, he said, "It's been a long journey of the soul, in a way, although I never thought of it that way until maybe *A Nightmare on Elm Street*. That's when I started equating what other religions might call 'being in the moment' or Zen—as opposed to being asleep or not really looking at what's going on—with the kind of spirituality I'm interested in. I rarely mention the word 'spiritual' or anything like that, because so much of it seems to drift toward being calcified [in one's thinking] or putting people in power or some other bullshit. Also, it just seems I'd rather be outrageous."

With *A Nightmare on Elm Street*, Wes fully embraced the horror genre and transformed it according to his own philosophical sensibilities. He might have taken some inspiration from film critic Robin Wood, who had spent the previous decade making a case for the cathartic value of horror films. In his 1972 essay "Disreputable Genre," Wood wrote, "No genre is richer in potential, its thematic material rooted in archetypal myth and the darker labyrinths of human psychology and having analogies with dream and nightmare."[2] Four years later, in his Freudian-cum-Jungian essay "Return of the Repressed," Wood equated the "revolution of a genre" with the "evolution of civilization's unconscious," concluding that "horror films are our collective nightmares."[3] He outlined his theory at length in 1979's "An Introduction to the American Horror Film," declaring that cinematic "dreams" can serve a therapeutic function for moviegoers, allowing them to escape "from the unresolved tensions of our lives into fantasies."[4]

That same year, Wood's work provided the theoretical basis for a week-long celebration of horror cinema at the Toronto International Film Festival. Organizers screened sixty horror films and hosted in-depth interviews with rising filmmakers John Carpenter, David Cronenberg, Brian De Palma, Tobe Hooper, George Romero, Stephanie Rothman, and Wes Craven. The landmark event effectively legitimized the modern American horror film as a subject for academic study, encouraging Wes—a former college professor—to share his own belief that horror films can function as a "pressure release," or even a "boot camp of the psyche."[5] Many years later, Wes articulated his own theory as follows: "What [people] go into that theater for is to have the terror of real life marshaled into some sort of order, so it can be dealt with. The chaos is caged for a few hours in a graspable narrative. And the hero or heroine makes his/her way through the worst we can all imagine and comes out on the other side not only alive, but steeled by that most basic of realizations—that survival is within us all."[6]

In a more oblique way, Wood's work might have inspired the subject matter of Wes's future work. The critic argued that Alfred Hitchcock's film *Psycho* (1960) inaugurated the modern American horror film by defining its central preoccupation with family-oriented neuroses. As Norman Bates said, "A boy's best friend is his mother"—even when she's his psychopathic alter. Wes may have been thinking of *Psycho* in these terms when he described *Last House on the Left* as "the next logical step after *Psycho*."[7] (In fact, the first draft of the *Last House* script includes a specific reference to Hitchcock's film in the dialogue.) His answer to Norman's crazy mama was Krug, the maniacal father who urges his son to "BLOW YOUR BRAINS OUT!"

Wood went on to celebrate *The Hills Have Eyes*—along with *Night of the Living Dead*, *Raw Meat*, and *The Texas Chainsaw Massacre*—as the culmination of the modern American horror film, arguing that their depictions of cannibalism reflect "the logical end of human relations under capitalism."[8] The statement probably left Wes and his peers wondering what could come next, after "the end." Wood's 1979 essay hinted at an answer—one that Wes had been contemplating for years.

Wood observed that Surrealist filmmakers like Luis Buñuel and Georges Franju were drawn to horror film imagery. Buñuel named *The Beast with Five Fingers* (1946), a Universal monster movie about a murderous severed hand, as one of his favorite films. Franju, director of *Les Yeux sans visage* (*Eyes Without a Face*), was similarly inspired by the Vincent Price movie *The Fly* (1958). Wes also wanted to exploit the inherently nightmarish quality of cinematic storytelling, twisting genre formulas into surreal images. He explained, "I'm interested in expanding the forms of consciousness within film because I think, with the exception of certain European directors, film is quite limited in the areas of consciousness it deals with."[9] He had incorporated dream imagery into all of his previous films; now he wanted to make dream imagery his main subject.

Wes got the initial idea for A Nightmare on Elm Street from reading a series of news articles in the Los Angeles Times, "about men from South East Asia, who were from immigrant families and who had died in the middle of nightmares."[10] Although at one point he claimed he read the first article in 1978 or 1979, journalist Bill Curry was the first to report on similarities among the dream-deaths, in his February 1981 article "Nightmare Syndrome?" Curry connected the mysterious deaths of thirteen men in different cities around the U.S.; all died in their sleep. In each case, the victim was a relatively young, apparently healthy, Hmong refugee who had fled the country of Laos in the wake of the Vietnam War. According to Curry, one physician attributed the deaths to chemical warfare agents, but the explanation didn't account for the fact that all the victims were young men, or for the fact that they died in their sleep.[11] A coroner in Portland, Oregon, offered an alternative explanation: bangungot syndrome.[12] The term "bangungot" means "nightmare" in Filipino culture, and reflects the theory that intense night terrors can cause sudden, mysterious death.

Wes was fascinated by the theory, and by a subsequent report in the Los Angeles Times that referenced a similar "death syndrome" (pokkuri) in Japanese culture. Taken together, these two articles suggested that people all over the world were suffering from a common affliction. In February 1982, novelist Ted Mooney reflected on the phenomenon and made a dramatic leap to a tantalizing theory: "In plain language, otherwise healthy people were being frightened to death by their own bad dreams." Mooney suggested that cultural beliefs and associated fears had "given the force of actuality" to the dreams of the Hmong refugees.[13] Another researcher suggested the victims were killed by their belief in evil spirits, including the Hmong "nocturnal pressing spirit" dab tsog.[14]

Many American doctors were reluctant to accept the theory. After all, what rational-thinking person could believe that a person's thoughts alone are capable of killing them? As Mooney pointed out, we usually attribute such fantastical ideas to horror fiction instead of scientific theory. Wes, however, knew from personal experience that such things could be possible. He'd contemplated a similar etiology for the mysterious illness that struck him in his early twenties, telling one family member that his fear of being "damned" had manifested itself as the creeping death that paralyzed him for six months. He couldn't prove it, but he conceived *A Nightmare on Elm Street* as a fictional answer to looming questions about the physical power of belief and dreams. Building on the simple storytelling formula of contemporary slasher movies, he manifested his own nocturnal demon, a new cinematic boogeyman.

In the beginning, all he had to build a story on was the vague image of a person "leaning out of the ether of the air and touching the sleeper."[15] In 1981, he began developing that image into a screen treatment, then pitched the idea to potential investors—including PolyGram producer Peter Guber, who was eager to work with the director again after *Deadly Blessing*, and producer Robert Shaye, founder and president of a New York-based distribution company called New Line Cinema. According to Wes, Shaye was "immediately interested and said, 'As soon as you have a first draft, send it to me.' That was very encouraging, so I went back and wrote the script."[16]

Robert Englund as boogeyman Freddy Krueger in *A Nightmare on Elm Street* (New Line, 1984)

191

Wes completed an early draft during the filming of *Swamp Thing*. Producer Michael Uslan remembers, "We were working late when I learned about it. We had wrapped for the day, then we had a production meeting, then we watched dailies, but we still had to map out a strategy for the next day or the next week. I had found a fancy restaurant in town that agreed to stay open late for cast and crew, so I said to Wes, 'Let's go to dinner there and we'll do it over dinner.' He said fine. We were shooting in the swamps and we were filthy, so I went to my hotel room to shower and change clothes. When I got to Wes's hotel room, he said, 'I just finished my new script and I'm really excited about it. While I'm taking a shower, you can read it.' I said fine. So I was the first person to read *A Nightmare on Elm Street* as it came out of the word processor.

"Eventually he came out of the bathroom, dressed, ready to go. He said, 'Did you read it?' I said, 'I read it.' He goes, 'What do you think?' I said, 'Wes, this is an awesome, phenomenal horror movie. You're gonna sell this script in two seconds.' He said, 'Well, let's do it together.' I said, 'Personally, I'm just not a fan of blood-and-guts horror movies, so the idea of spending the next two to three years working on it is not something I want to do.' Years later, somebody asked me, 'If you could reach back through time and talk to yourself at a younger age, what advice would you give?' I said, 'The first thing I would do is slap myself at that moment and say, *What the fuck are you doing?*' In my 46 years in the business, this is the one and only regret that I have. There you go: the stupidity of youth."

Wes continued to revise his script in the fall of 1981. Mimi Craven remembers her future husband, adorned in a blue bathrobe and a pith helmet, emerging from his home office every night with new pages from his Apple II computer. "He would write all day and then, at night, he would print out what he had written and we would read it aloud and act out some of the scenes. I would help him edit, figure it out, help to put it on its feet a little." In December, Wes sent a revised version of the first draft to his agent.

This early version of the script is not publicly available but there are indications that it was, in some ways, substantially different from subsequent drafts. Wes told an interviewer in 2014 that Bob Shaye gave him notes to be incorporated into "a second draft."[17] Max Keller says he also gave notes on early drafts, while he and Shaye "traded options" on the script. According to Wes,

Peter Locke also expressed interest in the script but couldn't raise the money to make it. In contrast, Sean Cunningham told Wes that a film about a dream-based killer was hopelessly flawed: "Nobody will take it seriously because they'll know it's a dream."[18] According to Wes, the project was eventually "rejected by everybody in town"—including execs at PolyGram, Warner Bros., Universal, and Paramount—so he continued to revise.[19]

By the summer of 1982, Wes had written a third draft script that included many of the iconic elements of the eventual film. This draft was set in the San Fernando Valley of Los Angeles, a setting haunted by the eerie influence of devilish Santa Ana winds and the eccentric music of Oingo Boingo. The draft follows four teenagers—Nancy, Glen, Tina, and Rod—who experience prophetic dreams of the same scar-faced psycho, ultimately revealed to be Fred Krueger, a child murderer that terrorized the community of Van Nuys a decade earlier but escaped prosecution due to a legal technicality. After the grisly deaths of her friends Tina and Rod, Nancy seeks answers in church, in a psychiatrist's office, and at UCLA's Institute for the Study of Sleep Disorders. The "experts" diagnose her as schizophrenic and prescribe a hearty dose of religion before Nancy finds the truth in her dreams. When she manages to pull the killer's hat out of the ether, her mother finally reveals that several parents, including her, torched old Fred Krueger in a shack off of Mulholland Drive.

In earlier incarnations of the screen story, Wes said, the parents figured more prominently: "There were scenes where various groups of parents talk about it and say they shouldn't have done it or that he couldn't possibly be hurting the children. There was even a line indicating that all the teenagers once had siblings who had been killed when Fred Krueger had originally terrorized the town, but nobody would believe that Nancy could not remember having siblings, so I cut it out."[20] By the third draft, Wes was more narrowly focused on the plight of the teenagers who were suffering for the sins of their parents. Glen gives Nancy some spiritual advice about how to fight the boogeyman, urging her to face him without fear, then Nancy draws Krueger out of the dream world. Once she turns her back on him in the real world, he disappears like darkness in the morning light.

Over the years, Wes also spoke about many other influences on his most famous creation. He said the look of his dream boogeyman was based on the drunken hobo he'd seen from his childhood bedroom window—a man with a "weird striped sweater" and felt hat. He borrowed the name Freddy from a childhood bully. The name Krueger, he said, was an extension of the name Krug, the main villain of *Last House on the Left*, as well as an echo of the name Krupp, a munitions-maker for Nazi Germany.[21] Summing up, Freddy Krueger "stood for the savage side of male adulthood. He was the ultimate bad father."[22]

Freddy's burned face and copper claws came later—a result of Wes's desire to avoid the slasher movie cliché of a masked, knife-wielding killer. He wanted his villain to be monstrous and expressive, so he decided to use scar tissue instead of a mask. In the original draft, Freddy reportedly used "fishing knives," like the maniacal father in *Noah's Ark*, but Wes decided that too was a cliché.[23] The dream-killer's claws emerged from the writer's ruminations on psychologist Carl Jung's theory of the collective unconscious. In a 1998 Q&A on his official webpage, Wes explained, "I figured somewhere in our human / primate subconscious, there had to be ancient memories of being stalked by animals with claws for fingers."

To add a touch of supernatural menace to the anthropomorphic predator, he then drew on memories of the comic book *Plastic Man*, explaining, "He used to change shape, but you could always tell it was him because the couch would be red with a green stripe down it—or yellow. So I wanted Freddy to be a shape-shifter that could be recognized from his colors"[24] As for the iconic red and green sweater: the color choice was inspired by an article in *Scientific American* magazine indicating that the two "most clashing" colors in the visible spectrum are red and green.[25]

The "plastic man" aspect of the character came to define the screen story. Because he exists in dreams, Freddy Krueger's body can break the rules of conventional reality. As a result, Freddy has an advantage over anyone who refuses to "wake up" to this new reality and new rules. Wes explained that Freddy represented, for him, the danger of denying or evading an unpalatable truth. He recalled how one Hmong refugee stayed awake for days, only to be betrayed by his loved ones. The boy's father gave him sleeping pills and put him to bed; later, he found his son dead. To Wes, the message of the story was clear: "Here was a youngster having a vision of horror that everyone was denying. That became the central line of *Nightmare on Elm Street*."[26] In this modern-day fairy tale, the boogeyman is real—and only those who accept that strange truth *as truth* have a chance of surviving until morning.

Like the ill-fated Hmong refugee, *Nightmare*'s heroine Nancy Thompson is determined to stay awake; she keeps a coffee maker under her bed and stays caffeinated for days. She, like Wes, is determined to confront an unpalatable truth that her parents have hidden from her. Once she learns that truth, she pulls the dream demon onto her own turf and forces him to play by her rules. Taunting her nemesis with a series of booby traps (like the vengeful parents in *Last House on the Left* and the "civilized" family in *The Hills Have Eyes*), Nancy expresses faith that Freddy has no real-world power, only the power that she herself has given him.

Wes said the ending was meant to express his own personal belief that real-world cycles of violence can only end through a conscious effort to break the cycle: "You can go as far back as the Greek philosophers to see that the chain of revenge has to be stopped or it'll go on forever. It's obvious that the old-fashioned, John Wayne philosophy—that violence can cure your ills—doesn't work anymore. You have to be like Nancy; you have to turn away from the darkness or you'll end up just as evil as what you've destroyed."[27] Instead of being swallowed by the abyss, like the ostensibly "victorious" characters in *Last House on the Left* and *The Hills Have Eyes*, Nancy awakens from her dark night of the soul by stepping into the light of day and greeting her no-longer-dead friends Tina, Glen, and Rod. Actor Robert Englund, who played Freddy in the film, remembers, "The original ending was great. It's all over, birds in the soundtrack, spring has sprung. [...] The car pulls up with the kids and you say to yourself, it's that old *Twilight Zone* ending; it's just a nightmare. It's all been a dream."[28]

When the scene was shot in the summer of 1984, however, producer Bob Shaye wanted to give it more punch. "I'd seen *Friday the 13th* and some other films," he argued, "and there's always a zinger at the end."[29] Wes added a zinger—a gotcha moment in which the characters are abducted by a Freddy-convertible with a distinctive red-and-green canvas top—but later said he regretted his decision because "it's the one part of the film that isn't me."[30]

In the early 1980s, Wes was no longer the same person who'd made *Last House on the Left, The Fireworks Woman,* and *The Hills Have Eyes.*

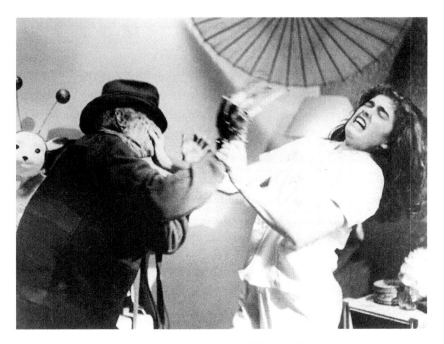

Freddy (Robert Englund) vs. Nancy (Heather Langenkamp) in
A Nightmare on Elm Street (New Line, 1984)

Having recognized and escaped from a lifelong cyclical pattern of belief and disillusionment, he'd found a new guiding philosophy that he attributed to early 20th century Russian mystic George Ivanovich Gurdjieff. In Wes's words, Gurdjieff "wrote about how consciousness was a spectrum that stretched from where most of us are basically sleepwalking through life, to a rarely visited peak of absolute consciousness, where one was in total mindfulness."[31] As early as 1978, Wes himself had concluded that "all belief is sleep, the lowest form of consciousness," and resolved to believe nothing while remaining open to everything.

It is not clear exactly when or how Wes discovered the teachings of Gurdjieff, but he may have heard the name or some variation of the teachings through the work of another Eastern guru. Musician Don Peake, who composed the score for *The Hills Have Eyes*, remembers that he first met Wes around 1977 in a Los Angeles-based meditation group led by Andrew Da Passano. That same year, Da Passano established a charitable organization called the Temple of Esoteric Science in Los Angeles, through which he taught an "eclectic system" of energy work to "those who are willing to experiment with the tools for liberation."[32] According to Peake, "Da Passano had a little place on Hollywood Boulevard, upstairs in a building. We would sit in a darkened room with candles and Andrew would wear saffron robes, because he had been initiated by the Tibetan monks, and he would talk to us about many things, including astral travel and the use of the Datura plant, which was a hallucinogenic, and Tantra Yoga."

Da Passano drew his authority from the traditions of Tibetan Buddhism and Taoism but also incorporated insights from a wide range of thinkers, teachers, and writers—including Shakespeare, Rumi, William James, Albert Einstein, Aldous Huxley, Madame Blavatsky, Ramana Maharshi, Ram Dass, Christopher Isherwood, Krishnamurti, Nisargadatta, Carlos Castañeda, Fritjof Capra, Annie Dillard, Stephen LaBerge, Stephen Levine, and George Gurdjieff. Da Passano taught that human beings have three separate bodies—a physical body, a mental body, and an emotional (astral) body. When we perceive the world through one body alone, he wrote, we are perceiving a limited reality, an illusion of total reality. To help his students expand their consciousness, Da Passano led awareness exercises. For example, he told students to make signs that said "I AM AWARE" and post them around the home and workplace until the message could sink into the student's subconscious mind. The desired result was enlightenment, the state of higher consciousness that Gurdjieff defines as The Fourth State of Being.

Gurdjieff described all four states as follows: "The two ordinary states of consciousness are sleep, the passive state in which we spend anywhere between a third and half of our lives, and the more active state in which we spend the balance of our lives, in which we walk, write and talk, which we call 'clear consciousness' or 'waking state of consciousness.' [...] The third state of consciousness is one of self-remembering or, in other words, 'self-consciousness,' consciousness of one's being. [...] The fourth state of consciousness is called 'objective consciousness,' a state in which a person is able to perceive things as they are."[33] Wes incorporated this philosophy into his life as well as his film.

In *A Nightmare on Elm Street*, the supporting characters (Tina, Rod, and Glen) represent the lower levels of consciousness, in which human beings are distracted by carnal desires and lazy habits—sex, food, television, etc.—and fail to contemplate a higher reality. In contrast, Nancy struggles to "wake up" from such distractions and illusions. Wes said, "She was the only one that had the guts to say, 'I saw this and I have to figure out how to confront it.'"[34] Because Nancy sees and confronts the reality that everyone else represses and denies, Wes proclaimed Gurdjieff the "spiritual father" of *A Nightmare on Elm Street*.[35]

Although he didn't expect most horror fans to pick up on the spiritual message, he hoped viewers would at least discern a note of triumph in the film. To Wes, the screen story conveyed the idea that "the world is what you imagine it to be," and it showed how one can "imagine your own solutions, defenses, even attacks on the Freddy Kruegers of life."[36] Jessica Craven says that message has resonated strongly throughout her life. "Ultimately, this whole idea of 'you don't give the Freddy any energy,' you sort of turn your back, you know—it becomes a life lesson. You have to stop, at some point, giving energy to all these horrible things that happened in the past and give energy to what is before you that is healthy and good. Dad has been a teacher of that, for me, more than anybody."[37]

Of course, not everyone saw the film in such positive terms. By 1982, in the midst of a backlash against slasher movies, few Hollywood producers wanted anything to do with horror films, spiritual or otherwise, and almost nobody wanted to finance *A Nightmare on Elm Street*. Wes remembered, "The conventional wisdom was that the horror film was burned out. There was a desire to be politically correct—although at that time the term wasn't around—a feeling that horror movies were nasty and ugly. There had been so many reactionary articles against *Friday the 13th*, about violence and its effects on kids, that no one would go near *Nightmare*."[38] Only New Line Cinema's Bob Shaye was willing to take a leap of faith on Wes Craven's idea, but raising the financing proved to be a long and arduous process. In the meantime, Wes's fortunes floundered. "I went through all my savings," he confessed. "Had to sell my house. I was making lists: 'How much can I get for my guitar?' Stuff like that. And borrowed money from Sean Cunningham to pay my taxes. And then I had nothing."[39] For a while, he scraped by on writing jobs, cranking out "twelve different full-length treatments for various people; rewrites for people, script doctoring, and several things of my own."[40]

One script he wrote for himself around this time was a children's movie titled *Circus Gang* (a.k.a. *Tightrope*). In late 1981, the project was "under consideration" at Disney, as part of a development deal with Peter Locke.[41]

Wes described the project as "a comedy-drama concerning a group of circus-performer kids who solve a crime in a rag-tag-army sort of way, using their circus skills, at the same time coming to terms with life."[42] Although it now seems an unlikely project for the reputed master of horror, it was not the first time he had tried to steer his career toward family fare. He may have taken some cues from Sean Cunningham's films *Here Come the Tigers* and *Manny's Orphans*. Unfortunately, *Circus Gang* failed to get a green light.

According to author Brian J. Robb, Disney execs at one point expressed interest in a toned-down version of *A Nightmare on Elm Street*, hoping to turn it into a relatively tame frightener that could play every Halloween on the Disney Channel. Wes later denied the rumor, but it is noteworthy that a 1986 Disney Sunday Movie bore some resemblance to Wes's *Nightmare*. Screenwriter Michael Janover's *Mr. Boogedy* revolved around a cackling, pizza-faced ghost of a dead pilgrim that haunts a middle-class family in an eerie New England town. It is perhaps also worth noting that both films bear similarities to Nathaniel Hawthorne's novel *The House of the Seven Gables*, about a "pestilent wizard," executed as a witch, who now haunts the dreams of his persecutors' descendants.

Among the other scripts Wes wrote while waiting for his ship to come in was *The Fallen*, a collaboration with producer Veda Nayak. On April 6, 1982, *The Hollywood Reporter* announced the project as a $6 million film to be shot in southeastern India, Yugoslavia, and the U.S., and summarized it as a story about "a UCLA scientist who uncovers a series of murders perpetrated by an India cobra-worshipping cult concerned with the supernatural."[43] A month later, a full-page ad touted the forthcoming film as "an unusual drama" in the tradition of *The Omen*, *The Exorcist*, *Raiders of the Lost Ark*, and *Close Encounters of the Third Kind*, and named Wes Craven as the prospective director. A subsequent article, published in late June, indicated that Wes was actively involved in casting the movie, stating: "Director Wes Craven was so hot to grab Klaus Kinski for the lead role in his *The Fallen* pic to pop later this year, he jetted to Paris to clinch KK personally for the role."[44]

Mimi Craven remembers the trip and the meeting: "Klaus Kinski came to our hotel room. It was Wes, Klaus, me, and someone else. Another man. I was the only woman. Klaus Kinski never said a word to me, other than 'How do you

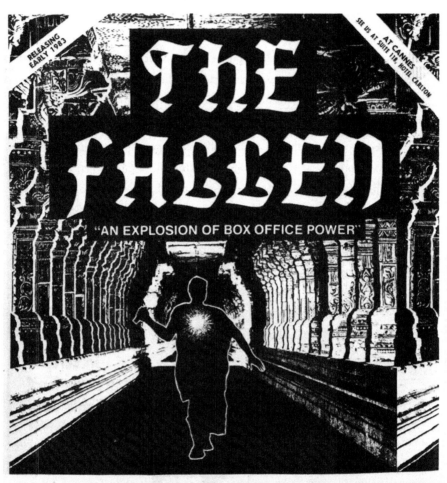

do?' Then the boys started having a very grown-up conversation about life and I'm just sitting there. Forty-five minutes later, I felt completely nude. Obviously, I wasn't but I felt like I was. I was so creeped out. My heart was racing. [Kinski] never looked in my direction, but he was the weirdest, creepiest guy. He had one of those faces where you can't look at him but you can't look away. And I felt vulnerable and scared. I was really glad when that [film] didn't go."

Four months later, *The Fallen* was still in pre-production, under a new title (*Journey into Light*), with Wes still attached to direct.[45] Around the same time, however, he solidified his deal with New Line Pictures to direct *A Nightmare on Elm Street*. On October 20, Bob Shaye told *The Hollywood Reporter* that the film would start shooting in January 1983 with a projected budget of $2.5 million.[46] It seems likely that Wes backed away from *The Fallen* as a result of this new momentum. It would be another year, however, before *Nightmare* went into production.

Wes undoubtedly wanted to focus on his own personal project instead of a work-for-hire, but the decision to bail out of *The Fallen* (if, in fact, it was Wes's decision) caused him a tremendous amount of trouble. In a 2010 interview, Wes discussed a lawsuit filed against him around 1986 by a writer who claimed that *A Nightmare on Elm Street* was based on a story Wes had stolen from him. Wes's description of the supposedly stolen story—involving a "snake cult" in India—closely resembles *The Hollywood Reporter*'s synopsis of *The Fallen*.[47] After Wes's death in 2015, an August 1984 draft of the unproduced Craven / Nayak script, titled *Twilight Adventure*, was acquired by the University of Pittsburgh Library for its Horror Studies Collection. Curator Ben Rubin summarized it as a supernatural thriller set in the Balkans, about "the death of a patriarch, the conflict of succession of his estate, and a long-held family secret" involving a snake cult.[48] The location change suggests that Nayak continued to revise the script after Wes moved on. *Twilight Adventure* includes a love story between the hero, a Sociology professor named Justin Strong, and an apparently reincarnated gypsy, as well as a Yoda-like spirit who advises Strong to face his fears and recognize the illusory nature of evil. There's also a mysterious Nazi treasure to justify comparisons to *Raiders of the Lost Ark*. The themes are Craven-esque but the humorless script is not. According to Wes, the lawsuit was eventually settled out of court.

With *The Fallen* and *A Nightmare on Elm Street* both in limbo, Wes continued moonlighting as a writer-for-hire. Other scripts written during this time include *I Was a Teenage Bombshell,* based on an original story by Chuck Minskoff and Randy Rovins, and *The Innocents,* based on an original story by Christopher Mankiewicz. According to Minskoff, the former was conceived as a vehicle for actress Sharon Stone, a close friend of Mimi Craven. He remembers, "The one sentence pitch was '*Animal House* meets *An American Werewolf in London.*' It was about two completely different types of transformations; one was a rather unattractive lady who turns into a beautiful woman, and the other was a kind of a female werewolf, but more cat-like than wolf-like. The story was set on a college campus and in the sorority house there was a den mother who watches over everyone. Her name was Polly Janus, which was Wes being clever and giving us a clue about who the monster was."

I Was a Teenage Bombshell was never produced but at least one scene had a life beyond the script. "Early in the script," Minskoff says, "some guys take out a mirror in one of the girls' bathrooms and set it up so they can spy on the girls. Typical gag, like a similar scene in *Porky's.* That sets up a huge jump scare where the [cat-creature] comes through the mirror at the girl. Wes repurposed the gag in *A Nightmare on Elm Street,* when Freddy comes through the mirror and attacks Nancy." Other notable Wes-isms include silly character names (Walter J. Codpiece, Ms. Anthrope), allusions to Greek mythology (Diana and Narcissus), slapstick comedy (including a sequence with a blind girl crossing the street), overt generational conflict, an incompetent sheriff, and a Faustian deal-maker who declares his eternal faith in "the possibility of change."

According to Minskoff, Wes also wrote a separate tongue-in-cheek monster movie for a different producer. Despite the similar titles, he says *I Was a Rock N Roll Werewolf* was a "completely different" story. "Wes could write as fast as he could type. And he was a very fast typist."

Wes's next script, *The Innocents,* concerned "a girls' choir that shipwrecks on a Pacific Island and reverts to savagery."[49] This is the same project Wes referred to in 1985 as "*Lord of the Flies* with girls."[50] In his script, the girls' choir group—called Yes America—is flying to New Zealand when an albatross hits their plane, forcing an emergency landing. No doubt this was a nod to "The Rime of the Ancient Mariner," which connects the script in an oblique way to *The Hills Have*

Eyes. Instead of a family lost in the desert, *The Innocents* focuses on a handful of twenty-something chaperones who become stranded with the teenage choir girls. Only two of the chaperones are men, and one of them—a blatantly horny photographer named Keith—believes that he and his male compatriot, Henry, have landed in paradise. Keith has obviously never read *Lord of the Flies* (or Thomas P. Cullinan's *The Beguiled*).

The matronly girls' choir leader dies quickly, followed by her 28-year-old protégé, which leaves the younglings in the hands of 24-year-old Sheila and 20-year-old Karen. While Karen pursues a love affair with Henry and builds a raft to get off the island, Sheila brainwashes the rest of group and creates her own cult, a "New America" devoted to discipline and order and "purity." The rest of the story adheres to the *Lord of the Flies* template—with Sheila standing in for power-hungry Jack, Karen as rational Ralph, Keith as doomed Piggy, and an old pirate sword as the all-important conch shell. In the end, Wes's screen story withdraws to a bird's eye view high above the seemingly deserted island— another similarity to *The Hills Have Eyes* script. Although the story has an ostensibly happy ending, the proposed musical accompaniment ("America the Beautiful") suggests an ironic tone.

An August 9, 1983 advertisement in *The Hollywood Reporter* listed *The Innocents* as a recent acquisition of the Overseas Film Group. Less than a month later, another article in the same publication indicated that the project was in the "initial stages of development," with Wes attached to direct.[51] Two months after that, filming was scheduled to begin in early 1984 on location in the South Pacific.[52] For whatever reason, it didn't. An article in *Screen International* indicated that the film was still in pre-production as of the summer of 1984, at which time the filmmakers hoped to start filming in September "on the Dalmatian coast of Yugoslavia" (in modern day Croatia) and the Greek islands.[53] By then, Wes had vacated the director's chair.

In the early summer of '83, Wes traveled to Acapulco, Mexico, to revise David Andrew Fisher's shooting script for *Toy Soldiers*.[54] The film, about a group of entitled American teens who unwittingly sail into a Central American hostage crisis, only to be rescued by a laconic "ex-Marine," is reminiscent of Wes's script for *Marimba*. Regardless, there is little of his distinctive voice in the final film. The happiest outcome of the assignment for

Wes—aside from the much-needed paycheck—seems to have been a lasting rapport with Willard Pugh. He wrote a role for the young actor in his next film, *The Hills Have Eyes Part 2*.

Over the years, Wes rarely talked about the ill-fated sequel. He said the project came about because the UK-based VHS distributor of the original film offered to finance a followup. In a moment of weakness—and poverty—Wes gave in. "I thought, 'Why not, let's just go make a movie,' because I was standing around Hollywood while Bob [Shaye] seemed unable to raise the money for *Nightmare*."[55] In a more candid moment, he admitted, "The reason I did *Hills 2* is because I was dead broke and needed to do any film. I would have directed *Godzilla Goes to Paris*."[56]

A Godzilla parody might have been more fun, but at least having a new film in production boosted Wes's confidence, as well as his profile in Hollywood (where it always helps to look busy). Defending the project years later, he said, "It was a much better script, I think, than the movie turned out to be."[57] Wes completed a 103-page first draft of *The Hills Have Eyes Part 2*, titled *The Night of Jupiter*, in early April 1983. He said he wrote it in about two weeks and that the prospective investors liked it so much they asked him to expand the story.[58] He obliged, turning in a 112-page second draft, titled *The Revenge of Jupiter*, on July 29. As both titles suggest, the sequel initially featured the return of the hill-dwelling family's flesh-eating patriarch, Papa Jupiter. The first draft also featured central roles for Bobby Carter; Ruby, Jupiter's daughter; and Pluto, Jupiter's only surviving son. The action began as Ruby casually led Bobby and his new teenage friends (a troupe of motorbike racers, including a blind prophetess named Cassandra) to her mother's hotel and spa in the desert. They find the place empty and haunted by the all-too-real specter of Papa Jupiter, who is bigger and meaner than ever. (In the first draft, even Pluto wants to get away from him.) The second draft minimizes the role of Bobby—he fearfully avoids returning to the desert—and takes place at a deserted mining camp instead of the abandoned spa. The third act calls for more stunts and special effects but the story is mostly the same. For the teenage characters, it's still Miller time all the time. In Wes's third draft, titled *The Reaper* and dated August 31, Papa Jupiter gets replaced by a new title character, clumsily identified as the late patriarch's brother.

John Bloom as The Reaper in *The Hills Have Eyes Part 2*
(New Realm, 1984)

Although the scripts are more nuanced than the final film, it seems unlikely that *Hills 2* was ever meant to be more than a formulaic slasher movie. Apart from the innovation of having a blind "final girl"—which had been done before, in the 1981 film *Eyes of a Stranger*—*Hills 2* could easily pass for a mutant *Friday the 13th* sequel. This was probably no accident. Wes was struggling to reimagine the modern horror film with *A Nightmare on Elm Street*, while his friends Sean Cunningham and Steve Miner (who directed the first two *Friday* sequels) were getting rich on formulaic *Friday* sequels. If that's what audiences wanted, why shouldn't he and Peter Locke reap the rewards too?

Unfortunately, as Wes later explained, he couldn't complete *The Hills Have Eyes Part 2* on the twenty-four-day production schedule in the fall of 1983. Mimi Craven says it was a particularly grueling shoot due to very limited production resources. "They were gonna shoot out in the desert," she remembers, "and Wes was gonna be gone. And I said, 'I don't want you to be gone and I'm stuck at home, so what can I do on set? I want a job on the set.' We decided I would be a wardrobe assistant. Seemed simple enough. In our first meeting with the crew, everybody knew who I was, so I said, 'Okay, I know I'm Mrs. Sir, but I'm not because I'm Wardrobe Assist, so I want you to treat me like you would any normal Wardrobe Assist.' That was week one. By week three, I was like, 'Who do I have to fuck to get off of this set?' It was hot. At pre-sunset, bugs the size of Buicks would come out, as Woody Allen would say. The catering was horrible. There was no craft service."

In the end, the filmmakers ran out of money. Wes said, "We planned to shoot a further five days, but the producer took the uncompleted film off to the L.A. film market and got such a good response that he decided to save the money and release it as it was!"[59] In the meantime, Wes moved on to another directing gig. Still trying to maintain career momentum and keep his *Elm Street* dream alive, he signed up to make a TV thriller called *The Club*. He remembered, "We were a few days away from doing the [sound] mix on *Hills 2* when the TV movie offer came through. Negotiations on *Nightmare on Elm Street* were dragging on and on, and my agent felt we weren't being taken very seriously, so I decided I would do it."[60]

Journalist Dennis Fischer says Wes did an uncredited rewrite on Richard Rothstein's script for *The Club*, which was eventually retitled *Invitation from Hell*.[61] If so, he must have worked fast. By Wes's own account, he interviewed for the directing gig on a Friday, received the job offer over the weekend, started pre-production on Monday, and started filming two weeks later.[62] The shooting script was finalized on February 15 and the movie aired on May 28. Although Wes later joked about the "preposterous" premise of *Invitation to Hell*—a yuppie family under attack by a soul-sucking country club diva/demon—he seemed relatively happy with the end result.[63] More importantly, *Invitation* helped to push his long-gestating dream project into pre-production.

On February 11 that same year, *Screen International* announced that Bob Shaye had secured financing—from VTC Productions, the same company that financed *The Hills Have Eyes Part 2*—for *A Nightmare on Elm Street*.[64] The deal eventually fell through but Shaye managed to strike a last-minute replacement deal with video cassette distributor Media Home Entertainment, and the show went on as planned. *A Nightmare on Elm Street* went into production on June 11, 1984. Behind-the-scenes tales—most of them gathered in author Thommy Hutson's exhaustively researched book *Never Sleep Again*—indicate it was an intense shoot, but also a fortuitous one. In an interview for the TV series *Hollywood's Best Directors*, Wes said there are two crucial elements to making a successful film: a tight script and an extraordinary cast.[65] After four years of honing the script, he had worked out every detail of this particular screen story—but he remained open to some improvisations, because he recognized that he had an extraordinary cast and crew.

In the lead role of Nancy, 20-year-old Heather Langenkamp conveyed strength as well as innocence, while veteran character actor Robert Englund brought sinister glee to the role of Freddy Krueger. Langenkamp recalls, "The schedule was incredibly grueling but Wes and I had a really great shorthand for how to get the work done. He would tell me exactly what he wanted, exactly what kind of mood or tempo. In general, he just wanted me to be me. He wanted the Heather that he met in the casting office to be Nancy. He picked me because I was so close to her in many ways, so I thought the best thing I could do was to be myself—while also taking some great ideas from him about how to act in a horror movie, which required a lot of choreography. The way that Nancy and Freddy move around each other is very balletic, in a way."

Englund adds, "Wes had encouraged, especially in the latter half of the film when it was down to Heather and me, an awful lot of improvisational cat-and-mouse stuff, which gave rise to the sort of cult of personality that developed."[66] The actor remains grateful to the director for giving him a certain amount of freedom in bringing Freddy Krueger to life. "I remember bringing ideas to Wes and Wes saying yes, but I don't remember Wes steering me a lot. I mostly remember him saying, 'Do it that way again.' I don't want to say he left me alone because that's not what happened; he trusted me."

Throughout the entire process, Langenkamp says, Wes managed to keep things relatively light on set. "He knew that when you're making a horror film, things get crazy—like the guy following you around on the floor with a tube up your leg to make you bleed, or whatever. Special effects. He knew we had to joke about those things, to get it out of our system, so that when he said 'Action!' we could be serious and sell the horror. So he was always making bad jokes. There was a part of Wes that was still a 14-year-old boy. He couldn't resist lame puns. Clever but lame. And then in the same breath, someone would ask him something serious about the next scene and he would give a great thumbnail academic answer. Very thoughtful. That's the best way to describe Wes; he was very, very thoughtful."

Mimi Craven had a small acting role in the film—as a nurse in the Katja Institute for the Study of Sleep Disorders—and also did her part to help create a supportive, familial atmosphere on set. "I would bake cookies and bring them to set and everybody would call me mom. To this day, Johnny Depp still calls me mom. The great story is that Wes wasn't going to hire Johnny at first. Annette Benson was the casting director and she got Johnny [to read for the part of Glen, Nancy's boyfriend]. Wes's daughter Jessica and her best friend were sitting in the back of the room for all the auditions, because Wes thought it would be fun for them, seeing all these cute young guys coming in to read. I remember Wes had a clipboard with everybody's name on it, and Johnny came in to read and Wes scratched Johnny's name off the list. The other adults in the room were looking at him, going, 'What are you doing?' Wes said, 'He was terrible.' We said, 'Look at Jessica and her friend.' They were in the back of the room squealing—that high-pitched thing that young girls do. 'Now multiply that by millions.' That's why he got the part."

Robert Englund in *A Nightmare on Elm Street*
(New Line, 1984)

Wes and his cast were supported by an equally talented crew. Cinematographer Jacques Haitkin remembers how he and Wes worked out a lighting scheme to keep viewers in suspense throughout the film: "I wanted to put a very strong effect so that you'd know you're in a nightmare, so that it would really be scary. Wes said, 'No, no, no, no, no. I don't want to let people know we're in a nightmare. It's just the opposite.'"[67] Wes explained, "From a very wholesome, all-American look we'd make a very subtle transition into a dreamlike look where things were just slightly awry and always water[y]…so it had that boiler room feeling." The filmmakers also decided to light only the top of trees while darkening the trunks, to give dream sequences "the feeling of floating." [68] The aesthetic conveyed the "sense of arboreal mystery and the subconsciousness of water" that had enchanted Wes as a child growing up in Cleveland.

The final film features eight different dream sequences. Two of the most iconic set pieces involve a rotating room, which allowed Freddy Krueger to drag one victim up a wall and across a ceiling, and to pour another victim's bloody remains out of a stationary bed mattress. Wes said, "Some of the effects shots were in the original script, but others were introduced by [special effects designer Jim] Doyle and his crew."[69] Doyle remembered, "I pitched him a rotating room as a good way to kill Rod's girlfriend Tina. He thought I was nuts. We had no budget. I thought, 'Well, what if we kill [Glen] using the same set?'"[70] The rotating-room provided a harrowing experience for the filmmakers as well as the viewers; at one point, the director and his cinematographer found themselves hanging upside down in the set, covered in fake blood and trying not to get electrocuted.

In another memorable set piece, Freddy attacks Nancy by pulling her down into a bottomless bathtub. This scene does not appear in the initial shooting script, which features a more straightforward shower scene. At the last minute, Wes apparently decided to repurpose the bathtub scene he'd added to *Deadly Blessing*. In *Nightmare*, Freddy's claws emerge from the water between Nancy's legs much like the phallic snake in *Deadly Blessing*, but *Nightmare* goes further. Whereas the heroine in *Deadly Blessing* screamed and fled the room, Nancy gets pulled down into the dream demon's netherworld, a beat reminiscent of the supernatural coda to *Deadly Blessing*.

The new addition highlights the sexual nature of the cat-and-mouse game between Nancy and Freddy—a game that reaches its climax with another scene reminiscent of Wes's earlier work. Shortly before Freddy turns Glen into a geyser of blood, the villain playfully calls Nancy on the phone and quips, "I'm your boyfriend now," his words echoing a phrase spoken by a Colombian rapist in *Marimba*. A moment later, the phone Nancy is holding transforms into a fleshy proboscis with a slimy tongue that darts into her mouth. The sexually-suggestive "Freddy phone" gag is a callback to the more-than-suggestive phone sex scene in *It Happened in Hollywood*. Wes probably never dreamed that anyone would connect the two films, but he clearly wanted to amplify the sexual tension in his latest tale of Beauty and the Beast.

When filming wrapped in July, Wes flew from Los Angeles to New York to oversee the editing of the film in the offices of New Line Cinema. It was, he said, a difficult decision because "I was just married and had to leave my wife back in L.A., and that did not work out well at all."[71] According to Mimi, "We were remodeling a house and he would call me every night and I would tell him what was being done and he would tell me everything was wrong. And I became claustrophobic, agoraphobic, you name it." As time and distance amplified the personality differences between the 45-year-old husband and his 27-year-old bride, the marriage began to crack under the strain.

Bob Shaye's unenthusiastic reaction to the first rough cut of *A Nightmare on Elm Street* added to Wes's anxiety. When the producer saw the film for the first time, he reportedly asked, "Do you think we have a picture here at all?"[72] Wes worked closely with his post-production team to create a tighter cut of the film with sound design and a pulse-pounding score that worked on a subconscious level. In the meantime, Wes held his breath for a few days in mid-August, as the film *Dreamscape*—about a psychic who kills people in their dreams—appeared in theaters. The film threatened to steal Freddy's thunder and prompted his creator to curse the fact that his story had spent so many years in development hell—and that he had talked about it so openly in interviews over the years. As it turned out, the filmmaker had good reason to worry—not because *Dreamscape* stole Freddy's thunder but because the other film's mediocre box office scared at least one major studio away from distributing *Nightmare*. In the end, Bob Shaye took a chance on distributing *Nightmare* himself.

Nancy (Heather Langenkamp) gets an obscene call from the Freddy-phone
in *A Nightmare on Elm Street* (New Line, 1984)

As the film approached its November 16 release date, Wes went into marketing mode. In an interview for *Fangoria* magazine, he tried to make the case that his forthcoming film wasn't *really* a horror film but "more of a fantasy, an impressionistic thriller."[73] (In contrast, the interviewer described *Nightmare* as a low-budget cross between *Dreamscape* and *Poltergeist*.) By January 1986, Wes was speaking more confidently about *Nightmare* as a watershed film, "a whole new type of horror film" destined to inspire an entire subgenre of "hallucinatory horror films."[74]

A Nightmare on Elm Street grossed more than $1 million in its opening weekend, outpacing the George Burns comedy *Oh, God! You Devil* and the controversial Santa Claus slasher movie *Silent Night, Deadly Night*. Wes said, "It opened and then came this call, I think on the third day, and it was from Bob." The producer sounded very enthusiastic. Wes reflected, "You hear that tone [of voice], you know what's going to happen: your credibility goes way up, and you feel like you've connected with the audience. It's a great feeling."[75] Two months later, the film had grossed over $10 million, prompting Wes to publicly speculate that his latest film might gain him admittance to "the club" of well-respected horror filmmakers like John Carpenter and Sean Cunningham, and perhaps grant him an opportunity to escape the "man-with-a-knife" genre.[76] In the short term, he capitalized on the buzz by embracing offers to write and direct some unconventional genre films.

In the fall of 1984, Universal Studios hired Wes to adapt V.C. Andrews's controversial coming-of-age novel *Flowers in the Attic* to the screen. The story revolves around four siblings raised in captivity by an abusive, fundamentalist grandmother (and mostly absent mother) in the attic of a rural Virginia mansion. The isolation of the children—and the specter of a family curse—leads to the older siblings to develop a taboo physical relationship while they act like parents to the younger siblings. Wes saw it as a modern fairy tale—"*Hansel and Gretel* on a big scale," "Tennessee Williams meets Stephen King," as well as a story about "the power of the human spirit to come out of the darkness."[77] His script visualized some of the novel's darkest speculations, but also changed the ending, incorporating a wedding scene from the book's sequel *Petals on the Wind* to provide closure for the children and comeuppance for their tormentors.

Almost immediately, Universal executives became nervous about the novel's "theme of incest" and scrapped the project.[78] New World Pictures picked it up and commissioned a second draft from Wes, which he delivered in late March 1985. Obviously excited about making the film, he hyped this version as follows: "In some sense, *Flowers* is—using the word as delicately as possible—exploitive. But it's not going to be treated as an exploitation picture whatsoever. Instead we all want to do it as a top-quality feature film because it just has the elements of a classic in it."[79] Ultimately, however, New World decided not to make his script.

According to Jeffrey Bloom, who eventually wrote and directed an adaptation for New World, Wes's script was deemed too horrific. He elaborated, "It's a psychologically dark, fanciful, Gothic fairy tale. But there's nothing horrifying about it in a movie sense. New World, however, kept asking for horror and they kept getting it. But upon reading the various drafts [...] they didn't like what they were seeing."[80] Bloom convinced the producers that they shouldn't think of *Flowers in the Attic* as a horror movie but rather as a "woman's movie," because "there's an enormous audience already out there of women who will come to see a woman's movie."[81] In the end, the filmmakers downplayed the horror elements and produced a tamer, PG-13 adaptation of the novel.

Meanwhile, Wes directed *Chiller*, a TV movie that also had some horror elements but was not (the director stipulated) "horror in the sense that there's a maniac stalking people." Like *Invitation to Hell* and *Flowers in the Attic*, *Chiller* was a family-oriented horror story, and Wes focused on the "humanistic dramatics and top-notch actors."[82] He has described *Chiller* as the "most interesting" of the TV movies he directed, probably because it was the most philosophical.[83]

The story, about a man who returns to life after being cryogenically frozen for ten years, is a familiar cautionary tale by screenwriter J.D. Feigelson. In a monologue that sounds very much like Professor Craven, a priest character lays out the story's central (and thematic) conflict: "We believe that man is made up of body, mind and spirit. Now, the body is physical. You see it. You can touch it. But the spirit... We believe that when someone dies, the soul goes off to paradise, to heaven, to some hereafter. Now suppose that a man died, really died—not one of those near-death experiences—and suppose that in fact he was buried for ten years, and after that time somehow he was reanimated, brought back to life. If the body and the mind functioned, then he would technically be alive. But what about the soul?" The horror movie conceit is that the soul does not return; the main character becomes a soulless yuppie—much like the members of *Invitation to Hell's* Steaming Springs Country Club.

Feigelson remembers that Wes came on board the project as a director-for-hire: "The script had been approved by the network, and Wes had written an additional scene that he wanted in the movie. It was a dialogue scene. I was a producer on the movie too, so I told him, 'Wes, as much as I love you, we can't do that. Because the script has been approved.' He got bent out of shape about that, but I explained that making TV movies is not like doing features. Once the network approves the script, that's the script you have to shoot. If we went back to the network [with a revised script], they could say, 'Then let's can it.' We could lose a lot of money. Wes finally agreed that he didn't really know that much about TV movies, so we went on and shot the movie as it was written." *Chiller* went into production on January 22, 1985. Throughout the shoot, Feigelson says, "Wes really was a gentleman. Not only to me, but to everybody that worked with him. He let everybody pretty much do their thing, unless there was something specific he wanted, then he would ask for that. But Wes was one of the most laid-back directors I've ever worked with. That was just his way, his nature."

By the time *Chiller* aired on May 22, *A Nightmare on Elm Street* had grossed over $25 million at the domestic box office and Wes had become a bona fide celebrity director. In June, he wrote to an old friend that the success of the film had made him "negotiable, which is what this town is at least half about." In July, he reflected on this high watermark of his career, saying, "I feel as if I've finally come out into the light."[84] Unfortunately, it wasn't all sunshine and roses. Soon after the release of *A Nightmare on Elm Street*, he learned that he had inadvertently signed away the ancillary rights to his own creation, granting producer Bob Shaye the ability to sequelize the film. Shaye didn't waste any time; by early December 1984, he was publicly contemplating story ideas for *Freddy's Revenge*. Although understandably frustrated, Wes kept the door open to the possibility of directing the sequel if Shaye's team could come up with a script that intrigued him. In the meantime, he looked for opportunities to do something completely different.

The most exciting offer that came along was a chance to direct several episodes of the new *Twilight Zone* TV series for producer Phil DeGuere, who had been a fan of Wes since *Last House on the Left*. When Wes had first moved to Los Angeles, DeGuere convinced his own agent Marvin Moss to accept Wes as a client. Later, he offered Wes a directing gig on his TV series *Simon & Simon* (1981-1984), but Wes declined because he wanted to focus on feature films rather than television. He changed his tune in early 1985 when DeGuere stepped into *The Twilight Zone*.

Wes said he "grew up" on the original show, which premiered in October 1959.[85] It was around that time that Wes suffered his mysterious paralysis and had to give up his dream of becoming a Navy pilot, so it is tempting to imagine twenty-year-old Wes as the character in the very first episode of Serling's show—a U.S. Air Force pilot stranded in a completely deserted town with no memory of how he got there. Eventually, the episode reveals that the pilot is trapped in an experimental sensory deprivation chamber and the town is pure hallucination. Although his reality is an illusion, his loneliness and frustration remain devastatingly real, and the juxtaposition made the episode resonate.

Rod Serling, who wrote the story, narrated his concept for the ongoing *Twilight Zone* series: "There is a fifth dimension beyond that which is known to man. It is a dimension as vast as space and as timeless as infinity. It is the middle ground between light and shadow, between science and superstition, and it lies between the pit of man's fears and the summit of his knowledge. This is the dimension of imagination. It is an area which we call The Twilight Zone." Wes understood the concept implicitly; he was already living most of his life in the dimension of imagination. Serling reassured him that he was not alone.

When Phil DeGuere set out to reboot the series, he explained that his goal was not to try to "step into Rod Serling's shoes" but to "put together a collection of the finest writers that we can find in America, and the best directors and the best actors, and create a collection of self-contained stories."[86] The first season's roster included writers Ray Bradbury, Arthur C. Clarke, Harlan Ellison, Robert Heinlein and Stephen King, as well as directors William Friedkin, Joe Dante, and Wes Craven. Coming off the massive success of *A Nightmare on Elm Street,* Wes was an obvious choice—and an enthusiastic collaborator. Years later, he gushed that "suddenly I was being trusted […] with material that was sensitive, comedic and tragic, and all these different things, and it was just an incredible opportunity to show what I could do in other areas."[87]

Wes directed both segments of the pilot episode, "Shatterday" and "A Little Peace and Quiet," each one a tense but deeply humanistic drama. Subsequent episodes "Wordplay" and "Dealer's Choice" illustrated his comedy chops, as did a brief acting role in the episode "Children's Zoo." (Wes, playing an inmate in a zoo for parents, ad-libbed a line—telling a little girl "I know where your teddy bear sleeps"—but the line was cut from the final episode.) "Chameleon" delivered him into the realm of speculative sci-fi, while "Her Pilgrim Soul"—a story about a scientist whose invention allows him to interact with a mother he never met—reveals the sentimental side of Hollywood's reputed Sultan of Slash. Wes later named "Her Pilgrim Soul" as his favorite episode, saying, "One of the things it really captures—and I guess we feel this in our own lives too—how brief life can be. And then if you find somebody you really love, how quickly the thing moves forward and moves away from you in some ways. You kind of have to seize the moment."[88]

Thirty years later, Wes remained grateful for his experience on *The Twilight Zone*, saying, "It's one of the things I'm proudest of doing. Period. I really loved that work." In addition to appreciating the show because it allowed him to escape the limitations of his horror persona, he regarded Serling's basic concept as a correlative to his personal views on dreaming, filmmaking, and the nature of reality. In a 2015 interview with Daniel Griffith, he summed up, "The great thing about being able to go into a dream-life reality or altered planes of reality—whatever you want to call *The Twilight Zone* experience— is that you get to cover areas of human consciousness that we don't usually think about as legitimate or something that is easily discussed. We don't have a vocabulary for it, usually. But in something like *Twilight Zone*, you can suddenly go into alternate versions of reality [and] that's really mind-expanding and quite fascinating. And it's very cinematic; it's very visual."[89] Wes would continue to explore this otherworldly terrain during the most prolific phase of his career as a storyteller.

The Soul of Wes Craven

CHAPTER EIGHT

LUCID DREAMING
(1985 - 1988)

*"You can't fool Freddy, because he knows what you know.
And so Freddy just keeps coming back, no matter what.
Actually, that's probably what he would do until you
accepted him, or tried to love him."*

– Stephen LaBerge, *Rolling Stone* (October 6, 1988)

"People are under the impression that I'm following a much more controlled path than I really am," Wes said in the 1990s, stipulating that he felt like his professional life was "more of a random thing."[1] Obviously, he had not chosen his career path; he'd made horror films (and hardcore sex films) because that's what he could get paid to make. The only thing he controlled was how to make the stories his own. Later, after honing his craft as a technical filmmaker on works-for-hire, he'd staked his future on an idea that was entirely personal and completely original. The gamble paid off; *A Nightmare on Elm Street* became an iconic film, earning Wes opportunities to work on more prestigious, bigger-budget projects. But *Nightmare* was also an albatross. Going forward, investors and audiences expected the filmmaker to repeat his success. For the next decade, Wes lived in the long shadow of Freddy Krueger as he struggled to take his storytelling to the next level.

In May 1985, Wes stepped away from *Flowers in the Attic* and turned his back on *A Nightmare on Elm Street Part 2* (although he did offer the screenwriter some story notes) in order to direct *Deadly Friend*, his first major studio film. He later said he took the job because his agent Marvin Moss had urged him to, and because the film was "out of the [horror] genre."[2] Based on Diana Henstell's novel *Friend*, about a brilliant but emotionally-disturbed 13-year-old boy who implants a robot brain into the body of a murdered 11-year-old girl, the property was being developed for Warner Bros. by producer Bob Sherman under the working title *Artificial Intelligence.*

Wes was intrigued by the *Frankenstein*-esque plot and the novel's "well-rounded characters" but he quickly decided he didn't want to adapt the material himself.[3] Instead, he and Sherman selected newcomer Bruce Joel Rubin to write the script. At the time, Rubin's only screenwriting credit was on the sci-fi drama *Brainstorm* (1983) but he was better known as the author of *Jacob's Ladder*, a spec script hailed by industry insiders as one of the best unproduced scripts in Hollywood. Like Wes, Bruce Rubin wanted to distance himself from the horror genre—he was more interested in mythic and mystical tales—but financial needs prompted him to take the job. In the summer of 1985, he began writing.

Wes, meanwhile, focused on writing a thematically-similar script. Although he later claimed that his responsibilities on *The Twilight Zone* series prevented him from writing *Deadly Friend*, it is more likely that he was sidelined by *Roger Corman's Frankenstein*. His collaboration with the godfather of indie filmmaking came about because, according to Corman, "Universal had done some research and found out that a picture called *Roger Corman's Frankenstein* would be successful. So they came to me and asked if I wanted to make such a film. And I said no." The legendary filmmaker was reluctant to return to the director's chair (for the first time since 1971's *Von Richthofen and Brown*) but Universal eventually made him an offer he couldn't refuse. Corman said, "They offered me more money than I had ever made in my life, so I thought if I could find a new way to do *Frankenstein*, I'll do it."[4] All he needed was a brilliant script. Producer Thom Mount promised to deliver "the best script we can get, the best cast we can get, the best music we can get, and the best advertising campaign we can get." Corman then commissioned a series of scripts from several young writers, including Wes Craven.[5]

In late August 1985, industry trades announced *Roger Corman's Frankenstein* would be made for Tri-Star Pictures, written by Wes Craven, set in the 21st century, and shot in Argentina.[6] Corman outlined his development process as follows: "I work with the writer and with my story editor [...] in a joint effort to create first an understanding. We do not put anything on paper in the beginning. We get to the point where all three of us understand what the picture is about and the line it will take. Only at that time, when we have really made most of the decisions, is the writer sent home to do a treatment. [...] He brings in the treatment, and we have another series of discussions. Then the writer goes for his first draft. [...] Our normal policy is a first-draft script, a second-draft script, and dialogue from the second draft."[7] Wes turned in his second draft of *Roger Corman's Frankenstein* on October, 28, 1985 and it was a doozy.

His screenplay revolved around a young scientist named David Frank, who lives in a dystopian future Los Angeles where he conducts biological experiments for an Orwellian tyrant known as Big McDad. McDad's goal is to create the ultimate "McWarrior" to protect his shining New City on the hill, but the scientist suffers from a guilty conscience and decides to secretly remove his research from the despot's lab. A super-soldier named Captain Mars pursues him into the slums of Old Venice (Wes's own mid-80s stomping ground), then into the Hollywood hills, which are inhabited by political

UNP

SECOND DRAFT

10-28-85

ROGER CORMAN'S
FRANKENSTEIN

a screenplay
by

Wes Craven

rebels. There, David teams up with a rebel activist named Jessica, who helps him bring his Creature to life, and learns that David Frank is a biological descendant of Baron Victor Frankenstein.

David's Creature emerges from a "portable womb" and grows to adult size in a matter of hours, then declares war on his intended nemesis. After a series of elaborate car chases, helicopter chases, military bloodbaths, and an encounter with mutant "hypergators" (an embellishment of the urban legend about pet alligators in the sewers), the screen story culminates with a ritualistic gladiator fight between Mars and the Creature. This clash of the testosterone titans leaves only the latter standing. In a sudden twist, however, the Creature pledges his allegiance to Big McDad. The tyrant explains that he spiked David's secret monster-making formula to guarantee this outcome.

Next, David learns that McDad is actually an AI entity running a cybernetic civilization beneath the façade of his New City, and now he has transformed David's Creature into a "machine-man" with no human impulses or moral code. Using old-fashioned human ingenuity, David and Jessica manage to escape and sabotage the fleshy-pink mother brain of the machine city, then decapitate David's Creature. The October 28 script concludes with an alternate ending in which the heroes witness the collapse of the machine city from afar, then do battle with the Creature one more time on the beaches of Old Venice, beneath a sky full of 4th of July fireworks.

In short, Wes's version of *Roger Corman's Frankenstein* is an action-packed assault on the senses with a hearty dash of liberal politics thrown into the mix. Despite some obvious similarities to *The Hills Have Eyes* and a scene that expresses the writer's conviction that violence only begets more violence, the script seems like a stronger expression of Corman's storytelling sensibilities than Craven's— and perhaps an even stronger expression of director Paul Bartel's sensibilities. It's closer to Bartel's *Death Race 2000* than to Mary Shelley's *Frankenstein*.

The screen story for *Deadly Friend* also gravitated away from its source of inspiration in Mary Shelley's novel *Frankenstein*. Bruce Joel Rubin submitted his initial story treatment to Wes Craven and Bob Sherman in May 1985, followed by a first draft screenplay on July 19 and a second draft on October 28 (the same day Wes turned in his second draft of *Roger Corman's Frankenstein*).

The director's earliest notes on the screen story reflected concerns about the ages of the two protagonists. If too young, he suggested, casting / production would become problematic; if too old, the story would veer into the realm of overt exploitation. He also expressed concern about the novel's description of the revived female protagonist, believing that it would be difficult for viewers to sympathize with a rotting corpse, while also acknowledging that she could not simply retain her human appearance. In general, Rubin's drafts softened the story, turning the nerdy male protagonist into an older, more relatable boy genius in a chaste romance with an older but still naïve/innocent girl next door. When the girl dies tragically at the hands of an abusive father, he implants a robot brain into her body with predictably monstrous results. The revised tale focuses less on horror than on the tragic romance.

In spite the inherent darkness of the story, Rubin says he was trying to emulate the lighter tone of contemporary blockbusters like *E.T.* and *Gremlins*, explaining, "I didn't like a lot of the tropes in the novel. My instinct was to get away from the [Frankenstein] clichés, and Bob and Wes liked that I had a different take on the story. None of that would have gone forward without Wes's blessing. My impression at that point was that he was trying to get out of the horror genre. He wanted to make something that had more basis in character and the sort of emotional underpinnings that he had not had in his other films."[8] In fact, around the same time Rubin was finishing the script, Wes was directing *Casebusters*, a family-friendly drama for Disney. The short feature, about a pair of mischievous children who solve a small-town crime, would eventually air on ABC's *Disney Sunday Movie*, giving the director his broadest audience yet. To Wes, it was an extension of the freedom he'd experienced on *The Twilight Zone*, another welcome opportunity to work outside of the horror genre.[9]

When he returned to the *Deadly Friend* script at the end of 1985, Wes clarified plot points and modified action with the goal of making "an unexpectedly tender movie" about "romantic obsession."[10] When filming began in January 1986, it was a celebratory moment. Wes was shooting his first major studio movie on the promised land of the Warner Bros. backlot, with an office two doors down from legendary filmmaker Sydney Pollack. Bruce Joel Rubin shared Wes's sense of adventure, and was grateful that Wes allowed him and his

Top: A Wes Craven romance?: Samantha (Kristy Swanson) and
Paul (Michael Labyorteaux) meet cute in *Deadly Friend*
Bottom: Wes Craven directs Kristy Swanson in *Deadly Friend*
(Warner Bros., 1986)

family to be part of the production. "The backlot at Warner Bros. was twenty minutes from our house, and every evening we would pack the kids in the car and drive to the studio to watch them shoot. Usually when you're the writer, you don't get invited to the set. In this case, [my sons] Josh and Ari became like the set mascots. It was very inclusive and very special, and made me feel like part of the Hollywood studio system. That was a gift from Wes."

Unfortunately, *Deadly Friend* marked the beginning of a nightmarish year for Wes. In early May, the brass at Warner Bros. called for reshoots—to bring the film in line with the director's reputation as a horror filmmaker. Wes remembered how the reaction of a single test screening had transformed the film: "They got in a heavy metal, hard-core audience who had been told they were going to see a 'Wes Craven Film.' So this horror audience was totally pissed off that there wasn't more blood and guts." The scene that tested highest in the screening was a nightmare sequence added to the script during principal photography. As a result, the studio asked the filmmaker to write and shoot more "gory stuff" to splice into the film. Wes reluctantly complied, creating two new murder set pieces and two more gruesome dream sequences.[11]

The resulting film was a Frankenstein's monster of mish-mashed story beats, tones, and genres. Wes ultimately dismissed it as one of his worst films. In a Spring 1987 issue of *The Horror Show* magazine, he provided his own scathing review of *Deadly Friend*, declaring that "Wes Craven should stick to his own or 'A' material," "he should never do another film with over two (2) producers," and "he should have in his contract from day one that no producer, studio or advertising department shall have the right to tack some bullshit ending scare/ sequel hook onto his movie."[12]

Wes stipulated that *Deadly Friend* did not belong to the hallucinatory "rubber reality" subgenre he had created with *A Nightmare on Elm Street*, and expressed concern that other filmmakers were capitalizing on his genre-expanding idea while he was preoccupied with a pair of doomed Frankenstein monsters. In late February, Sean Cunningham and Steve Miner delivered their own mind-bending horror film, *House*, into theaters. Although that film has more in common with Sam Raimi's directorial debut *The Evil Dead* than it did with *A Nightmare on Elm Street*, Wes was quick to identify *House* as an example of the "new direction" of horror that he'd inspired.[13]

Meanwhile, he tried to set up his next rubber reality film—about a town where people's childhood fears come alive. Based on a novel by John Wooley and Ron Wolfe, *Old Fears* could have been an interesting followup to *Elm Street* but the project never got past the development stage. In the meantime, Wes hovered around several other genre films in development—including *Haunted*, a romantic comedy "about a guy, a girl and a ghost," written by Tom Ropelewski for Highgate Productions; *Beetlejuice* for The Geffen Company; *Superman 4* for the Cannon Group; and *Batman* for the Guber-Peters Company.[14] He was also approached by New Line Cinema to write the second sequel to *A Nightmare on Elm Street*.

Wes had publicly expressed his misgivings about David Chaskin's script for *A Nightmare Elm Street Part 2*, saying the screenwriter shouldn't have blurred the line between the film's villain and its nominal hero, as it left the film with "no philosophical thread."[15] Nevertheless, *Freddy's Revenge* made more money at the domestic box office than its predecessor, guaranteeing a third outing for the Springwood Slasher. This time, Wes chose to participate in the development process so that he could have some influence on the evolution of his creation. In *Part 2*, the filmmakers emphasized humor, hoping to leaven what director Jack Sholder called the "very dark, very oppressive, very serious" vision of the original film.[16] Producer Bob Shaye reportedly wanted to retain the lighter touch in *Part 3* but Wes was determined to restore Freddy's "seriousness." He said, "I felt that with *2*, they immediately threw all the important issues out the window and made it a series of strange, freaky events and the same old raunchy teenagers. I tried to wrestle it back with *3*."[17]

Wes decided to bring back Nancy Thompson and give her some new allies in the battle against Freddy, rationalizing that this would amplify the theme of his original story. He explained, "The first one was 'look what you can do by yourself against evil,' and the third was [about] what that power within yourself can be if it's combined with other people who have similar power."[18] Unfortunately, due to his obligations on *Deadly Friend*, he was unable to write the script on his own. Much as he had turned to Bruce Joel Rubin on *Deadly Friend*, he sought a new writing partner for *Elm Street 3*.

Wes approached Bruce Wagner after reading Wagner's unproduced screenplay *They Sleep by Night*, which Wagner describes as "an incredibly abstract script that was sort of like a Douglas Sirk meets August Strindberg family drama." He adds, "It was something that would've been appalling or irrelevant to anyone else, but this is how Wes worked. He was kind of a dowser." He and Wes shared an interest in creating stories that would transcend genre and formula. "Wes was immensely curious about the world and all the components of the world, the apparatus of the world. He was also bold and generous. If you marry bold and generous to curious, you have a variant of what it means to be spiritual. Wes was not a cynic, and that's another aspect of what it means to be spiritual. There are hardcore definitions of what it means to be spiritual. For example: one meditates, so one is more spiritual than he or she who does not. Those are false definitions; they're inherited definitions of what it means to be spiritual. Wes was completely open. What he did, with Bruce Rubin and myself, was he exercised that inherent generosity and boldness of spirit. What we wanted to do is to come from an unconscious place. That's what thrilled Wes—the symmetry and the anarchy of the unconscious. As long as that is authentic, then you have all the things that [spiritual teachers talk about]: the collective unconscious, primal fears, mythological templates. Those are the things that interested Wes—that was our *lingua franca*—but we never discussed what we might explore in terms of Gurdjieff or spirituality or anything like that. We wanted to enter the world of the authentic fairy tale, which embodies all of those things that I mentioned."

Wes said the first draft of *A Nightmare on Elm Street 3: Dream Warriors* was inspired by contemporary media coverage of an "epidemic" of teenage suicide in middle-class America, which prompted President Ronald Reagan to designate June 1986 as "Youth Suicide Prevention Month." The president called on a coalition of "individuals, families, communities, churches, synagogues, private groups and government agencies" to "detect the early symptoms of suicidal tendencies and develop ways of helping those whose depression and despondency could lead to this terrible act." Reagan also offered a cursory diagnosis of the problem, saying, "We must continue to combat those tendencies and influences such as the 'drug culture' that preach despair."[19]

Wes, however, had his own ideas about the cause of the suicide epidemic and how to fight it. The goal of *Nightmare 3*, he said, was to show that the youth of America wasn't just being tormented by a drug or mental health epidemic, but by "a real perception of evil." He explained, "A real teenager committing suicide doesn't want to do it; he wants somebody to know what's going on inside him, so he can be understood and not seen as sick."[20] He cobbled together his own coalition—the Dream Warriors—to fight the problem at its source.

In a first draft script dated June 16, 1986, Nancy Thompson searches for her father while he simultaneously searches for the childhood home of Freddy Krueger. Only these two characters understand that the undead serial killer is the real cause of the rash of teenage suicides haunting America's heartland. While Lt. Donald Thompson plans to confront Freddy and end the epidemic, Nancy avoids Freddy by using an experimental dream-suppressing drug called Hypnocyl. The plan works until she meets Neil Guinness, a psychiatrist at a hospital where her fellow survivors are gathered. As she earns their trust, Nancy realizes that the others have not survived by running away from the boogeyman but by harnessing their individual dream powers and fighting back.

The concept of dream powers is a significant departure from *Nightmare 1*, in which Nancy had to pull Freddy out of the dream world to defeat him. In the script for *Nightmare 3*, she becomes a friend and mentor to the "dream warriors," helping them realize that they can control their dreams by becoming aware of their dreams *while they're dreaming*, and then leading them into battle on Freddy's turf. The new story was inspired by Wes's experiences with lucid dreaming, and by psychophysiologist Stephen LaBerge's scientific studies.

LaBerge began studying his own dreams in 1977 and by the early 1980s he had become one of the foremost researchers in the fast-growing field of oneirology, the scientific study of dreams. His 1985 book *Lucid Dreaming: The Power of Being Awake in Your Dreams and in Your Life* suggested that lucid dreaming is a learnable skill; that by making a disciplined effort to observe and remember dreams, it is possible for dreamers to consciously dictate the content of their dreams. Indeed, LaBerge encouraged dreamers to take control of their nightmares instead of running away. "When we 'escape' from a nightmare by awakening," he wrote, "we have not dealt with the problem of our fear or our frightening dream, but merely relieved the fear temporarily and repressed the fearful dream. Thus we are left with an unresolved conflict as well as negative and unhealthy feelings. On the other hand, staying with the nightmare and accepting its challenge, as lucidity makes possible, allows us to resolve the dream problem in a fashion that leaves us more healthy than before."[21]

It is easy to imagine Freddy Krueger gleefully mocking this psychobabble, but his would-be victims put LaBerge's idea to good use, suddenly realizing that they can fight Freddy with any weapon or ability they can imagine. LaBerge explains, "Lucid dreamers are often overjoyed to discover they can seemingly do anything they wish. They have, for instance, but to declare the law of gravity repealed, and they float. They can visit the Himalayas and climb the highest peak without ropes or guides; they can even explore the solar system without a space suit!"[22] In the June 16 script, the dream warriors—Kristen, Kincaid, Taryn, Joey, and Laredo ("Will" in the final film)—represent "the next generation of the fight," an "evolutionary leap" beyond Nancy's battle techniques in the first *Nightmare*. Each warrior is capable of doing the impossible. All possess superhuman strength, as well as the ability to materialize firebombs out of thin air. In addition, Kristen has the ability to summon other people into her dreams, enabling her to bring all the warriors to the same battlefield at the same time.

According to Lt. Thompson, Freddy's childhood house is a doorway between worlds, and by destroying the doorway they can destroy Freddy, so the dream warriors plan to visit Freddy's house in a dream and burn it to the ground. Despite their collective strength, however, the warriors suffer individual weaknesses stemming from unresolved feelings of guilt and frustration over real world problems—and Freddy knows how to target those weaknesses. He lures Taryn to her death by appearing in the guise of her guilt-inducing grandmother. He lures Joey to his death by exploiting his lust. He *almost* tricks Laredo by appearing as his dead brother… but Laredo wises up and competes with the shape-shifter on his own terms. The result is an imaginative wizard's duel, like something out of Disney's *The Sword in the Stone* (1963) or Roger Corman's *The Raven* (1963). Ultimately, Freddy wins, leaving only three warriors standing. The nightmare man then chases the survivors out of the dream, into waking reality, where Nancy and Kristen try to turn their backs on him. The ploy doesn't work as well as it did at the end of *A Nightmare on Elm Street*, but it buys them enough time to find Freddy's house in the real world and burn it, magically reducing Freddy to a screaming mutant baby.

Unfortunately, the June 16 script didn't pass muster with the execs at New Line Cinema, so Wes and Bruce Wagner delivered multiple revised drafts, one of which (perhaps the July 7 draft?) became the basis for Jeffrey Cooper's

1987 novelization of the film. Cooper's version places a greater emphasis on Kristen's story, beginning with her Freddy-assisted suicide attempt. It also eliminates the Lt. Thompson character and substitutes Nancy's childhood home (where the events of *Nightmare 1* took place) for Freddy's childhood home. The latter change seems to have prompted the creators to dream up a new origin story for Freddy. Cooper's novelization tells us that Nancy's house on Elm Street was once an experimental sanitarium for psychotic women, including a teenage girl who was raped "a thousand times" and subsequently gave birth to a "huge" child. According to local legend, the new mother accidentally knocked over a lamp, setting herself and her baby on fire. Although she died, nobody knows what happened to the baby—only that the patient's name was Amanda Krueger.[23]

The Cooper version also modifies the talents of the dream warriors. Instead of possessing unlimited powers, each character has a specific dream "gift"—similar to mutant abilities in the *X-Men* comics. Kristen, in addition to being able to summon people into her dreams, is an Olympics-worthy gymnast. Taryn can breathe fire. Laredo is a magician who works in "metal, rope and ectoplasm." Jennifer can make herself invisible. Joey, who is mute and frail in real life, is strong and virile in his dreams. Kincaid can float like a butterfly (and, given his size and strength, sting like a bee). All of these talents become apparent early in the story, before the dream warriors mount their united attack on Freddy, allowing them to collectively kick his ass. The nightmare man seems almost pathetically weak by comparison. Assuming the novelization closely mirrors Wes's final draft of the script, that could explain why the producers at New Line decided to bring in a new pair of writers.

In their revised script, screenwriters Chuck Russell and Frank Darabont focus more on the *vulnerabilities* of the dream warriors. One by one, Freddy exploits the weaknesses of his victims in a series of ingenious nightmare set-pieces. He turns amateur puppet-master Phillip into a gruesome life-size puppet, then drops him off the roof of a building. He gives aspiring actress Jennifer a literal "big break in TV." He seduces Joey by growing breasts and employing a very unpleasant French kissing technique. All of these sequences had appeared in an earlier draft by Craven and Wagner, but Freddy's tactics are clearer and cleverer in the shooting script and in the final film. Russell and

Darabont applied the same bravura approach to a pair of new set-pieces. In one, Freddy haunts Will (a paraplegic in real life) with a demonic wheelchair; in the other, he taunts Taryn (a recovering drug addict) with a gleaming set of narcotic-filled syringes.

In the end, only Neil Guinness can effectively combat Freddy by exploiting the dream master's own weakness. The ghost of Amanda Krueger— identified in the film as a nun who was raped hundreds of times and gave birth to the "bastard son of a hundred maniacs"—tells Neil that he has to bury Freddy's bones in hallowed ground. Director Chuck Russell has said it was his way of equating the Freddy Krueger mythology with "an old school vampire movie."[24] Like Dracula, he explained, Freddy is vulnerable to crosses and holy water. The solution is at odds with Wes Craven's original mythology, especially considering that one of the first things Freddy does in the original film is knock Nancy's crucifix off of her bedroom wall. In Wes's first draft of *Nightmare 3*, the writer re-stated Freddy's resistance to religious iconography by having Freddy crucify Kristen. In Cooper's novelization, Freddy first appears to Kristen as a red-eyed figured on a crucifix. In the filmed version of *Dream Warriors*, Freddy becomes a vampire.

Predictably, Wes wasn't happy with the bastardization of his mythology—nor with the way New Line Cinema treated him. Years later, he said that after he turned in his script, the film's producers never contacted him again. Adding insult to injury, the studio selected re-writer Chuck Russell—the man behind *Dreamscape*—to direct the film. It was one of many bitter pills Wes had to swallow in the spring and summer of 1986.

In late May, his Disney movie *Casebusters* aired on television. The audience response was lackluster and, according to the director, Disney exec Jeffrey Katzenberg subsequently told his colleagues that Wes "didn't know how to do comedy."[25] Perhaps as a result, Wes lost the opportunity to direct *Beetlejuice*.[26] The directorial reins went instead to filmmaker Tim Burton, who also landed the job to direct *Batman* for the Guber-Peters Company. Around the same time, Wes met with actor Christopher Reeve about the possibility of directing *Superman 4*, "only to discover that Reeve felt I couldn't handle a big picture."[27] In June, his talent agent Marvin Moss died suddenly. Then, in September, *Roger Corman's Frankenstein* was put on hold.

Rounding out a perfect streak of bad fortune, Mimi Craven filed for divorce. She says, "I hate to say this, but I think there was a part of Wes that didn't think he deserved to be happy. He still had a lot of guilt from [leaving] Bonnie and the kids. I think he put himself under a lot of pressure. Too much pressure in too many different areas. Something had to give—and I do blame a lot of it on myself, because I just wasn't mature enough to deal with it. I disappeared. First mentally, then physically. It's really quite sad, because I did love him."

In the midst of a divorce and a floundering career, Wes found time to direct one more episode of *The Twilight Zone* TV series, a Jungian tale of a Vietnam veteran struggling to integrate his dark half, titled "The Road Less Traveled." He also began brainstorming an original TV series for the Fox TV network called *Dreamstalker*. "It was based on a conversation I had with my editor," he remembered. "'Let's do a version of *The Thing* where a person is able to get into the body of another person, and you don't know who he is or who he is inside.'"[28] The original concept involved "some sort of deal with the devil" that would allow the undead killer to enter other people's bodies through "their electrical nervous system"—so "the killer would have been different every week."[29] The series would revolve around an unlikely psychic hero (a football player) who tracks the killer's movements in his dreams.

Before the TV project could get off the ground, Wes landed his next directing gig. With the help of Andrea Eastman, his new agent, he signed on to direct an ambitious feature film adaptation of Wade Davis's nonfiction book *The Serpent and the Rainbow*. Davis, a Harvard-educated ethnobotanist and cultural anthropologist, had traveled to Haiti in 1982 in search of a substance allegedly used in voodoo rituals to produce zombies. He found what he was looking for—a drug that induced a temporary death-like state. He also became enchanted by the people and the local culture. In his book, Davis wrote about "something in the air, something electric—a raw elemental energy I had never felt anywhere in the Americas."[30]

The book is divided into three parts. In the first part, Davis recounts an initial trip to Haiti during which he met a *houngan* (voodoo priest) named Marcel Pierre, collected a sample of the zombie poison, and also learned about cultural influences that, in combination with the drug, can produce "zombies." The second part of the book follows Davis back to Harvard, where he studied the chemical composition of the drug and contemplated his personal experience. In the third part, Davis returns to Haiti to retrieve an antidote to the poison, and learns more about "the magic" of the place and its people—including Herard Simon, former head of the Tonton Macoute, a military police force that used voodoo to prop up Haitian dictators François "Papa Doc" Duvalier and Jean-Claude "Baby Doc" Duvalier until 1986, when Baby Doc was ousted from power.

Ultimately, Davis's book is a narrative of one man's personal journey of discovery, which is how Hollywood filmmakers decided to re-tell it for the screen—with some embellishments, courtesy of screenwriter Richard Maxwell. In his 2007 book *The Elements of Persuasion*, Maxwell outlines a five-element storytelling model—passion, hero, antagonist, awareness, and transformation. Bringing his own passion to the project, Maxwell co-created the other four elements by modifying details from Davis's book. The hero who grounds the story in our reality is Wade Alan, a skeptical scientist who slowly becomes aware of the deeper reality of mind-body-spirit connections. The antagonist is Dargent Peytraud, a highly fictionalized version of Herard Simon. (In the first draft of the script, the writer actually used the name "Herard" for a different, more benevolent character—Herard Celine. Perhaps this was an attempt to avoid upsetting a real voodoo priest? Whatever the case, the benevolent character was eventually renamed Lucien Celine in the film.) Maxwell also added a love interest to the story, transforming Davis's real-life friend Rachel Beauvoir into a fictional Haitian psychologist named Rachelle Doyen, who initiates Wade Alan into the dream-like world of the love goddess Erzulie. Things get complicated as Wade realizes he has entered a love triangle with a flesh-and-blood woman and a goddess.

Maxwell's elements of "awareness" and "transformation" are more nebulous. The screenwriter defines the former as "literally the inspiration the hero has that lets him, or her, see the problem for what it is and take the right action." In the first draft of *Serpent*, Wade Alan experiences moments of inspiration that propel him toward a final confrontation with Peytraud. The first such moment is a fictionalized version of Wade Davis's actual encounter (many years earlier) with a black jaguar in the Amazon jungle. In the screenplay, the jaguar becomes a symbol of the hero's inner strength. It reappears in moments when the hero becomes aware of expanded reality, and finally empowers

Top: Peytraud (Zakes Mokae, left) and Gaston (Badja Djola) torture
Dennis Alan (Bill Pullman) in *Serpent and the Rainbow*
Bottom: A metaphysical romance: Marielle (Cathy Tyson) and Dennis Alan
(Bill Pullman) in *Serpent and the Rainbow* (Universal, 1987)

him to confront the antagonist. Maxwell believes that the final element—transformation—is "the element that needs the least explanation because it is the natural result of a well-told story. If you've taken care of the other elements, it just happens. Our heroes take action to overcome their problems, and they and the world around them changes."[31]

At the time *The Serpent and the Rainbow* screenplay was being written, a real-world story was unfolding. A February 1986 uprising against the repressive regime of Jean-Claude Duvalier and the Tonton Macoute empowered the people of Haiti to make their own future. Eventually, the filmmakers would incorporate that transformation into the fictional story, turning *The Serpent and the Rainbow* into two parallel narratives—the awakening of a heroic individual and an entire culture.

Wade Davis was not happy with the earliest attempts to adapt his book to the screen. He explained, "When Hollywood saw zombies and voodoo, they said *Night of the Living Dead*. They kept pushing that cliché into the early stages of the script and I kept going, 'Wait a minute, fellas.'" He was also unenthusiastic about Wes Craven helming the project, telling one interviewer he couldn't even finish watching *A Nightmare on Elm Street*.[32] Executive Producer David Ladd says, "Originally, we hadn't intended to go the direction that we ended up going. We imagined it as something more in the vein of Peter Weir's film *The Year of Living Dangerously*. We had a much more serious bent and I think that's what attracted Wes to the project. He kind of wanted to get away from horror as much as he could. And we did. But at that time, Wes was a name above the title. When he became attached, the financier was like, 'Ah! Wes Craven and Zombies!' Who could resist that combination? That's what marketing is all about."

When Ladd and his producing partner Rob Cohen hired Wes in 1986, he was hot off of the success of *A Nightmare on Elm Street*. The producers developed some misgivings, however, after viewing his followup film. Wes said, "They hated [*Deadly Friend*] and told me during a meeting that if I was seen to be delivering a work like that, they would fire me!"[33] He set out to prove himself by fusing everything he'd learned from making horror films "into a love story and a political drama, while exploring the hitherto unexamined voodoo religion and telling an adventure tale about one man's trip into the heart of darkness."[34] According to Ladd, simplifying complex ideas was one of Wes's major talents:

"He would set up a story that moved along in a rather sophisticated, intellectual way and then—boom! He'd hit you with something visceral. And off the wall! Like a snake coming out of someone's mouth. The things he would come up with—his thought patterns—were wild. I think that was his signature, in a way."

In December 1986, Wes went with Ladd, production manager Doug Claybourne, and author Wade Davis to scout potential filming locations in Mexico, Jamaica, El Salvador, Belize, Brazil, and finally Haiti. Once the filmmakers visited Cap-Haïtien on the northern coast of Haiti, they knew they'd found the right spot. Claybourne says, "Haiti seemed a great place to shoot but we didn't realize that nobody had shot a feature film there in thirty years, so there was no infrastructure whatsoever. We based the production out of the Dominican Republic, in Santo Domingo, and the idea was to shoot the first week or so in Haiti, try to get as much of the flavor of the real location as we could, and then drop back to Santo Domingo where they had some feature film experience and more of the infrastructure and experienced people who had made films."

Making arrangements to film in Haiti is a story all its own. "There was a gal who worked with us—she was an American but she had grown up in Haiti and her mother had an import-export business in Port-au-Prince. The way we got in was we got a letter from this gal's mother to General [Henri] Namphy, who was running the country at that time. He agreed to meet us so we could get permission to film. Normally, getting into the country is a big deal but we just walked into this guy's office—Wes, myself, David Ladd, and this gal's mother. He had nothing on his desk except a gold or silver pen set and an outbox with nothing in it. We explained what we wanted to do, then he took a blank piece of paper and wrote us a letter, and said, 'This is your approval to shoot here.' We showed that handwritten letter to everyone we met. That was what got us into the country. It wasn't bribes or any of that other kind of stuff."

The filmmakers soon found themselves seduced by the mysteries of Haitian culture. Wes's personal accounts closely mirror mind-bending descriptions of the place and the people in Davis's book. "Their whole sense of reality is different, and that affected what they physically could do. One of the first times we location scouted, we went to this restaurant that featured a troupe that went into a trance when they danced. And something happened that I had to put into the movie. A woman who had gone into a trance came over to our table, picked up my glass—the glass that I had been drinking out of for the entire lunch—and ate it. Just bit off huge chunks of it and ate it right in front of me. And she was totally somebody else. She had been this kind of shy, demure woman, and now she was very aggressive and sexual. Everything about her had changed." Wes also said he "met a zombie" in a clinic outside of Port-au-Prince: a nineteen-year-old girl who "had been taken ill with a fever, died in about three days, was buried, and returned about twelve days later, wandering through a cane field."[35] Such experiences led him to the same conclusion Davis expressed in his writing (and which Wes had hinted at in *A Nightmare on Elm Street*): personal beliefs can transform physical reality.

After the initial trip to Haiti, Wes said he realized he had to revise the script to bring it "up to the level of spirituality, beauty, and passion that we saw."[36] The main differences between Richard Maxwell's August 12, 1986 draft and the February 12, 1987 shooting script are in the third act of the story, after Wade Alan (renamed Dennis Alan for the final film) returns from the grave. In the earlier draft, the antagonist Peytraud summons a powerful demon, then turns the hero into a zombie and puts him to work in the fields. This sequence embodies the sort of Hollywood clichés that Wade Davis wanted to avoid; the imagery is straight out of the 1932 voodoo film *White Zombie*. The scripted sequence ends with Wade Alan escaping captivity and rescuing Rachelle from Peytraud before the villain can sacrifice her to the demon. Peytraud then sends his army of zombies—along with a "demon dog"—after them. The heroes defeat the demon by releasing the enslaved souls of all the zombies Peytraud has created, causing Peytraud's body to burst into flames.

The third act of the February 12 shooting script incorporates the early 1986 political uprising into the climax of the story. Now the American hero's victory over Peytraud is linked to the Haitians' historic revolt against François Duvalier's culture of fear. The final battle between hero and antagonist takes place in the basement of the Tonton Macoute headquarters as it is being overrun by a mob of rebels. In the moment when the fictional hero overcomes his nemesis, the zombies and the citizens of Haiti also become liberated, transforming the narrative into a spiritual and political drama as well as a love story and a horror film.

Shortly before production began on March 9, 1987, the filmmakers secured the blessing of a real voodoo priest, who met the Americans wearing a pair of silver-plated handguns on his waist, and asked for some gold jewelry in exchange for a protection spell. Wes returned to L.A. to shop for gold necklaces in Beverly Hills.[37] Back in Haiti, the priest placed the jewelry on "an American doll [...] painted black," and announced, "You and your crew are now protected."[38]

"Everyone in Haiti had their hand out," says David Ladd. "They were wonderful people—absolutely wonderful people—but Haiti is a country that, even to this day, seems to suffer one disaster after another, and the people can never recover from it. 99% of the population were living in poverty and the other 1% were drug smugglers. You have to remember that Haiti was the bread basket of the world at one point, but because of the politics, things got so desperate there that people were burning their fruit trees to make charcoal—because their needs were so immediate, and it was easier to sell charcoal. I must reiterate, because everyone would say the same thing: We all fell in love with the Haitians—the people, not the politicians."

The cast and crew benefited from the presence of Wade Davis, who served as an advisor on the film. He remembers, "I was able to do some good during the very embryonic stages of the production, just by being there as a resource—talking about the book, talking about the way it really was."[39] According to Wes, the author's presence meant "we got into places no white guy except Wade has ever been in before."[40] Timing was critical; *Serpent* was filmed just one year after the overthrow of the Duvalier regime and a few months prior to the 1987 Haitian elections, which saw the assassination of two presidential candidates and the murders of at least two dozen voters. According to Wes, the tension in the air was palpable during those brief halcyon days in the spring of '87: "They were delighted that somebody was there from America to give them jobs, but on the other hand they could very quickly snap into a fury if they thought you were disrespecting them."[41] Anything could happen, and—according to many behind-the-scenes accounts—plenty did. Doug Claybourne reflects, "Part of the way I learned filmmaking from Francis Coppola [while working as a producer's assistant on *Apocalypse Now*] was you go into the place and you soak up all the atmosphere of what's going on. That's part of getting people into the spirit of the film. That was the way I scheduled things: you go into the heart of darkness and you soak up all the local culture you can and that plays into the performances. So we were doing that."

On the eve of the first day of filming, the crew members were rousted from their beds and "taken to this field where all kinds of drinking and dancing and wild music was going on." At a certain point, Wes said, a pig was slaughtered in front of them and they were encouraged to drink the blood. The dismayed Americans politely declined and the festivities continued apace. "We were lucky because, based on what we had already learned about voodoo, you can be in serious trouble if you don't drink it."[42]

Several members of the cast and crew had profoundly unnerving experiences during the shoot. Reportedly, the film's star Bill Pullman (who played Dennis Alan) became rattled by a vivid hallucination of a cow with television screens for eyes. In 2022, he added, "I had a lot of [hallucination] sequences to do with traveling really quickly over the surface of Africa, and moving towards a gathering of people out in the middle of nowhere, and I realized there was a convocation of people of all skin tones and colors, and that there was this steppe with an oration. That was an experience where I was so disturbed, I canceled the rehearsals the next day. They said, 'What's the matter with you?' I didn't want to talk about it."[43]

Another actor visited a historic mountain fort, possibly Citadelle Laferrière, and saw "somebody from the slave revolution against the French riding in on a white horse, telling him, 'You and all your people will die!'"[44] And Brent Jennings (who played *houngan* Louis Mozart in the film) witnessed a Vodoun priest becoming possessed and turning violent. According to Wade Davis, "[The priest] went crazy. He threw a chair into the brand new production vehicle, heaved a table onto the roof and hurled a machete past my head so hard it broke in half when it hit the wall."[45]

Perhaps the most harrowing experience was screenwriter Richard Maxwell's encounter with another Vodoun priest. Wes remembered, "Richard went down and interviewed this guy, and Richard, who was interested in all sorts of spiritual things, said 'I'd love to be indoctrinated into voodoo sometime.' And the guy, who was a very sly guy, said, 'Well, then you will be.' So somehow he must have dosed Richard in that visit, because Richard came back and just basically went mad in the course of a week. He locked himself in his room; he stopped wearing clothes; he was telling us he was writing but he couldn't concentrate. And finally, the day before we started shooting—actually the morning we started shooting—I woke up, like, five in the morning. Somebody was knocking on the door of my room. […] I opened the door and here's Richard, dazed and haggard, unshaven. I looked down and all around his feet are cigarette butts. He'd been there all night. He said, 'I just want to wish you good luck because Vodouns and the producers are in league against me and they're gonna kill me.' And he was literally taken to a plane, flown from where we were, way out in the boondocks, to Port-au-Prince and then put on an airplane. His wife met the plane in Miami [and] took him back to Los Angeles. And four days later he woke up, lucid, and the last thing he remembered was that guy saying, 'Well, then you will be.'"[46]

During the first half of production, the filmmakers managed to capture the beauty of the local culture in an astonishing religious pilgrimage to the Sans-Souci Palace in Milot. The director proudly called the sequence his "David Lean moment," but said his desire to create an epic visual tableau precipitated a rude awakening: "That was a three-day shoot. On the first day, I said, 'How much are we paying extras?' I was told, 'Twenty-five cents a day.' I said, 'Are you kidding?' Let's get a thousand extras.' So we got a thousand extras for the second night. Then on the third night we got to the set and people were still coming. They were from villages throughout the country and they had walked all night and they all wanted to be employed. And they all wanted to be paid! At the same time, there were these kind-of socialist provocateurs that were organizing them. Telling them they're being exploited by the white people. So we had to double their wages twice that night. And then they asked for more than we could pay them. They picked up stones and threatened to kill us. Just like that. In the middle of the night, we were surrounded by two thousand angry people that are picking up stones and saying, 'We are going to kill you.'"

According to David Ladd, "We had hired 2,000 people at $2 or $3 per day. Then 3,000 people showed up. The next day, they wanted $5 a day. I had to stand on the top of a bus and negotiate with these people. I suddenly looked down and saw that every one of them had a rock in their hand. So I said, 'Fine, $5, no problem.' The next day, they wanted $10. I didn't even bat an eye. 'Fine, $10.' At that point, as they were being paid in cash, they started storming the [production

Wes Craven's "David Lean moment" in *Serpent and the Rainbow*
(Universal, 1987)

facility]. Doug Claybourne's eyes were going around in circles. He said to me, 'Listen, we've got to get out of here.'"

After paying the extras, Claybourne made an executive decision: "The last day of the shoot [in Haiti] was supposed to be at this very religious waterfall [Saut-d'Eau], a very spiritual place for the Haitians. It was a short shoot but it would have been a two-hour drive to get there, then you have to unload, shoot for an hour or two, then drive two or three hours back in order to make a 12-hour day. I didn't want to put the crew in a situation where they would get waylaid and I couldn't get them out. I was so nervous that I called the studio executives who were financing the film and said, 'I want to get us out of here a day early. We'll find a place to shoot [the waterfall sequence] in the Dominican Republic. I'm not going to tell anybody we're leaving. I'll just tell the crew to pack up while we're shooting the night scenes at the airport.' I then asked Wes, 'Can you get us done in ten or eleven hours, so we're not staying too late?' He said yeah I can do that. Unfortunately, he didn't know [what I was planning] so he shot for twelve hours. Then I had everybody waiting at the airport but the guys that are supposed to stamp our travel visas had gone home. Thankfully, I still had several thousand dollars in hundred dollar bills. I sent my production accountant to go get them and tell them they would get a couple hundred dollars each if they came back to the airport and signed us out. So we got out of the country safely."

From that point on, the production was based in Santo Domingo in the Dominican Republic. Wes Craven's son Jonathan—a recent graduate of Northwestern University with a strong interest in documentary filmmaking— joined the crew. He remembers "They didn't have enough people and they had to build Haitian villages for scenes that were supposed to have been shot in Haiti. I remember meeting the art department people and they were definitely my people. They were the *crazy* people, so I was like yeah, I'll go with them. I was assigned to be the on-set dresser, which is a job that usually goes to somebody with more experience. That was amazing because I got to stand right next to the camera during filming. The director of photography would say, 'Look through the lens. We're supposed to be in a jungle, but do you see that parking lot back there? You need to get a bunch of trees and cover that up.' So I would show up to set every day with two machetes strapped to my body. They would give me $50 or $100 worth of petty cash—which was like a million dollars in the Dominican—and I would hire four or five local guys, so we could go out and move things around and hide the parking lot to make it look like the jungle."

Filming in local graveyards was especially surreal: "The props department had an enormous truck with huge bags full of human skulls and bones. We had some plastic ones but it was easier in the Dominican Republic to get human bones than it was to get fake stuff—so when you see stacks of human bones in the movie, they are actually human bones. We had all these cemetery scenes and the Haitian cemeteries were very different from the Dominican ones so we had to dress them. John Lindley, the director of photography, would say, 'We're going to put a [camera] dolly track here, so I need you to move that headstone.' We're in a small village in the Dominican Republic at night and there's hundreds of villagers watching, and here I am taking out headstones, moving them around. There were human bones poking out of the ground, so I'd have to either move them or tamp them down and re-bury them so the dolly track could go on top. Then I would dress the rest of the set with human bones from the truck. I can still remember the smell of the bones, because we were constantly burning candles on top of them. After sixteen hours, the candles would melt down and start burning the bones, so the air had this weird smell of human remains—not burning flesh, but still unsettling."

Filming in the Dominican Republic came with its own challenges, but the filmmakers managed to get the footage they needed. When shooting wrapped on May 12, 1987, not everyone went home. Producer Rob Cohen recalled, "One of our art directors got so caught up in the crazy things in the air that he met a woman down there and was married, in a voodoo ceremony by a voodoo priest."[47] According to David Ladd, the same crew member was "cursed" when he decided to return to the U.S. Soon after, he suffered a near-fatal motorcycle accident. "Down to the key grips, no one could get this film and this experience out of their system. It was bizarre. I've been involved in lot of movies and I've never had another experience like that." When Wes returned to California, his sister-in-law Donna Craven thought he was going to die. "He had fevers on and off for six months after that shoot."

In the fall of 1987, while ushering the film through post-production, Wes wrote a pair of long letters to his daughter Jessica, updating her on the progress of his latest project and confiding in her about some profound changes in his life. On October 17, he said that four months in the editing room had produced a rough cut of *Serpent* that was screened for a small group of executives at Universal Pictures. The response was enthusiastic enough to prompt a slight budget increase and a teaser trailer, which would premiere ahead of John Carpenter's new film, *Prince of Darkness*.

Next, Universal orchestrated a series of sneak previews. Some audience members apparently complained about the "boring political scenes," which prompted re-shoots in early December and significantly altered the third act of the film. In a December 10 letter, Wes described a new scene involving a prolonged physical and psychic battle between Dennis Alan and Dargent Peytraud, featuring particularly graphic horror-movie imagery. Doug Claybourne reflects, "It was the romance and the true story [of Wade Davis's experience in Haiti] that we were all drawn to. It was only Universal that wanted a 'Wes Craven horror movie.' They had to have that."

The forced ending probably influenced Wes's mood going into the holiday season. On December 10, he confessed he was experiencing Christmas Blues while confronting several milestones in his life. As he finished his latest film, he was negotiating a protracted divorce from Mimi, the second such perceived failure in his life, and feeling his mortality. On the verge of his 50th birthday, he wondered how many films he had left in him and whether he'd ever write a "great book." He also suggested he was feeling the first pangs of "senility" and a fear of dying alone. But the letter was not all doom and gloom. At the end, he added, "Admitting Middle Age makes me laugh a little less, but what laughter there is is more heartfelt. I know I have to start facing the Big Ending. I know life is truly very short. But I also believe it's very wide…" In a contemporary interview about *The Serpent and the Rainbow*, he added, "Haiti really mellowed me out. I almost died down there, and I experienced a lot of strange things. So when I came through it all not only alive but healthy, I decided to begin taking my life a little bit easier."[48]

The Serpent and the Rainbow arrived in theaters on February 5, 1988, and Wes was acutely aware that the film's success or failure would determine his future. Although he hoped critics would review the film as a sophisticated "political thriller," and that his peers would acknowledge his ability to tackle subject matter that was "more adult and complex" than the usual horror film, *The Serpent and the Rainbow* did not transform his career in the way he hoped.[49] It was a modest box office success and the shadow of Freddy Krueger continued to loom large over Daddy Craven.

Once again, New Line's Bob Shaye and producer Sara Risher approached Wes about writing or directing a new sequel to his most famous work. In 1989, Wes said, "New Line always calls me when they're about to start a new one and asks me if I want to direct it. Usually I'm involved in another film and they don't want to offer any money anyway. They ask me if I have any ideas for a script and we usually have a conversation around that. Then they'll go off and get someone who'll write it for $500."[50] According to Risher, Wes pitched an idea for *A Nightmare on Elm Street Part 4*, which she rejected. "His idea was illogical. It was about time travel within dreams that broke all the rules of dreams. We decided not to go with that."[51]

Eventually, a first draft was written by William Kotzwinkle, author of the novel *The Fan Man*. When New Line execs showed it to Wes, he praised Kotzwinkle as a writer, but said he did not want to get involved with a story he hadn't originated.[52] Kotzwinkle depicted Freddy Krueger as an increasingly powerful "Dream Master," empowered by all the souls he has gathered over the years. New Line fused that concept with neophyte screenwriter Brian Helgeland's idea to introduce a new heroine who similarly absorbs the strengths of her murdered friends, setting up a climactic battle between the two dream masters. As New Line went into production on their latest sequel, Wes began work on his own new nightmare.

Wes Craven in 1990
(courtesy Donna Craven)

CHAPTER NINE

THE EXORCISM OF HORACE PINKER
(1988 - 1992)

"Mainly we are dealing with a profoundly degenerate world, a living web of foulness, greed and treachery... which is also the biggest real business around and impossible to ignore. You can't get away from TV. It is everywhere."

- Hunter S. Thompson, *Generation of Swine:*
Tales of Shame and Degradation in the 80s (1988)

As Freddy Krueger made a leap from the big screen to the small screen, becoming the host of his own syndicated TV series *Freddy's Nightmares* (1988-1990), Wes Craven became increasingly frustrated about his lack of participation—both creative and financial—in his famous creation's extended life. His agent Andrea Eastman, aware of this, introduced Wes to producer Shep Gordon, whose distribution company Alive Films had recently made a multi-film compact with director John Carpenter.

As a producer, Gordon trusted the "vision of the artist" instead of forcing a filmmaker into a committee-oriented process that produces "a homogenized film" without a clear and unique "point of view."[1] Carpenter loved the approach, saying, "I only submit basic concepts to them, in a short paragraph. For *Prince of Darkness*, it was something like: 'The Devil is buried under a Los Angeles church, and graduate students come to fight him.' If they approve the concept, then I deliver them a print. I can't ask for more than that."[2] Gordon confirms, "He didn't even have to give me a title. There were only two things I asked for. Number one, they had to be genre pictures. Number two, the directors had to put their names above the title."

Wes leapt at the same opportunity, saying, "This is the way films should be made—with enlightened producers and a relaxed atmosphere. You do it on a modest budget [under $4 million], so you're not risking large sums, and at the same time you're given freedom." Under the circumstances, he added, a filmmaker has a real opportunity to be an *auteur*: "You can really look deep within yourself and say, 'What would I really like to put into this picture that will make it unique and true to my own vision?'"[3]

Wes had hoped to break out of the horror genre. He'd always wanted to have a career like that of Roman Polanski, who was able to succeed both in and out of the horror genre. Although Polanski had risen to fame on the success of *Rosemary's Baby* (1968), he also adapted Shakespeare (*Macbeth*, 1971) and Thomas Hardy (*Tess*, 1979), and made comedies, thrillers, and adventure movies. In contrast, Wes felt like he was being treated as a one-trick pony. He wanted critics to see the entire person behind his films, instead of dismissing him as the Charles Manson of cinema. With that in mind, he decided to make "a concerted effort" to direct a non-horror film.[4] At the same time, he resolved to "create another Freddy," one that he could control.[5]

In February 1988, Wes formally established his own production company—a shingle under the roof of Alive Films and its distribution partner Universal Pictures—and appointed his 25-year-old assistant Marianne Maddalena Director of Development. She remembers how their business relationship evolved: "I worked for Harold Robbins, a best-selling author of pulp fiction. I told him, 'I want to be a film producer,' and he gave me a job at his film company in L.A. I worked there for a month, then I got a job at an exclusive little talent agency that represented Dean Martin, Gene Kelly, Alfred Hitchcock, Michael Jackson, David Niven, Shirley MacLaine. I worked for an agent named Mort Viner, who was friends with Bob Sherman and Bob brought me in to meet with Wes on *Deadly Friend*. Wes said, 'What do you want to do,' and I said, 'I want to be a producer.' So he hired me as his assistant, and I learned everything about becoming a producer because Wes would take me to every meeting—which pissed everybody off, because assistants never go to every meeting. But Wes was very shy and he liked having me in the room."

Wes would eventually promote Marianne to the role of Producer, Vice President of his production company (in 1990), then President (in 1994), solidifying a successful business partnership. In the early 90s, he explained the alliance to John Russo: "It's very important to anybody who wants to make a career doing movies to remember that it is the film *business*. So, you have a love of the creative process; you still have to take care of the business end or find someone who will do that with you. I've found that my most successful films have been ones where I was allied with someone who had a good business sense and a real strong social sense."[6]

Many who worked for Wes Craven Films remember the duo's ideal rapport, each complementing the other. Wes, who suffered from prosopagnosia—a neurological condition associated with the struggle to recognize faces—could be awkward in social settings. At times, he was painfully shy. He could also appear insensitive to people's feelings. Marianne was socially confident, habitually outgoing, and a morale-booster. She credits their successful partnership to one guiding principle: "We were working all the time, so we decided we're just going to have fun when we're working. And we're only going to hire people that we like. And we're going to have a lot of parties."[7]

The initial development slate at Wes Craven Films included three films: a second sequel to *The Hills Have Eyes*, a "romantic telefilm" titled *The Gravity of Stars*, and another feature (to be written and directed by Robby Benson) titled *Confessional*.[7] Wes and fellow rights-holder Peter Locke hired Bruce Wagner to write the first draft of *Hills 3*, about a group of scientists who discover a new type of mutant in outer space.[8] Wagner also wrote *The Gravity of Stars*, which he remembers as a "PG-13 rated version of [the 2014 film] *Maps to the Stars*," about "a love affair between a handsome, entitled boy and a woman whose face had been mutilated by a fire." Unfortunately, both projects became mired in development hell when the Writer's Guild of America declared a writer's strike on March 7, 1988. The strike lasted eight months, costing the new production company a significant amount of time, money, and momentum.[9]

Luckily, Wes had a spec script of his own that he was able to move forward. After considering the project for more than a year, Fox TV had passed on *Dreamstalker*, Wes's pilot script about a body-hopping alien entity. Wes then decided to use it as the template for a "new Freddy Krueger" film that he could pitch to Shep Gordon. Unfortunately, it seems *Dreamstalker* also inspired other contemporary film projects. On Halloween weekend in 1987, New Line Cinema released *The Hidden*, a sci-fi feature about a body-hopping alien set loose on the streets of Los Angeles, directed by Jack Sholder, who had helmed *A Nightmare on Elm Street Part 2*. Wes felt that New Line had cheated him again, and didn't hesitate to say so in promotional interviews. In addition, Sean Cunningham was working on a film about an executed serial killer who torments his captor from beyond the grave. That story (eventually realized as *The Horror Show*, a.k.a. *House III*) had enough similarities to *Dreamstalker* to prompt a confrontation between the two old friends. Wes said, "I had long conversations with Sean, and he claimed that his idea had been around a long time. He was not able to produce registered copies of the idea and at a certain point I left it at that. He gave me his word that he would never steal from me, and I believe him."[10]

Ultimately, Wes decided to turn *Dreamstalker* into the first and second acts of a feature film, then add a completely new third act. While looking for inspiration, he stumbled upon a passage in a scientific periodical stating that dreamers and TV viewers experience nearly identical brainwave activity.[11] Immediately, Wes recognized a parallel to Freddy's dream world. His new dreamstalker, an occult-obsessed television repairman named Horace Pinker, would become an evil entity that could not only leap from one human body to another but could also inhabit the electromagnetic spectrum and thereby travel into the homes and heads of every TV-watching person in America. Wes planned to make Horace Pinker "so strong that Freddy will be forced into retirement."[12]

In September 1988, he completed a fourth draft of his new script. The cover page identified it as *Alive Project #1*, but it would eventually become known as *No More Mr. Nice Guy*, and finally *Shocker*. Marianne Maddalena easily got a green light from Alive Films. "I went in and said to Shep Gordon, '*Shocker.*' He said, 'Chakra? Yeah, I like it.' Because he was a big rock 'n roll guy." (Gordon has managed shock rocker Alice Cooper—as well as many other A-list musicians—since 1968.)

In Wes's story, a complacent 20-year-old college student named Jonathan Anderson suffers a concussion at football practice and wakes up with psychic powers. That same night, his stepmother and step-siblings are murdered by a serial killer known as "the Midnight Slasher." Jonathan dreams of the murders, then leads his stepfather, police lieutenant Don Parker, to the killer. In the filmed version of *Shocker*, Horace Pinker reveals that he is Jonathan's biological father—a twist that explains the psychic connection between them, and frames the young hero's journey as an effort to escape his bad dad's terrifying shadow. In the final act of the September 1988 script, Jonathan pulls Horace Pinker out of the TV world into the real world, and asserts his independence by saying, "You know who my father is? Me. I'm responsible for who I am. No one else."

Wes suggested *Shocker* "was kind of the flip side of *A Nightmare on Elm Street*, where you saw Nancy trying to sort out the relationship with her parents and especially her mother." In the same breath, he noted that he had named the hero of *Shocker* after his biological son, highlighting the personal nature of the story's theme of generational conflict. "This whole film, for me, was kind of an exorcism of my own issues with my father."[13] Like *A Nightmare on Elm Street*, *Shocker* is about confronting inherited sins and taking control of one's own life.

Top: Horace Pinker (Mitch Pileggi) gets fried, but he's not done yet, in *Shocker*
Bottom: Lt. Parker (Michael Murphy) and son Jonathan (Jonathan Berg) in *Shocker*
(Alive Films, 1989)

According to Wes, "One of the most important questions for human beings in general [is] whether or not we can stop doing what we've been doing for so long that's in the area of destruction and murder and mayhem, and go in a different direction." Obviously, Wes's father was not a murderer, and neither was Wes—but, for someone raised in a fundamentalist church, thought crimes can be matters of life and death. Well into the 1980s, Wes felt guilty for leaving his first wife and two children, perhaps viewing his role in their lives as a partially "destructive" one.

As for what specific "sins" Wes might have wanted to exorcise, Jonathan Craven tells a story that echoes a story his father once told. "I remember accidentally breaking a mirror when I was four or five years old, and he screamed at me: 'Stupid!' I never forgot that." The father's reaction is hardly sinful behavior, but the son suggests Wes couldn't forgive himself. "I've had my own regrettable moments as a father, but I try to address it afterward. I say to my son, 'Hey, what I did there, I'm not proud of it.' 'I didn't mean to…' Or 'I was mad about something else.' Or 'Daddy sometimes makes mistakes.' Whatever it is, I own up to those things. Wes carried a lot of guilt but he would never own it in that way. He did things to try to make up for his mistakes but the only way he could ever talk about it was in a big-picture way. He'd say, 'I just fucked it all up.' He made the problem so big in his head that it became unfixable. He made the sin, on his part, so big that I think he felt like the emotional payment he would have to make by owning it was bigger than he could ever possibly make."

When *Shocker* went into production in April 1989, Wes cast his son Jonathan in the film as an innocent passerby who gets shot in the back by Horace Pinker. The victim dies screaming "I didn't do anything!" Because Wes was so carefully attuned to his own subconscious thoughts and impulses, he must have been aware of the dark irony of this casting decision. Years later, he acknowledged that *Shocker* wasn't just about his issues with his father, but also an expression of anxieties related to his own success and failures as a parent, wanting to be "a better father to my son than perhaps my father was to me."[14]

By helping Jonathan gain a foothold in the film industry, he was no doubt trying to be a supportive father—giving his son opportunities that he himself had fought and sacrificed for—but he was also casting a big shadow. Jonathan was constantly trying to prove himself worthy. "On *Serpent and the*

The Cravens: Jessica, Wes and Jonathan, 1988
(courtesy Donna Craven)

Rainbow, I ran my ass off, all day long, and I remember the electricians looking at me and saying, 'Dude, I have never seen anybody work so hard in the art department. Plus, a director's kid?' I think they were making fun of me, but I remember feeling proud about that." Nevertheless, from day one, Jonathan felt the sting of his father's criticism. "Unfortunately, I was taking my [college] finals while they were shooting in Haiti. As soon as I got through them, I got on a plane. When I joined the crew [in the Dominican Republic], I was so exhausted that I immediately threw my back out. I remember saying, 'I'm sorry but I literally can't walk.' And I remember dad being mad at me. He said, 'That's so like you.' That was the weird thing about him. He could be so cool and so kind, but somehow it also seemed like he was always building a case against me."

In his 1976 journal, Wes wrote that he had discarded (or thought he had discarded) the belief that "I'll be able to realize everything in my son that I haven't realized in myself." Inevitably, however, he had high expectations for Jonathan. Perhaps Wes secretly wanted Jonathan to declare his independence—and maybe even denounce his father. Jonathan remembers, "One time, we were sitting at dad's dining room table, and he said, 'I feel like one of these days you're just going to come up here and kill me.' I didn't even know what to say to that."

Was Wes remembering his earliest primal screams, perhaps projecting his own inner life onto his son? If so, he maybe hoped that Jonathan would not be too much like his old man. In *Shocker*, that's precisely the conflict that fictional Jonathan navigates while trying to "exorcise" the influence of bad dad Horace Pinker. Ultimately, he musters the strength (thanks to the loving support of his murdered girlfriend's ghost) to embrace "a new way of thinking."

The playful tone of the final film suggests that Wes's personal "exorcism" of childhood demons was at least partially effective. *Shocker* came to represent for him "a period of restoration" after three years of intense personal and professional challenges, resulting in a surprising amount of humor in the final film.[15] "I was feeling happy and zany," Wes said, and "the material seemed to lend itself to off-the-wall humor."[16] A few years later, he added, "I started out to make a very scary, hard film, but by the end realized that the theme of the film was basically that the heart is stronger than the hand (or weapon)."[17] *Shocker* took on a life of its own, declared its independence from its slasher movie origins, and emerged as one of Wes's most idiosyncratic films.

The final act of the film is a surreal, absurd romp through the history of American television, with Horace Pinker and his son Jonathan chasing each other through stock footage of riots and wars, clips of Universal's *Frankenstein* and *Leave It to Beaver*, and cameos featuring Alice Cooper (in concert) and Timothy Leary (in church!). Wes meant the madcap sequence to illustrate "the whole violence of civilization as seen through and perpetuated by television," with hero and villain battling their way through all the "elements of the coercion of the twentieth century on the human spirit."[18] Heavy-handed? You bet. Wes Craven was a satirist at heart.

The inherent humor was amplified by a major production problem. Special effects designer Bruno George claimed to have "devised a system where a character of Horace Pinker could move through any given scene on video and save ourselves about two-thirds of the cost of doing it on film."[19] Unfortunately, very late in the process of making the film, the designer realized that the new process was not working.

In the waning days of summer 1989, Jonathan Craven helped the producers find and collect the raw film footage scattered around various editing facilities in Los Angeles, so the filmmakers could make a determination about what had to be done to complete the special effects and deliver the film. "We had to track everything down, label it, and then I think we hired about ten different effects companies to try to meet the [film delivery] schedule." Jeff Fenner, Wes's assistant at the time, says "everything was done at the last possible second, so the effects were really hit or miss. They had no choice but to put in [the final film] whatever came in. You either had to cut a sequence or use it even though you didn't like the effect, because it was such a scramble to get the film delivered."

In later years, Wes admitted that *Shocker* did not measure up to his ambitions for the film, but said he still liked it.[20] Despite all its problems, the film reflected a personal vision that had been realized with new creative freedom and high hopes for the future. Wes was having fun again. He suggested that *Shocker* was the culmination of a long journey he'd begun with the "nihilism" of *Last House on the Left*: "After a while, that sense [of nihilism] that puts you in that state of despair keeps working and you keep trying to grapple with these issues. You end up having sort of a workable worldview that's put through these films and that offers, I think, some real hope and a sense of concern about things." Finally, he'd arrived at a point in his life—and in his work—where he could express faith in something "within the human spirit" and "respond to horrible things in a very positive way."[21]

In the final scene of *Shocker*, Wes himself appears onscreen, as a homeowner lured away from his television set by a city-wide blackout. Having just witnessed the surreal chase sequence involving Jonathan and Horace Pinker, he steps out onto the front porch of his house and asks his neighbors, "Was that real?" The neighbors appear to be equally dazed as they try to connect with each other while observing the majesty of the star-filled sky above them for the first time. Although Horace Pinker is, technically, still on the loose at the end of the story, the ending seems reassuring—in a Twilight Zone kind of way.

Wes's fourth draft of *Shocker* also included a brief alternate ending— and a sly nod to the infamous shock ending of Brian De Palma's film *Carrie*. In that final scene, Jonathan watches TV news report on the unexplained blackout from his hospital bed. Things seem normal until he hears a sinister laugh. Any good horror fan must be expecting Horace Pinker to come back to life for one last scare, but instead the laughter comes from a friend playing a sadistic prank. Granted final cut for the first time in his career, Wes stuck with the Twilight Zone ending.

Ironically, at the same time Wes was making his big-screen satire on the danger of television, CBS was producing a TV series bearing his name, a sitcom titled *The People Next Door*. According to Marianne Maddalena, Wes's agent had encouraged them to pitch some projects for television because "in those days, if you had a name, you could clean up in TV." Wes conceived a basic premise and central characters, then co-wrote two scripts ("I Do, I Do" and "Town without Pity") with Bruce Wagner, but his commitment to *Shocker* prevented him from becoming involved with the production of the show. CBS hired Steve and Madeline Sunshine, producers of the popular sitcom *Webster* (1983-1989), to oversee the series, rewrite the introductory episodes, and work with new writers on eight additional scripts. When *The People Next Door* premiered on CBS on September 18, 1989, the central concept was recognizably Craven-esque but the sitcom format and canned laughter were not. *Variety* critic Tom Bierbaum wrote that the show included a few inspired scenes of "rapid-fire lunacy" but noted that they were mostly "interruptions to an otherwise conventionally paced and structured half-hour."[22]

The pilot introduces widower Walter Kellogg, a professional cartoonist with a supernaturally powerful imagination; his 14-year-old son Matthew; 9-year-old daughter Aurora; and bride-to-be Abigail, a therapist. At first, only Matthew and Aurora are aware that Walter can "make things appear or come to life, just by imagining them"—for example, a talking moose head, a pint-sized pervert in a trench coat, and a celebrity cameo—but after an extended nightmare sequence in which Walter's worst fears come to life in front of him, he makes a full confession to Abby. At the end of the episode, she nervously accepts Walter's gift/curse, and embraces him and his children as her new family. In subsequent episodes, nosy neighbors in the sleepy town of Covington, Ohio, begin to realize there's something strange about the family.

On October 19, after only five episodes had aired, *The People Next Door* was unceremoniously canceled. Wes quickly moved on, having learned an important lesson: if the creators aren't present, a TV show "will take on the characteristics of whoever is there." As a result, he and Marianne Maddalena "vowed that if we ever did television again, we would be there with the show."[23]

One week after the cancellation, *Shocker* arrived in theaters. Its commercial reception paled in comparison to the box office stature of Freddy Krueger—even in his fifth outing—so discussions about *Shocker 2* faded quickly. No doubt that was a disappointment, but Wes scored a consolation prize. Around the same time, he was able to settle his differences and square his accounts with New Line Cinema. He'd learned about "a basic clause in the Writer's Guild that the creator of a character is guaranteed 5% of whatever the producing company gets from merchandising." He urged the Guild to take New Line Cinema to court over his creator's rights for *A Nightmare on Elm Street*.[24] Soon after, Wes told an interviewer that New Line had cut him in on the Freddy profits, thereby resolving old grievances. Perhaps for that reason, he publicly contemplated a return to Elm Street, and even suggested a story idea for a final *Nightmare* movie: "I would have the central character in the last film recognize Freddy as being himself. He would accept him, and at the end of the film, the two would merge."[25] New Line execs apparently decided to follow their own ideas for Freddy's *Final Nightmare* while Wes Craven took another stab at the small screen.

The director's longest detour in television production began with the early 1990 sale of MGM/UA to Pathé Communications. After that, Alan Ladd Jr. began overseeing the studio's film division and tapped his brother for help with the television unit. David Ladd presumably recommended his *Serpent and the Rainbow* collaborator, because soon Wes had a two-year development deal. By March 12, Wes and novelist Thomas Baum had scripted an original movie-of-the-week titled *Chameleon Blue*, a thriller about a seasoned homicide detective and a seemingly schizophrenic young woman on the trail of a serial killer.[26] The woman turns out to be psychic—a skill the detective exploits for the sake of his job. As the story progresses, he learns that she is the sole survivor of a family decimated by a (different) serial killer's attack, and he becomes more of a therapist and mentor, helping her avoid a psychotic breakdown.

Similarities between *Chameleon Blue* and *Shocker* suggest that Wes was still recycling leftovers from his *Dreamstalker* pilot. He also might have been inspired by Baum's screenplay for the 1982 film *The Sender*, about a mentally disturbed young man with a terrifying ability to project thoughts and images into the minds of other people. In that film, the sender's gift/curse is also a product of childhood trauma; years of abuse by a sadistic mother has turned him into a psychic psychopath. In *Chameleon Blue*, the psychic heroine experiences prophetic visions, hears disembodied voices, and develops a full-on multiple personality disorder while tracking the "Spread-Eagle Killer" through the streets of Los Angeles. In the end, she and her new partner catch their quarry and forge a bond that will allow them to tackle future investigations together.

Chameleon Blue was supposed to become a series revolving around that relationship: each week, the heroes would team up on a new criminal case. Unfortunately, the network "had a test screening and one of the characters tested weak," so they dropped the series idea.[27] The pilot movie, retitled *Night Visions*, aired on NBC on November 30, 1990, receiving lackluster ratings and mixed reviews. Although it was a stylistic and thematic forerunner of Chris Carter's TV series *Millennium* (1996-1999), *Night Visions* was perhaps too rushed (from script to screen in nine months!) and too much of a hodgepodge of ideas from Craven and company.

Wes and his writing partner Tom Baum continued their collaboration on another prospective TV series. *Nightmare Cafe* originated as a pitch by Jonathan Craven and his friend Peter Spears. Jonathan says, "I really wanted to get into this idea that every human has something about their life that they're really terrified to look at—and when you go into the café, you're forced to confront it. The characters inside the café would become familiar players in this purgatorial drama of facing your greatest fear."

Wes claimed it was his idea to add three recurring characters to Jonathan's original concept, saying, "We wanted to tell the wonderful stories that used to be in *The Twilight Zone* but we also wanted characters that people could get to know, to have that identification from week to week. This isn't just a series of stories coming in from outside. We build on our three characters, expanding our knowledge of them and their relationships."[28] The three characters—Frank and Fay, two recently deceased strangers who become the mysterious café's cook and waitress; and Blackie, the establishment's impish proprietor—became tour guides and active participants in the dramas of the café's visitors.

Wes and Tom Baum added another twist to the original concept: the visitors wouldn't necessarily be facing their fears; they could also encounter opportunities for redemption. Wes wanted the supernatural way-station to be more of a Second Chance Café than a Nightmare Café; a place where people could "turn their lives around." His logline pitch was ultimately softer than his son's: "*The Twilight Zone* meets *Cheers*."[29] The reputed master of horror justified his lighter approach by pointing out that he could never achieve the kind of horrific visuals on television that he pursued in film: "Television is sort of antithetical to the sort of scares you can do in a horror film, where you have a very specific audience who are coming in there knowingly to be scared. We're setting out to do something that has a much broader appeal."[30] Of course, Wes also wanted to avoid overt horror and tell different types of stories, as he had on *The Twilight Zone*.

Unfortunately, his reputation as a master of horror completely overshadowed the project—especially after Robert Englund was cast in the role of Blackie. Jonathan Craven remembers, "Once you had Robert Englund in something directed by Wes Craven, it was, 'Where are the damn claws? Where are the nightmares?'" In his autobiography, Englund wrote, "We were throwing

Frank (Jack Coleman), Fay (Lindsay Frost), and Blackie (Robert Englund) in *Nightmare Cafe*. (MGM Television, 1992)

around names like *Terminal Café* and *Last Chance Diner*, but the network was balking because they wanted the word 'Nightmare' in the title to capitalize on the involvement of Wes and me."[31]

Wes acquiesced, but he continued to quibble with the network over the tone of the series. He may have wanted a lighter tone because he was simultaneously developing two horror film projects that were unremittingly dark. The first was an adaptation of Giles Blunt's 1989 novel *Cold Eye* for producer Lawrence Turman. Years later, Turman remembered sending the book to Wes, who responded in an unusual manner: "He asked me where I liked to eat. What? Yeah; if we liked the same restaurants, he felt he could work with me. We did like the same places, and so we worked together developing a script."[32] It is hard to imagine that Wes made the decision so casually; easier to believe that he gravitated toward the subject matter of Blunt's novel.

Cold Eye is the story of a New York artist who paints tableaus of death. Like Wes Craven, Nicholas Hood is sometimes embarrassed by his association with lurid material—or, at least, frustrated by the lack of recognition he receives from serious critics for his lurid work. So great is Nicholas Hood's frustration that when a mysterious figure offers him a Faustian bargain, he trades his soul for fame and fortune, essentially becoming a psychic vampire that thrives on the pain and suffering of others. In the end, he has to pay his debt to the devil—a carbuncular midget transformed into a handsome man (a la *The Portrait of Dorian Gray*) by Hood's self-sacrifice.

Author Giles Blunt remembers meeting with Wes Craven and Larry Turman several times to discuss a film adaptation: "Wes said the story appealed to him because, like Nick Hood, he was an artist whose success entailed the graphic depiction of violence and he was sensitive to the idea that there might be personal, moral, or artistic costs associated with it." Blunt also remembers that the filmmakers balked at the novel's bleak ending, in which Hood is put to death by lethal injection. "That meant we had to work out a way for him to come to his senses and redeem himself at the last minute. It was decided the best way to do that was to have [Hood's] beloved and innocent wife be put in physical jeopardy. I remember Larry saying, 'You could run up the last sequence like one of the old silent films where the girl is tied to the railroad tracks, etc.' Not literally, of course, but with her increasing jeopardy intercut with the hero's desperate attempt to save her."

Blunt wrote the screenplay and revised his own ending—after some initial protest that "the right ending is the one in the book"—but the screenplay was rejected. "[Larry] actually said, 'I can't believe you wrote this—it's like one of those goddamn silent movies!'" Today, Blunt's first draft outline—dated September 23, 1989—resides in the University of Toronto Libraries archives, along with typed notes from Wes Craven, in which the director suggests the main character should be redeemed through a sudden insight in the third act. Additional documents indicate the script was being revised as late as November 3, 1990.

Soon after, Wes shifted his attention to another original screenplay for Alive Films. He said *The People Under the Stairs* was inspired by a 1978 newspaper article about a burglary report and a gruesome discovery in Santa Monica, California: "There was this couple of upstanding citizens that were away at work and the police came to find [their house] broken into and found a place in the house that was barricaded. They broke down the doors and discovered these three kids who'd never been outside."[33] What struck Wes about the news story was the incongruity of idyllic setting and horrific reality: "It was wonderfully ironic that the people seeing the house burglarized were quite ready to say, 'This is what we would expect from the sort of people breaking in—they're coming to our decent world with all their depravity,' and then the police discovered that what was going on in the house was actually more depraved."[34] Significantly, the burglars were black and the homeowners were white.

Inspired by this real-life horror, Wes conceived a screen story about a pre-adolescent burglar who becomes trapped in a labyrinthine house, and discovers other children imprisoned in the basement.[35] Unfortunately, he didn't know what happened next. During a trip to the Brussels International Fantastic Film Festival in 1989, the second and third acts finally came to him in a lucid dream. "[I] woke up at about four in the morning after having dreamed the entire outline of *The People Under the Stairs*, and revised it twice while still in the dream, aware that I was Wes Craven, the filmmaker, and that I was dreaming."[36]

Wes said the lucid dream conjured vivid memories of his childhood home on East 82nd Street in Cleveland: "It was a house three stories high, and then had an attic also, and had the full basement with the coal furnace. So that was kind of, to me, looking back on it, my way of sort of forming what my world was as a child. Which was: the basement was dark but it also has fire and heat. It has coal and a little workshop in there. It even had a bin of rotten potatoes that my brother, who was ten years older, would throw at a target on the wall with Hitler's face drawn in coal..."[37]

Wes had first used the metaphor of house-as-psyche in his college-era short story "Death Mask, Three-Quarter View," followed by the "extended metaphor" of ark-as-writer's-mind in *Noah's Ark: The Journals of a Madman.* He explained, "The house to me was always a symbol of the mind. [...] The first and second floor [...] contain a lot of the subconscious things that we have as humans. [...] And then the attic, where the core memories of the family are kept; the trunk full of old things, secrets of the past. And then the basement was kind of earth, wind and fire of the furnace."[38]

Like Wes, the hero of *The People Under the Stairs*—an innocent boy nicknamed Fool—is drawn to the basement. There, he encounters the feral children that have been discarded by a perverse, manipulative Mother and sadistic Father—who, it turns out, are actually a biological brother and sister "playing house" with kidnapped children. When Fool encounters Alice, the only child that has managed to stay in Mother and Father's good graces (by remaining silent and obedient), he plots their escape. The two children ultimately shed their innocence and "find themselves" by going deeper into the bowels of the house, rebelling against the psychotic parents, and releasing the people under the stairs—the filmmaker's symbol of the "energies of life and youth and passion" that "can never be fully contained."[39] Wes explained, "The boy and the girl escape from the house, but in a sense they also escape from the madness the house represents. The idea of children escaping the madness of parents, of the next generation liberating itself from the madness of the previous generation, is very old and powerful."[40]

Escape from the influence of the older generation is a dominant theme in Wes's writing—from *Noah's Ark: The Journals of a Madman* to *My Soul to Take*—reflecting his own personal journey. *The People Under the Stairs* followed an "inner voice" that was helping Wes to "exorcise personal demons."[41] Although he was in his early fifties, he was still trying to escape certain formative experiences of his childhood and early adulthood. With the third act of *Shocker,* he had veered away from overt horror because he wanted to focus on "coming out of the darkness and into a sort of triumph that included humor." There

Top: Alice (A.J. Langer) and Woman (Wendy Robie) in *The People Under the Stairs*
Bottom: Fool (Brandon Quintin Adams) and Man (Everett McGill) in
The People Under the Stairs (Alive Films, 1991)

is just as much humor in *The People Under the Stairs*, but the tone is darker because Wes was confronting his darkest childhood memories.⁴² In his mind, the resulting film had more in common with *The Hills Have Eyes* than with anything he'd made since; *The People Under the Stairs* was another grim fairy tale about horrifying family dynamics.

Wes believed that his obsession with examining childhood fears had allowed him to make an honest film with broad implications and meanings. The experience of making the film, as well as the film itself, solidified his belief that good horror films must be unfiltered, uncensored expressions of the filmmaker's vision. He said, "If you start censoring yourself because it's too painful or too uncomfortable or your friends will talk about you later, you might as well become an accountant or something. These are very very deeply set, deeply hidden, very powerful elements of the American psyche, and maybe the psyche of any big culture, and you have to go there. *You have to go there.*"⁴³

In addition to exorcising personal demons, *The People Under the Stairs* shed light on cultural nightmares such as institutional racism and the hypocrisy of some moral arbiters. At the end of the film, the children escape from the horror house and detonate a secret room filled with money. The money explodes through the roof and rains down on the neighborhood—a literal and symbolic redistribution of wealth from the psychotic white slumlords to their predominantly black tenants. Wes Craven, a liberal-minded former professor who grew up in a working-class neighborhood defined by racial tension, had strong feelings about inequality and socioeconomic injustice, so it was no accident that *The People Under the Stairs* became a thought-provoking political allegory for the 1990s (and today). By tackling such themes, he was playing to his strongest audience—the young, the marginalized, the rebellious, the subversive. He knew exactly what he was doing and how to do it.

Around the same time he was making *The People Under the Stairs*, Wes was trying to put his personal life in order and make amends for some past mistakes. When his daughter Jessica graduated from college, he invited her to live with him in his house in Santa Monica while she contemplated her next moves. Jessica recalls, "He shined at that moment [as a father]. He was attentive and very present." Jessica's most poignant memories of the time involve a shared love of music. "He decided he wanted to make me mix tapes, because I didn't have any music and he thought that was very, very sad. He was looking for a way to cheer me up, so he would work late, late, late into the night, and when I woke up in the morning, he would be gone for work already but I would come up the stairs—I stayed in the guest bedroom, which was down a spiral staircase into the basement—and I'd find a little stack of cassette tapes on Dad's desk at the top of the stairs." What kind of music was the master of horror listening to at night while plumbing the emotional depths of his own childhood? Apparently, he was enamored with opera's greatest sopranos, especially Jessye Norman.

In the fall, Wes shifted his attention back to *Nightmare Cafe*. Although he'd been unable to direct the pilot episode due to his commitments on *The People Under the Stairs*, he vowed to put everything else on hold while his team completed the five subsequent episodes. Regardless, the series never quite found its footing. Toward the end of development, *Nightmare Cafe* lost its strongest supporter at the network, NBC president Brandon Tartikoff. According to Jonathan Craven, "Warren Littlefield took over, and it just wasn't his deal. They shot the pilot and the network was like, 'Okaaaay, we like the pilot but we're not really sure what the series is. Let's make five more [episodes] and we can sort of treat each one of them like its own pilot. Then we'll see which one we like the most and we'll focus on that.'"

Not surprisingly, that plan produced conflicting visions. Tom Baum says showrunner John Leekley came from "the Michael Mann school of sentimental macho" and didn't appreciate the quirky tone of the pilot script, so he wrote the episode "Sanctuary for a Child."[44] During production of that episode, Baum says, "I overheard one of the crew members ask, 'What is this? *Highway to Heaven*?' Because it had a very sappy feel to it." Subsequent episodes were written by veterans of David Lynch's *Twin Peaks* series and directed by reliable horror veterans like Armand Mastroianni (*Tales from the Darkside, Friday the 13th: The Series*), John Harrison (*Tales from the Darkside*), and Christopher Leitch (who worked with Baum on the HBO series *The Hitchhiker*), but the tone of the series remained in flux. According to Patrick Lussier, who co-edited three of the five regular-season episodes, the network liked the thriller episode "Dying Well is the Best Revenge," but disliked Wes Craven's absurdly comedic episode "Aliens Ate My Lunch."

Instead of righting the ship with its sixth and final episode, Wes's story transplanted the supernatural café to a rural town where a sleazy reporter employs a trio of vertically-challenged, bovine-loving aliens—dubbed Earth, Wind, and Fire—to stir up controversy for his tabloid magazine. The twist: unbeknownst to the reporter, his accomplices actually belong to a species of bird-like aliens. The episode was as outrageous as anything in *The People Next Door* or the final act of *Shocker* and it reportedly sealed the show's fate. Wes blamed the Friday-night time slot for *Nightmare Cafe*'s poor ratings, but Marianne Maddalena says, "Warren Littlefield was like, 'Is this guy nuts?' The show was canceled because of that episode."

Undeterred, Wes focused on his film career. *The People Under the Stairs*, released around Halloween 1991, was his most commercially and critically successful film since *A Nightmare on Elm Street*, allowing him to buy a celebrity dream house (actor Steve McQueen's former bachelor pad) in the Hollywood Hills. The mid-century modern post-and-beam house, with its breathtaking view of downtown Los Angeles, served as a symbol that the crazy kid from Cleveland had finally attained some level of mastery over his profession. Robert Englund recalls, "He had a lap pool put in and had the house decorated perfectly. Beautiful wood shelving. I don't want to say it was a work of perfectionism, but he did have the energy and the desire to exert a certain amount of control over his environment. The house was on a promontory coming off of the mountains, with a cliff on either side. If you looked one way, you could see Griffith Observatory. Look the other way and you could see the South Bay and parts of Santa Monica, all the way down to Palos Verdes. Even Catalina, on a really clear day. It was just a magnificent spot. And the house wasn't ostentatious. It didn't look like he was showing off and it wasn't like some seduction pad or anything like that. I would call it an *aria*. I really think that's what Wes created there—the definitive bachelor's *aria*."

Wes didn't rest on his laurels. In October 1991, he signed a contract to make a new horror film for MGM-Pathé. Six months later, he told an interviewer his next project would be the $10 million thriller *Shades of Gray*, a ghost story set at the United States Military Academy at West Point.[45] In March 1992, *The Hollywood Reporter* noted that the project was based on Timothy O'Neill's novel of the same name, which follows a cadre of sardonic West Point professors (and their significant others) in search of the truth behind a school legend. O'Neill says Wes's initial script was rejected by studio execs because it was "too long" and "studio execs were intent on remaking the story to replicate the success of *Dead Poets Society*," a very different type of prep school story. The filmmakers scrapped O'Neill's story in favor of an original narrative using the novel's setting and title. Working with frequent collaborator Tom Baum, Wes completed a third draft of the new story on May 31, 1994.

Unlike O'Neill's source material, which revolves around faculty members at West Point, Baum and Craven's version revolves around a group of cadets. The script begins with first year cadet Stanley Jardine experiencing strange hallucinations and sleepless nights in his Bradley Hall dorm room. He sees the room ripple like a mirage in front of him, hears faint rumblings, and smells gag-inducing stenches for no apparent reason. He tells friend and fellow cadet Jenny Fallow, but she doesn't have any similar experiences in Stanley's room, so Stanley concludes that he is suffering from some kind of mental illness. As a result, he hangs himself. Later, a first-year cadet named Greg Alcott takes up residence in the dead boy's room and begins having vivid hallucinations, along with mysterious blackouts, suggesting that the room is haunted by something that wants to drive its inhabitants crazy.

Greg confides in Jenny and her would-be boyfriend Matthew, who subsequently have their own strange experiences (depicted in elaborate "rubber reality" sequences of the Wes Craven variety) inside the haunted room. They investigate further and learn that a student named Avery Trotter killed himself there in 1961. It seems as if Trotter's ghost is taking possession of Matthew and thereby tormenting Jenny. As a handful of faculty members become aware of the strange happenings, psychology professor Liz Gibbon suggests to college president Jack Ramsden that Jardine's suicide was a "releaser event." For the time being, she and Ramsden remain tight-lipped about exactly what the event has released.

The first-year cadets learn the truth for themselves after Matthew has a psychic nightmare in which he sees a much younger Jack Ramsden tormenting Avery Trotter, leading the boy to kill himself. Destabilizing dream sequences abound as the group of friends realize that the sins of the college president are haunting them, and the psychotic spirit of Avery Trotter wants revenge. One by one, Trotter possesses the first-year cadets and urges them to kill Ramsden. One by one, they fail to commit murder, until the ghost finally turns to a psychically-vulnerable cadet named Desmond Hakes, who follows orders and goes in for the kill. He too fails in his mission—but only because Ramsden distracts him, calling him a "queer" and boldly daring him to pull the trigger. In the end, the cadets and the ghost of Avery Trotter conclude that they aren't killers but Ramsden is. Trotter then possesses Ramsden and gets his revenge by making the college president commit suicide.

The script ends with a subtle, subversive jab at a military culture that trains young men and women to enter a hive mind and become reflexive killers. In the final scene, the cadets—the nominal heroes of the story—have returned to their daily drills, once again reciting the mantra of the Long Gray Line. Without irony, they chant, "Six bells and all is well. Another week shot to hell. Another week in my little gray cell. Another week in which to excel. Oh, hell." The ending is reminiscent of Wes's 1961 short story "Onward, Christian Soldiers," about an ROTC cadet who worries he has become "a member of a mob, a non-thinking lump of blank-brained ectoplasm"—in other words, a ghost. Was Wes drawing on his own experiences at Wheaton College while co-writing the third draft? If so, his memories of being "denounced" by president Raymond Edman might have provided some inspiration for Jack Ramsden's psychological attack on Avery Trotter, and Trotter's desire for revenge. Worth noting is the fact that both Ramsden and Trotter turn out to be reprehensible characters—the former having dedicated his life to grooming killers; the latter having dedicated his afterlife to murderous revenge. The story's heroes remain caught in a cycle of violence that began before they were born.

In terms of themes and storytelling techniques, *Shades of Gray* would have been a representative Wes Craven film and given him an opportunity to tackle a horror subgenre he hadn't yet explored. In promotional interviews for his *Shocker*, he frequently mentioned a marginal subplot about Jonathan's murdered girlfriend, who returns as a ghost to empower Jonathan, as if laying the groundwork for a future film. "I've always had the notion, and I think it shows in my films, that 'death is not the end' is a jumping off point for horror. If you believe that, you've also got to believe that goodness and strength and love are immortal too."[46] In *Shades of Gray*, the essential goodness of the first-year cadets stymies the undead villain—at least, for a while. In the end, however, the script suggests that Avery Trotter is still lurking in his haunted dorm room, ominously peering down on the cadets.

For whatever reason, *Shades of Gray* remained unproduced and Wes moved on to a remake of *Village of the Damned*, scripted by Tom Holland.[47] The film was supposed to be set in a nuclear missile silo and filmed in South Dakota, but, according to Holland, he and Wes left the project due to mutual dissatisfaction with the story. Patrick Lussier, the film's would-be editor, offers a different explanation: "They were waiting on Linda Hamilton, who was going to play the lead in it. When she decided not to do it, the project fell apart."[48] Whatever the case, director John Carpenter took over in 1993 and his *Village of the Damned* was released in the spring of 1995.

Around the same time, *Variety* reported that Wes had agreed to write and direct a film adaptation of the Marvel comic *Doctor Strange* for newly-formed Savoy Pictures.[49] According to one source, he collaborated on a script with Akiva Goldsman.[50] Producer Michael Uslan suggests otherwise, explaining, "I got a call from the president of New World Pictures [1983-1989] Bob Rehme. He said, 'We are hiring Wes to do a Marvel TV series based on *Doctor Strange*, but he doesn't know anything about the story, the characters, the villains. I know you and Wes worked together really well [on *Swamp Thing*], so would you come on as executive producer and work with Wes on this?' I said absolutely. I talked to Wes and I laid out a first season arc based on an early *Doctor Strange* story called 'The Hunter and the Hunted.' Then I said to Wes, 'At the end of the first season, we'll introduce Nightmare.' He said, 'Who's Nightmare?' I told him about the character and he said, 'This is great. Second Season is Nightmare. We can spin him off into his own movie.' Then I said, 'Season Three, he meets Dormammu, the next level of demon.' And Season Four, he meets Eternity, which is pretty much the gateway to God.' I laid it all out, sent him all this stuff, and we were really pumped to get started. Then New World sold Marvel and that was the end of that."

In the fall of 1992, Wes took another shot at developing a TV series. When MGM Worldwide Television disbanded over the summer, executive producer David Gerber embraced Wes's concept for *Laurel Canyon*, a series that would explore the "mysteries in the Hollywood Hills through the eyes of a poet/

Wes Craven on the set of *Nightmare Cafe* (courtesy Jeffrey Fenner)

mailman who knows all the secrets."[51] In the pilot episode, co-written by Ellen Herman, 24-year-old Winona Gray moves to Los Angeles on the invitation of her boyfriend Lucas, only to find that his invitation letter was actually written by Charles Pulaski, a nosy mailman. Winona quickly lands a roommate (Kelly) and a new job (realtor), then learns that her roommate is dating an imprisoned serial killer who leaves dead crows at the scenes of his crimes. Winona sells a house, solves a murder, and flirts with Charles at the Queen of Cups Café, the geographic hub of the story.

The episode was shot in and around Caiote Pizza Café in Studio City, directed by Tim Hunter. It starred Annabeth Gish as Winona, Jeff Yagher as Charles, DeDee Pfeiffer as Kelly, and Anne Francis as Winona's employer Lucille Bessel. Unfortunately, nobody ever saw it—because, according to Wes, it was deemed too dark for network television in 1993.[52] It wasn't the first time Wes butted heads with censors but it would be the last time he fought to realize a vision for network television. In 1994, Wes returned to the big screen to revitalize his most iconic creation.

The Soul of Wes Craven

CHAPTER TEN

THE NEW NIGHTMARE OF NANCY THOMPSON
(1992 - 1995)

"The image of the distressed female most likely to linger in memory is the image of the one who did not die: the survivor, or Final Girl. [...] She alone looks death in the face; but she alone also finds the strength either to stay the killer long enough to be rescued or to kill him herself."

- Carol J. Clover,
"Her Body, Himself: Gender in the Slasher Film" (1987)

The 1990s was a tough decade for horror films and horror filmmakers. Even though *Silence of the Lambs* won five Oscars (including Best Picture) in 1991, it did nothing to legitimize the horror genre in the eyes of critics. Instead—because many industry insiders refused to recognize the gritty, gory tale of a cannibalistic serial killer as a "horror" film, instead dubbing it a "psychological thriller"—the horror label came to denote low-budget productions aimed at a niche audience. In contrast, "psychological thrillers" of the early 1990s were marketed to a larger, more mainstream, more sophisticated audience. The sea change left many of the modern masters of horror wondering what to do next.

For a time, Wes was attached to an adaptation of Richard La Plante's 1992 novel *Mantis* for producer Richard D. Zanuck. In La Plante's story, a serial killer uses Praying Mantis-style kung fu to incapacitate his victims before consuming them, hoping to transform himself into a more powerful being. A world-weary Philadelphia detective and a Japanese-American coroner join forces to hunt the killer. The obvious appeal was the fusion of three then-popular cinematic genres: the psychological thriller, the cop-buddy movie, and the martial arts film. For better or worse, *Mantis* never made it past the development phase.

In 1992, the same year La Plante's novel was published, director Francis Ford Coppola's lavish production of *Bram Stoker's Dracula* established another trend in contemporary horror cinema. The film inspired major Hollywood studios and A-list directors to revive "classic" movie monsters in prestige productions like *Interview with the Vampire* (1993), *Mary Shelley's Frankenstein* (1994), and *Wolf* (1994). Independent filmmakers followed suit. In 1993, Wes's name was attached to two different schemes to resurrect classic genre films. In May, *The Hollywood Reporter* announced that Wes's agents at the ICM talent agency had packaged a deal for ten 75-minute remakes of American International "drive-in classics" from the 1950s, to be directed by Quentin Tarantino, Mary Lambert, John Milius, Walter Hill, Wes Craven, John McNaughton, Allan Arkush, and Ralph Bakshi.[1] Two months later, the same publication announced that Warner Bros. had optioned over 200 titles from the legendary Hammer Films library. Reportedly, directors Martin Scorsese, John Carpenter, Joe Dante, Wesley Strick, and Wes Craven all selected the titles they wanted to remake.[2] Wes picked *The Nanny*, a 1965 thriller starring Bette Davis as the manipulative caretaker of an emotionally disturbed young boy. Probably because low-budget genre films were not in vogue, neither of these cycles of films got made.

In April 1994, *Variety* predicted the immanent death of horror cinema, observing that only twenty "conventional" horror films had been released in 1993—half as many as had been released in 1990. Filmmaker Brian De Palma blamed Moral Majority politics for the change: "There used to be an exuberance that permeated these films and that's been stopped by all kinds of restrictions on violence and sexuality. No one will come to your defense no matter how eloquent you may be on the nature of violence in society and, besides, the prevailing industry attitude is the broadest audience is the best and that necessitates a lot of pulled punches."[3] Other industry insiders insisted that a single innovative horror film— something like *A Nightmare on Elm Street*—could re-set the landscape. Brian De Palma's film *Raising Cain* (1992), Bernard Rose's *Candyman* (1992), and John Carpenter's *In the Mouth of Madness* (1994) were evolutionary steps toward such a reset, but horror remained in the doldrums. Wes Craven was hoping to buck the trends while escaping the perceived horror "ghetto." By analyzing his own career, and using it as the basis for a new story, he eventually accomplished that goal.

Since *Last House on the Left*, Wes had been fighting a popular perception of him as an immoral purveyor of violence and gore. With *Deadly Blessing*, he began to veer away from overt violence and gore in favor of Hitchcockian suspense and psychedelic thrills, but he couldn't escape his own reputation. A *Los Angeles Times* review of *Deadly Blessing* accused him of peddling "misogynist male fantasies of women's nightmares," and casually labeled him a "sleaze-monger."[4] (Around the same time, *Chicago Tribune* critic Gene Siskel vilified Wes's *Last House* collaborator Sean Cunningham as "one of the most despicable creatures ever to infest the movie business"—showing how vitriolic such attacks could be.[5]) A *Los Angeles Times* columnist also publicly wondered whether horror films could be "hazardous" to a person's health.[6] Wes countered that horror films serve a therapeutic function for viewers, especially younger viewers. He explained, "What horror films do is function as an allowable insanity. [...] People watch and hear about the real horrors of the world on TV; these are never resolved and build up anxieties. At least at the end of a horror film, they're resolved."[7]

The debate continued throughout the 1980s. The idea that horror movie violence could be responsible for real-life violence made headlines in 1984, when a California handyman named Richard Delmer Boyer stabbed an elderly couple to death in their home. At trial, Boyer's defense team blamed the killer's actions on a drug-induced "flashback" memory of a scene in *Halloween 2*, where serial killer Michael Myers murders an elderly couple in their home. Following a very public debate in the media, the jury found Boyer guilty and the judge declared his movies-made-me-do-it defense "absolutely ridiculous."[8] The verdict did nothing to dispel the alternative conclusion of moral arbiters who were already picketing theaters, banning videos, and appearing in Congressional hearings about the cinematic scourge of God-fearing Reaganite America.

When *A Nightmare on Elm Street* was released in 1984, the general bias against horror films was voiced by a *Los Angeles Times* reviewer who damned the film's technical accomplishments with faint praise: "When a film is designed to drench the screen in blood—with maximum violence directed, as usual, mainly toward women—rather than to give a good, fun fright, what does it finally matter how well it is made?"[9] The film's star Heather Langenkamp says that, for her, the prejudicial reaction felt like a personal rejection. "No one believes me when I say the stigma of making horror films [in 1984] was the same as the stigma of doing porn, but that's only a slight exaggeration." When the original *Elm Street* was released, even the actress's agents were embarrassed by it. "When I went into the agent's office and said, 'What do you think? Big box office this weekend!,' they lied and said they had seen it when they hadn't. That kind of thing was always happening. People would say, 'Please don't put that on your resume.'" Reflecting on the history of horror cinema in America, she adds, "Horror had always been seen as the outside genre that people didn't really get—until it started making money and then people were like, 'Oh, we loved it all along.'"

In Hollywood, money talks—and Freddy Krueger gabbed all the way to the bank, which earned his creator a modicum of (qualified) respect in some circles. By the time Wes's next film was released, the *Los Angeles Times* had changed its tune about *A Nightmare on Elm Street,* with one staff critic hailing the film as one of the two "most effective" examples of a new "self-conscious" breed of genre film that mitigated reprehensible depictions of violence with wild imagination and humor.[10] (The reviewer's second example was *The Terminator.*)

Kevin Thomas, the critic who had written the initial scathing review of *Nightmare*, also came around, hailing *A Nightmare on Elm Street 4* as "a superior horror picture that balances wit and gore with imagination and intelligence." He went on to laud Wes's film *The People Under the Stairs* as "a virtuoso work of cinematic terror incorporating superior cinematography and production design—and, most important of all, comic relief."[11] (He still urged parents to leave the kiddies at home.) Freddy Krueger didn't win over everyone with his caustic wit but he did become a familiar household name, which made him seem less threatening. Wes Craven also became a household name—but that made him and his subsequent films a bigger target for backlash.

While making *Deadly Friend*, a high-profile horror film backed by a major Hollywood studio, Wes had his first major clash with the ratings board of the Motion Picture Association of America. Although he'd quibbled with the board over a particularly gruesome scene in *A Nightmare on Elm Street*, he'd been able to secure an R rating on that film without trimming too much footage. In contrast, he said the MPAA's ratings process forced him to eliminate a significant amount of footage from *Deadly Friend*, altering the darkly humorous tone of the film. Years later, he described changes to one particular scene in which his teenage Frankenstein's monster hurls a basketball at the head of a cold-hearted, kid-hating neighbor. The neighbor's head explodes on impact, then she literally runs around like a chicken with her head cut off. Wes found the scene "bizarre and wonderful," but the humor was lost on the MPAA, which gave the film an X rating. He tried to appeal the rating, presenting evidence (a compilation reel of decapitation scenes from R-rated movies), but his words fell on deaf ears. Apparently, MPAA ratings were based entirely on what board members felt "in the room at the time" they watched a film. Wes thought this amounted to knee-jerk censorship: "There is no precedent you can look at. There is no consistency."[12] Because no major Hollywood studio would release an X-rated film, he had to keep cutting his director's cut.

Three years later, Wes encountered the same problem with *Shocker*. He submitted the film to the MPAA ratings board five times—and had to trim "thirteen separate sections," robbing the film of "a certain intensity"—in order to secure a commercially-palatable R rating.[13] That Halloween, he screened the outtakes for sympathetic horror fans at the Vidiots video store in Santa Monica.

At the time, he voiced his frustration in a news article about the inner workings of the MPAA, criticizing longtime ratings board chairman Richard Heffner by name: "He is the kind of man who will not allow a certain kind of view to be expressed, period. He has problems with pictures that depict a certain level of rage."[14] Heffner responded that rating board decisions did not reflect his personal views but those of American parents.[15]

Wes's own views on media violence were complicated. Even as he rebelled against critics and censors, he agreed that a filmmaker could go too far. At the Sitges Film Festival in October 1992, he walked out of a screening of Quentin Tarantino's debut film *Reservoir Dogs* during a scene in which a sadistic bank robber uses a straight razor to cut off a screaming cop's ear. Tarantino gushed that his film was "too tough" for "the guy who did *Last House on the Left*," without wondering why.[16] Wes explained, "It wasn't that it was too gory; what I was offended by was the glibness of it. I felt like it wasn't the character enjoying the violence but the filmmaker was."[17] And later, "It wasn't that I was horrified by what was being depicted, it was that I was horrified by the person who had done the depicting."[18]

Wes's problem with the scene was that Tarantino depicted his killer as *cool*, like Clint Eastwood in the spaghetti western that inspired him to make *Last House*—or Arnold Schwarzenegger in *True Lies* (1994), another film he criticized. "I don't like films that trivialize violence," he said. "That quite often happens in a *True Lies* type movie. I hate movies where guys go around mowing down people and cracking jokes. I think that is a really dangerous lie. Horror films are, by and large, pretty honest films."[19] Putting his theory into an even larger context, he quoted French philosopher Antonin Artaud, who said "most art is about telling things that didn't really happen, but the crime is to lie about the essence of the matter. So you make films about shooting people, but don't show it as being cool. Because it's not cool. People suffer."[20] Artaud called for a "theater of cruelty" that "releases conflicts, disengages powers, liberates possibilities."[21]

Wes decided to distinguish his evolving brand of horror film from other cinematic explorations of violence by revisiting the franchise that made him famous. New Line Cinema had killed off its cash cow in *Freddy's Dead: The Final Nightmare* (1991), but Bob Shaye was looking for a way to bring Freddy back. Since 1986, the producer had been talking about a *Nightmare on Elm Street*

/ *Friday the 13th* mashup, pitting Freddy Krueger against Jason Voorhees. At first, he treated the idea as a nonstarter, saying "it begins to make fun of the faith the audience has put into the character of Freddy."[22] By 1992, however, he was ready to try anything. When New Line acquired the rights to the *Friday the 13th* franchise from Paramount Pictures, Shaye teased a *Variety* reporter with an impromptu pitch: "Sometime in the future, Jason might start having bad dreams, and who he might team with at that point is anyone's guess."[23] Before openly mocking the faith of Freddy's followers, he decided to contact Freddy's creator.

Shaye called Wes and initiated a frank discussion about IP rights and money, and eventually a new *Nightmare*. Once financial terms were worked out, there was only one obstacle: Wes also didn't know how to bring Freddy back "without violating the nature of the [existing franchise] story or offending the audience." (It would be a few years before rebooting popular franchises by ignoring the sequels became commonplace.) In 1994, he explained, "I never wanted to do any of the sequels unless I was able to bring it up to a different level—sort of take it to a more interesting paradigm."[24]

The initial spark of inspiration for *Wes Craven's New Nightmare* came from a dream: "I was at some sort of cocktail party, and Robert Englund was there in costume doing Freddy schtick. And I was sort of standing off to the side, thinking, 'This is exactly what's gone wrong with the films. Freddy has become this comedian.' Then, off in the corner, I felt this presence, and I looked and there was a dark shape, moving with Robert, parallel to his movements, but much more ominous and threatening."[25] Wes interpreted the "dark shape" as the *real* Freddy—not the wisecracking character popularized by the *Nightmare* film franchise but the impetus behind Wes's original screen story. He remembered, "When I first wrote *A Nightmare on Elm Street*, I was trying to account for something in human nature, in the human race, that had been here since day one."[26]

Contemplating Freddy as a relatively new incarnation of timeless evil, Wes began studying similar myths and metaphors from historical cultures. One of Wes's prospective subtitles for his new film, *Freddy Unbound*, suggests the former professor contemplated Freddy Krueger as a modern-day Prometheus. He might have studied Percy Bysshe Shelley's epic poem *Prometheus Unbound* and/or Mary Shelley's novel *Frankenstein, or The Modern Prometheus*. Or perhaps he conceived his new *Nightmare* as a rejoinder to *Roger Corman's Frankenstein*

Unbound, the 1990 film that got produced instead of his own attempt to update Mary Shelley's myth. He also read "a huge French study of mythology in all the world cultures" and seized on an idea stemming from ancient Greek theater, "that if you did not tell stories about horrific things, which were invisible, then the horrific things themselves, if they were not given name and shape and something we could grapple with, would have more power."[27]

Eventually, Wes theorized that the "real" Freddy might have been empowered by the screen death and/or dilution of the Freddy Krueger character. He explained, "Yes, Freddy died in the last film and he's still dead [but] just because you stop Freddy doesn't mean you stop evil. You just free it up."[28] This statement implies that anyone who suppresses the telling of sincere fictional stories about evil—or dilutes the intensity of such stories in order to make the horror more palatable or less disturbing for an audience—is inadvertently amplifying real-world evil. It was a sly jab at Wes's moralizing critics and a heady rebirth for his dream master.

Wes realized that if he was going to reintroduce Freddy as a real-world villain, he would need an equally real hero to battle him. He returned to the first *Nightmare* film and rediscovered Freddy's original nemesis. In the early 1980s, Wes had dreamed up the character of Nancy Thompson as a kind of philosopher queen, the only teen on Elm Street brave enough to acknowledge and confront an unbelievable evil. Wes knew it wouldn't be enough to bring back the fictional character of Nancy Thompson; he'd also have to bring back the actress who gave Nancy her strength.

Heather Langenkamp remembers that Wes invited her to lunch, to catch up. For the most part, she says, they didn't talk about Freddy; instead, they talked about what had gone on in their lives since they made the original *Nightmare*. Heather's story, it turned out, was as harrowing as Nancy's. She explained that in the early 90s she and her husband were tormented by a real-life stalker—a disturbed fan who blamed Heather for the cancellation of the TV sitcom *Just the Ten of Us* (1998-1990), in which she'd played a devoutly religious teenager. "It was extremely traumatic for me and my husband," the actress says. "We moved to England for a while, just to avoid all the things the FBI was telling me I had to do. So I told [Wes] how bad it had been, and [that] it had prevented me from being that gung-ho about pursuing my acting career."[29] In subsequent years, the actress withdrew from Hollywood to focus on her family; she and her husband had a son in 1991 and a daughter in 1994.

Wes listened intently, realizing that "there was more reality and pain in what she was telling me than in any story I could make up."[30] He was especially intrigued by the fact that his "Nancy" had become a mother, recognizing that Heather's real son would eventually become aware of his mother's legacy as the grittiest of the horror genre's "Final Girls." With that in mind, he decided to focus his new *Nightmare* on "the after-effects of having made a horror film [...] and what the influence of that was on herself and also on her child."[31] Although the idea was partly inspired by Heather's real-life experiences, the new story would also be about Wes's experiences as a horror filmmaker, a parent, and a child—an ongoing exploration of themes from the first *Nightmare*.

Heather recalls that when making the original film in 1984, "Wes was a single father who had left his two children with his wife on the other side of the country. He was living in L.A., a pretty unfettered life, and I do think it probably caused some guilt. The movie comes from more of a teenager point of view of that situation, but obviously he had thought about it a great deal—and, like anybody who is a child of divorced parents or has been divorced, you somehow have to sublimate a lot of guilt." A few key scenes in *Nightmare 1* made her realize the screen story was especially "close to home." In one scene, Nancy's divorced parents argue in front of her at a police station. "You could feel it in the precinct office when Marge and Donald are forced to be together because their wayward daughter is caught up in the murder of Tina Gray. It's a small scene that no one ever talks about but it's a good example of working through adult problems as teenagers. Marge's alcoholism is another example. The drama of the parents is *the* obstacle to our happiness."

Instead of revisiting the plight of latch-key kids with divorced parents, the new *Nightmare* would explore the primal fears of a child being raised by a horror icon, who has misgivings of her own. For the sake of the script, Wes created a fictional version of Heather Langenkamp, who has a fictional son named Dylan. The son's name was apparently inspired by the name of a longtime friend's son. Mary Blocksma remembers, "I found Wes's films too disturbing to actually watch, but at one point he told me he'd named a character after my son. Dylan and I once visited Wes, and they stayed up late watching Wes's movies. Dylan loved watching them with their creator."

Heather Langenkamp as herself and Miko Hughes as Dylan in
Wes Craven's New Nightmare (New Line, 1994)

The "real" Dylan adds, "The movie I was willing to watch with him was the pre-release version of *The Serpent and the Rainbow*. I would have been 15, just getting into my rebellious teenage years when I had long hair in my face, smoked Marb reds, and covered Butthole Surfers songs playing bass in loud garage bands with names like Razorblade Buckwheat. I think all this was a pleasant surprise to Wes. What I remember most is that he included me in conversations when most adults would not have, and generally treated me as an equal. My guess is that he had imagined me more like his Dylan character [in *New Nightmare*] and was quite amused at the little punk that showed up."

Indeed, the fictional Dylan character in Wes's screen story is younger, more innocent, and more vulnerable. The first draft script—titled *A Nightmare on Elm Street 7* and dated July 9, 1993—gives his age at one point as three years old, and at another point as seven years old. It also diagnoses Dylan with childhood schizophrenia, a doctor's explanation for the boy's seemingly epileptic and occasionally *Exorcist*-like behavior. The screenwriter vaguely diagnoses Dylan's condition as a "state of ideology where dreams are tangled hopelessly with reality," while the doctor prescribes a holistic therapy: more sleep, allowing natural nightmares to replace unnatural waking hallucinations. Of course, in a Freddy Krueger movie, that doesn't go well.

Wes says that for him Dylan represented "innocence perceiving evil but not being allowed to share in the perception of it with those who are supposed to protect him."[32] He also says he based Dylan on himself as a child, while examining the theodicy of Dostoevsky, who asks, "How can God allow an innocent child to suffer?" When Dylan poses this exact question to his mother, wondering how to "see" God and thereby know He is real, Heather urges him to "reach out" and pray. Taking her advice literally, Dylan climbs to the highest point on a neighborhood playground and extends his arms to the sky. Instead of receiving an answer from God, he falls from his perch. Later, the boy laments, "God wouldn't take me." Wes said, "That was me—that was a part of me, a child reaching out to God and wondering, 'Well, where is God?' There was certainly a point in my life where I thought, 'The God people talk about is a God I can't touch.'"[33] Like young Wes, Dylan must rely on his mother for protection from the incomprehensible forces of evil. Despite her best efforts, Heather is overwhelmed by Freddy's threat to her son. Eventually, Dylan manages to acquire strength through the power of storytelling, and he helps his mother to do the same.

In the beginning of the screen story, Heather is anxious as she struggles with her legacy as Nancy and the threats of a real-life stalker. The fictional character's anxiety goes beyond what the real Heather experienced. The actress explains, "There's no way that I would have played myself as I really am. That wouldn't have been great for the part, and it wouldn't have been true to the Heather that Wes was thinking about. The writer/director's version of Heather was kind of stressed out and was bordering on not quite having her act together."[34] The sudden, mysterious death of fictional Heather's husband compounds the mother's nervous instinct to protect her son from anything and everything that could be dangerous. In her increasingly paranoid state, she begins to wonder if Freddy Krueger is real, which prompts other characters to question Heather's sanity. Soon enough, she too begins wondering if she has gone crazy.

Actress Heather Langenkamp remembers how the central conflict of the screen story came about: "At the lunch we had before *Nightmare 7*, [Wes and I] had a very, very deep conversation about mental illness. I remember we kind of asked ourselves the question, 'Is there a moment when you know that you're mentally ill… or do you *ever* know?' I think he kind of toyed with that idea with 'Heather.' *Is she already broken? Has she already crossed that line?* Everybody around her thinks she has. There are some moments in the film that most people probably don't notice, like when the nanny looks at me like, 'You're gone.' And even with Chase [fictional Heather's husband]… They're all thinking Heather has snapped. The doctors certainly think it. John Saxon certainly thinks it. It's a very subtle part of the movie; it's not banging you over the head but Wes certainly wanted to, I think, portray Heather that way. Because the idea that Freddy comes up into the real world—only a crazy person would believe that! And yet, by the end of the movie, we know that it has really happened. So it's a very sophisticated trick, I think. You start the movie portraying your lead as being on the verge of madness, if not already there, and by the end of it, you've actually proven that she was sane—because all of this did happen and it was real." Wes said he took inspiration from one of his favorite films, Roman Polanski's *Repulsion*, about a dangerously paranoid young woman.

A month or two after the lunch, he sent Heather the first draft of *New Nightmare*. Her initial reaction was that the writer/director had betrayed her trust by putting too much of her personal life on the page. After some careful reflection, however, she recognized that the filmmaker's dream-within-a-dream narrative was conceptually brilliant and that "Heather Langenkamp" would be a worthy role. "If Wes had had Heather dying in this script, I doubt I would have done it because that would have been too crazy," she reflects. "But the one thing I know is that Wes wanted Nancy to prevail. I think that was really important for him. He really did believe that good should triumph over evil. I always say that *Nightmare 1* is a triumph for Nancy; Freddy does not win in that one. The can got kicked down the road because Bob Shaye saw this opportunity to create a franchise, but Wes's intention was always for good to triumph over evil."

Wes's first draft of the new *Nightmare* ends with a somber and ambiguous scene in which it seems Dylan has been permanently scarred by his encounter with Freddy. After a shot revealing that half of the boy's face is covered with burns, the screenwriter ends on an even more ominous revelation that the boy is wearing a red and green sweater. So maybe Wes didn't initially imagine a total victory over evil?

Heather Langenkamp asked Wes for a couple of changes to the first draft script, but only to make the fictional Heather Langenkamp "less like me."[35] She says one change in particular became a bone of contention between them: "In the script was this line that said, 'My mother died in a mental institution.' And I immediately went to Wes and said, 'Wes, I'm not saying this line. My mom's going to see this movie and I'm playing Heather Langenkamp, so you can't have me say that.' I said, 'Write something else. Whatever you want. Just let me know before the day of shooting.'" When filming began, however, the line remained in the script. "Wes just had no sympathy for my point of view. Every week, I'd say, 'Did you come up with something new for that line, Wes?' And he never did. It was like this very weird stubbornness on his part not to accommodate my wishes, and it was the only time where I really didn't understand why."

In the July 1993 draft, fictional Heather's mother—identified as Sarah Victoria Langenkamp, maiden name Miller—has a ghostly presence throughout. When Freddy Krueger makes his return in a preliminary dream sequence, he whispers to Heather from behind some trees like a fairy tale witch, identifying himself as "an old friend of your mother's." Following the voice into the grove, Heather witnesses a pair of junkies getting sliced and diced by an invisible attacker. After running away, she encounters a Biblical burning bush, then experiences an earthquake and falls into a giant sinkhole, like Alice into Wonderland. Heather wakes up in a world where she can no longer discern dreams from reality. As the story progresses, we learn that the fictional Heather's mother recently died, and that the mentally ill woman may have passed a genetic illness on to her daughter and her grandson. In the script, Heather also identifies her mother as an alcoholic—but then retracts the statement, which seems to suggest she is suffering from false memories or delusional thinking.

In the third draft script—titled *A Nightmare on Elm Street 7: Freddy Unbound* and dated October 1, 1993—John Saxon hears Heather's confession about her mother's illness, and quips, "Hell, if having a screwy mother made you crazy, the world'd be one colossal nuthouse." Was this Wes's subtle jab at a mother who called him "crazy"? If so, it didn't make it into the film because the lead actress modified the line while the cameras were rolling—saying, instead, "a close relative of mine died in a mental institution." Saxon also omitted his snappy retort, and the details of the mother-daughter relationship remain nebulous as the story shifts its focus to mother and son.

Heather Langenkamp (as herself) comforts son Dylan (Miko Hughes) in
Wes Craven's New Nightmare (New Line, 1994)

Quite a few other changes were made between the first draft and the third draft of Wes's script. Instead of opening with a dream sequence in a park, the shooting script opens with a dream sequence on the set of a horror movie directed by Wes Craven, advertising the screen story's *meta* quality. Another major change involves actor Robert Englund's non-Freddy appearance. In the first draft, Heather goes to visit her actor friend at his Frank Lloyd Wright home in the Hollywood Hills (presumably, Wes was hoping to shoot at the Ennis House near Griffith Park), only to learn that Robert has been reported missing. She later finds him in Freddy's labyrinthine boiler room, suspended in the web of a Huge Freddy Spider. In addition to acquiring a new spidey sense in the first draft script, Freddy manages to take possession of Dylan's nurse/babysitter Julie, a 23-year-old woman who dons Freddy's famous red-and-green sweater, fedora hat, and steel claws, then tries to kill Heather.

Perhaps the biggest difference between the two drafts is the characterization of Freddy's nominal creator, Wes Craven. In the first draft, fictional Wes tells Heather that he has never actually written any of his horror movie scripts. Instead, he has a dark half that he refers to only as "The Writer," who does the dirty work for him. In the third act, Nancy comes face to face with Wes's doppelganger: a huge, unkempt—yet articulate—brute. He is flanked by actor Michael Berryman from *The Hills Have Eyes*, which suggests that Wes might have imagined The Writer looking something like Papa Jupe. In the shooting script, however, there is only mild-mannered Wes, who delivers many of the expository / explanatory lines attributed to Freddy in the first draft. The change wisely relegates the main villain to the shadows for much of the film's running time, giving him a greater air of mystery and menace.

Wes Craven's New Nightmare was filmed in Los Angeles between October 1993 and January 1994. Producer Jeff Fenner remembers that the first scenes were shot in the offices of New Line Cinema, with Bob Shaye making an onscreen appearance as himself. "It was scheduled first in order to set the power dynamic," Fenner insists. "The whole day was Bob delivering his lines, and he seemed so insecure because he had to act for Wes. Wes was great with him, but I think that was intentional. I really do. I think Wes knew that Bob could not be the boss of him after he'd directed him, and that it would kind of put him in his place." Shaye was one of many *Nightmare* series

Wes Craven as himself in *Wes Craven's New Nightmare* (New Line, 1994)

veterans who appeared in the film, leading up to the scene in which Wes himself explains the unfolding meta-fiction to Heather. In the film, when the heroine asks the guru how to stop Freddy, he answers, "I think the only way to stop him is to make another movie. And I swear to you I'm gonna stay by my computer and keep writing until I finish the script. But when the time comes, you're gonna have to make a choice… whether or not you're willing to play Nancy one last time."

In promotional interviews, Wes said he continued to dream up changes to the story even as the film was being shot: "I was writing pages daily, based on dreams I had the night before. So there was a lot of fear, on a constant basis, that I was going to come in the next day and make changes."[36] This would not have been the first time that such a thing happened, but Wes might have been exaggerating for effect (and marketing). He obviously knew he was making a film unlike anything that had been made before—a meta monster movie by way of Federico Fellini's 8½—so he probably indulged in some playful hucksterism.

At the same time, Wes and his crew were nervous about whether or not their experiment would work. Heather Langenkamp says, "It's a movie about moviemaking, assuming that the real people who make movies are the subject of the movie. It would be one thing if it was a documentary—but it's fiction. Nobody had ever done this before, really, in this way. That's why I don't think Wes gets enough credit for the mind-blowing aspects of that script. And I think that's one of the reasons why there was a lot more pressure, because it could have flopped so spectacularly and been such a terrible movie if every detail wasn't rendered perfectly so that people really bought into the Heather Langenkamp character, bought into the scenario, understood it to be real life—which is what the film was portraying it as—and then twisting it with this Freddy plotline."

To be sure, one plot twist was hauntingly prescient. Since the first draft, the screen story had always begun with an earthquake—inspired by Tina Gray's line in the first *Nightmare of Elm Street* about dreams as foreshocks. Eerily, during the filming of *New Nightmare*, a real 6.4 magnitude earthquake rocked the San Fernando Valley and the Los Angeles basin. Footage of the aftermath made its way into the final film, adding to the pseudo-documentary nature

Robert Englund as Freddy Krueger in
Wes Craven's New Nightmare (New Line, 1994)

of the screen story. Wes described the wreckage from the historic Northridge Quake as a "symbol of the instability of the fabric of life itself—that everything you think is solid can at any time be challenged and become fluid."[37]

In the film, the earthquake tears a hole in the fabric of Heather Langenkamp's reality, leaving four long gashes in her bedroom wall—a visual indicator of Freddy's return, as well as an allusion to Polanski's *Repulsion* (1965), in which the main character hallucinates huge cracks in the walls of her apartment. As fictional Heather undergoes her trial of sanity, Dylan starts having nightmares of mom's old boogeyman. The nightmares become so intense that he suffers a psychotic break and winds up in a hospital, where an intimidating doctor named Christine Heffner—no doubt, a kindred spirit to the MPAA's Richard Heffner—blames the boy's breakdown on *A Nightmare on Elm Street*. Although Heather insists that she has never let her son see that film, Dr. Heffner says it is the only rational explanation for the boy's symptoms of "incipient childhood schizophrenia." She concludes, "I'm convinced those films can tip an unstable child over the edge." Her prescription for Dylan is sleep.

Heather knows better—because Dylan tells her what kind of help he really needs. Upon returning home from the hospital, Dylan asks his mother to read him a bedtime story. When she does, Heather becomes dismayed by the intensity of the Brothers Grimm fairy tale "Hansel and Gretel" and tries to stop short before the climactic scene in which the children kill the evil witch. Dylan pleads with her to finish the story; he needs to hear her say that the children survive and the witch does not. "It's important," he says.

Wes was undoubtedly familiar with real-world research that supports the boy's claim. He probably read the work of child psychologist Bruno Bettelheim, who theorized that classic fairy tales like "Hansel and Gretel" can be a vital part of a child's healthy psychological development. In his book *The Uses of Enchantment: The Meaning and Importance of Fairy Tales*, Bettelheim writes, "Morality is not an issue in these tales, but rather, assurance that one can succeed. Whether one meets life with a belief in the possibility of mastering its difficulties or with the expectation of defeat is also a very important existential problem. The deep inner conflicts originating in our primitive drives and our violent emotions are all denied in much of modern children's literature, and so the child is not helped in coping with them. But the child is subject to desperate feelings of loneliness and isolation, and he often experiences mortal anxiety. More often than not, he is unable to express those feelings in words, or he can do so only by indirection: fear of the dark, of some animal, anxiety about his body."[38]

Wes had experienced such feelings of loneliness and isolation as a child, along with fears that he might be crazy or damned. Haunted by intense nightmares, he once asked his mother if she could come with him into his dreams, to help him fight the monsters. She replied that "she would be there when I woke up, but I would just have to be brave." That answer left him even more terrified.[39] In *New Nightmare*, when Dylan asks his mother the same question, she answers, "I think that only happens in the movies." This being a movie, however, Heather eventually realizes that she can help her son fight Freddy—by re-engaging with the myth of *A Nightmare on Elm Street* and seeing the story through to the end, in which the Final Girl vanquishes the mythical monster. After a battle royale in a Greco-Roman Hell, *Wes Craven's New Nightmare* ends with a scene in which the newly-empowered mother reads Wes's latest horror script to her son as a bedtime story, driving home the storyteller's message about the importance of myths and fairy tales.

Bettelheim concludes, "If a parent tells his child fairy tales in the right spirit—that is, with feelings evoked in himself both through remembering the meaning the story had for him when he was a child, and through its different present meaning to him; and with sensitivity for the reason why his child may also derive some personal meaning from hearing the tale then, as he listens, the child feels understood in his most tender longings, his most ardent wishes, his most severe anxieties and feelings of misery, as well as his highest hopes. Since what the parent tells him in some ways happens also to enlighten him about what goes on in the darker and irrational aspects of the mind, this shows the child that he is not alone in his fantasy life, that it is shared by the person he needs and loves most."[40]

This was also Wes Craven's answer to critics of his work in the horror genre. He summed up, "This is one of those healing nightmares. It's about children and love. It's about terror persisting. And it's about dealing with things that are painful but have to be dealt with. I like that kind of story."[41] With the apotheosis of the *Elm Street* saga, he had made his ultimate statement in and on horror cinema.

Reviewers generally seemed to appreciate it. *New Nightmare* became a surprise hit at the Toronto Film Festival in September 1994, prompting festival organizer Piers Handling to hail Wes for "bashing away at the barriers of the genre."[42] A month later, *New York Times* reviewer Janet Maslin recognized *New Nightmare* as the director's "own best defense," and "an ingenious, cathartic exercise in illusion and fear."[43] *Orlando Sentinel* reviewer Michael Wilmington described Freddy's latest outing as "the series horror movie to end all series horror movies—and if it isn't, it's not for want of trying, skill and sheer breath-twisting imagination."[44] Even Roger Ebert—who had gone from being one of the few defenders of *Last House on the Left* in the early 1970s to one of the most outspoken critics of slasher-style horror movies in the 1980s—conceded, "I haven't been exactly a fan of the *Nightmare* series, but I found this movie, with its unsettling questions about the effect of horror on those who create it, strangely intriguing."[45]

Wes Craven's New Nightmare didn't scare up the kind of big box office returns that earlier *Nightmare* films had—and, to be fair, some reviewers were more annoyed than amused by Wes's self-aggrandizing narrative—but the film became impossible to ignore. Once again, Wes had proven himself a master of horror, by elevating the genre above popular presumptions and expectations of the day. Predictably, after years of trying to distance himself from the métier, he planned to leave horror behind him. In a contemporary interview, the 55-year-old filmmaker suggested that making horror movies after *Last House on the Left* might have been a "mistake," stemming from "a lack of moral courage or laziness."[46] He confessed, "There's always been a part of me that has always agreed with the worst of my critics, that this is a terrible thing to be doing." At the same time, he resolved to shake off his guilt and "just love it."[47]

In the fall of 1994, Wes said he definitely would not have anything to do with *Freddy vs. Jason*, although he seemed to realize that the monster mashup was inevitable. (New Line Cinema eventually made the film in 2003.) Instead, he would direct his first major studio film since *Deadly Friend*. Perhaps because reviews of *New Nightmare* depicted Wes as a thoughtful and intelligent filmmaker instead of a crude pornographer of violence, execs at Paramount Pictures granted him an opportunity to direct a relatively big-budget comedy starring Eddie Murphy. There was only one problem—the star wanted to make a horror film, not a comedy.[48]

In his autobiography, Eddie Murphy's brother Charlie writes that the idea for *Vampire in Brooklyn* originated in 1992 on the set of *The Distinguished Gentleman*: "Eddie and I were sitting in a hotel room together, trying to brainstorm new feature film projects that would be different and urban, but at the same time would cross over to a wide audience. We started with the thought that vampires are sexy to everybody, so we got the idea to take vampires and drop them in the 'hood.'"[49] The duo collaborated with half-brother Vernon Lynch on a modern-day version of *Blacula* that quickly drew interest at Paramount. The project gradually morphed from an "all-the-way horror" story with a "totally evil" vampire played by Charlie into a horror-comedy starring Eddie.[50]

In the summer of 1993, a second draft of the script made its way to Wes Craven, who saw it as an opportunity to direct comedy, his "first love."[51]

When word got back to the Murphys that Wes was interested, they called a meeting, and Eddie told the director he was a big fan of *Serpent and the Rainbow* and *The Hills Have Eyes*. Wes recalled, "The first time we met him in his office, he came down out of his suite and there was a grand piano in the entryway. He sat down and played this beautiful thing, like a jazz pianist, and then he turned around and said, 'Baby fat. You fat. Fat and juicy.' He did this *Hills Have Eyes* [Papa Jupiter impression that was] perfect. Then he said, 'That's my favorite scene in your movie.'"[52] The two men hit it off, so *Vampire in Brooklyn* went into pre-production.

In late September 1993, *Variety* announced the film would start shooting in June, but Wes felt the story still needed a lot of work. "It seemed to lack a center," he said. "Parts of it were too savage and parts of it were funny in ways that the audience would not have warmed up to. There was no romance. It was more of an action-buddy picture, the very thing that Eddie seemed to be trying to get away from."[53] After several writers took a crack at revising the script, with unsatisfactory results, Wes recommended a trusted but relatively untested screenwriting duo. Chris Parker had previously worked as an assistant on *The People Under the Stairs* and *Nightmare Cafe* before pursuing a screenwriting career with his writing partner Michael Lucker. One day in February 1994, he received a call from Wes's production company. The next day, Lucker says, they started pitching their version of the story—first to Wes, then to the Vice President of Paramount Pictures, then to the President of Paramount, then to Eddie Murphy. "In less than four weeks, this script was greenlit. Everybody loved it."[54]

Despite the enthusiasm, there was still some disagreement about what type of film they were making. Parker remembers, "Paramount said [...] 'We want this movie to be funny. Eddie Murphy does not want to be funny. It's your job to trick him into being funny."[55] Wes came up with a plan: "I wanted the humor in *Vampire in Brooklyn* to come from the plot, not from Eddie. I wanted Eddie to be essentially a serious character. What I didn't want was just a black version of [the 1979 *Dracula* spoof] *Love at First Bite*. I didn't think *Love at First Bite* was very funny. I didn't want the comedy to be nearly that broad. [...] I kept encouraging Eddie to play it straight."[56] Wes was confident he could balance humor and horror by highlighting the romantic elements of the story and

Wes Craven, Angela Bassett, and Eddie Murphy on the set of
Vampire in Brooklyn (Paramount, 1995)

coaxing a "vulnerable" performance out of Eddie Murphy, but the producers at Paramount still tried to strong-arm him into making a comedy.[57] The film's editor Patrick Lussier says, "The head of the studio at Paramount had dragged him in after seeing some of the dailies and was yelling at him that it needed to be funny [...] the way Jack Nicholson was funny in *The Shining*, when he says, 'Here's Johnny,' and Wes's response was, 'Do you hear yourself?'"[58]

Vampire in Brooklyn became a film that pleased almost no one. In the midst of production, Paramount execs pulled resources from the film and the script underwent drastic changes until filming wound down in January 1995. Lucker remembers there was "a huge final action scene on the Brooklyn Bridge that had to be scrapped. Suddenly, the end of the movie is at the vampire's apartment. Which, you know... it might not have the emotional resonance one might be looking for."[59] Although Wes tried to pitch the film to audiences as a horror-comedy-romance hybrid dealing with "life-and-death issues, issues of the soul, if you will, and the conscience," the clash of visions resulted in a toothless film that, most critics observed, was neither scary nor particularly funny.[60] Over Halloween weekend 1995, *Vampire in Brooklyn* opened well at the box office but failed to meet expectations for an Eddie Murphy movie.

For Wes, it was a demoralizing setback; once again, an attempt to re-establish himself as a mainstream studio filmmaker had failed, causing him to question his instincts and his future. According to his then-assistant Julie Plec, "*Vampire in Brooklyn* came out and was kind of a disaster. And that made him sad. So he wasn't in any hurry to jump back into it, into his own genre."[61] According to Patrick Lussier, Wes was being courted to direct PolyGram Entertainment's *Snow White: A Tale of Terror*, starring Sigourney Weaver, but he decided to pass on the project.

Wes had recently loaned his face and his brand name to a pair of smaller horror films that failed to attract much attention, adding to his uncertainty. The first was a low-budget horror film titled *The Fear*, about a group of psychology students who attend an experimental weekend workshop. Wes appeared early in the film as a tweedy professor who ominously advises that "people who become shrinks do so because they're in need of therapy themselves." The workshop doesn't end well. Reflecting on his nascent acting career, Wes quipped, "If I ever lose the ability to get a movie mounted, I may start doing character roles. I enjoy acting."[62] *The Fear* didn't lead to any additional acting job offers.

Around the same time, Wes played the role of executive producer on his son's screenwriting debut, *The Outpost* (eventually retitled *Mind Ripper*), the mutant offspring of Peter Locke's plan to make *The Hills Have Eyes Part 3*. Jonathan Craven says, "Peter was always trying to get Wes back into *The Hills Have Eyes* franchise and Wes had moved on. So Peter said, 'Let's get Jonathan in here.' I think he saw that as a way to get Wes re-engaged."

Initially receptive to the opportunity, Jonathan read an existing script for the proposed sequel, written by Bruce Wagner years earlier. "It had something to do with a brain-sucking monster in outer space. I didn't want to have anything to do with a movie about a brain-sucking monster.' I wanted to make a gritty, 70's-style horror movie like the original *Hills Have Eyes*, because

Wes Craven as Dr. Arnold in *The Fear*.
(A-Pix Entertainment, 1995)

all the horror movies that were being made at that time—this was in '92 or '93—had that sort of blue tint and I wanted to do something grittier. So I said, 'Let's have some kids at a reform camp and maybe there's a monster there. It could still take place in the desert and be a *Hills Have Eyes* sequel.' I don't remember exactly what I pitched but I know Peter and I were never on the same page. We ended up with this premise about a military outpost in New Mexico where someone created a super soldier that had gotten away from them."

Things got worse from there. Instead of setting up the film in New Mexico, the producer decided to go to Bulgaria. By all accounts, the shoot was a disaster. According to Jonathan, "Everyone was frustrated by the production problems and especially language ones. We had every nationality on this shoot and often had to translate between Spanish, Bulgarian, English and Italian just to move the camera." There were also difficulties keeping the cast and crew safe from radioactive fallout due to the Chernobyl disaster in 1986. "I was running around the whole time with a scientist and a Geiger counter, checking out the safety levels."[63] Actor Lance Henriksen, who played the lead role in the film, says, "All I remember was waiting to get out of there. My bags were packed and I was ready to go home every day. It was horrible."[64]

To no one's surprise, the resulting film was not a hit. When the film premiered on HBO in the fall of 1995, a reviewer for *The Hollywood Reporter* concluded, "This production is so bad it's impossible to say anything good about it." Despite the mostly negative reception, Jonathan says Peter Locke offered him a multi-film producing deal—on the condition that Wes would continue to loan his brand name to future films. Sensing that Locke mainly wanted Wes's name value, Jonathan said no.

Wes, however, continued to loan his brand name to filmmakers he wanted to support, with mixed results. There was even talk of re-branding the *Amityville Horror* franchise as *Wes Craven's Amityville* for a new television series, but the idea was scrapped.[65] Although Wes could leverage his reputation to set up low-budget horror films, he seemed disinterested in actually making those films himself.

In the fall of 1995, Wes was feeling his way toward a new genre—or a "next level" type of horror movie.[66] A full slate of projects in development included a psychological thriller written by Joe Eszterhas titled *Original Sin*; a dark comedy for Malcolm McDowell titled *The Monster Butler*; an adaptation of Audrey Schulman's novel *The Cage*, about a female photographer's expedition to capture polar bears in the wild; and a new adaptation of Shirley Jackson's Gothic novel *The Haunting of Hill House*, the only one that came close to getting made.

The Haunting of Hill House was announced in January 1994 as an "updated version" of director Robert Wise's film *The Haunting* (an earlier adaptation of Jackson's novel), to be produced and distributed by Miramax Films under its Dimension Films banner. Budgeted between $12 and $15 million, producer Bob Weinstein pitched it as a "wide-audience horror property along the lines of *The Omen*, *The Exorcist*, *Rosemary's Baby*, or *The Shining*," illustrating his company's move into the "upscale horror film genre."[67] Weinstein hoped the project would "attract a major talent in terms of director."[68] By mid-June, he'd hired Wes Craven.

In his book *Down and Dirty Pictures: Miramax, Sundance, and the Rise of Independent Film*, author Peter Biskind suggests that the creation of the Dimension Films label was inspired by the success of rival studio New Line Cinema, which had risen to power on the back of Freddy Krueger.

That may be one reason why the Weinsteins allied themselves with Freddy's creator. The opportunity was equally appealing to Wes, who wanted to work with "next level" source material on a production budget comparable to that of a major studio film. Also, since *Shades of Gray*, he had been wanting to tell a ghost story.

The Dimension producers reportedly commissioned at least two different screenplays for *The Haunting*, one by horror veteran W.D. Richter (*Invasion of the Body Snatchers*, 1978; *The Thing*, 1982) and one by TV writer Edithe Swensen (*Tales from the Darkside*). According to Wes, the former was rejected because it was "too similar" to *A Nightmare on Elm Street*, while the latter was deemed "too mild."[69] Dimension exec Richard Potter says, "Wes was interested in the psychological aspects of the people in the house, the dynamics between them, and those dynamics being expressed through the haunting. I remember talking to him in meetings about the popular theories of why poltergeist activity always seems to involve prepubescent girls. In these 'true' stories (whether you believe them or not), it always has something to do with some kind of psychic energy mixed with sexual abuse. These girls feel powerless because someone is abusing them and the poltergeist is some supernatural or preternatural alter ego of theirs, expressing its anger and frustration." Still touting the project in the fall of 1995, Wes said his take on the material would emphasize "what the psychodynamics are between a mother and a daughter that would cause a house to resonate with its own haunting." Unfortunately, soon after, Dimension dropped the project.[70]

Although the producers at Dimension failed to find the right script for *The Haunting*, development exec Richard Potter remained in touch because "I wanted to find something to do with Wes."[71] One potential collaboration was on a TV series that Bob Weinstein described as "a series of science-fiction anthology films that, *Twilight Zone*-style, will highlight the talent of several directors."[72] Another possibility was a spec script by newcomer Kevin Williamson, which the Weinsteins bought in June 1995. The title: *Scary Movie*.

CHAPTER ELEVEN

STILL SCREAMING
(1995 - 2000)

"We do not doubt the reality of what we see on television, are largely unaware of the special angle of vision it affords. Even the question of how television affects us has receded into the background. The question itself may strike some of us as strange, as if one were to ask how having ears and eyes affects us."

- Neil Postman, *Amusing Ourselves to Death* (1985)

Kevin Williamson says he conceived the opening scene of *Scary Movie* in March 1994. He was house-sitting for a friend in the Westwood neighborhood of Los Angeles, watching a Barbara Walters special about the Gainesville Ripper, a serial killer that murdered five college students over four days in the summer of 1990. Startled by a strange noise, Williamson searched the house—and found a bedroom window wide open. He remembers, "With a butcher knife in one hand and a cordless phone in the other, I called my buddy David [who] kept trying to scare me on the phone, saying things like 'Freddy's gonna get you'..."[1] Friendly taunting turned into an impromptu horror movie trivia contest, with both friends trying to demonstrate their superior knowledge of slasher movies.

One year later, the experience inspired the opening scene of Williamson's new script. "I finally asked myself, *'What would scare me?'* I'm a kid, I'm a product of the VCR generation, I grew up next to a Blockbuster, I have seen all these movies. Then I thought, 'That's what would scare me'—if I was watching a movie about myself." Williamson incorporated the voices of his movie-loving peers into the story, making the teenagers in *Scary Movie* supremely relatable to the horror fans of Generation X. The fictional characters could joke about the tropes and techniques of slasher movies, but they were still terrified to find themselves living through one. "I think it kind of worked because of the idea that their knowledge of horror may save them or... it may not be really like it is in the movies, but completely different. *You* decide if it is going to save them or not."[2]

In the spring of 1995, the screenwriter completed his first draft of *Scary Movie* and sent it to a talent agent. Late one Tuesday afternoon, the agent passed it along to several production companies. Former Dimension Films executive Richard Potter received the script from a colleague at Miramax. After reading it, he promptly called his boss Bob Weinstein at home. "He'd always said that if I read something I loved to let him know immediately. This was the only time I ever did that."[3] The following day, Miramax won a short-but-intense bidding war against competitors including Oliver Stone's production company Cinergi Pictures, Universal Studios, Paramount Pictures, Columbia Pictures, Sony Pictures, Morgan Creek Entertainment, and LIVE Entertainment.

Once the script was in the hands of Bob Weinstein, the search for a director began. According to Potter, "There was no question who it was for. I don't remember ever having a serious discussion about it being for anyone but Wes, because we thought he would jump right into this." Wes, however, passed up the chance to direct *Scary Movie*. "What he told me was, 'I've already done this.' It's not like we had an in-depth conversation. When someone passes on a project, there isn't really a conversation."

Dimension auditioned other potential directors during the following weeks. Kevin Williamson tested for the job but faced stiff competition from some of the hottest young directors in Hollywood, including Robert Rodriguez (*El Mariachi*), Danny Boyle (*Shallow Grave*), and Anthony Waller (*Mute Witness*). None was quite what the studio execs were looking for. Kevin Williamson recalls, "They were saying, 'We're looking for the new Wes Craven.' And finally, Bob Weinstein said, 'Well, what about the old Wes Craven?'"[4] Potter clarifies, "We were talking to other directors but everything was being slow-played. We just kept going back to Wes and saying, 'Really? You really want to pass on this?'"

Wes later claimed he had several reasons for turning down *Scary Movie*. First, he was emotionally invested in making *The Haunting*, believing that it would allow him to "branch out" and do "something a little more mainstream" than the usual horror film.[5] Although *Scary Movie* was a *smart* slasher movie, it was a slasher movie nonetheless, and he said he wanted to put that subgenre behind him: "I felt it was so violent and so much back where I had started, that I felt I'd screw up my karma if I did it."[6] He also regarded *Scary Movie* as "a continuation of the deconstruction of *New Nightmare*" rather than something actually new.[7]

Some of Wes's longtime collaborators say he had additional reasons for turning down the project. Bob Weinstein believes that "Wes wanted to stay away from anything that was funny within the genre of horror. It wasn't so much his assessment of the script as an assessment of where he was coming from career-wise that made him reticent to even look at something that gave him a flashback nightmare of his last film experience [*A Vampire in Brooklyn*]."[8] Julie Plec, Wes's then-assistant, says "he was uncomfortable with the parts of [*Scary Movie*] that felt like it was making fun of the tropes and of the devices that he himself had created. I think he needed to get to the other side of what he considered to be spoof and recognize it as a scary piece in and of itself."[9]

Meanwhile, Kevin Williamson received notes from Dimension and turned in a second draft of the *Scary Movie* script on July 31, 1995, adding a new murder set piece and eliminating unnecessary clues about the killer's secret identity. Producers focused on casting the lead role of Sidney Prescott. Once actress Drew Barrymore expressed interest, Dimension's dream director re-read the script. Wes still had strong reservations about the amount of violence in the story, especially in the opening sequence, but he was more amenable. Finally, a young fan prompted him to take the plunge. According to Wes, "I went to a comic book convention and a little kid came up to me and said, 'I think *Last House on the Left* is your best film and you haven't been kicking ass enough in your films lately.'"[10] He decided to rise to the challenge.

There were other factors too. Miramax pulled the plug on *The Haunting*, leaving Wes—and his team of collaborators—without a project for the immediate future. Julie Plec proposed *Scary Movie* as a solution. "I said, 'Remember that great script? […] They're having a hard time finding a director and they really want you to do it.' […] And he said, 'Ah, well, they should make me an offer I can't refuse then.'"[11] Plec clarifies, "That's how they got him—money."[12] Wes's agent Andrea Eastman says she "made a killer deal for him on *The Haunting*. I worked with Sam Fischer, Wes's lawyer, to negotiate back-end box office bonuses. We just moved that deal over to *Scary Movie*."

By the end of the year, Wes was officially on board to direct the film—and screenwriter Kevin Williamson was nervous that the horror auteur would ask for major changes. Driving to Wes's home in the Hollywood hills, he was preparing himself for the worst: "This is the Master of Horror. What if he's a real horror? What if he hates my script? But he wasn't, and he didn't. His notes were production concerns and typos. He was very thoughtful, kind and sweet, with a gentle, quiet nature."[13] Wes respectfully questioned "things that we were all questioning, like the motive [of the killers, Billy Loomis and Stu Macher]. He had some questions about Sidney shooting Billy and Stu in cold blood at the end, for instance, so I rewrote that scene to have Stu attack her again—after which she crushes him with the TV—and Billy springs back to life."[14]

The third draft of *Scary Movie*—dated February 14, 1996—featured a new line of dialogue in which killer Billy Loomis explains his motive, telling Sidney that her promiscuous mother is "the reason my mom moved out and deserted me." Sidney gets her revenge by taunting Billy about the size of his "weenie" before shooting him in the head. The third draft also shortened the film's coda. In the first draft, Sidney had comforted her traumatized father, reassured him that "it's over," then winced as Gale Weathers quipped, "Until the sequel." It also included a beat in which Randy asked Sidney out on a movie date, and she responded, "Only if it's a nice Meg Ryan movie." Although the third draft retained Randy's triumph, the film would end on a more serious and somber note, with Gale Weathers reporting on the tragic deaths of the teenage victims and their killers. The decision to end on Gale was, according to Wes, the result of casting a strong actress—Courteney Cox, who wanted to play a much harder-edged character than the one she was known for on the sitcom *Friends*. Directing, as they say, is 90% casting—and, with *Scary Movie*, Wes Craven was an actor's director.

Once the film went into pre-production, Drew Barrymore decided she was more interested in playing the role of Casey Becker, the young woman who gets murdered in the opening sequence, than in the lead role of Sidney Prescott. The search for a new Sidney kicked off auditions of some of Hollywood's hottest young talent. Neve Campbell, a veteran of the National Ballet of Canada, best known at the time for a starring role on the Fox TV drama *Party of Five*, says her first meeting with Wes Craven was fortuitous. "I remember walking in, and Wes—his gentle, paternal energy just gave me a lot of confidence. I was very nervous, and his guidance was great, his direction was great, and his energy just really set the tone for everyone on set always."[15] In an on-set interview, she added, "He's really able to create images that bring you to where you need to be within a dramatic scene. I was doing a scene the other day, we had one last take and Wes said to me, 'Okay, you've got a thousand bullets ringing through your body, now go do it.' That helped me so much. Wes really has a sort of incredible kind of insight into what an actor needs, so I really loved working with him."[16]

Wes was equally impressed with his new lead actress. "She wanted to play something different, just like Courteney Cox. She's been a dancer all her life, so she was able to be very physical and was able to control her body within the frame in a way that's unique. And from what I've seen on *Party of Five*, that show can be pretty lachrymose, and since this required a lot of crying, she

Wes Craven with Drew Barrymore on the set of *Scream*
(Dimension, 1996)

Sidney (Neve Campbell) and Tatum (Rose McGowan) in *Scream*
(Dimension, 1996)

had superb control of that."[17] Just as Courteney Cox brought lovability to her role as a ruthless tabloid journalist, Neve Campbell brought a down-to-earth relatability to her Final Girl.

David Arquette also convinced Wes to cast him against type in the role of Deputy Dewey Riley, who woos Gale Weathers. The decision would radically transform the character from an ill-fated tough guy into a lovably goofy survivor, with Wes contributing many of the character's most memorable moments. Arquette says, "Wes would come up with these funny things, like Dewey eating ice cream while the other sheriffs smoked. Or the scene in the first film with him and Gale [where Dewey asks] 'Do you know what that constellation is?' 'No, what is it?' 'I don't know, that's why I was asking you.' Moments like that, where his humor crossed over."[18] The innocence, earnestness, and boyish charm of Deputy Dewey became a major contributor to the tone of the final film—as did the casting of Skeet Ulrich (as Billy), Matthew Lillard (as Stu), Jamie Kennedy (as Randy), and Rose McGowan (as Sidney's best friend Tatum). In hindsight, the cast members have suggested that the making of *Scream* felt like a family affair—if not a "union of souls"—with Wes as the benevolent "father figure."[19]

As he approached the first day of filming in March 1996, Wes said, "As far as I'm concerned, it's a dream cast. I could not be happier."[20] He was equally enthusiastic about the script: "I didn't make any major changes, except to the ending which was still somewhat in flux. So we fiddled with that a little, but this screenplay, more than any other I've directed by another writer, was ready to go. [...] It was a real pleasure to be able to simply concentrate on directing the script, and not have to worry about fixing it."[21] Directing the script, of course, entailed a certain amount of interpretation—and improvisation. Actor W. Earl Brown, who previously worked with Wes on *Vampire in Brooklyn*, says the director learned an important lesson on *Vampire* that he applied to the new film: "[Wes said,] We are making a satire of this genre, that's what this is. However, if this movie is not scary, it will not be funny. So, never at any point fall into thinking [you are] playing comedy here because if you don't play the moment honestly and I don't shoot it honestly, if the horror doesn't work, the comedy's not going to work."[22] The cast took the lesson to heart and the director preserved their most authentic moments on film. Skeet Ulrich reflects, "He just had such compassion for the project, for all of us as human beings and individuals, and he worked at a deep level. He was always focused on the subtext and what was going on behind the character."[23]

Kevin Williamson was thrilled: "We've lost so much humor by playing it real, and I'm very happy about that. I got to sit down with Wes Craven—Master of Horror, you know?—and say, 'This is what I was thinking,' and he'd go, 'Well, how about this?' He would take one of my thoughts and run with it and blow it up. It was great. I've learned so much from him."[24] Later, he added, "Wes gave *Scary Movie* its tone. He brought it to life with a perverse wickedness and I'm forever grateful."[25]

Not everything went as planned. Editor Patrick Lussier remembers, "The first thing they shot of the movie was the Drew Barrymore sequence, so the first five days of dailies was that 13-minute sequence. And the Weinsteins hated the dailies. Hated them. Were ready to fire Wes. Were sending Wes dailies from some other movie, saying 'Make it more like this. You're worse than a TV director.' This is literally what they were saying. Wes called me up and I had never heard him so despondent." Lussier edited the entire opening sequence, incorporating temp music and extensive sound effects, then sent the cut to the

Top: Gale (Courteney Cox) and Dewey (David Arquette) in *Scream*
Bottom: Billy (Skeet Ulrich), Randy (Jamie Kennedy), and
Stu (Matthew Lillard) in *Scream* (Dimension, 1996)

Dimension execs, who promptly changed their tune. "They watched it and they were like, 'Oh my god, we were so wrong. This works so amazingly well. We can't believe how wrong we were. We're so sorry.'"[26]

Around the same time, Wes encountered another major setback. In late March, a few weeks before filming was set to begin at Santa Rosa High School in central California, some members of the local school board read the shooting script and threatened to deny—or, according to the filmmakers, retract—permission to film at the school. One school board member explains, "We were told that it was a spoof, a comedy. And what we read was not."[27] Julie Plec remembers that the problem had a lot to do with the murder of Polly Klaas.[28] In October 1993, the neighboring community of Petaluma had been traumatized by the brazen kidnapping of the 12-year-old girl from a slumber party at her own home. After an intensive two-month search, Polly's body was found thirty miles north of town. Two days after *Scream* went into production, her killer went on trial. Understandably, some locals were upset to learn that Drew Barrymore's screen character was being tormented and eviscerated near Santa Rosa around the same time.

Wes later said, "I can understand the trauma that was on that area because of that case—but they were very harsh. They treated us like scum."[29] As the conflict escalated, Wes became desperate to avoid the expensive process of securing a new filming location while in the midst of production. He also became increasingly incensed over the public accusations that he and his crew were being depicted as "some sort of lowlifes who've crawled out of a rock someplace to depict violence."[30] On the eve of the school board's final decision-making vote, he defended *Scream* as "a good wholesome movie" while threatening to sue the school board. "I do not like to be pushed around," he said. "We're nice people, dammit. Normally, we wouldn't be making these kinds of threats. But what kind of choice do we have?"[31] On the day of the vote, he was especially vociferous. "They make us seem like monsters and the anti-Christ. They have impugned our integrity and reputation. They have been reviling us in public. We have been pictured as godless Huns from Hollywood, trying to buy off the souls of the school board."[32] His choice of words suggests that, for Wes, the fight against the school board had come to represent a lifelong rebellion—not against Christian values, but against self-righteous moralizing. He genuinely believed that his position was more sensible and more just.

In the end, the school board voted against allowing the filmmakers to shoot at Santa Rosa High School, claiming that the production crew's presence would be too disruptive to campus life. Wes quietly backed down. The school-based scenes were delayed while the producers sought another location. The story might have ended there, but two weeks after denying Wes permission, the school board approved director Ron Howard's request to shoot the R-rated coming-of-age film *Inventing the Abbotts* at Santa Rosa High School for eight days in late May. Understandably upset, Wes made a new request to shoot for five days at the school (instead of the originally-planned fourteen days) in early June. The school district's assistant superintendent again rejected the request, citing a scheduling conflict. Eventually, the school scenes for *Scream* were filmed at the nearby Sonoma Community Center and the film crew quietly left town.

Wes, however, got the last word. In the end credits of what turned out to be the most successful indie horror film since *Halloween* (1978), he issued "no thanks whatsoever" to the Santa Rosa City School District Governing Board.

That fall, the marketing team at Dimension made big plans for their new release. First, executive producer Bob Weinstein imposed a new title, reflecting the tonal shift that had taken place during filming. *Scary Movie* became *Scream*. Weinstein also made the then-unusual decision to release the horror film during the Christmas season, gambling that it would lure teen audiences that usually stayed away from theaters around the holidays. Ultimately, this pit *Scream* against another teen-oriented film, the animated comedy *Beavis and Butt-Head Do America*, as well as the romantic comedy *One Fine Day*, featuring A-list stars George Clooney and Michelle Pfeiffer. Industry insiders predicted a sudden death for the indie horror film. Andrea Eastman recalls, "We'd have these staff meetings [at ICM talent agency] and all anyone would talk about was *One Fine Day*. They were very dismissive of 'this little movie, *Scream*.'"

At first, the predictions of industry insiders appeared accurate; *Scream* was a slow launch. Richard Potter remembers, "The movie opened to $6 million for the weekend and we thought we were dead. That Monday was not a happy day. A movie usually drops by 50% each week."[33] For a film with a production budget of $15 million, it seemed like bad news. Then, in its second week of release, *Scream* made $9 million. The following week, it raked in $10 million.

The film would hover in the top ten until mid-February, then return twice in April. By Memorial Day weekend, after twenty-three weeks in release, *Scream* had grossed just shy of $100 million. Eastman says, "Suddenly, everyone was very respectful of Wes Craven."

For Wes, the scale of the film's success led to opportunities to break out of the horror genre that even *A Nightmare on Elm Street* had not provided. In an interview with this author, he remembered that things started changing before the film was even released: "We had a test screening in Secaucus and it went through the roof. Bob and Harvey Weinstein sought us out in a restaurant where we were celebrating our scores and they said, 'We want you to do two more horror pictures with us.' And I said, 'Well, jeez, I've been thinking of not doing any more horror.' And they said, 'Okay, we'll sweeten the pot. We'll give you a non-genre film.' This is something that nobody had said to me in thirty years of trying to do something different." Before *Scream* was even released, Wes had signed a deal to make two more films for the Weinsteins. Around the same time, he loaned his name to a rather muddy wave of new horror films.

By January 1997, Wes was hyping his next two directorial projects— one for Dimension and one for Miramax. The Dimension project was supposed to be *Bad Moon Rising*, a werewolf biker movie penned by Scott Rosenberg, who had recently written *Things to Do in Denver When You're Dead* (1995) and *Beautiful Girls* (1996) for Miramax. Wes described *Bad Moon* as a story about "a group of outlaws being hunted down by the Establishment."[34] His Miramax project would be very different—a feature film adaptation of *Small Wonders*, a 1995 documentary about an East Harlem music teacher.

Bad Moon Rising never made it to the screen. According to Patrick Lussier, Wes and Scott Rosenberg never saw eye to eye: "The script needed some work and I think when Wes had said that to the writer, the writer was very reluctant to make any changes to it, if memory serves, so he was not keen on it." Lussier also says that, at the time, Dimension execs were courting Robert Rodriguez, who had recently helmed *From Dusk Till Dawn* (1996), to direct a sequel to *Scream*. Rodriguez declined the offer out of respect for his fellow filmmaker.[35] At that point, Wes became the prime candidate to direct the sequel. Although he suddenly had several irons in the fire—including a computer game called *Wes Craven's House of Fear* and a major publishing agreement to write his first novel (*Fountain Society*)—he signed on to *Scream Again*. By March 20, he had executed a new, three-film deal with Dimension, incorporating two *Scream* sequels and the promised non-horror project.

Dimension hoped to release the first sequel approximately one year after its predecessor, which meant the filmmakers had to work fast. Kevin Williamson says he wrote a first draft script in three weeks: "Luckily, I already had the story mapped out. I would show Wes and everybody chunks of the script as it was done, then we'd all read it and talk about it. We all put our heads together, which is how we got a bunch of the twists and turns in the story."[36] Wes remembered that the nature of the project and its late start resulted in scenes needing a lot of work: "Some of them were very, very thoroughly worked out by Kevin, and other things came in in very preliminary shape and were heavily worked on and improvised."[37] Williamson ultimately wrote three drafts of the script, including a "dummy script" that "existed as a decoy" to protect against Internet script leaks.[38]

Wes embraced the opportunity to help shape the story, storyboarding scripted scenes to add suspense and sometimes modifying the dialogue. He also added a new plot point that would link horror cinema to classical drama. Halfway through the film, college student Sidney Prescott rehearses for a drama club performance, in which she plays Greek mythological prophetess Cassandra. Unable to focus due to the emotional trauma of recent events (a continuation of the murders from the first film), Sidney begs her drama teacher to let her off the hook. Instead, the teacher—an obvious surrogate for Wes— suggests that Sidney is a literal modern-day Cassandra, a cursed visionary who must cope with overwhelming tragedy. Or, in the parlance of horror movie criticism, a "Final Girl."

Wes pointed out that the scene related thematically to the film's opening sequence, in which a young couple gets murdered in front of a moviegoing audience. It also anticipates the film's finale, in which Sidney battles the killers on a theater stage. "I was trying to establish the underlying form of the film, with a second scene that would discuss the place of theater and acting in our lives—in a way, to be frank, to answer the critics of horror films that seem to think they're only bad or nonsensical or beneath [the intelligence of the critics]. And to try to point out that stage and the portrayal of the darker side of things has been with us at least since the Greeks, and probably long long before that, and it's an honorable thing and an important thing." Sidney accepts her fate and, in the final battle, literally returns to the stage to play her role. Wes adds, "I felt that since we had established this theme of the stage, beginning with the movie theater and then the drama at the midsection, that we needed to come back here for the finale. We kept the theme with its three-part structure."[39]

Another significant deviation from the original script was the identities of the killers. In Williamson's first draft, Sidney learned that her roommate Hallie and boyfriend Derek were behind the murders. In the final film, the evidence points to Mickey ("the freaky Tarantino film student") and local news reporter Debbie Salt, who turns out to be the mother of Sidney's murderous boyfriend from the first *Scream*. Although it's not clear who decided to change the identity of the killers, or why, Wes supposedly wrote some dialogue for the Debbie Salt character that rattled a few of his fellow filmmakers. Marianne Maddalena says, "Wes had a whole scene with Laurie Metcalf [the actress who played Debbie Salt] down in the basement, telling someone—the husband or the son—'Here I am, down in the basement, scrubbing stains out of your shorts.' That one line threw us all into a tizzy."

Wes found the shoot for *Scream 2* much tougher than the first film, due to the aggressive schedule, a series of technical problems, and pressure to deliver another blockbuster hit. Meanwhile, Dimension execs were basking in the glow of Wes's elevated status in Hollywood. On September 19, the company released *Wes Craven Presents Wishmaster*, a $5 million horror film about an evil djinn. Although the film bore Wes's name above the title, it was written by *Hellraiser* mythologist Peter Atkins and directed by special effects guru Robert Kurtzman. Jeff Fenner explains, "Wes negotiated a payout to put his name on it, then he put me on that show so it wouldn't embarrass him. I was his eyes and ears in case anything went wrong, but he had absolutely no artistic impact on the film. He could have. They would have welcomed his involvement, but I don't think he wanted to be involved."

Fenner suggests, "His fantasy, I think, was to do what Steven Spielberg did with Amblin Entertainment. He had this idea of becoming a mogul and capitalizing on it. Unfortunately, he didn't have Spielberg's ability to help other people to do their own thing. If he got excited enough about a project, he wanted to do it himself. He wanted to make it his own. He couldn't just give somebody notes and help them make it better. He was often very critical of other people's stuff, and he would undercut people who were not completely on board with his ideas. Not always intentionally. I just don't think he wanted to be a mentor at that time."

Wes admitted that he "didn't do very much on" *Wishmaster*, but he was "pleased" that it "did well," strengthening his brand.[40] Soon after, production wrapped on a second *Wes Craven Presents* film, and Wes had even less to do with that one. According to *The Hollywood Reporter*, he'd become attached to Trimark Pictures's remake of the 1962 cult classic *Carnival of Souls* in April 1996, before he directed *Scream*. Trimark later signed Adam Grossman to write and direct the film. Although Wes's development exec Lisa Harrison received a credit on the end product, Wes had no creative involvement. In an October 1999 chat on his official website, he explained, "I think we saw early versions of the script. We were doing other films at the time and we just sort of gave them our blessing. We did two films that way and both times we felt it was not the way we wanted to continue doing business because we didn't have that much control over the product." When the new *Carnival of Souls* surfaced, it died a quick death on home video.

In October 1997, the annual ShowEast film convention in Atlantic City recognized Wes at the peak of his career, granting him a Lifetime Achievement Award. Wes understood that the recognition was mostly for having made a highly profitable film, and that he was now expected to repeat that success: "The way the industry works is that you hear a chorus of 'Do that again!' when something is successful. They're not into 'Now, that was really good! Do something completely different!' I wish it would work that way."[41] A few months later, *Scream 2* arrived in theaters. It was another unqualified success, breaking $100 million at the box office. Now, Wes felt liberated to do something different. "It's not going to have a huge budget, but it will be the little film that I could have—or should have—made twenty years ago. And if I fall on my face, I can still say on my dying day, 'Well, at least I did it.'"[42]

As he moved closer to making *Music of the Heart*, the feature film version of *Small Wonders*, he also began moonlighting as a novelist. It had been thirty years since Wes completed *Noah's Ark: The Journals of a Madman*, the novel he'd hoped would kick-start his literary career. At the time, no one was interested. Now, as a hugely successful Hollywood filmmaker, he had no trouble getting a book deal. Wes claimed he came up with the core idea of *Fountain Society*—"about cloning and a brain transplant"—around 1972 and tried to develop the idea many times over the years. (There are some notable similarities to his unproduced script *Roger Corman's Frankenstein*.) In early 1997, he shared the current incarnation of his story with literary agent Ellen Geiger, who pitched it to several major publishing houses, including Simon & Schuster. Prospective publishers were initially skeptical: "It sounds a little far out; most people don't think that people can be cloned."[43] But on February 22, scientists at the Roslin Institute in Scotland announced the successful cloning of a sheep named Dolly. Simon & Schuster reacted to the news with a $1 million advance for Wes's seemingly prophetic idea.

In March 1997, Wes described the novel as a cutting-edge medical thriller, tonally similar to *Three Days of the Condor*, the 1975 film starring Robert Redford as a CIA analyst turned whistleblower. He spent the following year writing the book, with some difficulty. Wes later admitted that he was overwhelmed by the amount of work involved, and turned to fellow writer Tom Baum and research assistant Jeff Fenner for support.[44] The collaborative effort resulted in a story very different from Wes's most famous screen stories—less primal horror, more Michael Crichton. Less *Scream*, more *Chiller*.

In the simplest terms, *Fountain Society* is a modern-day *Frankenstein*, a cautionary tale about unregulated scientific progress. It is also a character-driven romance. The novel's Frankenstein Monster is Dr. Peter Jance, a weapons designer for the U.S. military, whose brain gets surgically transplanted into the younger, healthier body of his biological clone. Resident mad scientist Dr. Frederick Wolfe carries out the surgery, much to the horror of Jance's wife Beatrice. The old Jance now dead, the reborn Jance is drawn to a new romantic partner, an adventuresome supermodel named Elizabeth. Wes sets her up as an idealized Final Girl: "The fact was that Elizabeth *liked* risk—yearned for the taste and challenge of it. And deep inside she was even convinced that on the other side of such places and situations lay the reality she so desired. From the slopes of Switzerland to the runways of Paris, she had found everything she treasured most by threading passageways of fear to the other side."[45] At various points in the novel, Elizabeth is also compared to the heroines of *Alice in Wonderland* and *The Wizard of Oz*. These archetypal stories are fused into a new mystery that reveals the strength of the heroine and the humanity of the Monster. Despite Jance's certainty that he has forfeited "some precious part" of his identity, the eventual melding of his two selves (old brain, new body) produces a new respect for life and nature. Beatrice and Elizabeth—who turn out to be variations on the same genetic code—also undergo transformations, and the story concludes with the suggestion that love is timeless and more powerful than death.

In September 1998, Wes delivered his manuscript to Simon & Schuster, where it continued to undergo revisions. Although he complained that the editors rewrote him, Jeff Fenner suggests the novel mostly benefited from the changes. "All good writers need a good editor, but only some are secure enough to take an editor's changes without taking the criticism personally. Wes needed an ally, somebody that he felt was on his side. If the criticism came from an outsider, he would turn them into an authority figure to rebel against—and that would turn into a poisonous dynamic." Wes's strongest allies, Fenner suggest, were those who "wanted to make him the best version of himself that he could be, without worrying about advancing their own interests." At the turn of the millennium, however, he sensed Wes wasn't sure who he could trust: "*Scream* splintered his staff a bit because he hadn't developed that film. Some people were brought into his orbit who were not natural allies." After *Scream*, Wes Craven Films was renamed Craven-Maddalena Films, which may have contributed to the sense of a growing schism.

In early 1998, Wes began focusing on his non-horror passion project. On February 13, screenwriter Pamela Gray completed the first draft of *Fifty Violins*, an early working title for *Music of the Heart*, about the life of violinist and educator Roberta Guaspari. The story appealed to Wes for several reasons. First, it tapped into his love of music—especially classical music, which he imbibed deeply during his time at Wheaton College—and reinforced his belief in the transformative power of art. Second, it reminded him of his experiences as a student and a teacher. Also, as a child of divorce and a divorcee, he could identify with divorcee Roberta as well as her son Nick, who blames Roberta for his father's absence. Wes reflected, "My father left our family when I was about the age of Nick [at the beginning of the film], so I found myself, when I was making this film, being very moved by these scenes. And also feeling like I knew the territory. There was a lot of focus on this character of the son and his resentment, terror, anger at the loss of the father. Also, looking at the mother from the aspect of being held accountable for something that she had absolutely no control over."[46] He clarified, "I understood when Roberta's kids wanted her to find a dad for them because I felt that way about my mother."[47]

Roberta's love interest in the first draft of *Fifty Violins*—a composite character named Brian—bears some similarities to Wes. In the script, Brian has authored a book of interviews with Vietnam veterans as well as a book of interviews with witnesses to a loved one's murder. When Roberta wonders aloud about Brian's decision to explore such morbid topics, he explains that he is deeply interested in people that have been "to hell and back." Roberta suggests he should write a book about her life. Wes took the bait, turning Roberta's biography into his latest film about a heroine's journey to overcome her fears.

Although the biopic was his first mainstream movie—and his reward for the success of *Scream*—Wes said he did not have the kind of creative control he yearned for. "At a certain point, Harvey [Weinstein] is saying, 'Wes, what do you think about Madonna?' He says, 'I know her. She's great. She's gonna be in *Chicago* for us. Why don't we just have a meeting? And just get to know each other.' So the next thing you know, we're in a meeting with Madonna in our offices and she's very sweet and she's read the script and she likes it. Very quickly, Harvey said, 'So? Madonna? You wanna do the film?' She says, "Yes.' 'So, Wes? You wanna do the film with Madonna?' It's like, are you gonna say no?"[48] Although several high-profile actresses (including Julia Roberts, Susan Sarandon, and Meryl Streep) were considered for the role, the executive producer made it clear that he'd made an executive decision. Marianne Maddalena says, "Harvey Weinstein really wanted Madonna. We didn't actually have a choice when it came to the casting of the lead role."[49]

By mid-July, however, the film's director and star were at odds over how to tell Roberta Guaspari's story. Madonna reportedly wanted to focus on Guaspari's "relationships with men."[50] Wes took a very different approach: "Roberta was not going to be 'rescued' by a man. It was not going to be 'some guy came into her life and made it suddenly make sense'... We wanted very much to depict her as she was in real life, which was someone who transcended the whole issue of whether she had a man in her life or not." Wes saw Roberta's story as being about "the importance of discipline, the importance of taking what you're doing very seriously, and the importance of believing that you are capable of doing something very different."[51]

"We were not far from shooting, and she was calling for more and more really drastic script changes. I felt if I went along with it, I would be giving up control of the picture I wanted to make, to make one Madonna would see but that I wouldn't. And I thought, what was the point? I wasn't going to come all this way and get my chance to make a non-genre film, just to make somebody else's movie."[52] Wes brought his dilemma to Harvey Weinstein, who was less than sympathetic. "I said to Harvey, 'She's not gonna work out.' He says, 'I can't fire Madonna. [...] You're gonna have to do it.' So I had to go to Madonna's apartment and say it wasn't working."[53] On July 20, *The Hollywood Reporter* announced that Madonna had "left" the project due to "creative differences" with the director.[54]

For a month, the filmmakers struggled to attach another star. Finally, as the project was about to be shut down, Wes made a desperate plea to his ideal leading lady, Meryl Streep. "I sat down and wrote her a very ardent letter, just pouring out my heart to her and saying I had been a teacher myself and my own life growing up in a working-class family in Cleveland had been so influenced by my exposure to classical music."[55] Streep recalls, "He said, 'This can't fall apart. I've waited twenty years to make an out-of-genre film. This is my chance and it's something I really care about.' It was stirring and an undeniable plea, and I couldn't say no."[56] With the new star on board, the filmmakers scheduled an early winter shoot in New York City.

Meanwhile, three other Wes Craven projects were struggling to come alive. In May 1998, Fox TV had announced that a new series titled *Hollyweird*, executive produced by the master of horror, would appear in the network's fall lineup. In the pilot developed by singer Shaun Cassidy, a young couple from Ohio move to Los Angeles to investigate Tinseltown's most bizarre murders. Actress Melissa George was cast as the Nancy Drew-type sleuth, with Fabrizio Filippo and Bodhi Elfman in supporting roles. At some point between May and July, however, Fox execs decided to replace

Wes Craven directing Meryl Streep in *Music of the Heart*
(Miramax, 1999)

the two actors and rethink the concept of the series. In August, following a second round of major changes, Cassidy walked away from the project and Fox withdrew the title from its slate.

One month later, filming began on *Don't Look Down* (a.k.a. *Wes Craven Presents Don't Look Down*), an ABC TV movie conceived as "the first entry in… an annual Craven film event each Halloween."[57] On his official website, Wes described an even more ambitious plan for a TV series titled *Wes Craven's House of Fear*, which would consist of four episodes per year. Despite his grand plans, Wes had minimal involvement with *Don't Look Down,* and *House of Fear* never materialized. The former aired on October 29, 1998, exactly twenty years after Wes's first TV venture, *Stranger in Our House*, but the new movie's ghostly exploration of psychological trauma failed to inspire future "events."

Undaunted, that same month Wes revamped his deal with Miramax and Dimension, promising to direct three films (including *Scream 3*) for them over the next four years, and to executive produce four additional genre films under the "Wes Craven Presents" banner.[58] The deal was particularly ambitious while Wes was also developing a film based on his newly published *Fountain Society*. Five months earlier, he and Marianne Maddalena had pitched it to legendary producer Robert Evans over dinner at his Beverly Hills estate. The evening did not go quite as planned. In his memoir, Evans wrote, "I lifted my glass and made a toast to my guest. 'To you, Wes, one of the few directors in town who is an above-the-title star. Welcome to Woodland.' A bolt of lightning shot through my body. Like a pyramid of wooden matchsticks, I crumbled to the floor." Maddalena recalls their host's next statement: "I think I'm having a stroke." The guests called for an ambulance and followed it to the emergency room at Cedars-Sinai Medical Center. Later, Evans marveled at the effect of his own performance on the reputed master of horror: "The King of Scream? He was scared shitless.'"[59]

As Evans recovered, *Fountain Society* moved to the back burner and Wes committed fully to *Music of the Heart*. Filming began in late October and continued until early 1999, culminating with a three-day shoot at Carnegie Hall in New York. For Wes, it was a homecoming, a dream come true, and the culmination of his career as a filmmaker. "I told everybody if I got hit by a truck the next day, after finishing this picture, I would feel like my life had everything in it that it needed. It was just a great chance and it all worked out so beautifully."[60] Marianne Maddalena agrees. "Even though *Music of the Heart* wasn't a big commercial success, it was as exciting as *Scream*, because on another level we had so much fun making it. We shot in Carnegie Hall. We took the film to the White House. We showed it to the President. Everything about it was so wonderful, exciting and, most importantly, inspirational."[61] Andrea Eastman adds, "The two deals I made for Wes that were completely different were for *Serpent and the Rainbow* and *Music of the Heart*. I'm very proud of having those movies under my belt with him. *Music of the Heart* was not a big hit, but it was very respectable." In fact, it would become the only Wes Craven film to earn Oscar nominations—for Best Actress and Best Original Song.

In making the film, Wes felt he had finally escaped the stigma of being a horror filmmaker. On one particular shoot day, however, his past continued to haunt him. Sarah Nicholson, who had starred in Wes's unclaimed film *The Fireworks Woman*, appeared on the set of *Music of the Heart*, looking for work.

At that time, the actress was running a catering business in New York. She remembers, "I returned to New York, after having a food production facility in western Vermont, to see [Wes] when he was directing a movie with Meryl Streep." Although she managed to get a meeting with her former collaborator, "He was embarrassed. He couldn't give me a job, even though I desperately needed one. I said, 'You don't have to put me on camera. Just put me on the crew.' He was nervous about even… anything."[62]

Wes's reaction is understandable. Directing *Music of the Heart* was not just the culmination of a lifelong dream. He was also making a film that his mother and siblings, as well as many of his oldest friends, would approve of. He certainly didn't want to risk being pulled backward or drawing attention to a controversial film that his friends, family, and fans didn't (at that time) know about.

Music's arrival in theaters in September 1999 was a moment of celebration. Wes flew several family members, including sister-in-law Donna Craven, from Cleveland to New York for the premiere. She remembers, "We stayed in this top-notch, five-star hotel. Wes's sister Carole and my brother-in-law, who was a minister, came. It was the first [Wes Craven film] they ever saw."

It was also the first movie of Wes's that his mother had ever watched. The film came out over the weekend of her 91st birthday. According to Wes, her response was, "Well, honey, why didn't you do something like that before?"[63] Wes's niece Corinne remembers, "Grandma was so excited. She came back to Cleveland and told everyone in the nursing home about her son who had made this wonderful movie." After his mother's death in 2002, Wes said, "So in some ways she died happy; her pretty little boy had finally done something decent."[64]

Why it was so important for Wes to have this moment of maternal validation? Donna suggests that for much of his life, he just couldn't get his mother's disapproval out of his head: "It was a huge problem for him. And she didn't offer too much. He used to put tape recorders on her kitchen table and try to get her talking about the past. He had all these questions—but she wouldn't talk to him." Caroline and Wes would sit in silence for hours. The experience was excruciating for him. "He was always haunted by stuff about his mom. I felt bad for him because he couldn't let it go. Could not let it go."

The Cravens: Wes, Paul Jr., Carole, and Caroline, 1991
(courtesy Donna Craven)

One time in the late 1990s, Donna remembers, Wes returned to Cleveland for a press junket to promote one of his films. "He picked us up in a limo—me, my husband, and his mother. We went to one of the local TV stations and he did his thing, promoting the movie. We were sitting in the audience, and his mother couldn't hear very well—until the interviewer asked Wes about his past. [He talked about] how his dad had passed away and his mom had raised him, and all the different places they had lived in Cleveland. The interviewer said, 'Why did you move so much?' Wes said, 'My mother was a bookie.' When she heard that, she stood up and screamed, 'I was not!' She stood right up in her chair and yelled at him, 'Wesley! That is not true!' Everything stopped. I had to drag her out of the studio, into the bathroom. She was yelling, 'Why would he say something like that?!' I said, 'He was kidding.' 'Now everybody's gonna think I was a bookie!' When I came out of the bathroom, Wes goes, 'How bad was it?' I said, 'Well, she's calmed down now.' But the station manager and the show's editor had to reassure her that [the bookie comment] wouldn't be in the show. She was worried about what her church friends would think. Up until the day she died, that's how she was."

When *Music of the Heart* came out, Caroline Craven didn't have to worry what people would think of her wayward son—or, by extension, her and her family. On one level, Wes had finally earned her approval. Understandably, he was reluctant to return to horror. Events over the course of 1999 amplified his reluctance. That April, the mass shooting at Columbine High School inspired a Presidential Summit on Youth Violence. In a Congressional hearing, a U.S. senator used clips from *Scream* to prove that Hollywood movies were corrupting the youth of America. Wes's former Clarkson colleague Stuart Fischoff, a well-respected media psychologist, offered a less inflammatory opinion, saying, "'There are, of course, many other factors that contribute to violence in general and Columbine in particular. But they embrace social forces, which are far more difficult to manage. These are socially and politically desperate, perilous and opportunistic times. Media-manufactured violence is an easier and, in truth, a slower moving target. And Congress is taking dead aim."[65]

Wes had grown tired of being a target for the self-proclaimed "moral majority" in America—and his fatigue may have influenced the more light-hearted, comedic tone of *Scream 3*. According to Wes, "Kevin's outline was set in high school, and the plot was that this girl and a group of friends was killing people."[66] Co-producer Julie Plec elaborates, "We wanted to basically tell the story of Woodsboro ten years later, after everything had happened and the town had gone up into like a curfew lockdown. The kids that were too young to know the teenagers when *Scream* happened were now teenagers themselves and had lived in the shadow of that and were fucked up as a result."[67] Actor Matthew Lillard adds, "I was supposed to do *Scream 3* […] because the idea was that I'd be running high school killers from jail."[68] After the tragedy at Columbine, Wes said, "That's not going to happen."[69]

By the time the filmmakers decided to rewrite the script, Williamson was committed elsewhere, so the *Scream* team turned to newcomer Ehren Kruger. He remembers, "I came on and said, 'We were in high school in the first one, in a small town. Then we took the characters to a little bigger place, and to college, in the second one. Let's just continue that. Instead of bringing Hollywood to Woodsboro, let's take these characters to Hollywood and give them a bigger haunted house to run around in."[70] According to Wes, "He turned in a fantastic first draft, and we basically just built on that. There were plenty of changes, but that's just part of the process."[71] When Kruger also became unavailable, screenwriter Laeta Kalogridis came on board. Wes also did a fair amount of rewriting, most notably adding a signature dream sequence starring Sidney's dead mother.[72] Rewrites continued even as the film was being shot.

The main goal, Wes said, was to do justice to the legacy characters, especially Sidney Prescott. Envisioning the films as a more mainstream trilogy built around the growth of the heroes instead of the indestructibility of the villains, he summed up Sidney's arc: "It's about moving beyond the heritage of your own house and your own parents. It's about the limitations of revenge, and the difficulty of confronting evil and violence without becoming evil and violent yourself. It's about moving past tragedy to a moment in your life where it seems there's a chance for renewal and it's safe to leave the doors unlocked."[73] In *Scream 3*, Sidney doesn't just stop another sadistic killer; she stops allowing the existence of sadistic killers in the world to dictate how she lives her life. Once again, she overcomes her fear. In the final scene, she leaves her door open for one last scare—but, because this was meant to be Wes's final *Scream* (if not his final horror film)—the villain doesn't get the final word.

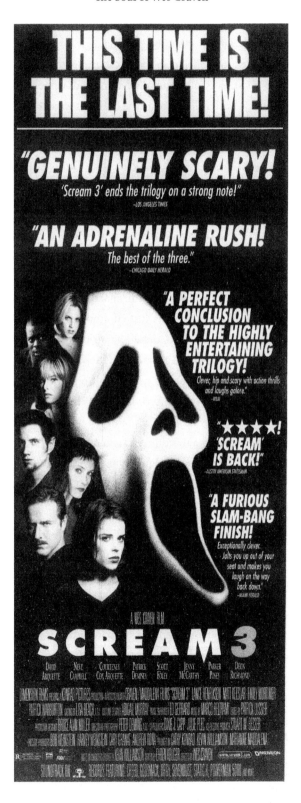

Wes celebrated his 60th birthday on the set of *Scream 3*, a milestone event separating old ghosts from new hopes. In promotional interviews, he said he was putting horror films—at least, a certain type of horror films—behind him. "If I do go back to genre," he declared, "I'm going to have more adult standards, more like *The Sixth Sense* than going back to people chasing people around with sharp instruments."[74] At the time, he was hoping to direct an adaptation of *Fountain Society* for DreamWorks by the summer of 2000.[75] Until then, he was hoping to travel and relax.

On November 27, 1999, Wes chatted with fans via his official website. Asked if he was living a "good life," he responded with the confidence and gratitude of a man who has achieved a hearty measure of success. "It's been as good as I could ever imagine it. It's a very tough life really; success brings with it just constant work and sort of a sacrifice of personal life a lot. But the pleasure of being creative and being surrounded by creative people and fun and funny people and imaginative people is wonderful."

Wes entered the 21st century feeling optimistic.

The Soul of Wes Craven

CHAPTER TWELVE

THE CURSE OF CHRISTOPHER WREN
(2000 - 2006)

"It's always night, or we wouldn't need light."

- Thelonious Monk (attributed)

Horror cinema was in a slump, Wes said at a Writer's Guild conference on June 4, 1999. He suggested the genre was languishing in an eight to ten-year popularity cycle that wouldn't end until someone "breaks through and does something personal." The challenge for any serious horror filmmaker, he said, is to avoid relying on formulas that have worked before and to "go into your own dark side as deeply as you dare go, and bring that out in a way that's interesting to yourself, and in a way that you can say 'I have not seen this before on the screen.'"[1] Over the course of three successive decades, he had helmed three breakthrough horror films—*Last House on the Left* (1972), *A Nightmare on Elm Street* (1984), and *Scream* (1996)—each released twelve years apart. To continue this pattern of success, he'd have to come up with another deeply personal horror movie idea by 2008.

Although he'd essentially given himself marching orders, a series of events distracted Wes from developing a new, deeply personal horror film over the following years. First, Bob Weinstein had his own plan to reboot horror cinema for the new millennium. The movie mogul thought he could make money off of a film titled *Dracula 2000*—even better: *Wes Craven Presents Dracula 2000*—if only he had a story. Seizing the opportunity, Wes's longtime editor Patrick Lussier wrote a script that captured the attention of both Bob and Wes.[2] Lussier's re-telling of the legend hinged on a revelation that the king of the vampires is actually Judas Iscariot, cursed with immortality for his betrayal of Jesus. Despite some concern among Dimension execs that the story would anger the Religious Right in America, Weinstein's title had a built-in expiration date and the project moved forward at a breakneck pace.

As the production approached a late June 2000 start date, a host of screenwriters—including Joel Soisson, Scott Derrickson, Paul Harris Boardman, and Ehren Kruger—revised the script. According to Soisson, Wes also helped to mold the script "in ways that didn't change the story, but took advantage of techniques that he's very aware of, and insights."[3] Patrick Lussier claims, however, that Wes couldn't keep up with all the constant changes; he remained involved as an executive producer until the film was cast, then stepped back and gave Lussier creative control over his directorial debut. A personal health crisis also prompted the withdrawal.

Donna Craven became concerned about her brother-in-law's health around Easter 2000, when she and Wes's brother Paul visited him on Martha's Vineyard. She remembers, "We were supposed to go to a big party thrown by a lady who sold real estate on the island. That morning, Wes was so tired that he could barely walk. I said, 'Do you really want to go to this party? We can hang out here.' He said, 'No, I want to go.' So we went. And when we were ready to go home, he gave Paul his car keys and said, 'I don't even think I can drive.' He got in the back seat and laid down; he was that exhausted. The next day, he flew back to Los Angeles and we went back to Ohio."

"Maybe a month later—beginning of June—we got a call from [his girlfriend] Cornelia Kiss, saying, 'Wes has to have quadruple bypass surgery on his heart tomorrow.' So Paul and I flew to Los Angeles in the morning and went to see him in the hospital at Cedars-Sinai. When we got there, I said to Wes, 'Are you going to take a break from work now?' He said, 'Yeah, I'm kind of being forced to.'"

At one time, Wes had feared he would die at the age of 40, just like his father. At age 60, he was finally being forced to confront a genetic predisposition to heart disease. Cornelia Kiss says he did it quickly and privately. "He tried really hard to keep it quiet. In the filmmaking business, you have to. You have to keep things moving. He knew how close he had come to death—he heard those words—but he didn't feel it for very long. Once he recovered, he wanted to get back to work as soon as possible." By the end of the summer, Wes and Cornelia's relationship ended, and Wes was actively pursuing a new beginning for his filmmaking career.

A year prior, Wes had hired a development executive named Alix Taylor to find some exciting non-horror projects for him to produce and direct. Around the same time, Miramax acquired the film adaptation rights for *Drowning Ruth*, Christina Schwarz's debut novel about carefully-guarded family secrets, mental illness, and the bonds of tragedy. Taylor thought it would make an ideal transitional project for Wes. The idea gained traction in September 2000, when Schwarz's novel became an official selection of Oprah's Book Club, guaranteeing an audience for any potential film adaptation.

Not everyone was optimistic about the prospect. Reviewing the novel for *The Washington Post*, Carolyn See wrote, "It's easy to imagine the scary movie this might make [...] but the book itself offers much more tender gifts—the shore, the lake, the island, all keeping their own mysteries while distraught humans go about, thinking that they're the center of attention."[4] To demonstrate the sincerity of his interest in the material, Wes made an appearance on *The Oprah Winfrey Show*, and said, "I really would just like to capture the sense of the book and the devastating power of secrets in a family, and show how horrible that can be, especially for young people who are left with secrets from the previous generation. They don't have clues from the people that could tell them and they have to piece it together themselves." A few days later, Miramax executives claimed they were "moving forward" with the adaptation—just as soon as Wes finished directing *Fountain Society* for DreamWorks.[5]

While Amy Holden Jones wrote the script for *Fountain Society* and Mark Kruger adapted *Drowning Ruth*, Wes's development team continued to look for additional non-horror projects. In August, Craven-Maddalena Films purchased the rights to Oprah-endorsed author Chris Bohjalian's new novel *Trans-Sister Radio*, a kaleidoscopic narrative about family and secrets. The central character, a film professor named Dana Stevens, falls in love with fellow teacher Alison Banks around the same time he's planning to undergo a sex change operation. The relationship transforms the lives of Alison's teenage daughter Carly and her ex-husband Will, and reveals a strain of intolerance within their small-town New England community. The novel seemed particularly provocative when it was released in 2000, which might have been part of the appeal for Wes. Certainly, one of the recurring themes of his work—and of horror films in general—is the struggle of the outsider, often perceived as a "monstrous" threat to the status quo and mainstream social mandates.

As in many of Wes's films, the younger generation in *Trans-Sister Radio* adapts more easily to change. In one passage, Alison reflects on her daughter's perspective on Dana's transformation: "After his surgery, she had observed, he would still have the same brain, the same soul, the same sense of right and wrong. The same sense of humor. The same understanding of exactly how much fresh mint should go into a summer pea salad. Why, she had asked me, would the things that she loved most about him have to change once he'd had his surgery?"[6] *Fountain Society* had revolved around similar questions about the fluid nature of personal identity and the durability of romantic love, posing the question of whether a marriage can survive a radical bodily transformation. Such questions were clearly important to Wes. Just as his novel's preoccupation with the subject of human cloning seemed prescient after Dolly the Sheep, so Bohjalian's novel seems to anticipate the LGBTQ+ Rights movement of the 21st century. Unfortunately, *Trans-Sister Radio* did not move forward.

On November 1, entertainment industry trades announced that Wes Craven's production company had snapped up the rights to *The Day I Went Missing*, a memoir of a young woman manipulated and financially exploited by her therapist. The story may have had a personal appeal for Wes, especially the final pages in which author Jennifer Miller sums up the lasting impact of her experience: "I doubt I'll ever trust someone a hundred percent. I know that I got fooled once, and I'm not stupid enough to think it's impossible it couldn't happen again. Never say never. I trusted someone a thousand percent, and was completely, utterly wrong. How can you possibly know who's good and who's bad? Really, really know?"[7] Just as Miller credits Gavin de Becker's 1997 book *The Gift of Fear* with helping her to understand her vulnerability to such manipulation, Wes once named William Sargent's 1957 book *The Battle for the Mind: A Physiology of Conversion and Brainwashing* as a book that "shaped" him.[8] Perhaps he hoped a film version of *The Day I Went Missing* would offer similar help to others.

Wes arranged a meeting with veteran TV writer Donald Martin, who says, "At that time, I hadn't done horror, so I thought, *What does he want to talk to me about?* In our first meeting, I even jokingly asked, 'Are we here to talk about a *Scream* movie?' He said, 'Absolutely not. I'm tired of making those movies. I'm much more than that.' We talked and he was so professorial and so intellectual and such a gentle soul. He started pitching me this book that he loved, Jennifer Miller's *The Day I Went Missing*, and telling me what intrigued him about the story. He said, 'In a way, this is a horror story but it's a horror story of a much more intimate and personal nature, because of what this con artist did to Jennifer, and what she went through emotionally.'" Martin proceeded to tell Wes about a bizarre and darkly humorous experience he'd had in his own life, with a therapist that became infatuated with him. By the end of the meeting, both men were laughing helplessly. Wes had found the right collaborator.

"He said, 'Here's the book, go read it, then let's talk next week and you can give me your take on it.' So I read the book. I identified with it a lot, in terms of Jennifer Miller's dysfunctional family background, which was not so different from my own. My therapist didn't steal money from me, but I could relate to Jennifer's experience and I just loved the story so much. I went back and pitched my take on the story to Wes and his team, and they immediately said yes. I wrote a treatment, I wrote a first draft, I wrote a second draft. It was such a joy to work with Wes because his notes were so succinct and intelligent. He and I were clearly on the same page, creatively and thematically. He signed off on my second draft and everybody was excited. Then it went to Miramax. And we waited. A month later, Wes finally got a response—and he couldn't believe it. We met for coffee and he said, 'They gave me this development deal to appease me, but they were never serious.' He felt that he had been misled, that they just wanted to keep him doing horror so they gave him a development fund to play with but they never had any intention of making anything [non-horror] with him. He was deeply hurt. And it was shocking to me, as an artist, because to me Wes was someone who had 'made it.' He was a big success, he was a brand name, he was *Wes Craven*. I thought he could do anything he wanted, but I was wrong."

In some ways, Wes might have felt like he was repeating his experience following *Last House on the Left*, when he struggled desperately to avoid making another horror film but no one would hire him for anything else. Since he'd completed the *Scream* trilogy, he'd had access to the best spec scripts and studio stars in Hollywood, but he still couldn't break away from his fright-master reputation. As a horror director, he'd made a lot of money for a lot of people, most notably the Weinsteins, who'd invested heavily in the director's name brand and didn't want him to close the door on horror. If he wanted to work, all Wes had to do was say yes to a new horror movie. For the time being, he held back.

Wes continued to look for opportunities to tell different kinds of stories, which included making himself available as a director-for-hire. In October 2000, he forged a deal with UPN television network to produce and direct an untitled pilot written by Karl Schaefer, creator of *Eerie, Indiana* and *Strange Luck*, "about a wealthy mogul and a woman who specializes in artificial intelligence as they explore the supernatural."[9] Around the same time, Around the same time, Wes collaborated with RC Matheson and real-life psychic cop James Van Praagh on a prospective

TV series. Van Praagh's story eventually migrated to CBS, where it became *Living with the Dead* (2002), a TV movie starring Ted Danson and directed by Stephen Gyllenhaal. The Karl Schaefer project did not get made. Wes kept looking.

In January 2001, he accepted a surprising opportunity to direct the President of the United States. Wes and Marianne Maddalena had held a private screening of *Music of the Heart* for Bill and Hillary Clinton at the White House in 1999. Two years later, the first couple invited the filmmakers back to create a short, intimate documentary for the William J. Clinton Library and Museum. During the final days of the Clinton White House, they were granted a personal tour of the Oval Office, the Treaty Room, and the Music Room. The president also gave a sit-down interview in which he shared stories about his early years and personal relationships, as well as his outlook on America and its future. Unfortunately, the documentary was never completed.

At the time of his second visit to Pennsylvania Avenue, Wes's name was haunting theaters in the guise of *Dracula 2000*. Although the revamp grossed less than its reported production budget, it launched a new horror franchise and inspired Dimension execs to resurrect more classic horror movie monsters. The studio announced that Wes would direct a new adaptation of Robert Louis Stevenson's *The Strange Tale of Dr. Jekyll and Mr. Hyde*, with screenwriter Craig Rosenberg contributing "a few twists" to the familiar story.[10] Around the same time, Wes worked on an update of Henry James's ghost story *The Turn of the Screw*. He also attached his name to a film version of American McGee's video game *Alice*, a dark and violent re-telling of *Alice's Adventures in Wonderland*. Any of these projects could have been a natural fit for the reputed master of cinematic horror.

By summer, Wes was in negotiations to direct a remake of Dominik Moll's 2000 thriller *With a Friend Like Harry* for Miramax. The original French-language film, in which an interloper systematically dismantles his rival's perfect life, had been a modest hit, drawing comparisons to the work of Alfred Hitchcock and Roman Polanski. Eager to follow in those same footsteps, Wes signed on. Plans were made to film in uptown Manhattan, with a cast including Rufus Sewell, Christopher Walken, and Mary McCormack.[11] Unfortunately, the filmmakers couldn't nail the script. Marianne Maddalena says, "We hired a writer named Greg Pruss to write it, but it was a difficult story to tell as far as audience sympathy goes. It was very French, not very American."

In August 2001, *Alice* and *Harry* were still in development but *Jekyll & Hyde* and *The Turn of the Screw* apparently were not. Cody Zwieg, then a new hire at Craven-Maddalena Films, remembers that his first reaction to the development slate was, *Where's the horror?* "There were at least twenty total projects in development, maybe more, but I don't know that there were any horror projects. That was a head-scratcher for me. It seemed like a statement, a conscious shift. I found it fascinating that the master of horror was looking to do something completely different."

Wes was now actively pursuing director-for-hire jobs on mainstream, major studio thrillers—including *The Farm* (which became the 2003 film *The Recruit*, starring Al Pacino and Colin Farrell) and *Perfect Stranger*, initially set up as a star vehicle for Julia Roberts.[12] The latter apparently caused a rift between Wes and his longtime agent. On November 13, 2001, entertainment industry trades announced that ICM client Philip Kaufman would direct *Perfect Stranger*.[13] Two weeks after that, the same publications announced that Wes and Marianne had left ICM and signed with the William Morris Agency.[14] Cody Zwieg says, "Wes ended up working with a new agent, Mike Simpson, who was very helpful to Wes. I think he brought him around to understanding and appreciating how strongly horror fans felt about him."

Wes returned to horror in the wake of 9/11, the biggest real-life horror in decades. Most filmmakers were carefully avoiding the genre at that time, but Wes apparently decided that a certain type of horror film could help viewers face timeless fears in that troubled time. He explained, "Most horror films are unrealistic and copycat. They don't inspire you to be a better human being. And I think that's possible by looking into the spiritual elements of fear. Horror movies are about the horror of being mortal."[15]

On November 28, *Variety* announced that Wes Craven would direct a remake of director Kiyoshi Kurosawa's Japanese-language thriller *Kairo* (a.k.a. *Pulse*) for Dimension Films.[16] Kurosawa summed up the central idea of his film as follows: "Ghosts are death made real; they are the presence of death among the living, and I thought: is there a way, by using ghosts in a public manner, to portray how society at large deals with death?"[17] Released in February 2001, *Pulse* portrayed the dehumanizing effects of rapid technological progress in the Internet Age. As one character says, "Death traps us in our loneliness."

The film's overwhelming tone of despair shifts in the final act, when a young couple's romance transcends death, suggesting the dawn of a new era in which the living co-exist with the dead. Kurosawa reflects, "We were really on the cusp of a new century. The idea was to abandon, by destroying, everything from the 20th century in order to head into a good, new future. It wasn't that the apocalyptic vision was negative or despairing; it was positive, a way to get rid of old baggage."[18] The apocalyptic vision hit even harder after September 11, 2001.

In many ways, Kurosawa's story seems like a natural extension of Wes's perspective on the *Scream* trilogy. Commenting on the first *Scream*, Wes said, "There's definitely a tone, I think, that comes over a culture towards the end of a century and certainly towards the end of a millennium where you feel like nothing is quite in the right place anymore, and you're sort of moving toward some dark revelation." Wes added that "the modern age was conceived to be [...] 'everything's going to be alright through technology.' And 'post-modern,' in the loosest sense, can be that that dream, that illusion, is over, and we're sort of moving to where we're having a much more realistic view of the way mankind is going—that it's not all going to be solved by technology. I think [*Scream*] very much reflects that in the young people's attitudes, that technology is not bringing peace and love."[19] In comparison, *Pulse* is a post-modern horror film that finds love in the ether between two worlds connected by a dial-up modem.

Cody Zwieg suggests Wes was eager to remake *Pulse* because "the Weinsteins gave him the opportunity to write the script, which they hadn't done before, and I think he wanted to be respected as a writer, even more than a director." Seizing the opportunity to get back to his pre-*Scream* roots as an *auteur*, Wes completed his first draft of *Pulse* in early 2002. His goal was to faithfully translate Kurosawa's story to the American landscape.[20] Some of his closest collaborators, however, found the new script too faithful, suffering from lapses in storytelling logic (like the film it was based on) and inconsistencies of tone. Cody Zweig says, "I don't think he knew what the Weinsteins wanted from him. He thought they wanted more of the same, so he was trying to do a *Scream* version of *Pulse*. The two tones didn't work together."

The script quickly entered the Miramax/Dimension mill of storytelling-by-committee. As with *Scream 2, Scream 3,* and *Dracula 2000*, an eventual shooting script was cobbled together by several writers, including future

Breaking Bad creator Vince Gilligan. The screen story remained in flux in late June, with filming scheduled to begin in September, and producers worrying they wouldn't be ready in time.

In the interval, Wes flirted with other film projects. In April 2002, Miramax purchased Leslie Dixon's rom-com spec script *Accidentally Yours* for Wes to produce and possibly direct. In that story, a hopelessly clumsy man falls in love with a graceful woman who works in a china shop. In his effort to woo her, the man takes ballroom dancing lessons—with predictably disastrous results.[21] Ultimately, neither *Accidentally Yours* nor *Pulse* would get made on Wes Craven's watch.

Two years earlier, in the midst of a post-production crisis on *Dracula 2000*, Wes had offered this pithy—and prescient—advice to anyone wanting to make movies with the Weinstein brothers: "They don't pay you for what you do. They pay you for what they do to you." Decrying the "terribly difficult and completely unnecessary" way that Dimension execs made (and remade) films on agonizingly aggressive schedules, he urged his fellow filmmakers to "cross your legs and wear a cup."[22] Maybe he should have been prepared, then, for what happened in the fall of 2002. According to Marianne Maddalena, five weeks before the anticipated start date, "Bob Weinstein suddenly pulled the plug on *Pulse* and said 'Make *Cursed* instead.'"

Wes told his future protégé Nick Simon that the studio scrapped *Pulse* because Weinstein thought it was too similar to the 2002 film *The Ring*—an unlikely rationale considering that *The Ring* made nearly $250 million at the American box office (and that the Weinsteins eventually made *Pulse* anyway). Patrick Lussier suggests a more likely explanation, that the studio heads killed *Pulse* in order to force Wes to make *Cursed*: "The Weinsteins knew Wes had a core team, people he worked with all the time, who were committed to *Pulse*. At this point in his career, it was no longer just him and Marianne. It was thirty to forty other people, and a potential 150 crew members on top of that. All of those people would be out of work. I think they used Wes's kindness and compassion for his team in order to make him do what they wanted." Wes himself said the Dimension execs "made us an offer that we kind of had to accept, to do this film *Cursed*."[23]

Scream writer Kevin Williamson reportedly brought his concept for *Cursed* to Dimension in 2000, at which time the story focused on a New

York college student carrying a werewolf gene that heightens her abilities as a dancer, and on a serial killer who attacks her. The young woman bites back and the killer begins changing into a werewolf. Later, once he realizes what has happened, the killer hunts down the dancer, setting up a climactic duel between werewolves. The project was first announced on October 15, 2002— with Wes Craven, post-*Pulse*, in the director's chair—but the story shape-shifted until filming began the following spring. By then, *Cursed* had become a satirical horror film about a trio of werewolves.

Wes initially rejected the comedic version because it reminded him too much of *Vampire in Brooklyn*, which had failed to achieve the delicate balance between comedy and horror. An eye-popping director's fee, an all-star cast, and perhaps some nagging reminders that he initially turned down *Scream* changed his mind. Wes later said he should have known better. Marianne Maddalena adds, "We just never had a script. Bob Weinstein just took a gamble and we agreed to it, and it was the wrong bet."[24]

Filming began on March 17, 2003, with the three main werewolf roles played by Christina Ricci, Jesse Eisenberg, and Skeet Ulrich. Sometime in June, after 54 days of shooting, the production was shut down and the script was taken back to the development phase. Julie Plec recalls, "We stopped shooting to rewrite the ending, but in needing to rewrite the ending, we sort of realized that most of the movie didn't work. So, then we rewrote, like, most of the movie."[25]

Wes said the story had to be readjusted to account for a major change in character dynamics: "While we were trying to develop a love story between Skeet and Christina's characters, Jesse's character was moving totally separate from them. […] So when we changed things around and went with the idea of Christina and Jesse being brother and sister, it all just kind of flowed together."[26] Unfortunately, the changes prompted Skeet Ulrich and several other cast members to walk away. In late 2003, Joshua Jackson joined the cast to play a completely new character and filming resumed on December 2. In early 2004, the "Josh Jackson cut" was completed and test-screened. Editor Patrick Lussier says, "It scored in the 60s, which is good enough that people think they can make it better if they sink more money into it, but not good enough to stand on its own for the money they've already spent." After two more reshoots, which altered the ending and turned Jackson's character into a villain, Wes delivered his director's

Christina Ricci as Ellie in *Cursed* (Dimension, 2005)

cut, only to have the producers re-cut it. He said the film was "basically taken away from us and cut to PG-13 and ruined."[27] In February 2005, *Cursed* finally arrived in theaters to disappointing box office numbers and scathing reviews.

At the end of the two-year debacle, Wes lamented, "There's so much I could have done with my time."[28] Numerous film and television projects had fallen by the wayside during the interval—including a television pilot titled *Kamelot*, "in which King Arthur is resurrected as a hip revolutionary who reigns supreme in a Camelot-like future society"[29]; a supernatural thriller called *The Waiting*, in which a woman believes she is being haunted by her dead child; an untitled "cop / exorcist project" based on the real-life accounts of NYPD detective / demonologist Ralph Sarchie; a romantic comedy titled *Whole New You*, about a famous actress who escapes the burden of being famous by posing as herself in a celebrity lookalike contest; and *Wildcard*, a comedy of errors in which a pair of con artists target a wealthy mark. Wes also had to decline the chance to make a standalone episode of the Showtime series *Masters of Horror*.[30]

As he endured *Cursed*—and *Cursed* again, and *Cursed* again—the filmmaker's personal life was equally disquieting. Since the summer of 2000, Wes had been living a solitary life and, to some who saw him every day, appeared lonely. His mother Caroline's passing in November 2002 prompted him to think seriously about his relationships and his future. One month later, he told Wheaton alum Ron Watson, "I suddenly have this feeling, Oh my god, I'm next. There's a long line of life and suddenly you realize you're next in line, or you're at the head of the line. Suddenly, I have this feeling, What am I doing living alone?"[31] Although he'd said for years that he would never get married again, fate intervened.

Wes's longtime friend Barry Cahn approached him at a New Year's party and asked if he was dating anyone. Wes replied, "I'm retired from love." Apparently, that did not deter Barry from playing matchmaker.[32] Barry had a similar conversation with Iya Labunka, a 30-year veteran of the entertainment industry who had worked her way up from production coordinator (for Roger Corman's film company, as well as director Alex Cox's debut film *Repo Man*) to line producer and associate producer (on *Stand and Deliver* and *Heathers*, among others) to an Executive Vice President position at Disney (where she managed films directed by Jonathan Demme, M. Night Shyamalan, Wes

Anderson, Spike Lee, and many more.) Like Wes, Iya was divorced, independent, and had no interest in dating. She recalls, "Barry said, 'You gotta meet this guy.' I was working; I was raising a child; I was a studio executive. I was busy and I just said, 'No, I'm not interested.' But he wouldn't give up. He just wouldn't give up. I finally said, 'Okay, who is it?' And Barry goes, 'Well….' I said, 'No, don't tell me, I don't want to know. I'll either like the guy or not.'"[33]

Iya agreed to meet the mysterious stranger on the condition that it would be a double-date with Barry and his wife Sherri, so the matchmaker made reservations at a restaurant in Hollywood. When the night arrived, Iya remained hesitant. "I'm driving to the restaurant, going, *I can't even believe I agreed to this. This is ridiculous. I don't even know who this is. This is a waste of time.* I'm a block away from the restaurant and a black cat walks across the street in front of my car. And I'm like, *This is not gonna go well. This is such a bad sign.* I'm just trying to recover from that, saying [to myself], *I promised Barry, so I'm gonna go.* Meanwhile, the radio is on, and KCRW, the local NPR station, is running a contest. The prize is two free tickets to a play. Now, I have never won anything in my life. I don't know what possessed me [to call]. Car phones were a new thing so I somehow dialed the number, got through—which is crazy—and won two tickets for the play. I'm like, *Okay, there was a black cat, but I just won something. This could be interesting.*

"I walk into the restaurant and I see Barry waving me back. We go to the back of the restaurant and there, leaning against the bar, was Tall, Dark and Handsome. And Barry says, 'This is Wes Craven.' I just burst out laughing. It was like, *Are you freakin' kidding me?* It was crazy." Iya was not a horror movie fan; she had never seen any of Wes's films. Nevertheless, because she worked in the industry, she was very much aware of his stature in the world of genre filmmaking—and she quickly got to know him as a person. "We sat down to dinner, the four of us, and—I have to tell you—we did not stop talking for five hours."[34]

Wes said, "We just hit it off. We spent the dinner laughing. We had a lot in common—we both had kids, and her father had been a college professor— and we started dating immediately."[35]

Well, maybe not *immediately.* Iya explains, "I met Wes on Friday night and I went to my friend's house on Sunday and told them, 'I'm in trouble. Why hasn't this guy called?' Because, you know, we talked for *five hours*! And then I heard nothing on Saturday, nothing on Sunday. Wes finally called me on Monday and said, 'Let's go out.' So we went to the see this play that I'd won the tickets for, then went to dinner afterwards, and talked and talked and talked. That was the night we both realized that this was very serious. I can still feel the moment that I fell in love with him—which is incredible, to know exactly when it happened. He was being so open and honest and straightforward about himself, in a way I'd never seen in a man. He said, 'I have nothing to lose. I'm laying it all out on the table.' He was so vulnerable and so fearless. No games. No bullshit. Here it is. I fell in love with him in that minute." Sometime later, just to satisfy her curiosity, Iya asked Wes why it had taken him two days to call her for a second date. "He said, 'I knew if I picked up that phone, we were going to get married. And I needed the weekend to think about it.'"

On the couple's third date, they went to the J. Paul Getty Museum in Los Angeles. There, they had a long lunch and Wes explained that he was at a crossroads in his professional life and he felt he needed to make some changes. "He didn't feel he had the support he needed. Mind you, he was not asking me to step in [and play a role in his professional life]. He was simply telling me about his life. And he made a very wise decision to keep our relationship private for the first three months—which wasn't easy because he had an entourage of people who surrounded him. That was a defining, foundational act. It allowed us to figure out who we were and what we wanted out of our relationship."

By March, the relationship had gotten serious enough for Wes to meet Iya's 12-year-old daughter Nina Tarnawsky. She recalls, "I thought it was weird that my mom had a boyfriend, but he seemed like a nice enough person. Quiet but friendly. I remember we were driving home from his house, and she basically said, 'I really like this guy'—in a way that made it clear: *This is happening.*"

Wes and Iya continued to find common ground, including a shared love of nature. On one early date, they went on a bird-watching expedition in Malibu—a private trip hosted by world-renowned ornithologist Frank Gill, senior vice president of the National Audubon Society. Iya recalls, "My first true 'birding' experience was with Frank Gill and Wes Craven, which is kind of like sitting on the 50-yard line at the Super Bowl for your first football game. Later, we were approached by the people at Audubon to support the creation of Debs Park in Los Angeles. Then they asked both of us to be on the board of California Audubon and that became a huge part of our lives. It opened up parts of California to him that Wes was had not previously been aware of." Subsequent birding trips took the couple to Machu Picchu and the Galapagos Islands. Iya says, 'Wes had actually been to the Galapagos Islands before, with his friend Bruce Wagner in the early 90s, so he was contrasting that experience with being there twenty years later and seeing it with me."

2003 was a reflective and transformative year for Wes. Since at least the mid-90s, he had been thinking of writing a memoir or a semi-autobiographical film about his early life, and growing up fundamentalist. In several interviews, he referred to the project as *Total Immersion*. At that time, however, he said he "didn't have the courage" to tell the full story and "deal with the pain it would cause my mother."[36] He remembered that in college he had written "a naturalistic one-act play based on my actual life and my mother and grandmother." When his mother read it, she was "horribly hurt," so he vowed not to attempt anything similar during her lifetime.[37] Now, with his mother gone, he started contemplating the biography idea again. Marianne Maddalena's assistant Cody Zwieg says he saw some pages of a rough draft.

Wes was probably working on the memoir in the fall of 2003, when his daughter Jessica came to live with him for several months. She recalls, "When he was single—and maybe even when he wasn't—he would sit up all night and write. He was a night owl, so he would start writing at 2:00 in the afternoon and keep working until 2:00 in the morning. Although half of that time, he was not writing; he was playing FreeCell on his computer. Or organizing his studio. Putting different kinds of pens in different kinds of bins. He used to love the container store more than anything on earth. He just loved to organize things. And he had a little placard in his office that said, 'I hate writing but I love having written.'" This might explain why Wes never completed a draft of *Total Immersion*.

In December 2003, he decided to stop examining his past and start focusing more on his future with Iya. She remembers, "He asked me to marry him right after my father died—and it was because he realized that time is short." Although the couple didn't get married right away, their bond was strengthened. Wes also made an effort to be a meaningful presence in the life of Iya's daughter Nina, who says, "Even before they got engaged, he was trying to connect with me. I

Wes Craven and Iya Labunka, c. 2004
(courtesy Iya Labunka, photo credit: Dale Hopkins)

remember going to his house one day, when I was about 13, and I wanted to watch *Monty Python and the Holy Grail*, so he sat down and watched it with me. He would do stuff like that. For him, I think, it was a second chance to be present."

At a time when his private life was more fulfilling than his professional life, Wes contemplated the possibility that *Cursed*—which was turning out to be a disaster of epic proportions—might be his final film. Sensing the same possibility, Marianne Maddalena began searching for their next project. In early 2004, plans for Steven Spielberg's DreamWorks Pictures to make *Fountain Society* had fizzled, but the lines of communication between DreamWorks and Craven-Maddalena remained open. Marianne says, "Sara Bottfeld, one of our agents, told me about this project at DreamWorks called *Red Eye*. She said, 'The script isn't ready yet—Spielberg's going to have the writer do another pass on the ending—but let's track it.' A few months went by and she said, 'I've got the script.' And it was so good! I said to Wes, 'You have to read this script.' He said, 'I can't read it. I'm too busy.' What?! It's DreamWorks! He said, 'My daughter just got a divorce and I've met this new woman... I can't possibly take the time to read this.'" Wes explained, "I wasn't even finished with *Cursed*, and I'd been on it for two and a half years. So my first reaction was that I just wanted to get some sleep."[38]

Marianne persisted. "I was worried that if we didn't close a deal before *Cursed* came out, we might not have careers after that. So I called Mike Simpson. He called Wes and said, 'Why don't you read it, I'll read it, and we'll talk tomorrow? And if you don't like it, I'll tell Spielberg we're gonna pass.' But Wes read it and he loved it." Later, Wes said, "I [wanted] to do something that acknowledges 9/11 and the way our lives have changed since then, and the fact that we're fighting an enemy, whatever your political or religious beliefs are, that is causing us to get into a fight where it's impossible not to hurt innocents, and it's impossible not to lose your innocence."[39] *Red Eye* fit the bill, bringing Wes's preoccupation with cycles of violence into the 21st century.

In Carl Ellsworth's original screenplay, a domestic terrorist named Jackson Rippner holds hotel manager Lisa Reisert hostage on a late-night flight from Dallas to Miami, intending to use her as an unwitting accomplice in an assassination attempt on the Deputy Secretary of Homeland Security. Most of the screen story takes place between the two characters in a single setting, making *Red Eye* a carefully contained narrative like Alfred Hitchcock's *Lifeboat, Rope,* or *Rear Window.* Relishing the opportunity to make a Hitchcockian thriller, Wes signed on in late July and the project went into pre-production. In November, cameras started rolling. Later, Wes said the project restored his enthusiasm for filmmaking and "saved my ass."[40]

Although Wes closely adhered to Ellsworth's script for *Red Eye,* he added a few significant twists to the third act, including a location change for the final confrontation between the terrorist and his hostage. Once Lisa foils Rippner's assassination attempt, the killer follows her to her home to exact revenge. By giving her a chance to fight back on her own turf—and defend her home—the villain seals his own fate. Wes thought the modified action would add psychological complexity to both characters, revealing Rippner's humanity and Lisa's heroic resilience.

Like the killers in *Last House on the Left,* whose faces express shock and remorse after the callous murder of Mari, Rippner becomes vulnerable in the final scene of *Red Eye.* Wes said, "You can see that there is some decency in him, or shreds of it… Right up to the last look: he's looking at her, and it's not entirely defeated. There's the half-smile there where he just almost admires her and has to admit to himself, 'This woman is really something'—and he's got two bullets in him. I just really liked that."[41]

Wes also added a layer of complexity to the heroine's journey by establishing similarities between Lisa and Nancy Thompson, the Final Girl of *A Nightmare on Elm Street,* who defeats Freddy by turning her back on him. In the third act of *Red Eye,* Lisa fights Jack Rippner but stops short of killing him. Instead, Lisa echoes Nancy by telling Rippner, "You're pathetic." Wes didn't want to turn the heroine into a killer, explaining, "The alternative is that endless cycle of violence that we are caught in now. 'You did 9/11. We'll attack Iraq. It will make it all better.'"[42] At the same time, he understood the villain had to be vanquished. In a twist on the climax of *Scream,* Rippner comes back for one last scare—and Lisa's father shoots him dead, to protect his daughter.

In the midst of filming *Red Eye,* plus another round of *Cursed,* Wes got married. On November 27, 2004, he and Iya Labunka tied the knot in a small ceremony at the home of Barry Cahn, the man who'd introduced them. Iya says,

Top: Jack Rippner (Cillian Murphy) threatens Lisa (Rachel McAdams) in *Red Eye*
Bottom: Wes Craven directs Rachel McAdams and Cillian Murphy in *Red Eye*
(DreamWorks, 2005)

"We couldn't figure out a time to get married—we were both too busy—so I said, 'Why are we trying to plan a wedding? Let's just elope and invite the kids and not tell anybody else.' That might sound practical and unromantic, but it was actually perfect. Small, intimate, and impossibly romantic, with only those who were nearest and dearest to us. We pulled it all together in two days. I found a place to get married, a person to marry us, a photographer, music, dinner, everything, in two days. We drove up to Santa Barbara and got married over Thanksgiving weekend. Truly, truly perfect." The honeymoon would have to wait. On November 29, they went back to work.

Cursed was finally released in February 2005. Commenting on his relationship with the Weinsteins at that point, Wes said, "I would not do another film there unless I had final cut and a definite budget, and the studio went away and let me make my film."[43] Allegedly, Bob Weinstein offered to put *Pulse* back in production and do exactly that. For whatever reason, it didn't happen. *Pulse* was extensively rewritten by Ray Wright and Jim Sonzero, and Sonzero filled the director's chair. In July, the Weinsteins concluded their "Wes Craven Presents" series with the direct-to-video release of *Dracula III: Legacy*, a film Wes had no input on. One month later, *Red Eye* arrived in theaters, cementing Wes's departure from Dimension and Miramax.

Still willing to leverage his brand to help a friend, Wes offered to executive produce a horror film for his former A.D. Nicholas Mastandrea, who made his directorial debut with *The Breed*, a naturalistic horror film about a quartet of island tourists beset by wild dogs. Mastandrea told interviewer Rachel Belofsky that Wes's attachment was helpful for getting financing and casting the film, and that Wes gave notes on the final cut of the film. *The Breed* was distributed by First Look Studios in late 2006, but it would be the only post-Dimension film to feature the "Wes Craven Presents" banner. At that point, Wes wanted to reclaim personal control of his horror brand by focusing on projects "we could produce and handle ourselves."[44]

Wes's first new project as executive producer, developed entirely in-house at Craven-Maddalena Films with producing partner Peter Locke, was a remake of *The Hills Have Eyes*. Planning had begun in early 2004, when they realized that the intellectual property rights for the original screenplay had reverted back to them thanks to a new copyright law. Based on the commercial success of new versions of *The Texas Chainsaw Massacre* and *Dawn of the Dead*, several Hollywood studios were already racing to remake classic horror films of the 1970s. Wes decided he didn't want to write or direct the new *Hills*, but he wanted to help find the right filmmaker(s) to take the reins. Over the summer, the producers vetted candidates recommended by their agents and in-house horror fan Cody Zwieg. Among the dozens of filmmakers considered for the job were writer Grégory Levasseur and director Alexandre Aja, the duo behind the 2003 French-language slasher film *Haute Tension*. Locke recalls watching the film on the recommendation of Wes's agent, and being impressed. "It was really, really rough. Scary and mean. We realized Alex Aja has a high tolerance for other people's pain, and that was what we needed."[45]

For Aja and Levasseur, it was a dream come true. The duo had been friends since middle school, when they bonded over a mutual love of American horror films. Years later, that shared passion became the foundation of their filmmaking careers. According to Aja, "*Haute Tension* was directly inspired by the classic American horror movies from the 1970s and especially by *Last House on the Left*." Hollywood took note and soon the filmmakers were entertaining offers to work with the likes of Sam Raimi and Wes Craven. "One day, our agent sent us a script by Stiles White and Juliet Snowden called *The Waiting*, which was being produced by Wes Craven. It seemed to be the perfect next step and it was an amazing opportunity." The filmmakers arranged to meet with Wes and Marianne Maddalena for a business lunch, but the conversation veered away from *The Waiting*, toward *The Hills Have Eyes*. "Wes asked us, 'Do you know *The Hills Have Eyes*?' Although I was a much bigger fan of *Last House on the Left*, we knew the movie well, so we said yeah. And he said, 'We are thinking of remaking it. Would you be interested?'"

Wes challenged the duo to come up with a pitch that would make his original story worthy of re-telling thirty years later. Aja says, "We watched the movie again and we came up with the idea of digging into something that was only mentioned [in the original film], about the nuclear testing zone and the effect of nuclear fallout on the people that lived in the hills. [In our version,] they would become actual mutants, not just weird rednecks in the desert. We pitched the idea to Wes and I think he really connected to it—this idea of an American family having to face an enemy that, indirectly, they [as Americans] had created through that testing. To us, it was a direct line to the

September 11th attacks, where Americans faced terrorists that the CIA had trained years before, when the terrorists were still on their side. That was the subtext that really got us excited. We wanted to come to Hollywood and do a movie about American culture in a deep way. It was also an opportunity to write the script, which was not the case with the other projects [*The Waiting* and Sam Raimi's *The Messengers*], so we put them aside and just dove into *The Hills Have Eyes.*"

After Aja and Levasseur wrote the script, they went on a location scout with Wes and Peter Locke, on the outskirts of the Mojave Desert. Although they decided the filming location for the original *Hills* was not right for the remake, the trip made an impression on Aja. "We were driving around in an SUV and Wes stopped in the middle of the road because he had seen a dead raven. A really big raven. He got out and bent down and looked at the bird for quite a long time, then he took out some plastic gloves and collected the bird, emptied the cooler of all our water bottles that we had brought for the day, and put the dead bird inside the cooler. I later learned

Craven's raven (courtesy Alexandre Aja)

that Wes had a passion for birds and he was going to [preserve] it—but at that point, I didn't know what he was doing. So that was very weird. And the bird smelled terrible. A few years later, I asked him what happened to the raven and he said it was still in his freezer."

The location scout continued—throughout California, Arizona, New Mexico, Mexico, and even South Africa. Finally, Aja convinced his producing partners to base the production in Morocco. "At first, Wes and Marianne were kind of like, 'Are you insane?' But if you look at the part of New Mexico where the story takes place, Ouarzazate [in southern Morocco] has the same altitude, same climate, same flora. I took photos of both places, gave them to Wes and Marianne and said, 'Please tell me what's New Mexico and what's west Morocco.' And they couldn't. So I won that battle. And in Ouarzazate, ten minutes away from our hotel, we had a 360-degree view of the desert. It was the perfect place to make the film." Locations were selected and casting began. In the summer of 2005, Fox Searchlight picked up the project.

In the fall, Marianne Maddalena accompanied the filmmakers to Morocco, while Wes turned his attention to developing some new off-brand projects, including *Susan's Last Letter*, a romantic comedy in which a widower receives a series of letters written by his late wife, and *Starstruck*, a road movie about a young cancer patient who cons a movie star into taking her to breakfast at Tiffany's. During this time, Wes apparently developed some misgivings about the filmmakers' plans for *The Hills Have Eyes*. Aja says, "He was worried about the subtext—stuff like [Doug] killing [Pluto] with an American flag and Big Brain [one of the savage mutants] singing the National Anthem. [He wanted to cut] all those things that I thought were making the movie more powerful." To be fair, Wes knew that these elements—implied criticisms of American values—would also make the film more controversial. Cody Zwieg explains that they met with dozens of directors for *The Hills Have Eyes* before they picked Aja. "Wes was like, 'Bring on the Frenchman to class it up a little.' And that's why he pushed back on certain things in the script—like using the American flag as a weapon. At that time [less than four years after 9/11], we thought, *People are going to hate us for this*. Also, there were protracted scenes of sexual assault and trauma toward women and Wes didn't want to keep using that as a trope again and again."

Wes had been accused of peddling misogynist fantasies throughout his career, so he was sensitive to such criticism. In 2005, *New York* magazine journalist David Edelstein had not yet coined the derogatory term "torture porn," but the films that inspired the term—*Saw, The Passion of the Christ,* and *The Devil's Rejects*—had already been released. By the time *The Hills Have Eyes* reached theaters, the term "torture porn" was making headlines, and *TIME* journalist Rebecca Winters Keegan was calling out the so-called "Splat Pack," "an emerging and collegial band of horror auteurs," including Alexandre Aja, who were being "given almost free rein and usually less than $10 million by studios or producers to make unapologetically disgusting, brutally violent movies." Keegan predicted that the "horrorteurs lovefest" would end in "overkill" and widespread condemnation.[46] Old guard horror filmmakers like Wes Craven saw the writing on the wall before it materialized.

Aja, however, did not want to pull any punches; he wanted to make *The Hills Have Eyes* as savage and incisive as possible. He says, "I did something very ballsy at the time—which I don't know if I would do now, but I was kind of in the energy of pre-production and I had the conviction that we were doing the right thing. I wrote to Wes and I said, 'Wes, you're right. This is a remake of your movie and if you really think that all the notes you're sending me are right, then we should make the changes. But then I really think that you should come and direct the movie.' I had a hunch that he would not take that stand. I think my commitment to the material was a challenge to him, but I think he also really believed in supporting a director's vision. After that, I didn't hear from him again until the end of the shoot."

Wes said that once they started filming, he gave almost no input. "In fact, I thought it was important not to be in his face during that period. I just put myself in his position, and I think it would be a nightmare to have some guy, who 30 years ago made a horror movie that's become famous, sitting on your set, watching every move you make."[47] Wes also wanted to focus on the success of *Red Eye*, and what it might mean for his filmmaking future. Following that film's successful opening, he said, "I woke up with this incredible sense of just peaceful energy, like I had just come out of—I don't know—a long, long struggle, you know. I mean, *Cursed* was really hard. And then before that, there was a very difficult writing period on the film I was going to make [*Pulse*]. And before that

I had quadruple bypass, so it's like I had gone through a lot and suddenly I just felt like I had gotten it right."[48] In another contemporary interview, he joked about adopting a pseudonym—maybe "Christopher Wren"—and embarking on a completely new career, making "other kinds of films."[49]

As it turned out, he didn't have to change his name. While promoting *Red Eye* in Europe, Wes received an invitation to make one of twenty five-minute segments of the film *Paris, Je T'Aime*, an anthology of stories set in the twenty different arrondissements of Paris. Wes told an interviewer that he committed to the project simply to film in Paris: "Okay, I'm there. What plane do I need to be on?'[50]

The assigned arrondissement for Wes Craven was the Quartier du Père-Lachaise, home of the sprawling Père-Lachaise Cemetery, where American rock god Jim Morrison, French siren Édith Piaf, and English novelist Oscar Wilde are buried. Wes wrote three separate scripts related to each of these figures, but the Morrison and Piaf storylines fell by the wayside. Assistant Carly Feingold says Wes was more than happy to embrace Wilde's offbeat sense of humor and to tell a story with a lighter tone.

In the third story, a young bride-to-be gushes over Oscar Wilde's tombstone, but her fiancé is cranky and morose. She pleads with him to make her laugh, to bring "lightness" into her life, but he seems ill-equipped for the job… until the ghost of Oscar Wilde feeds him some helpful hints. Although the entire story takes place in a labyrinthine cemetery, there is no hint of the macabre, only wonderment. At the end of the segment, the fiancé redeems himself and promises his bride, "I'll make you laugh."

Around the same time, Wes had made a similar vow to his wife Iya. She says, "Every single morning of our marriage, he made me laugh. Every. Single. Morning. It was like an assignment he gave himself, to start every day that way. And it was always something different—it was gesture; it was a joke; it was physical comedy; it was goofiness. But every single day, he made me laugh. It was a choice on his part, to live that way, to start that way. And it was a discipline and a focus, which translated to other areas of his life."

As he completed his work on *Paris, Je T'Aime*, Wes attached himself to another project that would expand his range as a storyteller. John McColgan,

Young lovers Frances (Emily Mortimer) and William (Rufus Sewell)
in *Paris, je t'aime* (Canal+, 2006)

co-creator of the Irish theater show *Riverdance*, announced in late October 2005 that the master of horror would develop a Broadway musical for him, transforming the Dublin stage play *Magick Macabre* into a bigger, bloodier show for an 1,800-seat theater in Las Vegas. "I came up with a terrific idea," Wes said. "A young magician, who is serving as the clown of the world's most famous magician at the time, gets kicked around and treated vilely by this guy. He makes [a] deal with the devil to be the world's most famous magician and the devil says, 'I'm going to make you do some sins. […] The first one is murder, and here's the name [of your victim].' And it's his boss."[51]

According to Wes, the young magician would then create a series of magic shows, each one culminating with the commission of another deadly sin. As he becomes increasingly famous, the magician undergoes a horrifying transformation. Eventually, Wes explained, the magician would literally transform into the cruel man he murdered.[52] Like his character in *Paris, Je T'Aime*, Wes took cues from Oscar Wilde—specifically, *The Portrait of Dorian Gray*, about an aristocrat who sells his soul for eternal youth and beauty, only to become a monster inside. He also might have been remembering his unrealized film adaptation of Giles Blunt's novel *Cold Eye*, another tale about an artist and a Faustian curse.

While he worked out the details of *Magick Macabre*, Wes returned to Paris, where editing was underway on *The Hills Have Eyes*. Alexandre Aja remembers, "We were showing it to friends and the reactions were really good, so we were quite happy and proud of what we were doing. When the director's cut was finished, Wes and Peter came to Paris to watch it. We had a screening in a room on the outskirts of the city, and we were so excited to show them our movie. They watched it and they came out with the most [horrified looks on their] faces. Like, 'What have you done?'"

According to Aja and Marianne Maddalena, Wes initially thought the film needed a different ending, which meant extensive reshoots. Cody Zwieg recalls, "I think he was reacting to the nonstop brutality of it all." Maddalena adds, "At that time, Wes kind of denied that he made horror films. When he looked at the first cut of *The Hills Have Eyes*, he said, 'This is so violent, I can't even show this to my wife.' I said, 'What?! Have you seen your other movies, Wes?' Somehow, he saw himself in a completely different way."

Whatever his reasons, Wes reportedly had trouble embracing the new *Hills*. Alexandre Aja remembers, "Grég and I took the movie to L.A. and we still couldn't understand what [Wes thought] was so bad about it. At that point, two executives from Fox Searchlight came to see the [director's cut] and they actually loved it, so then there was some debate." The brass at Craven-Maddalena Films continued pushing for reshoots, but Aja pushed back. "I was like, 'No, I really want to test the movie because I really want to understand what is happening.'"

Eventually, the studio arranged screenings of the director's cut of *The Hills Have Eyes* for two very different test audiences. The first screening took place on a backlot in Santa Monica. Aja recalls, "People were cheering and applauding. It got an amazing reaction. When the movie ended, somebody shouted, 'Wes Craven is back!' Someone else said, 'That was the best Wes Craven movie in a long time.' It was a lovefest. Afterward, Wes came up to me and shook my hand and told me he hadn't understood something and that he was wrong. We were very happy at that point. A week later, we went to Orange County—and the screening went even better. That was the end of the craziness."

After some minor re-editing, *The Hills Have Eyes* was released in the U.S. on March 10, 2006. Reviews were mixed but the film eventually made over $70 million worldwide, easily recouping its $15 million budget. In promotional interviews, Wes theorized that the success of *Hills*—as well as other "extreme" horror films like *Saw* and *Hostel*—might be "a reaction to Republican stricture," or to "the post-modern deconstruction of the genre."[53] Although he didn't quite understand it, he realized he was suddenly riding the crest of a new wave of cutting-edge horror.

Fox Searchlight immediately started talking about a sequel. Aja says he and his filmmaking partner pitched a story idea, but Wes wanted to go a different way. "He wanted to bring the Army into the desert and we thought that was too obvious. Also, he wanted to write the sequel with Jonathan [Craven], so Grég and I decided to take a step back." Jonathan remembers, "Fox wanted the second film to come out one year after the first, and the script had to be written in about a month, so Dad was like, 'I'll just write it myself.' Then he called me and said, 'Would you want to help me write the script?' It sounded like fun."

Wes explained that his choice of co-writer was not a casual one: "Jonathan had been writing for a long time in many different venues. He's written screenplays and he's been a journalist. So I knew I'd be going into the room with a professional and somebody who understands deadlines. And there was no way in hell I could have done this myself. And he's my son, so it was a guaranteed time to be with him under a very interesting situation."[54]

Jonathan remembers, "Once we'd decided to do this, I went to his house one morning around 9am, and Iya came to the door and said, 'Wes was up all night. He got an idea and was writing until 5:00 in the morning.' Wes came out and he handed me about twenty script pages, which was his idea for the opening. It was set in a huge housing project that was slowly encroaching on the area in the Mojave Desert where the [cannibals] live. There was a developer who was already living there, in an unfinished house, and he got spooked by a noise. He searched the house but couldn't find anyone. A couple minutes later, he walked into the bathroom and saw the largest human turd you could possibly imagine. Then, when he turned around, he saw this big MF cannibal standing there, getting ready to kill him. It was supposed to be sort of a funny opening—but I think Marianne [Maddalena] shot it down. She said, 'We're not building a housing development on the edge of the desert.'"

Building on the idea that the popular new wave of American horror films was a reflection of current events, the Cravens decided to set the sequel story against the backdrop of America's contemporary wars in the Middle East. "I don't really have to have a morbid imagination these days," Wes explained to one interviewer. "I just have to read the newspaper."[55] Closer to home, he saw several members of his own family—children of his nieces and nephews—leaving for war in the Middle East. Wes and Jonathan tried to imagine what the soldiers were going through, and Jonathan concluded, "The horrors they face are 1,000 times worse than anything you could cook up for a horror movie."[56]

The initial idea was to follow one of the survivors of the first film as she led a group of soldiers into the desert for revenge. That scenario, reminiscent of *Aliens* (1986), was scrapped because actress Emilie de Ravin was unavailable to appear in the sequel.[57] Next, Jonathan says, they decided to feature National Guard members in training. "Dad liked that because he could make them more vulnerable." Wes explained, "What if they were recruits and they're only halfway through their training[?] They were not sent in to do this at all, but they were just in there and just get swept up into it.' [...] It seemed to have parallels to things that are in the news, and we couldn't help making those comparisons."[58] In a room at the Chateau Marmont, the duo tapped into "that dark, dark humor that seems to run in the Craven genes," and delivered a story that was as savage as its predecessor.[59]

Wes also may have built a version of himself into the story, basing the peacenik character Napoleon on the young Wes Craven who planned to become a Naval Air Cadet. Official production notes for the film state: "Wes [came] from a working-class family and was the first kid in his family to go to college. The character of Napoleon also comes from a working-class family, is very intelligent and wants to go to college, and he joins the National Guard to get an education." Like the other cadets, Napoleon instead gets a fubared mission.

Wes and Jonathan completed their shooting script on June 16, 2006, and the experience renewed Wes's enthusiasm for writing horror. In September, as *Hills 2* started filming in Morocco, he began developing his first wholly original horror film since 1993's *New Nightmare*. It would be his most personally-revealing screen story and his penultimate film.

The Soul of Wes Craven

CHAPTER THIRTEEN

THE COLLECTIVE SOUL
OF ADAM HELLER
(2006 - 2011)

"A child is never born with a soul.
A soul can be acquired only in the course of life."

- George Ivanovich Gurdjieff, *Views from the Real World*

In September 2006, Wes Craven declared his independence as a filmmaker by renaming his production company Midnight Pictures. *Variety* reported that he and longtime partner Marianne Maddalena intended to "make films separately, with Maddalena developing her own slate." The filmmakers entered into a new first-look deal with Rogue Pictures, a Universal Studios-affiliated production company, to remake *Last House on the Left* as well as an original horror film that Wes described as "more *Sixth Sense* than a slasher film."[1] Unfortunately, Wes's original film led to several years of creative frustration.

The writer/director wanted to create something unique and deeply personal, a counterpoint to the recent wave of "torture porn" films and formulaic remakes / reboots / re-imaginations of "classic" horror titles. Pitching a new story idea to Andrew Rona, a former Dimension exec, Wes found a particularly receptive audience. He explained, "It was a unique situation where a studio head who I'd known for years basically said, 'I'd love to do a film with you,' and I pitched this idea and he said okay. That was it. There were no other studio people involved." All he had to do was write a script that could be made for under $15 million.

Before he could begin writing his script, Wes was alerted to a purported crisis on the set of *The Hills Have Eyes 2*. In early October, producers Marianne Maddalena and Peter Locke were concerned that the film's director, Martin Weisz, might not be getting the footage they needed to make a successful film. Co-producer Jonathan Craven remembers, "He just wasn't making the film the way Wes would, or the way Marianne could relate to. Wes had a very specific way of shooting movies and making movies. They'd hired a guy who had a very different style, then they started to panic. It got really ugly."

Ultimately, Wes traveled to Morocco to "shadow direct" new scenes and re-shoot existing footage. It was not a decision he was proud of. Wes knew he was becoming a director's worst nightmare—a micro-managing producer. In his own defense, he said, "I try to stay out of the way, but at the same time you feel like it's your film and you're responsible for it to the studio. There are things that you know will or will not work because you've been doing them for a long time, and you try not to be obnoxious about it […] But sometimes you've got to make sure everything is done the way it should be done."[2] Wes spent countless hours working on the sequel, ushering the film to its final edit.

Unfortunately, the result seemed hardly worth the effort. In the spring of 2007, *The Hills Have Eyes 2* made half as much money as its predecessor, and the reviews were uniformly negative. As one critic had predicted a year earlier, the "horrorteurs lovefest" of 2005 had ended in a commercial and critical backlash—and Wes's latest film was part of the "overkill." No doubt smarting from the experience, and the sullying of his brand name, Wes tried to steer the forthcoming remake of *Last House on the Left* into safer waters, hoping to redeem himself by producing a more thoughtful and responsible version of his most notorious film.

The *Last House* remake initially had been developed at Sean Cunningham's Crystal Lake Entertainment by Mark Haslett, who wrote a draft restoring the metaphysical speculations of Ingmar Bergman's *The Virgin Spring* to Wes's variation on the same story. Haslett explains, "The script was set in California in the early '70s. The Collingwoods had bought this property that they hoped to grow something on but the area was going through a historic drought. It was causing a lot of stress within the family— the parents were dealing with what might be the early stage of a divorce— and that was the state of things when Mari went out with her friend. When the story came around to its violent conclusion, the dad forced Mari's friend to take him to see the body of his daughter. Then, instead of a spring opening up [as in *The Virgin Spring*], it began to rain. The idea in my mind was that there was a curse on the property and the murder / sacrifice of the daughter had lifted the curse."

The script sparked some interest at several studios, so Sean Cunningham took the project to Wes. At that point, Wes's production company took over and Haslett's script practically disappeared, along with its Bergman-esque ending. Haslett says, "I had a very memorable meeting with Wes and I talked about trying to get more of the Bergman in, and he just sort of demurred. I think he already knew he wanted to go in another direction."

Wes and Marianne Maddalena tapped newcomer Adam Alleca, whose spec script *Home* had caught their attention, to write a new script from scratch. Alleca says, "Very rarely have I worked with a director who wants to get into the nitty-gritty of why certain choices were made and what we're trying to say with a film, but Wes had very specific thematic ideas. He wrote very clear, lengthy notes about what he wanted and why. And you could tell he used to be an English professor, because if you had a typo or used the wrong tense, he would write a little paragraph explaining what you'd done wrong. He was a perfectionist. Which is probably why he was such a great director. No detail escaped his gaze."

While developing *Home,* a story about a mentally-disturbed young man haunted by the specter of his violent father, the two writers developed a strong working relationship. Afterward, Wes approached Alleca about remaking *The People Under the Stairs.* "We met a few times about that in 2006, and I wrote a few treatments. Then they had some kind of rights conflict, so I ended up moving on to *Last House* very quickly in early 2007. I spent about six months writing different drafts. The script never deviated from the original *Last House* film in terms of plot or structure, but it was tonally different. In our initial discussions, I said the type of movie I wanted to write was something like *In the Bedroom* or *House of Sand and Fog.* Heavy, dark dramas about loss, grief, and revenge. My script was all about the futility of revenge. That was the theme: first, you lose someone you love, and then, through the act of taking revenge, you lose yourself as well. It's a double tragedy. I had visual motifs to illustrate that theme, showing how the parents were full of life in the beginning and then completely empty at the end. It was very, very depressing. You can probably understand why something in that vein wasn't going to work as a commercial horror movie."

When the Writer's Strike ended in February 2008, nearly a year after the release of *The Hills Have Eyes 2*, Alleca's draft was revised by *Red Eye* screenwriter Carl Ellsworth, who made two major changes to the story. Ellsworth says, "I can't believe I did this, but I told Wes, 'This is the bleakest, most depressing thing I've ever seen. And I don't go to the movies wanting to come out more depressed than when I went in. I said I wanted a more cathartic ending because I am a huge believer in that. It doesn't necessarily have to be a happy ending, but audience catharsis is necessary. If you put your audience through hell, the audience deserves—and your characters deserve—to survive." Wes agreed, so Ellsworth conceived a new third act built around an excised moment from the original *Last House* film, in which Mari's parents find her alive.

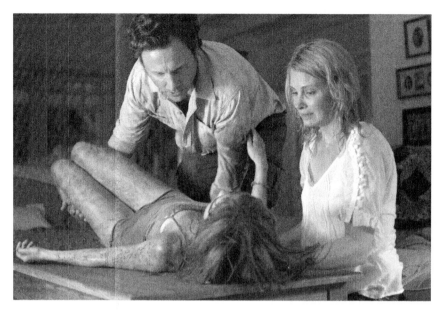

John (Tony Goldwyn) and Emma (Monica Potter) fight for the life of their daughter Mari (Sara Paxton) in *Last House on the Left* (Rogue, 2009)

The more cathartic version of the story also included a more outrageous ending, one that is at odds with Wes's stated beliefs about responsibly depicting violence in cinema. Ellsworth says the final scene—in which Mari's father tortures his daughter's would-be killer by paralyzing him from the neck down, then sticking his head in a jerry-rigged microwave—arose out of desperation: "I was having dinner with my in-laws and I was stressed out because I was trying to come up with a creative way to end the film, a creative way to kill Krug. My wife's dad said, 'You could do something with a microwave.' He might have even said, 'You could stick his head in a microwave.' So I put that in the script, knowing full well that it would *never* make it into the movie. Later, Marianne told me that it was the scene that got the movie made!" Rather than protest, it seems Wes chose to focus on his next film.

Marianne Maddalena says, "He really was an *auteur*. He liked to do his own projects. He thought, *Why am I working with a writer instead of writing? Why am I working with a director instead of directing?*" Wes had reached a point where he had to make a career-defining decision: "Am I going to spend my time remaking stuff that I've already done, kind of helping other directors, or am I going to go back and do what I do best?"[3]

In about a month, he wrote his first pass on an original screenplay, initially titled *BUG* and later retitled *25/8*. According to several sources, the quick turnaround was a necessity. Everyone in the film and television industry was reeling from the effects of the long Writer's Strike—which had lasted from November 5, 2007, until February 12, 2008—and dreading the possibility of a Screen Actor's Guild strike, starting June 30. Rogue greenlit Wes's new film on February 12, before the script was finished, then rushed into pre-production to beat the impending shutdown. Iya Labunka says, "There was a lot of pressure to get it shot before June 30th. Everyone was saying, 'You gotta deliver, you gotta deliver, or you're gonna be shut down for two years.' Because of that, the script wasn't worked out as well as he wanted it to be."

Wes continued to revise during the following weeks, but, according to co-producer Carly Feingold, "He was really struggling, because he felt like he just had to finish it and he couldn't really afford the time to think it through. It ended up having the same issues that *Cursed* had, because the script wasn't finalized. It was just greenlit and 'go.'"

For better or worse, the first draft of *25/8* was unfiltered Wes Craven, charting a narrative journey that Wes described as "the most autobiographical" of all his films, a coming-of-age story about a teenager haunted by the local legend of a supposedly-dead serial killer who is also his father.[4] As for the cryptic title, Wes explained, "The idea was if you want to fight the devil, the devil fights 24/7, so if you want to win, you have to fight 25/8 to do it."[5]

The writer's onscreen surrogate is Adam "Bug" Heller, a teen who "starts off a bit like Candide and ends up like Voltaire."[6] Wes once described himself the same way, defining his college years as the beginning of a "Candidian search" that led him from innocence to disillusionment to Voltaire's philosophical resolve to "tend his own garden." Bug's search also parallels that of Noah Songsti, the central character in Wes's unpublished novel *Noah's Ark*, who forges a new identity by shedding multiple personalities. Like Noah, Bug uncovers family secrets, learns his father's identity, and distinguishes himself from his friends, all of which contributes to his becoming a "whole" person.

Wes took some additional inspiration from research into his own family history and genealogy—a subject that was increasingly important to him. In recent years, he'd pored over countless files and family photos to create an album he shared with close relatives. In the process, he learned about many family secrets that had been withheld from him as a child, especially details about his father. "You can't really grow as a person until you know your roots," Wes said, which explains why the research was so important.[7] It also echoes the theme of *25/8*, which hinges on Adam Heller's relationship with his father.

Wes's father, Paul Eugene Craven, was born on July 3, 1905, in Montpelier, Vermont, to parents Eugene Elsworth Craven, a professional stone cutter, and Maude Lizzie Magoon. The couple briefly lived in an apartment building at 131 Elm Street on the western shore of the Winooski River, then moved to "Athenwood," a lavish Rural Gothic home designed by recently deceased artist Thomas Waterman Wood. During the family's time at Athenwood, Maude gave birth to Paul and his younger brother John Edgar Craven (born in 1907).

These basic facts suggest little about the family members, but contemporary news reports offer a bit more context. Within a few months of John's birth, the Cravens had vacated Athenwood, and Eugene, apparently suffering financial troubles, was fending off rumors that he planned to sell his business. Soon after, Eugene's mother died of heart failure and his father-in-law Edgar Magoon sued him to collect an "overdue note." Around the same time, Maude filed for divorce, citing "intolerable severity" as the cause. In the spring of 1908, she was granted a divorce and full custody of Paul and John. Thus, by the time he turned forty, Eugene Elsworth Craven had lost his family.

According to the 1910 census, Maude took her two boys to live with their grandfather Edgar Magoon in Washington, Vermont. Ten years later, the trio was living in Chicago, Illinois, with a new family member: 5-year-old Allen Booth. Craven family lore says that, in the intervening years, divorcée Maude went to live with her sister Mina and Mina's husband Richard Booth, and the three Booth children. Sometime before 1918, Mina moved out. The birth of Allen—around 1915—might have had something to do with it. Maude subsequently took Richard's surname as her own. Mina remarried and took custody of her three biological children, leaving Allen Booth behind.

What Wes gleaned from all of this was that that his father Paul had twice witnessed the breakup of his family—first due to violence, and later due to infidelity—by the age of 14. The Booth-Craven family subsequently moved to Cleveland, where Paul met and married Caroline Miller on December 3, 1927.

In the midst of his research, Wes also learned that his mother had carried some dark secrets from her childhood. He explained, "She had a father who drank heavily who was kind of terrifying. She was the one who had to put him to bed when he came home drunk because he was violent to his wife. And then she married a guy [Paul] who turned out to be a ladies' man and died about eleven years after they were married."[8] By 1945, Paul Eugene Craven had abandoned his wife and three children to go live with another woman. At that time, he was one of 8,700 workers employed by the Jack & Heintz manufacturing company in Maple Heights, making airplane parts for the U.S. military. In July 1945, he died there on a loading dock, and the remaining details of his 40-year life died with him.

Wes could relate to Eugene and Paul's stories in some ways. He too had grown up without a father and he too had left his wife and children. Perhaps he felt he had inherited a family curse, stemming from the "intolerable severity" of his grandfather. Perceiving an unpleasant pattern in the lives of three generations of Craven men—the sins of the fathers being visited upon the children—he spent much of his own adult life trying to re-invent himself. For Wes, the Candidian journey of self-discovery continued long after his college years. In 2010, he said, "Wrestling with the question of 'Am I ever going to be distinctly different from my parents?' or 'Am I going to be haunted by realizing, Oh my god, I've become my father?' is something that can happen to you in your thirties or forties."[9] His script *25/8* indicates that the question continued to haunt him, at least as a storyteller, well into his sixties.

In the script, Wes weaves his familiar "bad dad" boogeyman idea into a dense and complex mythology about Adam "Bug" Heller's coming-of-age in a broken family and a cursed community. The story begins with a bonfire party held on the river banks of an idyllic Massachusetts town, where seven teens are celebrating the 15th anniversary of their simultaneous births. At the same time, they are celebrating the death of notorious serial killer Abel Plenkov, The Riverton Ripper, whose killing spree ended abruptly on the night they were born. All seven teens participate in an annual ritual in which one of them must confront and "kill" an effigy of The Ripper. This year, it is Bug's turn. Unfortunately for everyone, the local police break up the illicit gathering before he can complete the ritual. His failure apparently unleashes the real boogeyman.

In an extended flashback sequence, set fifteen years prior, we see Bug's mild-mannered dad Abel Plenkov painting a wooden rocking horse for his unborn son, as well as a doll house for 4-year-old daughter Leah. At a certain point, Abel trips and hits his head, then discovers a distinctive bloody folding knife. The discovery awakens a mysterious voice in his head. We learn that Abel has long suffered from multiple personality disorder. The new voice belongs to the Riverton Ripper, who threatens to murder Abel's wife and children. Abel seeks help from his psychiatrist, William Blake, but he's too late. The Ripper, controlling Abel's body, kills Abel's wife and attacks his daughter before a cop named Frank Paterson guns him down.

Paramedics rush Abel and his victims to the hospital, where six local women have simultaneously gone into premature labor. This plot twist may have been inspired by Wes's early 90s attempt to remake *Village of the Damned*, about a town where multiple women are simultaneously impregnated by an unseen alien presence. In *25/8*, the simultaneous births suggest the migration of Abel Plenkov's hidden personalities—or hidden souls—into new physical bodies. The implied question is whether one of the miracle babies has inherited the malignant soul of the killer. The script also suggests the possibility that Abel Plenkov, whose body disappeared in the river, is still alive somewhere, waiting to strike again.

For fifteen years, the citizens of Riverton—and their potentially cursed children—have lived ordinary lives, but everything is about to change. In the first post-flashback scene, teenage Bug sleeps soundly in his bedroom as a long blade slices through the wall above his head and a monstrous hand emerges to grab him. The scene is a callback to the vision that inspired Wes to write *A Nightmare on Elm Street*. Like Freddy, the Ripper is crossing over from a land of dreams and legends, into the real world. Luckily, Bug wakes up before getting diced.

Next, a sequence of expository scenes defines Bug's six peers. Brandon O'Neil is a desperately horny jock; Brittany Cunningham is brainy and beautiful but cold; Jerome Brown is a blind male "Cassandra"; Alex Dunkelman, Bug's best friend, is a prankster coping with an abusive father; Jay Chan is a superstitious artist from a broken family; and Penelope Bryte is a devoutly religious but feisty redhead with a soft spot for Bug. The script also sets up a mysterious female character named Fang, who exerts a tremendous amount of influence over all the other characters.

For Wes, the characters are elements of an extended metaphor. In 2006, he explained, "My feeling is that when you do a horror film, it's almost like you construct a very complex character that has all sorts of things hanging off of him or her—the past and what the mom thought and what their friends think you should do—and one by one, you kill them. It sounds like you're just a butcher, but really if you look at it in a mystical sense, you're actually stripping away parts of a personality or a persona that don't work [...] until you end up with this core persona, the hero or the heroine that knows exactly what's going on, still has goodness, but is able to kick ass and takes names. And stays awake. And that's what it's all about."[10]

In 2010, he offered a similar explanation: "You're dealing with an uber-personality, a composite personality that is made up of the hero or heroine and all of his or her friends. They all are aspects of an overall personality, and the parts of that personality that don't work when faced with grim reality are killed off. It's a parallel with our own life. [...] A certain point in your life where you said 'That was pretty stupid and I'm getting rid of it' is the equivalent of a character in a horror film dying. That's how I look at it. It's really, in a way, [the story of a hero] honed by fate and fear and necessity to perform at the heroic level. With this film, I kind of consciously did that."[11]

Wes's original script extends the metaphor in a scene where Bug delivers a school presentation on the California Condor. Dressed in a hideous condor costume, Bug vomits and defecates on Brandon to illustrate his point: "I am the condor!" Wes said he intended the scene to show that Bug has a collective soul: "It's based on a Native American legend about condors [as] the gatherer of souls. It's not a hideous creature that eats dead things [...] but it is something that keeps the soul of every animal that it eats and protects it, so that it has accumulative wisdom and gravitas about it."[12] He adds, "As the seven kids start to be targeted and attacked, and everyone dies, [Bug] gets their attributes.

Max Thieriot (who plays "Bug") and Wes Craven on the set of
My Soul to Take (Rogue, 2010)

So he kind of matures and turns into a man in the course of absorbing both the male and female elements of his closest friends."[13]

Eventually, the only characters left standing are Bug and Alex. Most of the script's clues point to Bug as the likely killer, but Wes was indecisive about the ending. In the original script, the Ripper / Abel Plenkov reappears in the flesh, mortally wounds Alex, and vows to kill Bug. In the same breath, he asserts that he is *not* Bug's biological father. Bug then asserts his independence, like Jonathan in *Shocker*. Moments later, Officer Frank Paterson (now Detective Paterson) reappears to shoot the Ripper a second time. The script concludes with an image of a tall, white steeple atop the town's Baptist church, and a suggestion for end credits music: the gospel hymn "Oh Happy Day." Like the protagonist of *Noah's Ark*, Bug seemingly follows the churchy music to his salvation.

In April 2008, Wes traveled to Connecticut to start pre-production on *25/8*. Rather than relying on people he'd worked with since *Scream* (or earlier), he decided to make the film with a mostly new team. Co-producer Carly Feingold says, "He'd worked with a lot of the same people for twenty years and

I think he just wanted to try something different, to see if it changed things and gave [the film] a different energy." Based on Iya Labunka's years of experience working with directors and studio execs, Wes convinced her to come on board as producer. She remembers, "Wes and I had a lot of very long talks about that. It was not something I jumped at. We really discussed it from every angle, and made a promise to each other that our marriage would always come first and that I was coming in as a supportive entity. At the end of the day, the director takes the slings and arrows, and he basks in whatever glory comes—because he's the one who has to put himself out there."

Filming began in late April and continued through June. During that time, Wes continued to revise his script—but he was never completely satisfied with it. Nina Tarnawsky, who worked as a production assistant on the film, says, "He would get home from the shoot and have to write the next day's script, which is never a good sign." Carly Feingold adds, "He would try to fix things during filming, but it was hard because he was working with a lot of new people and I don't think everyone understood their roles. Also, there were a lot of changes happening at Rogue. They were downsizing and letting people go. It was like a revolving door over there. For a while, we were shooting the movie and we didn't know who to talk to, who to get approval from, who to send dailies to. It's nice not having a studio breathing down your neck, but I think that was a disservice to Wes."

Immediately prior to the anticipated Screen Actor's Guild strike, the filmmakers completed principal photography and Wes went into editing. Since the beginning of his career, he had prided himself on his ability to shape (or re-shape) a film in post. "The time that I spend in an editing room," he once said, "has probably more to do with the way that my films come out than anything else that I do, including directing."[14] This time, however, he struggled to make the film work.

Jonathan Craven remembers, "I got a call and he said, 'Can you come up? We're stuck. We don't know what to do with this. Would you mind watching it?" I remember watching it and thinking, *This film just doesn't work at all. I don't think he knows what he's trying to do here.* When the screening ended, I didn't know what to say. I only had one idea. I said, 'There's way too much backstory. Nobody cares.' When Dad was not super sure of himself, he would overthink everything. Just kill a story with overthinking. I prompted him to look at things a different way and then he was able to get back to work."

By late 2008, Wes had a rough cut of *25/8*. He also had a new draft of the script, calling for reshoots to clarify the story. A December 9 draft of the script shortens the lengthy flashback sequence, putting the necessary details into new dialogue for the riverside ritual scene. The script also adds onscreen kills that were noticeably absent from the previous draft. Other additions expand on Bug's rapport with his peers, and give Officer Paterson a more consistent presence throughout the story.

Most significantly, a revised third act confrontation between Alex and Bug redefines the film's villain. While inhabiting the body of Alex, the Ripper explains that he (or his soul) can inhabit the bodies of any of the children born on the night of his death. For years, he's been body-hopping, Horace Pinker-style, from one kid to another. Now, with only two bodies remaining, he vows to kill Bug. Instead, Bug plunges a knife into Alex's gut. It's unclear, however, if the Ripper dies with Alex or if he inhabits Bug's body next. In the climactic scene, Bug's sister Leah/Fang pulls a gun on him, demanding to know if the Ripper lives inside of him now. When the church bells toll midnight, she concludes that the end of Bug's birthday / the Ripper's death day means all will be well.

Wes's revised script also included a surprising coda, in which we see Bug walking down the street with Alex and Jerome, talking as if they never got killed. When Bug hears a car coming, he steps aside and the car drives right through Alex and Jerome, indicating that they are, in fact, dead. The shot widens to reveal the ghosts of all six murdered peers walking beside Bug, illustrating the central metaphor for Wes's unique horror film.

In early 2009, Wes delivered his director's cut to Rogue. Around the same time, another studio acquired Rogue. As a result, *25/8* fell into distribution limbo. Wes said, "We sent in the finished film and never heard anything."[15] For a time, it looked like *25/8* might not get released.

Wes had more luck with the *Last House on the Left* remake, which arrived in theaters in March 2009. Critics and audiences were generally receptive to the surprisingly lyrical, often ethereal quality of the film. At that

John Magaro (who plays Alex), Wes Craven, and Max Thieriot on the set of
My Soul to Take (Rogue, 2010)

point, Wes said his plan all along had been to turn his grindhouse movie into something that "could almost play in an art house." He credited director Dennis Iliadis with realizing the goal: "That has proven to be the thing Dennis has managed to do, sometimes almost to spite us. Sometimes I—we—felt it's too slow, it's too arty. And then we watched it with the first test audience and we were just astonished by the power of it."[16]

Although some viewers prefer the rawness of Wes's original film, others have championed the Iliadis version. Stephen King gave the remake a huge stamp of approval, saying, "The Iliadis version is to the original what a mature artist's painting is to the drawing of a child who shows some gleams of talent."[17] Wes might have agreed with the substance of the review, but those words undoubtedly stung—especially at a time when he was having doubts about his latest film as writer/director.

In July 2009, Wes directed a second round of reshoots for *25/8*, intending to put "a really fun little button on the ending."[18] This time, the Ripper offers Bug a Faustian deal. Bug declines, fatally stabs Alex, and becomes—in Wes's words—a "fallen angel." In the theatrical cut of the film, Bug then tilts his head to the sky, and says, "I know you're up there and I know we're down here." The line sums up the protagonist's final insight, which Wes articulated as follows: "If there is a God, he doesn't really intervene in the horrible things that happen on Earth very much at all, so we kind of have to embody it all ourselves."[19] In other words: *Tend your own garden.*

As Wes continued to tinker with *25/8*, amidst worries that it would never be released, he had to cope with the immanent return of Freddy Krueger in a glossy, big-budget remake of *A Nightmare on Elm Street*... that he had nothing to do with. Samuel Bayer directed the remake from a script by Wesley Strick. Wes said none of the filmmakers asked for his input. In contemporary interviews, the subject came up constantly, forcing him to admit, "It's actually really painful to think about."[20] The remake arrived in theaters—to little fanfare—in early 2010. By then, Wes's production company was practically shuttered.

According to Carly Feingold and Cody Zweig, a number of potential projects had become mired in development hell at Midnight Pictures. The titles included *Midnight*, a murder mystery written by Richard Tanne and Travis Baker; a modern-day Sherlock Holmes series for NBC; a supernatural drama about a boy who gets struck by lighting and develops power to heal the sick; a remake of the Spanish film *3 Días* (a.k.a. *Before the Fall*); a dark comedy about an undead Vegas hitman trying to solve his own murder; a sci-fi thriller called *The Rising* for Sean Byrne to direct; and *Sunflower*, a serial killer drama written by future *Lovecraft Country* showrunner Misha Green. In the end, none of these projects moved forward—but Wes wasn't idle for long.

In March 2010, he signed on to direct *Scream 4* for the Weinstein Company, and the studio announced that original *Scream* team—Wes, Kevin Williamson, Neve Campbell, Courteney Cox, and David Arquette—would all return for the sequel. Williamson's plan was to return the story to the town of Woodsboro and reunite the survivors of the original trilogy. His first draft immediately reintroduced the franchise's Final Girl. "My opening scene was Sidney Prescott," Williamson explains. "Because I felt like I really wanted to meet her and know who she was all these years later. So we meet Sidney Prescott, we get to know her, and we catch up with her for two or three minutes before the phone starts [ringing] and the calls start. […] And it's a bloodbath, where these killers came in and we watched how she was different now. She was stronger and she had technology behind her. With her house locked down, she was able to protect herself […] And she ultimately killed the killer."[21] The story then jumped forward two years, at which point Sidney returns to her hometown of Woodsboro to promote a memoir about surviving trauma.

According to Wes, Bob Weinstein thought the Sidney-centric opening would "slow the pace of the story," so he prompted the screenwriter to construct an alternate movie-within-a-movie opening and "go with young characters" instead.[22] A similar concern apparently influenced the characterizations of Gale Weathers and Dewey Riley, who were parents in the early script but not in the film. The big challenge, according to Kevin Williamson, was integrating the stories of the legacy characters with the new, younger cast members—including Emma Roberts as Sidney's niece Jill, Hayden Panettiere as Kirby, and Marley Shelton as Deputy Judy Hicks. The screenwriter says, "Everybody was second-guessing everything because everyone wanted it to be perfect."[23]

In May 2010, Williamson left the film to fulfill a contractual obligation to his TV series *The Vampire Diaries*. At that point, *Scream 3* writer Ehren Kruger stepped in. Wes said, "He was the person solving the problems of the second part of the film, as far as [...] who did what where, and who got knocked off and who didn't."[24] Kruger wasn't the only re-writer; Williamson says no fewer than eight writers vied for credit on the final film.[25] Paul Harris Boardman reportedly contributed the ending, in which Sidney emerges victorious over her ego-driven Millennial nemesis.

Once filming began in July, Wes claimed he had "an enormous amount of input" on the evolving screen story.[26] Iya Labunka, who served as the producer on the film, remembers, "Because of the way all that went down, he would shoot all day, do rewrites at night, then come back and shoot the next day. There was a stretch where he shot three days and wrote two nights without a wink of sleep, and then slept for two days." Co-producer Carly Feingold adds, "After we would pick a filming location, if the action didn't work there as written, we'd be up until 4:00 in the morning, rewriting the script and sending it out. He always used to say, 'I'll sleep when I'm dead.'" Obviously, the 70-year-old filmmaker was still energized by making a movie.

Wes said his main storytelling goal for *Scream 4* was to maintain a "core of reality" for the Sidney Prescott character. "She actually feels the loss of people," he said, adding that his goal as director was to make audiences share her empathy.[27] During a press conference for the film in March 2011, he added, "The interesting thing about the [legacy] characters is that they are always changing. Obviously, [in *Scream 1*] Neve was a teenager—her character—and everybody else was quite a bit younger, so they've all gone through these enormous changes in their lives. I think that's part of what makes *Scream* unique, in that people actually have lives. They actually change. They change who they are, in some ways. The fact that Gale Weathers decided to marry Dewey and take that chance and live in a small town, despite the fact that she probably knew she was gonna be bored stiff in some ways—that's really fascinating. You just don't get that at all in any of the other [horror franchise] films that I can think of, so I think we're all amazed that we're in this drama that's taken place over fifteen, sixteen years." In a moment of sentimentality—and gratitude—he said, "It always felt like a family. And sometimes I feel like the father. Or the grandfather."[28]

Top: Neve Campbell returns as first and final girl Sidney Prescott in *Scream 4*
Bottom: New blood: Jill (Emma Roberts) awaits Ghostface in *Scream 4*
(Dimension, 2011)

During post-production on *Scream 4, 25/8* sprang back to life—with a new title. *My Soul to Take* was slated for an early October release—in 3-D, no less—so Wes went into marketing mode on the two films at once. He pitched *My Soul to Take* as "*Stand by Me* with knives" and a twisted spiritual autobiography: "This is really inspired by my own life, coming out of this fundamentalist church and going out into the world feeling very naïve, not being aware of a lot of things. And then just sort of learning and taking on attributes from the people I met in the course of teaching and making movies that I wouldn't have had just by living in a vacuum. […] 'The gaining of wisdom' is a phrase that kept coming to my mind."[29] The phrase echoes Wes's college-era novel *Noah's Ark*, in which he wrote, "I felt the beginning of wisdom, and a compassion for everybody that came into me and was covered with my ignorance, my weakness, my stupidity."[30] In a way, the storyteller was acknowledging the people and experiences that helped to make him Wes Craven.

Unfortunately, the critical response to the director's most personal film was resoundingly negative. One of the first print reviews began as follows: "What explains *My Soul to Take*, Wes Craven's latest dead teenagers movie? Did he turn this incoherent fiasco in as incomplete? Did the studio sign off on a horror movie based on the words 'We can do it in 3-D' in the pitch? Or has the director of *Nightmare on Elm Street* and *Scream* finally gone off his rocker?"[31]

Things got worse from there, with some critics declaring *My Soul to Take* the worst film of Wes's forty-year career. *Soul* debuted in the No. 5 spot during its opening weekend, making only $7 million before vanishing from theaters and leaving many to wonder what went wrong—including Wes himself, who believed he had made a worthwhile film. Months later, in a promotional interview for *Scream 4*, he said, "I tried to do a whole different kind of horror film… And in the horror community, it doesn't feel like there's a big search for something more complex than just more scares and blood."[32]

The reception to *Scream 4*, released in April 2011, was also disappointing. From the beginning, Wes had understood that expectations were frighteningly high. "You have to come up with something worthy of coming back," he said. "You're addressing a generation of young fans, but also the generation that has gone with you for three, as well as a decade worth of other films. You have to be as good, or better, than all of these films."[33] Although critics and fans would later recognize that *Scream 4* astutely commented on the rising dangers of social media and influencer culture, contemporary reviews were mixed and it went on to become the first film in the series to gross less than $100 million at the box office, squashing speculations that *Scream 4* would launch a new trilogy. Fans would have to wait another decade for *Scream 5*—and it would have to be made without Wes Craven's creative guidance.

Following two back-to-back disappointments—compounded by the heart-wrenching death of his brother Paul in December 2010—Wes "went to ground," explaining, "That's when an animal gets shot and goes as deep as it can into its burrow and just sits there to see whether it's going to die or live."[34] Wes's stepdaughter Nina says, "After *Scream 4* bombed at the box office, he kind of felt like he was done. 'People don't want what I'm doing. It's over.'" Wes and Iya retreated to their new home on Martha's Vineyard to contemplate the future and "just try to be human beings for a while."[35] Although friends and collaborators say Wes never intended to retire permanently, by 2011 he seemed to have made peace with his legacy as a filmmaker. When one interviewer asked if he had a message for his fans, Wes responded humbly and graciously.

"If I were to think of something to say to the fans, I would say thank you. Thank you for being there. Appreciating what I do. Sometimes, give me a little rap on the head to get me to go back in the right direction. Most of all, I think that you are the proof that everything that people say that don't like horror movies, everything they say that horror movies do to people is disproved by you—because you turned out to be some of the greatest people I've met, and the most gentle souls. [You] get all the humor and everything else in my films too, so thank you. Thank you for all you've given."[36]

CHAPTER FOURTEEN

THE BIRDS
(2011 - 2015)

"No, you could never tell where you were going, that was a sure thing.
The only sure thing. Nor could you tell how you'd get there—
though when you arrived it was somehow right."

– Ralph Ellison, *Invisible Man*

Wes's sabbatical on Martha's Vineyard started out well; he and Iya spent the summer of 2011 in their home on the west side of the island, communing with new friends and neighbors—"fun, interesting people, almost none of whom had seen a single movie I'd ever made."[1] It was a time and place of refuge and creative restoration.

Wes had first come to the Vineyard in the 1990s, visiting his friend Jack Coleman. According to Iya, "Jack and his wife had a place in Edgartown and they invited Wes for the holidays. The moment Wes stepped off the plane, he fell in love with it. It was snowing at the time, and Edgartown in the snow is storybook. Wes said he felt like he had entered Narnia. He was like, 'My god, places like this actually exist?'" Within a few years, Wes had bought an old whaling captain's house on William Street, in the historic district of Vineyard Haven. He subsequently bought another house near Lagoon Pond, where he and Iya spent the early days of their marriage. Then, in 2007, they fell in love with a parcel of land in the West Tisbury area—"a place where Wes could be in the woods, in the wild, in nature, among the birds. And a place where he could write."

The couple hired architect Maryann Thompson to design their dream house, an elegant modern structure integrated into its natural setting. She says, "It was pretty obvious where we should put the house. Near the top of the hill, you get the breezes and a little bit of an ocean view, off in the distance. But we decided not to dominate the hill. Wes and Iya liked the idea of building further down the hill and sort of wrapping the house around the hill, so there's a dialogue with nature. There's this beautiful grove of long-branched oak trees, growing horizontally along the ground, which is covered with ferns, so the site already had some mystery to it. We wanted to preserve that and incorporate that into the living space, so that the house is kind of bowing down to the site, rather than being a dominant object. Instead of being an object, it's a mysterious unfolding sequence of spaces. It's kind of cinematic, actually. You have to walk through the house in order to experience it. The house is all about mystery and the direct experience of walking through it. It's not a normal house. It's a mystery house."

By the summer of 2011, the couple was living full-time in the new house. Iya's daughter Nina Tarnawsky says Wes became more interested in bird-watching and woodworking, reading and playing guitar, than in making

Nina Tarnawsky, Wes Craven and Iya Labunka, March 2015
(courtesy Iya Labunka, photo credit: Nancy Neil)

another movie. Wes did not, however, lose his lifelong interest in storytelling. Instead, he embraced the role of elder statesman and offered his experience and expertise to a younger generation of writers.

At an end of summer barbecue, host Bill Eville, a new neighbor and writer at *The Vineyard Gazette* newspaper, connected with Wes for the first time. "I was talking with some people about an article I had written about getting kidnapped here on the island when I was a kid. Wes overheard the conversation. Three days later, I got an email from him, saying, 'Hey, I loved your article. Have you ever thought about making a screenplay out of it?' I responded, 'Well, I am now!'" After that, the two men met up occasionally to discuss the idea. Although they never cracked the story, Eville says "it was a quiet affirmation of what I was doing. I think it was meaningful for Wes too. He loved writing and he shared that love with other writers. It was a beautiful thing."

Wes similarly encouraged Nina, who says, "I was figuring out what I wanted to do after college—who I am, where I wanted to live. He really wanted me to be a writer. He wasn't pressuring, but he said, 'If this is what you want to do, then you should be around other writers. You need to be around other young people who are trying to write and be creative.'" Wes might have been speaking to himself as well as his stepdaughter. While Nina interned at *The Vineyard Gazette*, Wes continued to bond with Bill Eville. He also connected with nonfiction author Paul Schneider, the new editor of *Martha's Vineyard Magazine*. Nina remembers, "It was a little bit of a mentorship type of thing. These guys were in their 40s and he was in his 70s, but they were all writers. And Wes really thought of himself as a writer, more than a director."

On short business trips to Los Angeles, Wes also mentored five young screenwriters through a new program in the Writer's Guild of America created by Robert Disney. According to Nick Simon, "Every few months, we would have dinner at Wes's house, and we would talk about everything. Wes told us the story about what had happened on *A Nightmare on Elm Street*. He said, 'I had just done two movies that bombed, back to back, and I needed a movie that was going to work. I had taken the script to every single studio and everybody passed on it. Bob Shaye wanted to make it. My lawyer and my agent both looked at the contract and said, 'Don't sign that thing.' I signed it anyway, because I had to get that movie made.' Everything we were all going through as young writers, Wes had already gone through it—30, 40 years earlier."

Wes was happy to share his personal experience, but he also wanted to learn from the new generation. "At the first or second dinner, he asked us, 'What do you guys think is scary? What scares you?' And we're all looking at him, like, 'What are you talking about? *You* scared us! We're making films because of *you*!' Nobody really answered him, so he finally said, 'The reason I'm asking is because people didn't really seem to like *My Soul to Take* and *Scream 4*…' He said he felt like he didn't know what was scary anymore. He literally said that: 'I don't know if I know what's scary anymore.' We were like, '*What?* You're Wes Craven!'"

Wes's reticence about making another horror film didn't keep him from developing new material, including a comic book about monsters and "a children's book about nightmares."[2] He had been kicking around the idea of a supernatural *Odyssey* story for several years. In November 2011, he decided to meet with comic book writer Steve Niles to develop the story. Niles says, "His idea was 'A vampire, a werewolf, and a zombie walk into a bar…' And we went from there. We were talking about what he'd like to do and I came up with the title *Coming of Rage* at that meeting."

In *Coming of Rage*, which ultimately became a five-issue graphic novel, a college kid named Ritchie Westmord is summoned to the bedside of his dying father. Victor Westmord, a wealthy vintner, asks Ritchie to take over the family business, but Ritchie—who has never had a good relationship with his father—declines. Later, at a bar, he gets into a deadly brawl, sprouts fangs, and learns that he is a vampire. Ritchie also meets Oscar, a teenage werewolf, and Jacqueline, a teenage zombie. Together, the trio embarks on a cross-country journey of discovery. As they each learn how they became who they are, they also learn the truth about the Westmord family business: Ritchie's father doesn't sell… wine. Following the patriarch's death, Ritchie's Uncle Seth—an even more bloodthirsty capitalist than his brother—wants to expand the family business. On top of selling bottled blood to vampires, he wants to kill lower-class innocents and turn them into prime meat for discriminating carnivores. Ritchie is the only obstacle to Uncle Seth's hostile takeover, so he and his new friends are targeted for termination.

In a panel discussion at the Boston Festival of Books in 2013, Wes summed up the story: "It kind of follows a pattern in some ways of a lot of my work, which is young people finding out what the parents really are and what they have made of the world." Commenting on the central character's arc, he added, "Ritchie's rise from idle ignorance to a young man / young vampire with a deep knowledge of the world, both the good and the bad, is fascinating to me. And that he finds his place, his mission can be something we can actually admire. He and his two friends will not be predators of the innocent. But they will be hunters—hunters of evil. And when they ferret it out, they will do battle with it to the death, until the world is just a bit safer for the rest of us."[3] For Wes, the story was personal and also topical, turning the aftermath of 2008's Great Recession into a fairy tale for the current apocalypse. "Vampires are huge now," he explained, "while we have a whole generation of brokers on Wall Street that shaped our economy. And zombies—I think people have a sense that we're sleepwalking through life."[4] *Coming of Rage* was conceived as a wake-up call and a battle cry.

Before *Coming of Rage* came to fruition, however, in late 2012, Wes suffered a Vespa accident. One minute, he was touring some friends around his property on Martha's Vineyard, cruising at ten miles an hour on a dirt road. The next, he was face-down on the ground. Regaining consciousness, he saw "something gray and gory" sticking out of his left leg.[5] The Vespa's kickstand had impaled itself in his calf.

Doctors were able to stitch up the leg, but Wes's subsequent overreliance on his other leg compromised his right knee, demanding total knee replacement surgery. Afterward, he posted on Twitter, "Enough with the creaking hinges! Looking forward to being able to climb through the cables on set soon!" But the string of bad luck continued. In early 2013, Wes fell and cracked his pelvis. In mid-February, he wrote, "Give me the insanity of impossible schedules, screaming studio heads, script pages never showing up until the morning we're ready to shoot them—anything but the horrors of retirement."[6]

At the very least, the spate of injuries gave him a chance to catch up on his reading. At the Boston Book Festival, he chatted about his favorite publications, and declared his undying interests in cutting-edge science, nature, history, and "weary stories about family dysfunction."[7] Wes also subscribed to a huge number of periodicals, including *Scientific American, Popular Mechanics, Wired, Journal of the American Medical Association, Psychology Today, Audubon, Nature, Birdwatching, Natural History, National Geographic, Discover, TIME, Newsweek, Foreign Affairs, Smithsonian, The Atlantic, The New Yorker, Vanity Fair, Dwell, Architectural Digest, American Woodworker, Fine Woodworking, Woodworker's Journal, Woodworking Shop, Woodsmith, ShopNotes, Condé Nast Traveler, Travel and Leisure, Boating, Wooden Boat, Fretboard Journal, Granta, Popular Photography, Outdoor Photographer, American Cinematographer, Aperture, Cinefex, Fangoria,* and *Rue Morgue.* Iya says, "Wes was a man with an insatiable curiosity about the world and our experience in it—and a continuous desire to figure that out, and tell stories to help other people understand it as he was trying to understand it."

Around the same time, Wes named several fellow filmmakers whose work had meant a lot to him over the years: Polanski, Hitchcock, Truffaut, Buñuel, and John Huston. He singled out Huston as something of a "father figure," and praised Huston's 1980 autobiography *An Open Book.*[8] A socially-liberal man's man, Huston once asserted, "I don't like being afraid of seeing other people be afraid. What I really like are horses, strong drink, and women."[9] He might have added boxing, guns, and cinema.

Wes's ex-wife Mimi says she and Wes attended a weekend-long retrospective of Huston's films in the mid-1980s, and had a chance to meet the legendary filmmaker. "It was a big deal because Wes loved his movies and John Huston was everything he wanted to be. You know, a twelve-foot tall, bulletproof filmmaker. So we paid an ungodly amount of money to go and see all of his films at an event on the *Queen Mary*. They set up screening rooms and we were running from screening to screening. And then there were meet-and-greets, Q&As, and meals-with. I remember at one of the meals, somebody asked John Huston a question and he answered it. Then, like two seconds later, Wes asked a similar question, and John Huston looked at him and said, 'I already answered that.' He hadn't answered that *exact* question— but that was all Wes could talk about for the next eighteen hours, how he had been put down by his father figure. It upset him greatly because John Huston was everything to him."

In *An Open Book*, Huston reflected on his body of work, indicating that he failed to see "any continuity" from film to film. Although he claimed he didn't have any regrets about the films he'd made, he wrote that the "best approach" a filmmaker could take was that of the *auteur*, a creator pursuing specific subjects and themes for distinctly personal reasons: "The director conceives the idea, writes it, puts it on film. Because he is creating out of himself, controlling all aspects of the work, his films assume a unity and a direction. I admire directors like Bergman, Fellini, Buñuel, whose every picture is in some way concerned with their private lives, but that's never been my approach. I'm eclectic. I like to draw on sources other than myself; further I don't think of myself as simply, uniquely and forever a director of motion pictures... The idea of devoting myself to a single pursuit in life is unthinkable to me."[10]

Wes might have related especially to the latter sentiment. Certainly, he was a man of many interests and many obsessions. But unlike Huston, he was an obvious *auteur*. The unity of Wes's films may not reflect the filmmaker's entire personality, but they do reflect the deepest corners of Wes's soul. Furthermore, his work follows a clear direction: out of darkness, into light.

Still, in later years, Wes seemed somewhat disappointed with the limitations of his career. At a Masters of Horror dinner in the early 2010s, Wes and fellow filmmaker Tom McLoughlin compared notes. McLoughlin had made three horror films in the early part of his career, then took a job directing a network TV miniseries and spent the following two decades making TV movies in a wide variety of genres—comedies, dramas, Capra-esque fantasies, Hitchcockian thrillers, ghost stories, and coming-of-age stories. "Wes said, 'I gotta be honest with you, I'd much rather have a career like you've had.' I said, 'Are you kidding me? You are Wes Name Above the Title Craven! You have to love the fact that your name is associated with so many classics of the genre.' He goes, 'As wonderful as that is, it's not what I wanted my career to be. I just hate that it means I can't explore other things.'"

A few years out from *Scream 4*, Nina Tarnawsky says Wes would make similar comments at the breakfast table. "He would say things like, 'I would have had a much more interesting career if it hadn't been for Bob Weinstein.' There was definitely some resentment about having been pigeonholed in the genre... but it was complicated. I don't think he regretted his career. He just felt hemmed in. [French photographer] Henri Cartier-Bresson once said he was always haunted by the pictures he didn't take. I think there was a lot of that with Wes. He was very aware of the shadow of the career he didn't have."

In the spring of 2013, he couldn't help looking back. Over the weekend of May 5th and 6th, Wheaton College's graduating class of 1963 held its fiftieth reunion, and Wes—somewhat nervously—made an appearance. "He had some trepidation," Iya remembers. "He went back and forth. 'Should I go? Nah, that's stupid.' Then, eventually, he was like, 'Yeah, whatever.' I think, on some level, he wanted to show that world to me. And, more than anything else, he was curious. Toward the end of our lives, I think we all crave the experience of seeing people who knew us when. It was interesting."

Because Wes and some of his other classmates did not want to set foot on the college campus, Harry Strachan and Ron Watson organized an unofficial, off-campus banquet. Wes attended with Iya and Nina. Later, Strachan compiled a series of essays from the attendees, who summed up their spiritual journeys post-graduation. "One reassuring surprise," Strachan reflects, "was to find how many of us felt that, in spite of all sorts of mistakes and potholes, 'we have arrived at where we belonged.' In that acceptance, we also saw in a new light the role that Wheaton, its faculty and fellow students, had played in our lives."[11]

Wes may have felt more conflicted. In 2002, he had told Ron Watson that he'd had a difficult time communicating with old friends from Wheaton, saying, "It's like that whole life is just another life and I'm terrified of being dragged back to it somehow."[12] At the 2013 reunion, Watson says, Wes seemed less comfortable revisiting his past than many of his peers: "I don't think Wes ever got very far away from his experience of growing up in the church and being shaped by that. It was something he continued to talk about [decades later] in a very emotional way. And that's different from most of his peers. Most people got far away from those early experiences and could be more objective. 'This was my experience and this is how I was socialized, but then I moved on.' Wes was unusual in that, in a way, he didn't move on. He was still hooked."

Watson adds that, at one point during the reunion, he had a brief exchange with Wes about one of the pivotal moments in Wes's life—when Prexy Edman publicly "denounced" him from the pulpit. "Later, as he was leaving, I said to him, 'You know, Wes, Prexy is dead.' He looked at me and said something to the effect of, 'Are you saying I should give it up?' This was fifty years after the fact."

Jessica Craven says her father always seemed to have a strong need to "jettison his past," and to separate himself from people who reminded him of hard times. "Religion became the enemy," she says. "That was the thing he blamed, and anything associated with that got—at the very least—compartmentalized." Toward the end of his life, however, Wes became more interested in—and capable of—reminiscing. Nina Tarnawsky, who attended the Wheaton reunion with her stepfather, observed something more like reconciliation and closure: "I think that was a big deal for him. Like everybody who goes to a reunion, he was able to say, 'I made it. This is what I've accomplished.' He was able to revisit that period in his life, knowing that he had recovered from it. He had, basically, found himself." Iya adds, "I think the moment of getting away from the church—and from Wheaton—was his moment of revelation. But you're always on the road to Tarsus, in some ways. You never really get there."

Soon after, Wes returned to the filmmaking world. At one of the later dinners with his Writer's Guild mentees, Nick Simon brought up a new project: "He said, 'What are you working on?' I said, 'Oh, I've got this script called *The Girl in the Photographs*. I've been working on it with a couple other writers and we've been going back and forth on it for a long time.' Wes said, 'Well, send it over. I'll read it and give you notes." And I was like, 'Really?' Because he was still our mentor and, when we first entered the mentor program, they said, 'Don't send him scripts. Don't ask him to produce something for you.' And I didn't. So I was like, 'Are you sure?' Wes said, 'Yeah.' I didn't think he would actually read it."

In *The Girl in the Photographs*, a young woman named Colleen is stalked by a pair of sadistic killers in her small town of Spearfish, South Dakota. When the killers start leaving crime scene photos where Colleen can find them, Spearfish's most famous former resident, Peter Hemmings, takes an interest. Now a caustic L.A. fashion photographer, Hemmings brings his entourage—including a charming but timid personal assistant named Chris—to meet Colleen and document the perverse events in Spearfish. Predictably, the tourists become the next victims. Chris initially survives the wrath of the killers by staying close to Colleen, but eventually the killers confront the Final Girl and create their masterpiece.

Wes raved about the script, expressing enthusiasm for the opening kill (an obvious homage to *Psycho* and *Scream*), the strong female lead, and the insufferably human Peter Hemmings character—who, Wes astutely noted, was named after David Hemmings in *Blow-Up*. According to Nick Simon, "He said he felt like it was something fresh and new and exciting, and he said he hadn't had that feeling since he read the first *Scream*. He wasn't comparing *The Girl in the Photographs* to *Scream*—because it was never meant to work on that level—but he was saying it made him feel something he hadn't felt since *Scream*." Wes offered some editorial (and grammar) notes on the script, then offered to help Nick make the film. Eighteen months later, Wes's name appeared on the film as an executive producer.

Claudia Lee is Colleen, the final girl in *The Girl in the Photographs*
(courtesy Nick Simon)

In the meantime, Wes began moving forward on his own new projects. In the fall of 2013, *The Hollywood Reporter* celebrated him as one of the top twenty Masters of Horror, and Wes embraced the opportunity to talk about an animated film he was developing "about a little girl who is possessed," as well as a feature film "about environmental horror, global warming and the planetary reaction to that."[13]

Sara Bottfeld, Wes's agent-turned-manager, says the former project was an adaptation of Ray Fawkes's *Possessions*, a graphic novel about a hell-raising five-year-old girl possessed by a "pit demon" named Gurgazon the Unclean. Despite her best attempts to spurn love and acceptance, Gurgazon finds a happy home among fellow freaks at the Llewellyn-Vane House for Captured Spirits and Ghostly Curiosities. Bottfeld thought it was "a great metaphor for life at that age, because the child was really just misunderstood. Unfortunately, we never got to the script stage on that one, but we developed a very elaborate pitch that was so fun and delightful. Wes was tickled pink about the possibility of bringing this really fun character to the screen."

The second project seems to have been in gestation for years. In 2001, Wes said, "I think my basic fears are about the next 50 years, what with the population reaching 6 billion in the past 40 years and it's still going up at an arithmetic rate. This is what really scares me. There just ain't enough room for this many humans on the planet."[14] He believed that the next big wave of horror films would focus on the future of humanity and the loss of our earthly environment.

Serving as a judge for submissions to the Catalina Film Festival in 2013, Wes praised Australian filmmaker Ariel Martin's short film *The iMom*, in which a generation of deadbeat parents employ robotic "new mothers" to care for their children. When a technical glitch causes one iMom to misread a context clue, a baby gets roasted like a Thanksgiving turkey. Tim Kennedy, Wes's personal assistant and founder of the Catalina festival, says, "Wes was just horrified by that, and I think he would have gone the same route [in his future films]. You can only make so many gory, killer-in-the-woods movies. The scary thing, for Wes, was what the future is going to be. He had his eye trained on the direction humanity is going, what's going to happen to us when everything is automated, when we have self-driving cars and robots working at McDonald's. If you can't even get a job at McDonald's anymore, people will be stealing from each other—because they've got to make money somehow!"

One element of *The iMom* that may have fascinated Wes was a vague hint that the Biblical prophecy of end-times was about to come true. Responding to the story of Adam and Eve, the film's robotic new mother says, "The world is the tree [of knowledge] and I am the fruit. So what does that say about the world?" Soon after, Wes received an invitation to write and direct his own take on a Biblical story.

In January 2014, the Weinstein brothers announced their plan to produce an epic, 10-part TV series titled *The Ten Commandments*. With each segment, a different filmmaker would put a "modern spin" on one of the commandments. Filmmakers attached at that time were Gus Van Sant, Lee Daniels, Jim Sheridan, Michael Cera, and Wes Craven—who had already picked his segment: "Thou Shalt Not Kill."[15] Bob Weinstein described Wes's story as an exploration of "the stresses of a soldier who operates drones to launch attacks in foreign wars and how this affects his relationship with his son."[16] Friends say Wes was very passionate about the project.

Wes's idol John Huston had also directed an anthology film based on the Old Testament in the later part of his career, and he claimed that most interviewers responded by asking if he "believed in the Bible literally." Huston answered that for him the Bible represented a transition from Myths to Legends to History. When asked more pointedly if he believed in God, he answered, "I don't profess any beliefs in an orthodox sense. It seems to me that the mystery of life is too great, too wide, too deep, to do more than wonder at. Anything further would be, as far as I'm concerned, an impertinence."[17]

Wes probably agreed with Huston's answers. In 2002, he said, "I don't believe anything that I don't experience directly. What I experience directly is a sense of awe at life and the way it's organized and the way it manifests itself. I'm very attracted to biology, animal biology, astronomy, and science in general. I've come to really love science because I think it has a very rigid approach to what it declares to be reality. And it always leaves itself a hedge that something could be disproved by another theory. I really love that."[18]

Around the same time, he compiled a list of "favorite quotes" which included a passage from Nobel Prize-winning physicist Richard P. Feynman: "I think it's much more interesting to live not knowing than to have answers which might be wrong. I have approximate answers and possible beliefs and different degrees of certainty about different things, but I'm not absolutely sure of anything and there are many things I don't know anything about, such as whether it means anything to ask why we're here, and what the question might mean. [...] I don't have to know the answer. I don't feel frightened by not knowing things, by being lost in a mysterious universe without having any purpose, which is the way it really is so far as I can tell. It doesn't frighten me."[19]

In lieu of knowing—and not knowing—Wes made a habit of observing the world around him. In a 2010 interview with author John Wooley, he explained, "I certainly don't believe in some God up in the sky dictating what we should do or not do. But it's not like I don't think there's some supreme essence to consciousness and to the world that is simply awe-inspiring. To me, it could simply be a bird."[20] In an interview with me on the same day, he talked about birds in a different light: "You watch birds at a feeder and, if you're into birds, you start to realize that every second they're expecting to get whopped upside the head. They're just constantly looking over their shoulder, all the time. I live up in the hills and there's a hawk that's come into the area called a Cooper's Hawk. It's about three quarters the size of a Red-Tail Hawk. And they're ambushers. They'll sit up in the tree and watch the feeder, and just come in this low flight between the trees, hit a mourning dove, and the mourning dove just explodes. The hawk flies off and all that's left behind is feathers."

One wonders if this was, for Wes, evidence of a violent God or of an indifferent universe?

Prompting what? Wonder? Awe? Fear? All of the above?

Wes offered a concise worldview by answering the question "Why Do Birds Matter?" In a 2013 article published on the Audubon Society website, he wrote, "Since the beginning, birds have lifted our eyes to the skies. They've shown us we're not gravity's slave, that flight is possible and limitless. It can hover and soar, dive and display, and take us from one end of the planet to the other in a single, impossible burst of energy and purpose. Inspiration is the gift birds have given us from the start. But now they give us a question as well. Like the canary in the mine, they hold the planet up to us like a mirror and ask: 'Can you not see that if we pass away, soon you will as well?'"[21]

In a roundabout way, the topic became fodder for one of Wes's last projects, a thinly disguised horror movie. The project began with a sarcastic suggestion. In October 2013, Paul Schneider asked Wes if he might be interested in writing a series of articles about birds for *Martha's Vineyard Magazine*. "I just thought it was a funny idea," Schneider says. "Gee, wouldn't it be great to do [a riff on] Alfred Hitchcock's *The Birds*? I thought there was maybe a 15% chance that he would say yes—because why would Wes Craven need to write a bird column for a local magazine? I wasn't really expecting much."

A month later, Wes requested a meeting to discuss "The Birds." Four months later, he began writing. In the first installment of what would turn out to be an eight-part series, Wes wrote that he had recently discovered "a book about what birds think" (probably Tim Birkhead's *Bird Sense: What It's Like to Be a Bird*) but was disappointed that it failed to address one important question: What do birds think *about humans*? Hitchcock, he wrote, had addressed that very question by implying that our feathered friends might get sick of us, or at least sick of our habitual disrespect for the natural world. Communicating with his own backyard inhabitants ("I get fan mail from them quite often"), Wes prophesied a similar turn of events in the near future. To help his fellow humans avert horror-movie disaster, he suggested that we should show a little love for the birds, instead of hastening "the biggest species die-off since the age of the dinosaurs."[22]

Schneider was floored by Wes's first column. "It was astonishingly creative. I just thought, Wow, this guy is thinking on so many different levels. And I thought it might be the best thing the magazine ever published while I was editor." "The Birds, Part 1" appeared in *Martha's Vineyard Magazine* on April Fool's Day 2014. Subsequent installments appeared in the May, July, and August issues. Wes observed casual chit-chat among anthropomorphic birds at a Boston bar, interviewed a group of cynical seagulls on the coast, and followed a barn owl on a quasi-mystical journey to a sacred tree.

Then things started to get weird. When the barn owl suggests that Wes's imagination has transported them into the past—Martha's Vineyard before it was overtaken by human settlers—the mystical vision suddenly evaporates. "There was a rumble, and the tree suddenly just wasn't there. The birds were flying and I was falling."[23]

Amidst these flights of fancy into his private wonderland, Wes had to put his work on hold and cope with a major health crisis. In July 2014, he was diagnosed with prostate cancer. His treatment prevented him from taking an active role on the MTV series *Scream: Resurrection*, although he reportedly gave some notes on the pilot script. Director Jamie Travis took the reins in August, and filming began in the fall. Wes said, "I just put my name on it. I was too busy to do much else."[24]

Near summer's end, a very short prose piece by Wes—titled "The Man Who Vanished"—appeared in an art gallery show on the Vineyard. Written as part of a group experiment involving a "chain" of 140 artists, Wes's story was based on a sensory experience conjured by a fellow artist's tea. The taste reminded the narrator of a night when he was twenty years old and "bedded down in a barn in New Hampshire after running away from home. Or from her." The "her" is the man's wife, who recently passed away, and whose death prompts him to walk into the freezing-cold ocean outside his home, where a shark claims his body like a hungry lover. Wes said he wrote the story during a "dreadful" time the previous Christmas holiday season. When asked if the story meant something to him that a casual observer might not know, he answered, "Yes, and by god the observer isn't going to be told what those things are."[25]

In September and November, Wes composed three more tributes to The Birds. The first was a riff on the political climate of Hawks vs. Doves, culminating with an image of a carrion-eater awaiting its next meal. In his next column, Wes addressed readers who had suggested that his literal dialogues with nature "constituted a cry for help."[26] A lifelong believer in psychotherapy, he wrote that he had consulted a reputable Boston shrink, Dr. Malleus Maleficarum, who gave him a prescription and urged him to talk about his mother, but said he fled the psychiatrist's office to seek the advice of a horned owl instead. The wise old owl asserted that birds everywhere are suffering from PTSD, then invited his Cessna-flying friend to go south with him for the winter.

In Part 7, Wes continued his "flightmare" by interviewing fellow migrators. Eventually, the columnist found himself staring into the future, witnessing the catastrophic results of global warming (or Mother Nature's wrath?) as well as rising gas prices (which he predicts to be $25/gallon in 2030), followed by a gunfight between birds and one particularly callous human. As the surviving birds head out to sea, one advises Wes to fly home and write about what he's seen. When Wes crash lands in a future version of Martha's Vineyard, however, the locals decide he *really* needs psychiatric help. An E.R. doctor responds to the columnist's latest anecdotes by administering a strong sedative and drowning the narrative in darkness. For seven months, that seemed to be the end of "The Birds."

The 2014 holiday season was not as "dreadful" for Wes as the previous one. His doctor announced that Wes had beaten prostate cancer. Feeling grateful for the new lease on life, Wes and his wife and stepdaughter celebrated Christmas with friends and neighbors at a public gathering on the Vineyard. Bill Eville says, "The annual Christmas Eve service is held at the Agricultural Society Hall, and about 900 people usually come. It's not a church service but it's very traditional; there's a children's pageant and then they pass out candles and sing 'Silent Night.' Everyone is welcome, and a lot of people use it as an opportunity to check in with Christmas without having to go to church." Eville's wife Cathlin Baker, an Episcopal pastor on the island, says Wes was deeply moved by the event's message of love. "This was a Christian message Wes could embrace."

Unfortunately, in the waning days of 2014, Wes noticed signs of a new illness, beginning with a hiccup in his speech when he tried to retrieve words. Friends on the Vineyard recall seeing him at a New Year's Eve party at his and Iya's house—and then, not seeing him again.

Less than forty-eight hours into a new year, a medical scan showed an abnormal growth of cells inside Wes's brain. He and Iya quickly returned to Los Angeles to pursue treatment. Iya says, "That was one of the saddest moments of my life. As we were driving away from our home in Martha's Vineyard, Wes said, 'I don't think I'll ever be back here again.' He knew how serious it was."

Back in L.A., Wes's assistant Tim Kennedy visited Wes at home. He remembers, "Wes was just sitting there, very calmly. He said, 'Hey, Tim.' I said, 'What happened? Why did you rush back here?' And he started joking, 'Oh, I've got this little thing—brain cancer.' I just stood there dumbfounded. Like, why are you joking about this? But that was the way he dealt with it."

Nick Simon had a similar experience a few days later. "Wes said, 'Here's the thing: they found this tumor, we're going to do surgery, and we think it will go okay. I could live six months. I could live six years. Nobody knows.' Then he said, 'Please keep this to yourself. We don't want anybody to know about it. We'll issue a statement when we're ready.' I said of course. But he was like, 'I'm still here.'"

Apart from family and close friends, few people knew about Wes's condition. To a certain extent, he tried to go about his business as usual, which included moving forward on several new film projects. On January 23, Al-Ghanim Entertainment announced plans to make *The Girl in the Photographs*, a film "inspired by the *Scream* franchise" and executive produced by Wes Craven.[27] As the project moved forward, Nick says Wes remained a constant presence and mentor: "One day, I was getting frustrated with some of the stuff that was going on behind the scenes to get the movie made. I had breakfast with

Wes and I said, 'I don't know what to do.' He said, 'Here's the thing: You're a really nice guy. You're almost too nice. It's a great quality to have, but in the situation you're in right now, you have to be more primal. You have to look people in the eye and say that's not going to happen. Don't apologize. Just say no, we're not doing that. Don't smile. Don't laugh. Don't let them think you're making fun of them. Just be very stern and emotionless. Look them in the eye, tell them what you feel, and move on. Worst case scenario, if they bail on the project, we'll find someone else.'"

Wes's no-bullshit approach to dealing with producers reflected his strong commitment to getting the film made. He played a major role in casting the film and also helped to bring in key collaborators, including cinematographer Dean Cundey. He also called on his old friend Mitch Pileggi—*Shocker*'s Horace Pinker—to play Spearfish's surly sheriff.

While ushering *The Girl in the Photographs* toward production, Wes underwent a craniotomy to remove a large portion of a cancerous glioblastoma from his frontal lobe. Throughout the ordeal, he retained his dark sense of humor. In March, when Paul Schneider inquired about the possibility of another installment of "The Birds," Wes emailed an apology and an excuse: "Didn't see this from you due to having another hole in my head, but I'd love to do another column." Around the same time, Bill Eville also received an email from Wes: "The subject line said 'open-minded.' I clicked on it and there was a photo of Wes's brain that the doctor had taken during one of his surgeries. I was shocked and aghast—but it was also funny."

Wes's social media posts in the spring of 2015 reflect his hobbies: birdwatching, cat-watching, sky photography, and adding to his collection of printing letterpress blocks. He also poked fun at himself with a series of posts in which he replaced one word in the title of each of his films: *Last Goat on the Left, The Heels Have Eyes, The Bunny and the Rainbow, The Pancake Under the Stairs*, and *A Nightmare on Elm Tweet*. He tried very hard to keep things as light as possible for the loved ones around him. Jonathan Craven found him to be genuinely hopeful about the future: "He had two operations and, after the first operation, there was a period when things seemed to be much better. He was very optimistic."

Wes spent weekends with family—Iya and Nina, Jonathan and Jessica, and three grandchildren. "We wanted the kids to have that time with him," Jonathan says, "so we went to his house every Sunday. We had a lot of really nice times with him. But then there was a big collapse in progress, and in his sense of well-being. The doctors were feeding him this idea that they could keep him alive for two more years, maybe five, and I think Iya was very invested in keeping that fantasy alive. But my sister and I had a pretty strong sense that that was not going to happen."

Iya concedes, "He submitted to some of the treatments more for me than for himself. I never pushed him; I never insisted; it was always a conversation: 'These are the choices. What do you think?' But I knew he was doing it for me. That's who he was."

Assistant Tim Kennedy had the sense that Wes wasn't afraid of dying: "He was more worried about everybody else. One day, I was visiting him at the hospital and I told him about something bad that had happened, and he said, 'When I'm not here, who's gonna look after you?' All I heard was 'When I'm not here…' That was my first clue that he was terminal."

Despite many debilitating hardships, Wes's final summer was exceptionally busy. On April 20th, just days after MTV released the first trailer for its new *Scream* TV series, he signed a first-look deal with Universal Cable Productions. Although Wes wasn't actively seeking new projects, he suddenly had multiple TV series in development: one based on his film *The People Under the Stairs*, one based on Daryl Gregory's novel *We Are All Completely Fine*, and one based on Steve Niles and Christopher Mitten's graphic novel *The Disciples*, a sci-fi variation on the Jonestown tragedy. Iya says he was going to meetings and pitching stories for months, nonstop.

None of the projects made it to the screen. Screenwriter Michael Reisz helped develop a pilot script for *The People Under the Stairs*, but Wes reportedly had some misgivings about revamping his story as "a contemporary *Downton Abbey* meets *The Amityville Horror*."[28] Wes planned to write and direct his own pilot for *We Are All Completely Fine*, an ensemble drama about a psychotherapist and three ostensibly-insane patients, but ultimately didn't have enough time. According to Steve Niles, *The Disciples* was outlined as a TV series, but failed to get picked up.

But Wes still had more projects in development. Nina Tarnawsky remembers he was especially enthusiastic about a pitch by writer Daniel Knauf, creator of the HBO series *Carnivàle*. Conceived as a six-season ensemble drama, Knauf's *Sleepers* would follow a group of liberal arts college students as they confronted a multiversal threat based on H.P. Lovecraft's *Dream Cycle* Mythos. Knauf explains, "The series raised big, existential questions about the nature of good, evil, courage and cowardice while exploring the very fabric of quantum reality. Best of all, the fulcrum of the show was an exploration of the single most egalitarian of human superpowers: the ability to dream."[29] It should come as no surprise that such a pitch intrigued the creator of Freddy Krueger. Knauf adds, "To the end, [Wes] was always enthusiastic, brimming with brilliant ideas and quick to provide support and motivation for me to push the outside of whatever envelope we confronted."[30] Unfortunately, *Sleepers* remained dormant.

Only *The Girl in the Photographs* moved forward. In late April, Wes went to a table read in Los Angeles, just days before filming began. Nick Simon had been warned that Wes might not feel well enough to attend. "So when he showed up, everyone was so excited. Out of all the table reads I've ever participated in, that one was the most dialed-in. Everybody was on. Everybody was in character. Because—*holy shit, it's Wes Craven*, you know?"

Afterward, the cast and crew left for Vancouver, where the film was shot. Throughout the production, Nick sent each day's footage to Wes, and received immediate feedback. "Wes would say things like, 'Some of the scenes are dragging on a little longer than they need to. I understand that, on the day, while you're shooting, it feels like the right speed. But make everyone go faster. Because it's not.' And he was right."

Nina remembers that Wes also had some concerns about the content of *The Girl in the Photographs*. "When he first told Nick he wanted to be involved as an executive producer, he didn't have cancer. When it started filming, he did, and that got him thinking a lot about his legacy. Had he brought more violence into the world? Had he made the world worse somehow? He wasn't expressing himself in those grandiose terms, but he worried that he might have contributed to some sort of glorification of violence. He worried that *The Girl in the Photographs* follows some of the same tropes that every horror movie

Top: Wes Craven with the cast of *The Girl in the Photographs*
Bottom: Wes Craven with Nick Simon, director of *The Girl in the Photographs*
(courtesy Nick Simon)

follows. For example, he worried that the cops in the film were too stupid. He worried that the movie was a little too violent—maybe without earning it. There's a scene where the main villain keeps a female victim in a dog cage in his basement. He was wrestling with that. I believe he was thinking about how people would remember him. Would they think he was a guy who perpetuated horror instead of confronting it?"

During this period of time, Nina watched all of Wes's "classic" horror films with him—except one. "He did not want me to watch *Last House on the Left*. We watched everything else, but *Last House* was a touchy subject with him. I still have never seen it, because he didn't want me to. He was worried that it would make me see him differently. He said, 'I was an angrier person then.' I know it would not have changed how I felt about him, because I know how to separate the art and the artist, but I can understand why he felt that way." Over the years, Wes had often expressed misgivings about the original *Last House on the Left*—a film that assaults its audience with unflinching depictions of extreme violence, and all but insults its audience with a flippant secondary narrative about stupid cops.

Wes evolved into a much more nuanced, sensitive, and sympathetic storyteller—all the while remaining a horror filmmaker. Nina says, "I see so much of Wes in his [later] movies—in the sense of humor, in the social commentary, in the undermining of traditional family values. From today's perspective, he's not very radical, but he was always pushing against traditional formulations of life, which is why he was so perfect for horror. He was perfectly suited to make horror films, but I think that was something he fought internally because he felt a lot of shame about it. It was something he dealt with his entire life."

Nina's favorite film is *The People Under the Stairs*, "because it's so outrageous and so funny. During the scene where Everett McGill comes around the corner wearing the gimp suit, I was laughing so hard I was crying. Initially, Wes was a little uptight that I was laughing so hard—like, was I making fun of the movie?—but then he loosened up and said, 'This is the first movie I wrote after I got on Prozac. I felt so light while I was making it.' And you can feel his freedom in that movie. You still get the broken family theme and the political commentary, but it's so *free*. Wes may have felt a lot of shame about making horror movies, but I can't imagine any other genre being as elastic for his storytelling."

The Girl in the Photographs completed filming on May 15th. Six weeks later, Wes gave a final round of notes to the director. At the same time, he put some finishing touches on his long-rumored "children's book of nightmares" (which he trademarked on June 19th) and his newspaper column "The Birds." After a brief recap of the previous year's ill-fated migration journey and apocalyptic vision of the future, Part 8 begins with the narrator on trial for terrorism, in a courtroom filled by angry birds. The judge sentences him to return to Martha's Vineyard in the year 2015, and instructs him to "ask your friends and representatives what the hell they were thinking back then, because they sure weren't thinking very much about the future the rest of us had to live in." Wes does his penance and documents about the horrors of "Planet War One," the impending standoff between Nature and humanity.[31]

In the same week that Wes's final installment of "The Birds" appeared in the *Martha's Vineyard Magazine*, Wes eulogized fellow horror icon Christopher Lee in *The Hollywood Reporter*. The two had met decades earlier, when Wes tried to cast Lee as the villain in *Swamp Thing*. Lee turned down the role of Arcane because "he didn't want to turn into the monster at the end."[32] In his eulogy, Wes marveled at the longevity of the actor's career, as well as the range of his roles, personal interests, and accomplishments, noting that Lee began releasing heavy metal albums in his eighties and nineties. "Many of us hope we'll live life to the fullest—Lee actually did. His fans will continue to find him where we always did: onscreen."[33]

Wes tried to enjoy the time he had left. On July 13, he attended an Elvis Costello concert at the Hollywood Bowl with Iya and friends Neve Campbell and J.J. Feild. On August 2, he celebrated his 76th birthday with family, and thanked fans on social media for helping to make it a "wonderful day." Although his strength and his ability to communicate effectively were waning, he visited with a few close friends, including Carly Feingold, who remembers, "The week he passed, I saw him at his house. He was resting, but he woke up and we talked a little bit. I was pregnant with my daughter at the time and he asked me, 'What are you going to name the baby?' I said, 'I don't know yet. Maybe we'll name her Wes.' That made him smile—that was the last time I saw him smile—so my daughter's middle name is Wes."

Jonathan Craven says, near the end, Wes struggled to talk. "The glioblastoma had manifested in the part of his frontal lobe that affected speech, so he didn't lose anything intellectually; he was still cognizant, but he couldn't communicate—at least, not verbally. During those last couple of weeks, when he was conscious, I got the sense sometimes that he was trying to say something, trying to reach out. It's anybody's guess what he might have said, had he been able to speak."

At 1pm on Saturday, August 30th, 2015, Wes Craven died at his home in Los Angeles, surrounded by those who loved him. "He died in peace and love," says Iya. "We should all be so lucky."

Many who knew Wes—and many more who knew his work—were shocked by the news. In the days and weeks that followed, filmmakers and fans released a steady stream of heartfelt tributes. Robert Englund, who had embodied Wes's most famous cinematic creation, celebrated his friend's life by sharing an anecdote about Wes's famously dark sense of humor. One Saturday night in 1991, Englund said, Wes visited him at his apartment in Vancouver, where they were filming *Nightmare Cafe*. The nightmare men had a few drinks and sat down to watch a *Saturday Night Live* episode featuring a sketch called "Massive Head Wound Harry." In the sketch, Dana Carvey plays a young man arriving late to a snooty cocktail party, apparently unaware that he has a gaping, bloody head wound. The other party guests are too polite or too horrified to tell him, so the man leaves a trail of gore all around his host's posh apartment. As he lies down to take a nap on a pristine white couch, the host's dog smells food and starts snacking on the massive head wound. At that point, Englund says, Wes fell off the couch, laughing so hard "there was snot coming out of his nose."[34]

Reflecting on the thin line between comedy and tragedy, Wes quoted Voltaire: "God is a comedian playing to an audience that's afraid to laugh." Wes was never afraid to laugh. "To me, it's just a way of coping," he explained. "It's not like I go around thinking the world is horrible all the time, but there's that subtext that you feel all the time of 'God, it's just madness out there.' To be able to joke about it erases it somehow."[35]

Despite his macabre sense of humor, Wes was deeply compassionate. Several of his most famous collaborators eulogized him by emphasizing his humanity above his instincts for horror. Kevin Williamson wrote, "As the

Master of Horror, he has made his mark in cinema. And, by knowing and working with him, I can also attest he is the master of kindness, grace, class and poise."[36] *Scream* actress Rose McGowan tweeted, "Thank you for being the kindest man, the gentlest man, and one of the smartest men I've known."[37] Andrea Eastman adds, "In a business where most people are sharks, Wes was very pure and honest. I always felt that he was a gentle soul."

To many of his collaborators, Wes was family. Courteney Cox says he was "like a father figure in so many ways. He would sit there and just share his wisdom, but he'd also love to go out and have a glass of wine and be silly. He was just an incredible person."[38] David Arquette adds, "There's only a few people that really stand out as almost angels coming into your life at a time when you need them. They care about you. They want the best time for you. They don't want anything out of you either. They're just looking out for you... He was such a generous person."[39] Their *Scream* co-star Neve Campbell sums up, "He had a twisted sense of humor and a sweet, sweet soul. He really did. He was respectful, loving, like a father in a lot of ways to all of us. And mischievous. And so talented. [...] He was magic."[40]

In 2002, when asked how he wanted to be remembered, Wes answered, "A good and decent father. That would be good. The rest? I don't care. I'd like it to be known that I took the chances. I took the chance of going out into the darkness."[41] Iya says he really tried to be a good father. "He grew up without a father, so fatherly behavior was difficult for him. He told me he had to read books about fathering to figure out how to be a father. And he valued his relationship with his children very, very deeply." Jessica Craven adds, "It wasn't easy. But I never doubted that he loved me. At the end of his life, we talked about all that stuff and all was forgiven."

Stepdaughter Nina says that, in his final years, Wes was still working through his early life experiences, still questioning some of the decisions he'd made regarding his family and his career. "I think marrying my mom, having a happy marriage—having that kind of home life, after he had accomplished a lot of what he wanted to do professionally—settled some of that. I think having a second chance with a kid helped him a lot. It also helped that he was getting a kid who was already somewhat formed; not having to go through the baby and elementary school years. But he was a very good stepfather. He was very respectful."

And Iya: "The thing that I will always adore and admire him for—until the day I die—is his fearlessness. When he knew the chips were down, Wes would perform the highest trapeze act. Put everything on the line. When we met, he said, 'I'm laying it all out on the table. No games. No bullshit.' He was so vulnerable and so fearless. I fell in love with him in that moment, because of the fearlessness of a man in his sixties being able to open his soul that way. To trust me completely. Which then allowed me to trust him completely. It was incredible.

"Compare that to the ability of an artist to put their innermost selves out into the world, in the form of their art. They can be so vulnerable, so insecure, and extremely sensitive—and yet they can open themselves up to everything and everybody. It's extraordinary, and every culture that values art understands that.

"That is an example to follow. That's who he was.

"Totally. Fucking. Fearless."

Opposite: Wes Craven. (courtesy Robyn Twomey)

AFTERWORD

by Jonathan Craven

September 10, 2015.

Director's Guild of America, Los Angeles.

My father was a singularly special man who will be greatly missed. I have to say that, on a level, it's somewhat ironic that I'm eulogizing him… as dad and I haven't always had the… uh… simplest of relationships. It's not always a walk in the park to be the offspring of a living legend. In fact, there were several more, shall we say, unresolved moments in my life where I composed imagined eulogies to my father, which I would not now want to repeat. Suffice it to say I am not here to give one of those today.

It's unnecessary for me to recount his achievements in film, as his legendary body of work speaks for itself. But, for those of you who didn't grow up with him, I want to share a few things you might not already know. He was largely self-taught in many areas, and developed several notable talents outside of filmmaking: mechanical drawing, fine carpentry, handwriting analysis, classical guitar, ceramic dinner plate juggling, photography, and extremely high-level dinner table punning. He loved to drive fast, attacking the curves of the Hollywood hills at precise but breakneck speeds, and delighting at the ashen looks of his passengers.

Sorry, dad, I'm just trying to paint the full picture here.

He was also a fine cartoonist—a talent which I believe contributed to him getting kicked out of Wheaton College—and an accomplished whistler. As some of you know, he was once a Humanities professor, and his love of learning never waned. He devoured books and periodicals on an array of topics. The meanings of dreams, astrophysics, the workings of the human brain, and military booby-traps were amongst his favorites. For the last several years, he'd also developed a passion for ornithology, and sat on the board of the California Audubon Society. By the way, his grandchild Myra Jean, a notable amateur ornithologist, is a favorite to assume his seat… just as soon as they finish kindergarten.

I bring a different perspective to Wes's history than some. Jessica and I were around at the very outset. Weekends with dad sometimes meant setting up camp at the midtown Manhattan editorial rooms of *Last House on the Left*, where we'd launch yellow film spools across the slick linoleum corridor floors while he fine-tuned Krug's somewhat conflicted relationship with *his* son Junior on a Steenbeck. (He didn't show us much, don't worry.)

He'd often lull us to sleep by improvising a variety of musical adventures concerning a super hero mutt named "Flying Banana"—based very loosely on our dog Banana.

And there were nights at his gothic 2nd Avenue apartment, when the rooms were filled with incense and other kinds of smoke, to this day unknown. (It was the seventies.) On Saturday nights, we'd watch *Chiller Theater* on a black-and-white TV and cringe in delight when, during the opening credits, the gnarled six-fingered hand emerged from a pool of blood, and a creepy voice uttered, "Chiiiillleer…" (Ahh, childhood.)

Dad even invented a special holiday for us. After he and my mother had parted ways, we usually spent time with him the day *after* Christmas. One year, we awoke on the 26th to a letter from "Wally the Walrus," who, apparently, had swum down the Hudson River from the North Pole, on a mission from Santa, with sacks of swag for kids from broken households. Wally's dispatch contained clues to a glorious treasure hunt around the Chambers Street loft, and kicked off the first of several thrilling St. Walrus Day adventures.

Then there were the letters. No one, in my experience, could write a letter quite like my father. Typewritten and expertly hewn, he spun episodes from the Mojave Desert set of the original *Hills Have Eyes*: "Dear Jon. Today was a bit of a tough one. It was very hot and the animal wrangler lost a rattlesnake on set. We looked everywhere for it. Don't worry… Eventually, we found it."

But, I'm sorry to tell you, my father was not without fault. He had shortcomings just like everyone else. He certainly did not practice what they now call "helicopter parenting."

When I was twelve, in lieu of the requisite father-son talk about the onset of puberty, I received a Schick razor and a 12 oz. can of Gillette in the mail, with a note stating, "You may be needing this soon." I kept the set for years, although I wouldn't actually have a need for it until I was nearly thirty.

One of his greatest weaknesses ended up being a silver lining for us as kids. This was an arena in which he was, until the very end, utterly feckless. He had a profound and utter lack of any culinary prowess whatsoever. This meant, for his lucky young spawn, a strict weekend and holiday diet of freshly-sourced Big Macs, subtly-heated tins of Dinty Moore beef stew, non-artisanal Hostess Yodels, and many cold glass bottles of Coca-Cola. Delicious.

There were other issues with regards to being dad's son. I'll never forget being razzed by elementary school classmates about an ad for the original *Hills Have Eyes*—which was, that week, billed as a double feature with *I Drink Your Blood* in Times Square. Much to my astonishment, they snickered and scoffed. In my mind, how could they miss the fucking cool factor there? In fact, Michael Berryman's primal glare and hand-tooled animal-gut necklace adorned with rifle shells and human teeth made me so very proud.

I'm not kidding. Damn Philistines.

Point being, there was a time when dad's work was not something that exactly opened doors. *Last House on the Left* was said to have been the work of a lunatic. I was in first grade. Enough said.

Fact was, it took what seemed like forever for him to become a household name. To put it in perspective, I was a freshman in college by the time Freddy Krueger slashed his way into theaters. That previous summer, when Jessica and I visited the *Nightmare on Elm Street* editing room, he had a distinctly downcast look on his face. When we asked how it was going, he shrugged and said, "It's a mess. I'm not sure I even have a movie here."

We shared a special kind of father-son awkwardness—long, deep silences which were impossible to breach. I couldn't help but take it personally at times; it was so difficult to wrap my head around those voids. Until one day, at a family gathering in Cleveland, whilst sampling a bowl of seven-layer dip, I observed him and his older brother Paul sitting next to teach other in utter silence while all the other relatives chatted away. *Ah*, I realized. *The silence.* THIS might just be the way Craven men say "I don't know how to say the words 'I love you.'"

When I had kids of my own, I understood it all a bit more. Even if dad and I weren't on the same page (as it were) in a given moment, my wife Rachel and I always made a point of bringing the kids up to his house. Miles and Max loved their grandfather, "Papa Wes." And he so clearly loved having Miles, Max, and Jessica's kid Myra Jean around the house.

When he was diagnosed this January, we knew we had limited time left. Knowing that every hour was precious, every single moment counted, our family spent every minute we could together. It was a special seven months. Dad had so many things going on—so many things he wanted to do. Aside from all the film and TV endeavors, there were countless personal projects in progress. Iya could barely keep the power tools out of his hands.

I understood why he wanted to keep his illness a secret. But personally, maybe even selfishly, I had an urge to have him go public, so he could experience the incredible outpouring of love and appreciation we witnessed after he passed. What an amazing and well-deserved roar of tribute.

As his strength waned, he worried about all the things that remained unfinished. Possibly also, some things that were left unsaid. In the days before he died, we took care to let him know we were alright, that our families were strong, that it was ok for him to go.

The night before he died, I reiterated, "It's ok, dad. We're all good." He couldn't speak. But I knew from the look in his eyes that he heard me.

The next day, with his family all around him, he was finally ready—and off he went. Off to be with Paul.

Later that day, still in a bit of shock, I went to his shop in the garage to find a whisk broom—and there, on the work table, I found a wooden truck he'd made for my son Miles years earlier. He'd recently been in the process of repairing it.

And it really, finally hit me. I saw his love for me, for the family… made… unmade… unfinished, but so clear… all in the pieces… all spread out on the table, a work in progress.

It's ok, dad. We're all good.

A NOTE ON SOURCES

I have quoted from my own interviews and e-mail correspondences with Wes Craven, his family members, friends, and collaborators. All other sources—itemized in the Bibliography, Appendix I, and Appendix II—are endnoted.

Aja, Alexandre. Phone interview, October 14, 2022.

Alleca, Adam. Phone interview, May 5, 2023.

Baum, Thomas. Phone interview, April 27, 2022.

Benest, Glenn. Phone interview, December 27, 2015.

Bennett, Rowland V. Phone interview, January 22, 2020.

Bilton, Bromley. Phone interview, February 3, 2020.

Bilton, Doris. Phone interview, March 2, 2020.

Bilton, Ted. Phone interview. February 10, 2020.

Blocksma, Mary. Phone interview, January 16, 2020.

Blunt, Giles. Email, June 15, 2022.

Bray, Michael. Phone interview, September 15, 2022.

Burton, Michael. Email, February 15, 2020.

Cameron, David. Email, March 25 and 26, 2023.

Chapin, Bonnie Broecker. Phone interview, February 13, 2020.

Claybourne, Douglas. Phone interview, April 27, 2022.

Craven, Donna. Phone interview, April 22, 2022.

Craven, Jessica. Phone interview, February 7, 2020.

Craven, Jonathan. Phone interviews, February 4 and February 11, 2021.

Craven, Mimi Meyer. Phone interview, October 6, 2022.

Craven, Wes. In-person interview, March 12, 2010.

Culbertson, Judi Chaffee. Phone interviews, May 30, 2020 and July 12, 2020.

Cunningham, Sean S. Phone interview, March 4, 2016.

Dutschke-Klotz, Gretchen. Email, January 21, 2020.

Eastman, Andrea. Phone interviews, March 23 and April 4, 2023.

Ellsworth, Carl. Phone interview, December 6, 2022.

Englund, Robert. Phone interview, January 12, 2023.

Everett, Rob. Phone interview, December 10, 2015.

Eville, Bill. Phone interview, December 19, 2022.

Feigelson, J.D. Phone interview, May 17, 2023.

Feingold, Carly. Phone interview, October 14, 2022.

Fenner, Jeffrey. Phone interview, April 18, 2022.

Frumkes, Roy. Phone interview, July 21, 2020.

Gilbert, Kathy Randall. Email, April 2023.

Gordon, Shep. Phone interview, March 22, 2023.

Haslett, Mark. Phone interview, December 1, 2022.

Helfrich, Dick. Phone interview, February 13, 2020.

Hemrich, Frank. Phone interview, March 1, 2020.

Keller, Max A. Phone interview, May 1, 2021.

Kennedy, Tim. Phone interview, January 17, 2023.

Kuhn, Dylan. Email, July 3, 2022.

Labunka, Iya. Phone interviews, December 14, 2022 and January 26, 2023.

Ladd, David. Phone interview, March 26, 2023.

Langenkamp, Heather. Phone interview, May 20, 2022.

Leax, John. Phone interview, February 6, 2020.

Lindberg, William E. Phone interview, October 24, 2022.

Locke, Peter. Phone interview, November 9, 2015.

Lussier, Patrick. Phone interview, May 26, 2023.

Lyon, Ken. Phone interview, February 11, 2020.

Maddalena, Marianne. Phone interviews, April 21 and July 8, 2022.

McGill, Jon G. Email, January 1, 2021.

McLoughlin, Tom. Phone interview, May 15, 2023.

Minskoff, Chuck. Phone interview, February 17, 2023.

Niles, Steve. Email, December 14, 2022.

O'Neill, Timothy. Email, July 3, 2022.

Peake, Don. Phone interview, May 15, 2021.

Perkins, James A. Emails, February 14 and 27, 2020.

Potts, Lynne Buri. Phone interview, February 25, 2020.

Reich, David. Phone interview, July 15, 2020.

Rubin, Bruce Joel. In-person interview, September 10, 2014.

Ruddy, Joe. Phone interview, November 29, 2022.

Sadar, Ned. Phone interview, December 8, 2022.

Schneider, Paul. Phone interview, January 3, 2023.

Schopf, Bill. Phone interview, January 16, 2020.

Sebrasky, Corinne. Phone interview, November 11, 2022.

Simon, Nick. Phone interview, November 26, 2022.

Smith, Jack. Phone interview, December 7, 2022.

Starr, Nancy Bryant. Phone interview, February 8, 2020.

Storms, Katherine Hobbie. Email, January 6, 2021.

Tarnawsky, Nina. Phone interview, October 12, 2022.

Thompson, Maryann. Phone interview, May 12, 2023.

Uslan, Michael E. Phone interview, October 29, 2022.

Veltman, Calvin. Phone interview, February 10, 2020.

Wagner, Bruce. Phone interview, April 11, 2022.

Walker, Jeanne Murray. Emails, January 21 and 22, 2020.

Watson, Ron. Phone interview, November 28, 2022.

Werle, Dave. Phone interview, February 2, 2021.

Williams, Janyth. Email, January 7, 2021.

Zwieg, Cody. Phone interview, October 18, 2022. Emails, October 25 and 27, 2022.

ENDNOTES

FOREWORD

1   Dawidziak: "Nightmare"

CHAPTER ONE

1   Bergstrom
2   Grey
3   Bergstrom
4   Smith
5   Bergstrom
6   Bergstrom
7   Dawidziak: "*Nightmare*"
8   Emery: *Films*
9   Dieter Miller
10   Emery: *Take*
11   Emery: *Take*
12   Engelbrektson, Chisholm
13   Emery: *Take*
14   Russo
15   Tony Williams
16   Dawidziak: "Wes"
17   Dieter Miller
18   Dieter Miller
19   Schoell
20   Craven: "Night"
21   Rose
22   Craven: "Night"
23   Craven: "Night"
24   Garris: "Wes"
25   Craven: "10"
26   Reesman: "Exclusive"
27   Rose
28   French: "*Scream:* Frightmaster"
29   Greenberg: "Freddy", Sutherland
30   Goldesten
31   Robb: *Screams*
32   Wooley
33   Finn
34   Watson
35   Terry Gross
36   Craven: "Press Club"
37   Russo
38   Craven: "Craven's" (I)
39   Craven: "Craven's" (V)
40   Craven: "Craven's" (IX)
41   Craven: "Craven's" (VIII)
42   Watson
43   Wooley
44   Fox
45   Mueller
46   Craven: "Craven's" (XI)
47   Zinoman: "Killer"

CHAPTER TWO

1   Wheaton: *Vol. 35*
2   Goldesten
3   Kevin Kelly
4   Huffman
5   Kantzer
6   Watson
7   Wagner
8   Cane
9   Mueller
10   Moca
11   Hutson
12   Craven: "Foreword"
13   Dyrness
14   Kilby: *Minority*
15   Kilby: "Christians"
16   Howard
17   Kilby: "Into"
18   Kilby: "Modern"
19   Vahanian
20   Kilby: "Christians"
21   Kilby: "Aesthetic"
22   Bechtel
23   Eliot: "Hamlet"
24   Dutschke-Klotz
25   Craven: "Three"
26   Watson
27   Gnoli
28   Craven: "Onward"
29   Anonymous: "Birth"
30   Anonymous: "Cuyahoga"
31   Kroll
32   McIlnay
33   Craven: "Death"
34   Anonymous: "Patterns"
35   Craven: "Warning"
36   Freedman
37   Call
38   Craven: "*Kodon*"
39   Edman
40   Craven: "*Kodon*"
41   Bechtel
42   Anonymous: "Editor"
43   Kilby: "Decline"
44   Craven: "Warning"
45   Craven: "To"

37	Szulkin: *Wes*		36	Watson
38	Seligson		37	Maddrey: "Lost"
39	Al Goldstein		38	Anonymous: "Buckley's"
40	West		39	Ziehm
41	Abrams		40	Ziehm
42	Saint Charles		41	Bentley
43	Tobias		42	Black
44	Ebert: "*Last*"		43	Rainer
45	William Murray		44	Seligson
46	Montgomery			
47	Anonymous: "Coming"			

CHAPTER SIX

48	Anonymous: "Loops"		1	Maddrey: "Lost"
49	Saint Charles		2	Maddrey: "Lost"
50	Lovell		3	Emery: *Films*
51	Cramer		4	Robb: *Screams*
52	Lofficier: "Wes"		5	Maddrey: "Lost"
			6	Dennis Fischer: *Horror*

CHAPTER FIVE

1	Variety: "*Devil*"		7	Bob Martin
2	McNeil		8	Zinoman: *Shock*
3	Variety: "*Devil*"		9	Craven: Audio, *Hills*
4	Ebert: "*Devil*"		10	Craven: Audio, *Hills*
5	Turan		11	Wood: *Hollywood*
6	Abrams		12	Perry Martin
7	Ackerman		13	Sharrett
8	Dieter Miller		14	Tony Williams
9	Meyer		15	Berryman
10	Pearce		16	Szulkin: "Hills"
11	Graves		17	Kevin Kelly
12	Siskind		18	Frumkes
13	Siskind		19	Dieter Miller
14	Honan		20	Farley
15	Graves		21	Biodrowski: "Sean"
16	Pearce		22	Seligson
17	Watson		23	Craven: Audio, *Summer*
18	Siskind		24	Jones: "Wes"
19	Rainer		25	Seligson
20	Siskind		26	Jones: "Wes"
21	Graves		27	Dennis Fischer: "Stuff"
22	Meyer		28	Baldwin
23	Siskind		29	Barr
24	Siskind		30	Benest
25	Mack		31	Scapperotti
26	Meyer		32	Robb: "Living"
27	Meyer		33	Sharrett
28	Anonymous: "Divine"		34	Kent
29	Jordan		35	Jones: "Wes"
30	Wayne		36	Robb: "Living"
31	Anonymous: "Divine"		37	Osborne
32	Delos Kelly		38	Wooley
33	Holliday		39	Uslan
34	Wiater: *Dark Dreamers*		40	Barbeau
35	Dennis Fischer: "Wes"		41	Moriarty
			42	Sharrett

43	Hutson
44	Anonymous: "Hollywood"
45	Grant: "Rambling" [11/16/81]

CHAPTER SEVEN

1	McVicar
2	Wood: "Disreputable"
3	Wood: "Return"
4	Wood: "Introduction"
5	Seligson, Heldenfels
6	Craven: "Big"
7	Sharrett
8	Wood: "Introduction"
9	Robb: *Screams*
10	Biodrowski: "Wes"
11	Curry
12	Montemayor
13	Mooney
14	Adler
15	Saint Charles
16	Hemphill
17	Hemphill
18	Biodrowski: "Sean"
19	R.H. Martin
20	Dennis Fischer: "Stuff"
21	Wooley
22	Gire
23	Schoell
24	Biodrowski: "Wes"
25	Biodrowski: "Wes"
26	Marks
27	Goldesten
28	Altman
29	Marks
30	McVicar
31	Craven: "Foreword"
32	Da Passano
33	Gurdjieff
34	Kutzera: "Wes"
35	Heldenfels
36	Dieter Miller
37	Marechal: *I*
38	Tom Taylor
39	Saint Charles
40	R.H. Martin
41	Loynd
42	Bob Martin
43	Anonymous: "Craven to write"
44	Grant: "Rambling" [6/24/82]
45	Anonymous: "Two"
46	Anonymous: "New"
47	Wooley
48	Rubin
49	Anonymous: "Daily"
50	Lovell
51	Kleyweg
52	Anonymous: "Overseas"
53	Anonymous: "OFG"
54	Robb: *Screams*
55	Lovell
56	Newman
57	Newman
58	R.H. Martin
59	Bryce
60	R.H. Martin
61	Dennis Fischer: "Wes"
62	R.H. Martin
63	Wooley, Dennis Fisher: "Stuff"
64	Anonymous: "Elm"
65	Saint Charles
66	Cooper: *Nightmare on Elm Street Companion*
67	Hutson
68	Dennis Fischer: "Stuff"
69	Scapperotti
70	Marks
71	Hemphill
72	Hemphill
73	Goldberg: "On"
74	Goldberg: "Year"
75	Hutson
76	Lovell
77	Crawley, Goldberg: "Year," Anonymous: "Craven developing"
78	R.H. Martin
79	Roberts
80	Teitelbaum: "*Flowers*"
81	Teitelbaum: "Jeffrey"
82	Goldberg: "Year"
83	Robb: *Screams*
84	Goldesten
85	Goldberg: "Year"
86	Lofficier: "Spotlight: Phil"
87	Griffith
88	Craven: Audio, "Her"
89	Griffith

CHAPTER EIGHT

1	Robb: *Screams*
2	Goldberg: "Wes"
3	Goldberg: "Wes"
4	Tongeren
5	Gray
6	Pond
7	Di Franco

8   Maddrey: "Deadly"
9   Robb: *Screams*
10   Goldberg: "Year"
11   Wiater: *Dark Visions*
12   Betts
13   Goldberg: "Year"
14   Goldberg: "Wes"
15   Robb: "Living"
16   Cooper: *Nightmare on Elm Street Companion*
17   Shapiro: "Wes"
18   Robb: "Living"
19   Reagan
20   Robb: *Screams*
21   LaBerge
22   LaBerge
23   Cooper: *Nightmares on Elm Street Parts 1, 2, 3*
24   Farrands: *Never*
25   Wooley
26   Hutson
27   Shapiro: "Is"
28   Wiater: *Dark Visions*
29   Westerby
30   Davis
31   Maxwell
32   Longsdorf: "Wade"
33   Doyle
34   Szebin
35   Jacobs
36   Szebin
37   Doyle
38   Kogan
39   Wiater: "Wade"
40   Bergstrom
41   Doyle
42   Shapiro: "I"
43   Cheel
44   Doyle
45   Patrick Goldstein
46   Mendez
47   Patrick Goldstein
48   Shapiro: "I"
49   Shapiro: "Craven's", Kogan
50   O'Rawa
51   Gire
52   Robb: *Screams*

CHAPTER NINE

1   Buckley
2   Swires
3   Biodrowski: "No"
4   O'Rawa

5   Shapiro: "Shocker"
6   Russo
7   Ressner, Biodrowski: "No"
8   Ressner, Shapiro: "I"
9   Beck
10   Westerby
11   Robb: *Screams*
12   Mancini
13   Craven: Audio, *Shocker*
14   Craven: Audio, *Shocker*
15   Farrell
16   Biodrowski: "Staircase"
17   Dieter Miller
18   Banka
19   Emery: *Take*
20   Robb: *Screams*
21   Emerson
22   Bierbaum
23   Newton
24   Dieter Miller
25   Shapiro: "Is"
26   Dieter Miller
27   Shapiro: "Craven"
28   Keller
29   Dawidziak: "*Nightmare*"
30   Werts
31   Englund
32   Turman
33   Grey
34   Biodrowski: "Staircase"
35   Russo
36   Kutzera: "Craven's"
37   Craven: Audio, *People*
38   Marechal: "Wes"
39   Shapiro: "*People*"; Biodrowski: "*People*"
40   Biodrowski: "*People*"
41   Shapiro: "Craven"
42   Russo
43   Craven: Audio, *People*
44   Baum
45   Dawidziak: "*Nightmare*"
46   Robb: *Screams*
47   Jones: "Craven"
48   Hills: "Interview with Patrick Lussier"
49   Variety: "Marvel"
50   Charles Fleming
51   Lowry
52   Robb: *Screams*

CHAPTER TEN

1   Parisi

2	Parker
3	Klady
4	Linda Gross
5	Siskel
6	Isenberg
7	Kent
8	Tripoli
9	Thomas: "Another"
10	Wilmington: "Shocks"
11	Thomas: "What's"
12	Merchan
13	Broeske
14	Sean Mitchell
15	Heffner
16	Rosen
17	Grey
18	Lippy: "Directing"
19	Longsdorf: "Wes"
20	Dobuzinskis
21	Artaud
22	McDonagh
23	Chris Mitchell
24	Kutzera: "Wes"
25	Lawson
26	Robb: *Screams*
27	Honeycutt: "Horrors," Anonymous: "Wes"
28	Craven: Press, *Wes*
29	Kyle Williamson
30	Shapiro: "Wake"
31	Kutzera: "Wes"
32	Craven: Audio, *Wes*
33	Abrams
34	Peitzman
35	Kyle Williamson
36	Shapiro: "Wake"
37	Craven: Audio, *Wes*
38	Bettelheim
39	Stratford
40	Bettelheim
41	Craven: Press, *Wes*
42	Greenberg: "Wes"
43	Maslin
44	Wilmington: "This"
45	Ebert: "Just"
46	Greenberg: "Freddy"
47	Lacher
48	Emery: *Take*
49	Murphy
50	Shapiro: "Brothers"
51	Shapiro: "*Vampire*"
52	Garris: "Wes"
53	Shapiro: "*Vampire*"
54	Greene
55	Greene
56	Vincent
57	Emery: *Take*
58	Hills: "Lussier"
59	Greene
60	Persons
61	Siegel
62	Shapiro: "Wes"
63	Jones: "Craven"
64	Spelling: "Black"
65	Lovece
66	Shapiro: "Wes"
67	Frook
68	Frook
69	French: "Wes"
70	Shapiro: "*Vampire*"
71	Hills: "Interview with Richard Potter, Part 2"
72	Hirschberg

CHAPTER ELEVEN

1	Kevin Williamson
2	Goodson
3	Hills: "Interview with Richard Potter, Part 1"
4	Palmer
5	French: "Wes"
6	Emery: *Take*
7	Szulkin: "*Last*"
8	Weinstein
9	Maroney
10	Kruszelnicki
11	Siegel
12	Maroney
13	THR: "*Scream*"
14	Lippy: "Writing"
15	Power
16	French: "Neve"
17	Kronke
18	Riley
19	Crucchiola, Harbet
20	Honeycutt: "Cox"
21	French: "Wes"
22	Maroney
23	Rice
24	Garcia
25	Kevin Williamson
26	Galluzzo
27	Farrands: *Scream*
28	Maroney
29	Farrands: *Scream*
30	Anima: "Santa"

31	Anima: "*Scary*"
32	LeBaron
33	Hills: "Potter, Part 2"
34	Garcia
35	Maroney
36	French: "*Scream 2*"
37	Spelling: "Wes"
38	Collis, Mullins
39	Craven: Audio, *Scream*
40	Spelling: "Joining"
41	Arnold
42	Giles
43	Wiater: *Dark Dreamers*
44	Wooley
45	Craven: *Fountain*
46	Craven: Audio, *Music*
47	Stein
48	Saint Charles
49	Prigge
50	Wooley
51	Craven: Audio, *Music*
52	Malanowski
53	Saint Charles
54	Geier
55	Grove
56	Dawn
57	Richmond
58	Carver
59	Evans
60	Craven: Audio, *Music*
61	Prigge
62	Jordan
63	Wooley
64	Watson
65	Fischoff
66	Rein
67	Maroney
68	Crucchiola
69	Rein
70	Spelling: "Joining"
71	Shapiro: "*Scream*"
72	Maroney
73	Portman: "Reality"
74	Stein
75	Carter

CHAPTER TWELVE

1	Craven: *Words*
2	Rome: "Horror"
3	Rome: "Presents"
4	See
5	Lyons: "Miramax"
6	Bohjalian
7	Jennifer Miller
8	Kevin Kelly
9	Schneider
10	Lyons: "Craven a Classic"
11	Anonymous: "Rufus"
12	Lyons: "*Perfect*"
13	Lyons: "Perfecting"
14	Lyons: "Craven, partner"
15	Strickler
16	Lyons: "Craven, partner"
17	Alexander: "Ghosts"
18	Matthews
19	Craven: Audio, *Scream*
20	Robb: *Screams*
21	Michael Fleming: "Miramax"
22	Ascher-Walsh
23	Sci-Fi Wire
24	Showers
25	Maroney
26	Shapiro: "*Cursed*"
27	Carolyn: *It*
28	Shapiro: "*Cursed*"
29	Adalian
30	Bernstein
31	Watson
32	Wooley
33	Labunka
34	Labunka
35	Wooley
36	Giles
37	Watson
38	Robb: *Screams*
39	Lee
40	Merchan
41	Kelly-Saxenmeyer
42	Bergstrom
43	Shapiro: "*Cursed*"
44	Merchan
45	Maddrey: "Lost"
46	Keegan
47	Alexander: "His"
48	Paul Fischer
49	Kelly-Saxenmeyer
50	Rebecca Murray
51	MW Staff
52	MW Staff
53	Merchan
54	Carr
55	Goodman
56	Meh
57	Meh
58	Douglas
59	Meh

CHAPTER THIRTEEN

1 Michael Fleming: "Midnight"
2 Carolyn: "Heading"
3 Anonymous: "Q&A"
4 DiChiara
5 Gallagher
6 Prokopy
7 Anonymous: "Corey"
8 Watson
9 Marano
10 Rein
11 Wes Craven and Max Thieriot
12 Barkan
13 Prokopy
14 Jacobs
15 Reesman: "Wes"
16 Turek: "Event"
17 King: *Danse*
18 Anonymous: "Interview"
19 Zimmerman
20 Parfitt
21 Lipsett
22 Stack: "*Scream 4*, What"
23 Stack: "*Scream 4*, Writer"
24 Gingold
25 Lipsett
26 Buchanan
27 Barkan
28 Anonymous: "Craven can"
29 Dwyer
30 Craven: *Noah's*
31 Moore
32 Reesman: "Wes"
33 Portman: "Stormy"
34 Reesman: "Wes"
35 Zimmerman
36 Saint Charles

15 Braxton, Andreeva: "Wes Craven TV"
16 Eville
17 Huston
18 Watson
19 Feynman
20 Wooley
21 Anonymous: "Why?"
22 Craven: "Birds, 1"
23 Craven: "Birds, 4"
24 Bucksbaum
25 Sally Taylor
26 Craven: "Birds, 5"
27 McNary
28 Andreeva: "Wes Craven Inks"
29 Knauf: "*Sleepers*"
30 Knauf: "Farewell"
31 Craven: "Birds, 8"
32 French: "Supernal"
33 Craven: "Wes"
34 Topel
35 Reesman: "Exclusive"
36 THR: "*Scream*"
37 Rahman
38 Cox
39 Gomez
40 Campbell
41 Watson

CHAPTER FOURTEEN

1 Craven: "Retirement"
2 Gingold
3 Craven: "Guest"
4 Abrams
5 Craven: "Retirement"
6 Craven: "Retirement"
7 Sutherland
8 Bergstrom
9 Huston
10 Huston
11 Strachan
12 Watson
13 THR: "Hollywood's"
14 Sabbott

BIBLIOGRAPHY

Abrams, Simon. "Wes Craven: I Always Encouraged Robert Englund to Make Freddy Krueger His Own." Westworld.com. January 16, 2014.

Ackerman, Bill. (Host.) "Episode 32: Ashley West." *Supporting Characters.* December 18, 2017. Podcast.

Adalian, Josef. "A-list will fuel UPN dramas." *Variety.* December 9, 2002.

Adler, Shelley R. "Refugee Stress and Folk Belief: Hmong Sudden Deaths." *Social Science and Medicine* #40. 1995.

Alexander, Dave. "His Master's Mutants." *Rue Morgue* #54. March 2006.

Alexander, Dave. "The Ghosts of World's End." *Rue Morgue* #51. November 2005.

Altman, Mark A. "Wes Craven's *A Nightmare on Elm Street*." *Galactic Journal* #21. September 1986.

Andreeva, Nellie. "Wes Craven Inks UCP Deal, Sets Dramas *People Under the Stairs, We Are All Completely Fine*." *Deadline.* April 20, 2015.

Andreeva, Nellie. "Wes Craven TV Series at UCP Will Go Forward 'In His Honor and Spirit.' *Deadline.* August 30, 2015.

Anima, Tina. "Scary Movie Director: We'll Sue Santa Rosa Board." *The Santa Rosa Press Democrat.* April 16, 1996.

Anima, Tina. "Santa Rosa Resistance is Wes Craven's Own Nightmare." *The Santa Rosa Press Democrat.* April 5, 1996.

Anonymous. "Auden Says Poet is Witness; Not to Pass Moral Judgments." *The Wheaton Record.* March 21, 1963.

Anonymous [Wes Craven?]. "A Birth." *Kodon* Vol. 16, No. 1. Fall 1961.

Anonymous. "Buckley's *Kitty* Pic Softened Its Sex." *Variety.* January 16, 1974.

Anonymous. "Coming Cunninghams." *Variety.* February 9, 1972.

Anonymous. "Corey Taylor of Stone Sour and Slipknot Meets Wes Craven for 'Rogue on Rogue." Artistdirect.com. October 2, 2010.

Anonymous. "Craven can still hear the Scream." *USA Today.* April 13, 2011.

Anonymous. "Craven developing full '85 film slate." *The Hollywood Reporter.* January 9, 1985.

Anonymous. "Craven to write *Fallen* for Jadran." *The Hollywood Reporter.* April 6, 1982.

Anonymous. "Crime Movie?" *Morgantown Dominion News.* February 27, 1972.

Anonymous. "Cuyahoga County Hospital System (CCHS)." *Encyclopedia of Cleveland History.* Case.edu/ech. Accessed June 7, 2022.

Anonymous. "*Daily Mail* Campaign: Ban the Sadist Videos." *Fangoria* #31. December 1983.

Anonymous. "The Divine Sarah! Interview with Cover Girl Sarah Nicholson." *Flick* #6. June 1976.

Anonymous. "The Drama Club." *The Clarkson Integrator.* January 10, 1967.

Anonymous. "Editor to Review Criteria at Request of Pub Board." *The Wheaton Record.* December 13, 1962.

Anonymous. "Elm Street finance deal." *Screen International.* February 11, 1984.

Anonymous. "Hollywood Soundtrack." *Variety.* March 4, 1981.

Anonymous. "Interview: Wes Craven on *Last House on the Left*." DenofGeek.com. June 8, 2009.

Anonymous. "*Loops*." *The Independent Film Journal.* August 20, 1973.

Anonymous. "New Line Intro's *Xtro* Shocker, Seeks Fiscal Partners at Mifed." *Variety.* October 20, 1982.

Anonymous. "Nine Scouts on Camping, Canoe Trip." *The Massena Observer.* August 27, 1968.

Anonymous. "OFG, Thorn EMI *Innocents* deal." *Screen International.* May 26, 1984.

Anonymous. "Open Evening Class Announced." *The Clarkson Integrator.* November 8, 1966.

Anonymous. "Overseas Group offering 3 features." *The Hollywood Reporter.* October 25, 1983.

Anonymous. "Patterns." *The 1962 Tower.* Wheaton College, Spring 1962.

Anonymous [John Heneage?]. "The Potsdam Underground Surfaces with *Pandora Experimentia.*" *The Integrator.* May 8, 1968.

Anonymous. "Q&A: The King of Scream, Wes Craven, Talks Race and Horror." BET.com. April 14, 2011.

Anonymous. "Rufus Sewell to star in Wes Craven Thriller." Ananova.com. November 14, 2001.

Anonymous. "*Sandbox, No Exit* Terse Drama at Clarkson." *The Potsdam Courier-Freeman.* December 15, 1966.

Anonymous. "Two int'l. coprods. for Inter-Cultural." *The Hollywood Reporter.* October 12, 1982.

Anonymous. "U Promo State Took a Different Tack to Lure Adults to Serpent." *Variety.* February 17, 1988.

Anonymous. "Wes Craven: The Last Word on *Last House.*" TotalSciFiOnline.com. June 9, 2009.

Anonymous ["The Editors"]. "Why Do Birds Matter?" Audubon.org. March 6, 2013.

Arnold, Gary. "Movie Director Finds Scream-ing Success." *The Washington Times.* December 12, 1997.

Artaud, Antonin. *The Theater and Its Double.* Trans. Mary Caroline Richards. Grove, 1958.

Ascher-Walsh, Rebecca. "The Making of *Dracula 2000.*" EW.com. November 17, 2000.

Baldwin, Tornetha. "5 Questions: Matthew Barr." Greensboro.com. April 21, 2004.

Banka, Michael. "Interview on Elm Street." *Cineaste* Vol. 17, No. 3. 1990.

Barbeau, Adrienne. *There Are Worse Things I Could Do.* Carroll & Graf, 2006.

Barkan, Jonathan. "Wes Craven Looks Back on *Scream* Franchise." Bloody-Disgusting. com. September 3, 2010.

Barr, Matthew. (Interviewee.) "So It Was Written, with Matthew Barr and Glenn M. Benest." *Deadly Blessing.* Shout! Factory, 2013. Video.

Batson, Beatrice. *A Reader's Guide to Religious Literature.* Moody, 1968.

Baum, Tom. "How to give notes to writers. How not to." tombaumwrites.com. August 8, 2017.

Bechtel, Paul M. *Wheaton College: A Heritage Remembered, 1960-1984.* H. Shaw, 1984.

Beck, Marilyn. "George Peppard Plays 'Papa' with a Passion." *Chicago Tribune.* May 5, 1988.

Benest, Glenn M. (Interviewee.) "So It Was Written, with Matthew Barr and Glenn M. Benest." *Deadly Blessing.* Shout! Factory, 2013. Video.

Bentley, Toni. "The Legend of Henry Paris." *Playboy.* June 2014.

Bergman, Ingmar. *Images: My Life in Film.* Arcade, 1994.

Bergstrom, Elaine. "Wes Craven Says the Roots of Monsters Are Within Us." *Channel Guide.* October 13, 2006.

Bernstein, Abbie. *Master of Horror: The Official Biography of Mick Garris.* ATB, 2022.

Berryman, Michael. *It's All Good!: A Memoir, in My Own Words.* Self-published, 2023.

Bettelheim, Bruno. *The Uses of Enchantment: The Meaning and Importance of Fairy Tales.* Vintage, 1976.

Betts, Michael Arthur and Wes Craven. "Tattler." *The Horror Show.* Spring 1987.

Bierbaum, Tom. "Television Reviews: *The People Next Door.*" *Variety.* October 4, 1989.

Biodrowski, Steve. "No More Mr. Nice Guy." *Cinefantastique* Vol. 19, No. 4. May 1989.

Biodrowski, Steve. "*The People Under the Stairs.*" *Cinefantastique* Vol. 22, No. 3. December 1991.

Biodrowski, Steve. "Sean Cunningham: *House Keeper.*" *GoreZone* #21. Spring 1992.

Biodrowski, Steve. "Staircase Misery." *Fear* #34. October 1991.

Biodrowski, Steve. "Wes Craven on Dreaming Up Nightmares." Cinefantastiqueonline.com. October 15, 2008.

Black, David. "Totalitarian Therapy on the Upper West Side." *New York Magazine.* December 15, 1975.

Bohjalian, Chris. *Trans-Sister Radio.* Random House, 2000.

Bowen, Meredith. "Legendary Filmmaker Wes Craven Delves into Details of Craft." *The Daily Orange.* April 17, 2005.

Boyd, Pattie and Penny Junor. *Wonderful Tonight: George Harrison, Eric Clapton, and Me.* Three Rivers, 2008.

Bracke, Peter M. *Crystal Lake Memories: The Complete History of Friday the 13th.* Titan, 2005.

Braxton, Greg. "TCA: *10 Commandments* to become scripted event for WGN America." *Los Angeles Times.* January 12, 2014.

Broeske, Pat H. "Not for the Craven." *Los Angeles Times.* October 21, 1990.

Broughton, Bradford. *A Clarkson Mosaic: Bits and Pieces of Academic, Personal, Sports, and Administrative History, Creating a Portrait of Clarkson University's First Hundred Years, 1865-1995.* Clarkson U, 1995.

Brown, Thomas. (Director.) *Reflections on the Living Dead.* Image Ten, 1993. Video.

Bryce, Allan. "Wes Craven's Nightmare." *Video Today.* October 1987.

Buchanan, Kyle. "Wes Craven on Behind-the-Scenes Controversy and How Online Spoilers Have Shaped *Scream.*" Vulture.com. April 12, 2011.

Buckley, Heather. [Producer.] "*It's Alive!* with Shep Gordon." Shout! Factory, 2015. Video.

Bucksbaum, Sydney. "*Scream* Co-Showrunner Reacts to Wes Craven's Passing: 'I'm Ticked Off at the World.'" *The Hollywood Reporter.* August 31, 2015.

Call, Keith. "Wes Craven at Wheaton College." Recollections.wheaton.edu. September 1, 2015.

Campbell, Neve. (Interviewee.) *Scream [2022] Electronic Press Kit.* Paramount Pictures. Video, 2022.

Cane, Clay. "Q&A: The King of Scream, Wes Craven, Talks Race and Horror." BET.com. April 14, 2011.

Carolyn, Axelle. "Heading for the *Hills.*" *Fangoria* #261. March 2007.

Carolyn, Axelle. *It Lives Again!: Horror Movies in the New Millennium.* Telos, 2008.

Carr, Kevin. "Wes and Jonathan Craven Interview." FatGuysattheMovies.com. 2007.

Carter, Benedict and Chris Petrikin. "*Fountain* a Gusher." *Variety.* April 14, 1999.

Carver, Benedict. "Craven pact expands into bigger Dimension." *Variety.* October 14, 1998.

Cheel, Jay. (Director.) *Cursed Films II: The Serpent and the Rainbow.* Shudder, 2022. Video.

Chisolm, Graham. "Freddy Krueger Creator Wes Craven Loves Birds." *Audubon.* September-October 2008.

Ciardi, John and Ralph Ellison, Josephine Jacobsen, William J. Lederer, N. Scott Momaday, Louis D. Rubin Jr., and Wallace Stegner. *Teaching Creative Writing.* Library of Congress. Gertrude Clarke Whittall Poetry and Literature Fund, 1974.

Coan, Peter M. *Taxi: The Harry Chapin Story.* Ashley, 1987.

Coleman, Elliott. "The Meaning of Metaphor." *Gordon Review,* Vol. 8. Spring 1965.

Coleman, Elliott, and John Ciardi, Paul Engle, George Garrett, Theodore Morrison, and Wallace Stegner. "A Perspective of Academic Programs in Creative Writing." *Teaching Creative Writing.* Library of Congress, 1974.

Collis, Clark. "*Scream 2* at 25: Kevin Williamson remembers his second stab at screenwriting the iconic series." *Entertainment Weekly.* December 9, 2022.

Conroe, Scott. "He Was a Little Odd." *Syracuse Herald American.* March 26, 1989.

Cooper, Jeffrey. *The Nightmare on Elm Street Companion: The Official Guide to America's Favorite Fiend.* St. Martin's, 1987.

Cooper, Jeffrey. *The Nightmares on Elm Street Parts 1, 2, 3: The Continuing Story.* St. Martin's, 1987.

Cox, Courteney. (Interviewee.) *Scream [2022] Electronic Press Kit.* Paramount Pictures. Video, 2022.

Cramer, Jeff. "Chapter VII: After *Friday V.*" jeffcramer.blogspot.com. March 28, 2009.

Craven, Wes. "10 Movies That Shook ME Up." *Entertainment Weekly.* October 22, 2009.

Craven, Wes. Audio Commentary. "Her Pilgrim Soul." *The Twilight Zone.* CBS, 2015. DVD.

Craven, Wes. Audio Commentary. *The Hills Have Eyes.* Anchor Bay, 2003. DVD.

Craven, Wes. Audio Commentary. *Music of the Heart.* Dimension, 2000. DVD.

Craven, Wes. Audio Commentary. *The People Under the Stairs.* Shout! Factory, 2015. Blu-Ray.

Craven, Wes. Audio Commentary. *Scream.* Dimension, 1998. DVD.

Craven, Wes. Audio Commentary. *Shocker.* Shout! Factory, 2015. Blu-Ray.

Craven, Wes. Audio Commentary. *Summer of Fear.* Artisan, 2003. DVD.

Craven, Wes. Audio Commentary. *Wes Craven's New Nightmare.* Image Entertainment, 1995. Laserdisc.

Craven, Wes. "The Big Question." *Johns Hopkins Magazine.* September 2001.

Craven, Wes. "Wes Craven's The Birds: Part 1." *The Vineyard Gazette.* April 1, 2014.

Craven, Wes. "Wes Craven's The Birds: Part 4." *The Vineyard Gazette.* August 1, 2014.

Craven, Wes. "Wes Craven's The Birds: Part 5." *The Vineyard Gazette.* September 1, 2014.

Craven, Wes. "Wes Craven's The Birds: Part 8." *The Vineyard Gazette.* June 18, 2015.

Craven, Wes. "Craven Renews Pen Career with Letter Urging Reforms." *The Record.* March 7, 1963.

Craven, Wes. "Craven's Ravins" (I). *The Collinwood Spotlight.* February 15, 1957.

Craven, Wes. "Craven's Ravin's" (V). *The Collinwood Spotlight.* June 7, 1957.

Craven, Wes. "Craven's Ravin's" (VIII). *The Collinwood Spotlight.* November 3, 1957.

Craven, Wes. "Craven's Ravin's" (IX). *The Collinwood Spotlight.* November 22, 1957.

Craven, Wes. "Craven's Ravin's" (XI). *The Collinwood Spotlight.* January 17, 1958.

Craven, Wes. "Death Mask: Three-Quarter View." *Kodon* Vol. 16, No. 4. Summer 1962.

Craven, Wes. "Foreword." *Never Sleep Again: The Elm Street Legacy: The Making of Wes Craven's A Nightmare on Elm Street*. Thommy Hutson. Permuted, 2016.

Craven, Wes. *Fountain Society*. Simon & Schuster, 1999.

Craven, Wes. "Guest Post by Writer/Director Wes Craven." *Kindle Daily Post*. Amazon.com. October 28, 2014.

Craven, Wesley. "*Kodon* Answers Its Self-Styled Critics." *The Record*. November 29, 1962.

Craven, Wes. "The Night I Met Freddy." *CosmoGirl*. October 2004.

Craven, Wesley Earl. *Noah's Ark: The Journals of a Madman*. 1964. Electronic Theses & Dissertations Office. Sheridan Libraries. Johns Hopkins University.

Craven, Wesley Earl. "Onward, Christian Soldiers." *Kodon* Vol. 16, No. 1. Fall 1961.

Craven, Wes. "Press Club Shocked at WRU." *The Collinwood Spotlight*. October 12, 1956.

Craven, Wes. Press Kit. *Wes Craven's New Nightmare*. New Line, 1994. Print.

Craven, Wes. "Retirement: Scarier Than Freddy Krueger." *The New York Times*. February 16, 2013.

Craven, W.E. "Three Poems on Memory... All for the Price of One." *Kodon* Vol. 15, No. 3. Spring 1961.

Craven, Wesley Earl. "To the Woman Who Came to My Office and Wept." *Kodon* Vol. 17, No. 2. Winter 1962.

Craven, Wesley Earl. "A Warning from the Editor." *Kodon* Vol. 17, No. 1. Fall 1962.

Craven, Wesley. "Watch Those Black Cats!!" *The Collinwood Spotlight*. April 13, 1956.

Craven, Wes. "The Weapon." *Kodon*, Vol. 16, No. 3. Spring 1962.

Craven, Wes. "Wes Craven Remembers Christopher Lee, 'A Man of Infinite Class and Talent.'" *The Hollywood Reporter*. June 17, 2015.

Craven, Wes. (Interviewee.) *Words into Pictures 1999: The Writer as God*. Writers Guild Foundation. June 4, 1999. Video.

Craven, Wes and Max Thieriot. (Interviewees.) "My Soul to Take." *Meet the Filmmaker* podcast. October 7, 2010.

Crawley, Tony. "Things to Come." *Starburst* #83. July 1985.

Crucchiola, Jordan. "Matthew Lillard and Skeet Ulrich Answer All Our Questions About *Scream*." Vulture.com. January 27, 2022.

Curry, Bill. "'Nightmares Syndrome'?: Deaths of Laos Refugees Puzzle Officials." *Los Angeles Times*. February 26, 1981.

Da Passano, Andrew and Judith Plowden. *Inner Silence: A Guide to Peace and Empowerment*. Harper, 1987.

Davis, Wade. *The Serpent and the Rainbow: A Harvard Scientist's Astonishing Journey into the Secreet Societies of Haitian Voodoo, Zombis, and Magic*. Simon & Schuster, 1985.

Dawidziak, Mark. "*Nightmare Café*." *Cinefantastique*, Vol. 22, No. 6. June 1992.

Dawidziak, Mark. "Wes Craven, 1939-2015: Soft-spoken horror master from Cleveland." *The Cleveland Plain Dealer*. August 31, 2015.

Dawn, Randee. "Indie Scene '99: Meryl Streep." *The Hollywood Reporter*. September 14, 1999.

DiChiara, Tom. "Wes Craven: *My Soul to Take* is 'Autobiographical.'" MTV Movies Blog. October 9, 2010.

Di Franco, Philip J. *The Movie World of Roger Corman*. Chelsea, 1979.

Dobuzinskis, Alex. "Wes Craven on *Last House* and the Lure of Horror." Reuters.com. March 12, 2009.

Douglas, Edward. "Exclusive Interview: Horror Master Wes Craven." ComingSoon.net. March 19, 2007.

Doyle, Michael. "The Blackest Magic." *Rue Morgue* #140. December 2013.

Dutschke-Klotz, Gretchen. *Salvations*. Self-published online, 2021.

Dwyer, Jessica. "*My Soul to Take*: Growing Up with Wes Craven." *Horrorhound* #25. September / October 2010.

Dyrness, William. "Foreword: Remembering Clyde S. Kilby." *The Arts and the Christian Imagination: Essays on Art, Literature, and Aesthetics*. Ed. William Dyrness and Keith Call. Paraclete, 2017.

Ebert, Roger. "*The Devil in Miss Jones*." June 13, 1973. http:// www.rogerebert.com/reviews/ the-devil-in-miss-jones-1973.

Ebert, Roger. "Just When You All Thought It Was Over, *Nightmare* Goes One Step Further." *Chicago Sun-Times*. October 14, 1994.

Ebert, Roger. "*Last House on the Left*." *Chicago Sun-Times*. January 1, 1972.

Edman, V. Raymond. "Christian Ethics." *The Word for This Century: Evangelical Certainties in an Era of Conflict*. Ed. Merrill C. Tenney. Oxford UP, 1960.

Eliot, T.S. "Hamlet." *The Complete Prose of T.S. Eliot: The Critical Edition, Vol. 2: The Perfect Critic 1919-1926*. Ed. Anthony Cuda and Ronald Schuchard. Johns Hopkins, 2014.

Eliot, T.S. "Reflections on Contemporary Poetry [III]." *The Complete Prose of T.S. Eliot: The Critical Edition, Vol. 1: Apprentice Years 1905-1918*. Ed. Jewel Spears Brooker & Ronald Schuchard. Johns Hopkins, 2014.

Emery, Robert J. *The Directors: Take Three*. Allworth, 2003.

Emery, Robert J. *The Directors: The Films of Wes Craven*. AFI, 1999. DVD.

Emerson, Jim. "Alive gives producers freer hand." *The Orange County Register*. November 5, 1989.

Engelbrektson, Lisa. "Craven takes birds seriously." *Variety*. May 28, 2010.

Englund, Robert with Alan Goldsher. *Hollywood Monster: A Walk Down Elm Street with the Man of Your Dreams*. Pocket, 2009.

Evans, Robert. *The Fat Lady Sang*. HarperCollins, 2013.

Eville, Bill. "With Humor, Irony and Some Gore Too, Wes Craven Defined a Genre." Vineyardgazette.com. September 3, 2015.

Farley, Ellen. "Impresarios of Axploitation Movies." *Los Angeles Times*. November 13, 1977.

Farrands, Daniel and Andrew Kasch. [Directors.] *Never Sleep Again: The Elm Street Legacy*. 1428 Film, 2010.

Farrands, Daniel. [Director.] *Scream: The Inside Story*. 1428 Films, 2011. Video.

Farrell, Mary H.J. and Michael Alexander. "After *A Nightmare on Elm Street*, Director Wes Craven Dreams Up *Shocker's* Maniacal Killer." *People*. November 13, 1989.

Feynman, Richard P. *The Pleasure of Finding Things Out: The Best Short Works of Richard P. Feynman*. Ed. Jeffrey Robbins. Basic, 1999.

Finn, Robin. "Despite Its Charms, Horror Can Pale." *New York Times*. January 2, 1997.

Fischer, Dennis. *Horror Film Directors*. McFarland, 1990.

Fischer, Dennis. "The Stuff of Nightmares." *Monsterland* #3. June 1985.

Fischer, Dennis. "Wes Craven, Creator of Nightmares." *Monsterland's Nightmares on Elm Street: The Freddy Krueger Story*. Ed. James Van Hise. Pop Cult, 1988.

Fischer, Paul. "Craven Takes His Nightmares Above the Clouds." Filmmonthly.com. August 15, 2005.

Fischoff, Stuart. "Psychology's Quixotic Quest for the Media-Violence Connection." An Invited Address at the Annual Convention of the American Psychological Assocation, Boston, August 21, 1999.

Fleming, Charles. "… And Wise Words from the Bullpen." *The New York Times*. November 14, 1993.

Fleming, Michael. "Midnight Entertainment; Helmer haunts Rogue's house; Craven hires Maddalena to run Midnight Pictures." *Variety*. September 28, 2006.

Fleming, Michael. "Miramax trips for Dixon spec." *Variety*. April 21, 2002.

Fox, Christina. "Wes Craven: From Wheaton to Elm Street." *The (Wheaton) Record*. March 27, 1992.

Freedman, Jason. "Director Wes Craven Reflects on His Time at Homewood." *The Johns Hopkins News-Letter*. January 31, 2008.

French. Lawrence. "Neve Campbell, No Scream Queen." *Femme Fatales* Vol. 5, No. 9. March 1997.

French, Lawrence. "*Scream*: Frightmaster Wes Craven." *Cinefantastique* Vol. 27, No. 7. January 1997.

French, Lawrence. "*Scream 2*." *Cinefantastique* Vol. 29, No. 9. January 1998.

French, Lawrence. "Supernal Dreams: Wes Craven on 'glorifying violence' in *Last House on the Left*." Cinefantastiqueonline.com. March 13, 2009.

French, Lawrence. "Wes Craven's *Scream*." *Cinefantastique*, Vol. 27, No. 7. January 1997.

Friden, Peter J. and Steven Haut. "Culture Course Should Be Offered." *The Clarkson Integrator*. December 14, 1964.

Frook, John Evan. "Boo-who? Miramax takes stab at horror." *Variety*. January 6, 1994.

Frumkes, Roy. "Movie Review: *Hills Have Eyes*." *The Hollywood Reporter*. June 20, 1977.

Gallagher, Brian. "Comic-Con 2008: Wes Craven Talks *25/8*." July 27, 2008.

Galluzzo, Rob (Host). *Shock Waves*. Episode 163. "Trick or Treat! A One on One Chat with Patrick Lussier!" October 11, 2019.

Garcia, Chris. "One Last Scream." *Fangoria* #160. March 1997.

Garner, Dusty. "What's Doing?" *The Potsdam Courier-Freeman*. January 5, 1967.

Garris, Mick (Host). *Post Mortem with Mick Garris*. "Sean S. Cunningham." March 28, 2018. Podcast.

Garris, Mick (Host). *Post Mortem with Mick Garris*. "Wes Craven." October 20, 2014. Podcast.

Geier, Thom. "Madonna bows out of Craven's *Violins* story." *The Hollywood Reporter*. July 20, 1998.

Giles, Jeff. "Keep 'Em Screaming." *Newsweek*. December 15, 1997.

Gingold, Michael. "Q&A: Wes Craven's *Scream 4* Postmortem." Fangoria.com. October 4, 2011.

Gire, Dan. "Bye Bye, Freddy!" *Cinefantastique* Vol. 18, No. 5. July 1988.

Gnoli, Domenico. *Orestes, or the Art of Smiling*. Simon & Schuster, 1961.

Goldberg, Lee. "On the Set: *A Nightmare on Elm Street*." *Fangoria* #40. December 1984.

Goldberg, Lee. "The Year of Wes Craven." *Fangoria* #51. January 1986.

Goldberg, Lee and David McDonnell. "Wes Craven's *Deadly* Doubleheader." *Fangoria* #57. September 1986.

Goldesten, Patrick. "Riding High with a Sultan of Slash." *Los Angeles Times*. July 9, 1985.

Goldstein, Al. *I, Goldstein: My Screwed Life*. Thunder's Mouth, 2006.

Goldstein, Patrick. "A Spellbinding Way to Make a Movie." *Los Angeles Times*. February 3, 1988.

Gomez, Patrick. "The Last Survivors." *Entertainment Weekly: The Ultimate Guide to Scream*. 2021.

Goodman, Justine. "Interview: Director Wes Craven." Justinegoodman.com. March 2, 2007.

Goodson, William Wilson Jr. "Scream King." *Femme Fatales* Vol. 6, No. 7. January 1998.

Grant. Hank. "Rambling Reporter." *The Hollywood Reporter*. June 24, 1982.

Grant, Hank. "Rambling Reporter." *The Hollywood Reporter*. November 16, 1981.

Graves, Alice. *Don't Tell Anyone: A Cult Memoir*. Pond Park, 2019.

Gray, Beverly. *Roger Corman: Blood-Sucking Vampires, Flesh-Eating Cockroaches, and Driller Killers*. Thunder's Mouth, 2004.

Greenberg, James. "Freddy Krueger's Creator Breaks Out of His Genre." *New York Times*. October 9, 1994.

Greenberg, James. "Wes Craven Has Evoked Fear, Now Earns Respect." *New York Times*. October 14, 1994.

Greene, James Jr. "Drugs, death and that wig: An oral history of *Vampire in Brooklyn*." Hopesandfears.com. October 29, 2015.

Gregory, David (director). *Celluloid Crime of the Century*. Blue Underground, 2003.

Grey, Ian. *Sex, Stupidity and Greed: Inside the American Movie Industry*. Juno, 1997.

Griffith, Daniel. (Director). "Wes Craven's Twilight Zone." *The Twilight Zone: The Complete 80s Series*. Ballyhoo, 2015. Video.

Gross, Linda. "Spiritual Abuse in *Deadly Blessing*." *Los Angeles Times*. August 18, 1981.

Gross, Terry. "Wes Craven on Violence and Horror On-Screen." *Fresh Air*. September 11, 1980. Radio.

Grove, Martin A. "Craven Plucks Strings so Streep Can Make *Music*." *The Hollywood Reporter*. October 15, 1999.

Gurdjieff, G.I. *In Search of Being: The Fourth Way to Consciousness*. Ed. Stephen A. Grant. Penguin, 2021.

Harbet, Xandra. "*Scream*'s Neve Campbell and David Arquette Reminisce About Working with Wes Craven." Looper.com. January 24, 2022.

Harrison, George. *Anthology*. Hal Leonard, 1992.

Hauser, Brian R. "In Search of *Pandora Experimentia*." *ReFocus: The Films of Wes Craven*. Ed. Calum Waddell. Edinburgh UP, 2023.

Hauser, Brian R. "*Pandora Experimentia*: The Legend of Wes Craven's First Film." [Paper presentation.] Clarkson University. Potsdam, New York. March 26, 2017.

Heffner, Richard D. "Guidance to Parents, Not Profits, Governs Movie Rating System." *Los Angeles Times*. July 2, 1990.

Heldenfels, Rich. "In 2006 interview, Wes Craven discussed the finer point of horror moviemaking." *Akron Beacon Journal*. August 31, 2015.

Hemphill, Jim. "I Don't Feel Like I Gave Birth to Jesus: Wes Craven on *A Nightmare on Elm Street*." Filmmakermagazine.com. August 31, 2015.

Hills, Ryan. "Exclusive: Interview with Richard Potter Part 1: The True Story of the Sale of *Scream*." Scream-thrillogy.com. October 17, 2021.

Hills, Ryan. "Exclusive: Interview with Richard Potter Part 2: Creating *Scream*." Scream-thrillogy.com. February 9, 2022.

Hills, Ryan. "Interview with Patrick Lussier." Scream-thrillogy.com. January 3, 2021.

Hirschberg, Lynn. "The Mad Passion of Harvey and Bob." *New York Magazine*. October 10, 1994.

Holliday, Jim. *The Top 100 X Rated Films of All Time*. WWV, 1982.

Honan, Artie. *How Did a Smart Guy Like Me…: My 21 Years in Sullivanian Therapy and The Fourth Wall Theater Company*. Independently published, 2020.

Honeycutt, Kirk. "Cox, Craven make friends on *Scary Movie*." *The Hollywood Reporter*. March 28, 1996.

Honeycutt, Kirk. "Horrors! Genre alive, but 'sleepy.'" *The Hollywood Reporter*. October 30, 1992.

Howard, Thomas. *Christ the Tiger: A Postscript to Dogma*. Lippincott, 1967.

Huffman, John A. *A Most Amazing Call: One Pastor's Reflections on a Ministry Full of Surprises*. Self-published, 2012.

Huston, John. *An Open Book*. Da Capo, 1980.

Hutson, Thommy. *Never Sleep Again: The Elm Street Legacy: The Making of Wes Craven's A Nightmare on Elm Street*. Permuted, 2016.

Isenberg, Barbara. "Horror Films: Are They Hazardous to Your Health." *Los Angeles Times*. August 24, 1980.

Jacobs, David Henry. "Shock-Waves: *Toxic* Interviews Wes Craven." *Toxic Horror #3*. April 1990.

Janov, Arthur. *The Primal Scream: Primal Therapy, The Cure for Neurosis*. Dell, 1970.

Jensen, Paul. "Teacher Prejudices." *The Clarkson Integrator*. November 1, 1966.

Jones, Alan. "Wes Craven." *Starburst #44*. April 1982.

Jones, Alan. "Craven Images." *Shivers #2*. August 1992.

Jordan, Jennifer. (Interviewee.) *The Rialto Report #9: "The Naughty Victorians."* May 5, 2013. Podcast.

Kantzer, Kenneth. "The Authority of the Bible." *The Word for This Century*. Ed. Merrill Tenney. Oxford UP, 1959.

Keegan, Rebecca Winters. "The Splat Pack." TIME.com. October 30, 2006.

Keller, Julie. "Craven welcomes viewers to his 'nightmare.' *Columbus Dispatch*. March 13, 1992.

Kelly, Delos H. *Deviant Behavior: A Text-Reader in the Sociology of Deviance*. St. Martin's, 1979.

Kelly, Kevin H., ed. *Books That Shaped Successful People*. Fairview, 1995.

Kelly-Saxenmeyer, Anne. "Making a Name: Wes Craven Directs His Debut Thriller." *Back Stage West*, Vol. 12 Issue 34. August 18, 2005.

Kent, Martin. "Director-writer Wes Craven: love-hate affair with horror." *The Hollywood Reporter*. August 13, 1981.

Kilby, Clyde S. "The Aesthetic Poverty of Evangelism." *A Well of Wonder: Essays on C.S. Lewis, J.R.R. Tolkien, and the Inklings*. Ed. Loren Wilkinson and Keith Call. Paraclete, 2016.

Kilby, Clyde S. "The Christians and the Arts." *The Arts and the Christian Imagination: Essays on Art, Literature, and Aesthetics*. Ed. William Dyrness and Keith Call. Paraclete, 2017.

Kilby, Clyde S. "The Decline and Fall of the Christian Imagination." *The Arts and the Christian Imagination: Essays on Art, Literature, and Aesthetics*. Ed. William Dyrness and Keith Call. Paraclete, 2017.

Kilby, Clyde S. "Into the Land of Imagination." *Christianity Today*. 1985.

Kilby, Clyde S. *Minority of One: A Biography of Jonathan Blanchard*. Eerdmans, 1959.

Kilby, Clyde S. "Modern Art's Pursuit of Form." *The Arts and the Christian Imagination: Essays on Art, Literature, and Aesthetics*. Ed. William Dyrness and Keith Call. Paraclete, 2017.

King, Stephen. *Danse Macabre*. Gallery, 2010.

Klady, Leonard. "Scary future for horror pix." *Variety*. April 11, 1994.

Kleyweg, Hedy. "Overseas Film Group acquires w'wide rights to Kent projects." *The Hollywood Reporter*. September 2, 1983.

Knauf, Daniel. "Farewell to Wes." *Dread Central*. September 1, 2015.

Knauf, Daniel. "*Sleepers*." Knauf.TV. Undated, c. 2021.

Kogan, Rick. "Filming Voodoo Leaves Its Spell on Director." *Chicago Tribune*. February 23, 1988.

Kronke, David. "*Five* and *2*—It Adds Up." *Los Angeles Times*. December 7, 1997.

Kroll, Kristine. "Highland View Hospital." ClevelandHistorical.org. Accessed June 7, 2022.

Kruszelnicki, Fabien. "Horror Maestro Wes Craven on *Scream*, Freddy and Bloodying the American Dream." *Hero Magazine* #12. November 14, 2014.

Kutzera, Dale. "Craven's Nightmare." *Imagi-Movies* Vol. 2, No. 1. Fall 1994.

Kutzera, Dale. "Wes Craven's *New Nightmare*." *Cinefantastique* Vol. 24, No. 4. August 1994.

Labunka, Iya. "Pioneer Award Ceremony 2022 Celebrating Wes Craven." October 1, 2022. Hillman Library, University of Pittsburgh. Acceptance Speech.

Lacher, Irene. "… In Their Wildest Dreams." *Los Angeles Times*. October 22, 1994.

Lawson, Terry. "Cravin' a *New Nightmare*." *Dayton Daily News*. October 14, 1994.

Leary, Timothy. "How to Change Behavior." *LSD: The Consciousness-Expanding Drug*. Ed. David Solomon. Putnam, 1964.

LeBaron, Gaye. "A Lawsuit! Now, That's Scary!" *The Santa Rosa Press Democrat*. April 16, 1996.

LaBerge, Stephen. *Lucid Dreaming: The Power of Being Awake in Your Dreams and in Your Life*. Ballantine, 1985.

Lee, Michael J. "Wes Craven." Radiofree.com. August 6, 2005.

Lippy, Tod. "Directing *Scream*: A Talk with Wes Craven." *Scenario* Vol. 3, No. 1. Spring 1997.

Lippy, Tod. "Writing *Scream*: A Talk with Kevin Williamson." *Scenario* Vol. 3, No. 1. Spring 1997.

Lipsett, Joe and Trace Thurman. (Hosts.) "An Interview with Kevin Williamson." *Horror Queers*. January 14, 2022. Podcast.

LoBrutto, Vincent. *The Encyclopedia of American Independent Filmmaking*. Greenwood, 2002.

Lofficier, Jean-Marc and Randy. "Spotlight: Phil DeGuere." *Into the Twilight Zone: The Rod Serling Programme Guide*. iUniverse, 2003.

Lofficier, Randy and Jean-Marc. "Wes Craven: The Early Years." *The Bloody Best of Fangoria*, Vol. 8. 1989.

Longsdorf, Amy. "Wade Davis Stops Hollywood Voodoo on His *Serpent* Book." *The Morning Call*. February 6, 1988.

Longsdorf, Amy. "Wes Craven Realizes a Dream with his *New Nightmare*." *The Morning Call*. October 22, 1994.

Lovece, Frank. "Craven Images." *Newsday*. October 13, 1994.

Lovell, Glenn. "The 'Professor' Who Makes Horror Movies." *The Philadelphia Inquirer*. January 21, 1985.

Lowry, Brian. "NBC seeks young and the rest." *Variety*. March 24, 1993.

Loynd, Ray. "Craven shocking Universal, swinging at Disney Studios." *The Hollywood Reporter*. December 28, 1981.

Lyons, Charles. "Craven a Classic." *Variety*. February 27, 2001.

Lyons, Charles. "Craven, partner board WMA." *Variety*. November 28, 2001.

Lyons, Charles. "Miramax tosses buoy to thriller *Drowning*." *Variety*. October 2, 2000.

Lyons, Charles. "Perfecting *Stranger*." *Variety*. November 13, 2001.

Lyons, Charles and Dana Harris. "*Perfect* Fit for Roberts." *Variety*. September 25, 2000.

MacGuire, James. "Remembering Elliott." *The Fortnightly Review.* 2011.

Mack, Jon. "Dreaming of Community: The Fourth Wall." *Reflections in a Cracked Glass.* 2015.

Maddrey, Joseph. "*Deadly Friend*: An Autopsy." *Deadly Magazine.* September 2015.

Maddrey, Joseph. "The Lost Years of Wes Craven and Sean S. Cunningham." Blumhouse.com. March 2016.

Mailer, Norman. "A Course in Filmmaking." *Maidstone.* Signet, 1971.

Malanowski, Jamie. "Shifting from Blood and Guts to Heart and Brains." *The New York Times.* October 24, 1999.

Mancini, Marc. "Professor Gore." *Film Comment,* Vol. 25, No. 5. September-October 1989.

Marano, Michael. "Sins of the Fathers." *SciFi Magazine.* December 2010.

Marechal, Arlene. (Director). *I Am Nancy.* Some Pig, 2011. Video.

Marechal, Arlene. (Director.) "Wes Craven Extended Interview." *I Am Nancy.* Some Pig, 2011. Video.

Marks, Craig and Ron Tannenbaum. "Freddy Lives: An Oral History of *A Nightmare on Elm Street.*" Vulture.com. Oct. 20, 2014.

Maroney, Padraic. *It All Began with a Scream.* BearManor, 2021.

Martin, Bob. "Wes Craven! Part 3: On the Set of *Swamp Thing.*" *Fangoria* #17. February 1982.

Martin, Perry. (Director.) *Looking Back at The Hills Have Eyes.* Anchor Bay, 2003. DVD.

Martin, R.H. "Craven's Triple Play." *Fangoria* #38. October 1984.

Maslin, Janet. "Freddy Krueger Enters the Real World. Yikes!" *The New York Times.* October 14, 1994.

Matthews, Paul. "Kiyoshi Kurosawa." ReverseShot.com. October 20, 2005.

Maxwell, Richard and Robert Dickman. *The Elements of Persuasion.* HarperCollins, 2009.

McDonagh, Maitland. "New Line's *Nightmare, Part 3* Reunites Craven with Freddy." *The Film Journal.* February 1, 1987.

McIlnay, Philip. *The Bishop, the Hunchback, and the Lunatic: The Autobiography of a Mad-Doctor by an Apostate Son of a Baptist while Western Civilization as We Know It Hangs in the Balance.* CreateSpace, 2013.

McNary, Dave. "Al-Ghanim Entertainment Launching with Wes Craven's *Girl in the Photographs.*" *Variety.* January 23, 2015.

McNeil, Legs and Jennifer Osborne with Peter Pavia. *The Other Hollywood: The Uncensored Oral History of the Porn Industry.* HarperCollins, 2005.

McVicar, Brian. "Inside the Dark Mind of Wes Craven." *Fangoria* #337. November 2014.

Meh. "*Hills Have Eyes 2*: The Team!" Horror-Movies.ca. February 20, 2007.

Mendez, Mike and Dave Parker. (Producers.) *Masters of Horror.* Sci-Fi Channel, 2002. TV.

Merchan, George. "Exclusive Interview: Wes Craven (*The Hills Have Eyes*)." CHUD.com. March 10, 2006.

Meyer, Luke. [Director.] *The Fourth Wall. Part 1: The Revolution of the Self.* SeeThink Films, 2023. Video.

Miller, Dieter. "Wes Craven." *Authors & Artists for Young Adults, Vol. 6.* Gale, 1991.

Miller, Jennifer. *The Day I Went Missing.* St. Martin's, 2001.

Mitchell, Chris. "Shrewd marketing fuels Freddy phenomenon." *Variety.* August 19, 1992.

Mitchell, Sean. "The X Rating Gets Its Day in Court." *Los Angeles Times.* June 21, 1990.

Moca, Diane Joy. "*Nightmare Café* is No Horror." *Minneapolis Star Tribune.* February 28, 1992.

Monk, Katherine. "Wes Craven was horrified by horror crown." Ex-press.com. September 1, 2015.

Montemayor, Robert. "Indochinese Deaths Still Big Mystery." *Los Angeles Times.* September 15, 1981.

Montgomery, Paul L. "*Throat* Obscene, Judge Rules here." *The New York Times.* March 2, 1973.

Mooney, Ted. "A Culture Ends Not with a Bang but with the Gurgle of a Nightmare." *Los Angeles Times.* February 5, 1982.

Moore, Roger. "Fright-king Craven goes astray with *Soul to Take.*" *Chicago Tribune.* October 9, 2010.

Moriarty, Tim. "*Swamp Thing*: Grime Doesn't Pay." *Famous Monsters of Filmland* #183. May 1982.

Mr. Skin. "Marilyn Chambers: The Mr. Skin Interview." Mrskin.com. November 11, 2004.

Mueller, Jim. "The Thought is Just Scary." *Chicago Tribune.* June 8, 1997.

Mullins, Travis. "Exclusive: *Scream 2*'s Jerry O'Connell and Kevin Williamson Talk Leaked Scripts and Different Killers." DreadCentral.com. December 12, 2017.

Murphy, Charlie. *The Making of a Stand-Up Guy.* Simon & Schuster, 2009.

Murray, Rebecca. "Filmmaker Wes Craven Discusses the Film *Paris Je T'Aime.*" About.com. April 23, 2007.

Murray, William. "Playboy Interview: Sam Peckinpah." 1972. *Sam Peckinpah Interviews (Conversations with Filmmakers).* Ed. Kevin J. Hayes. U of Mississippi P, 2008.

Mynhardt, Joe. "Wes Craven." *Horror 201: The Silver Screen, Vol. 1.* Ed. Joe Mynhardt and Emma Audsley. Crystal Lake, 2015.

MW Staff. "Wes Craven Remakes *The Hills Have Eyes* and Goes to Vegas." Movieweb.com. March 10, 2006.

Newman, Kim. "The Kim Newman Archive: *The Hills Have Eyes Part II* (1985)." *The Encyclopedia of Fantastic Film and Television.* http://www.eofftv.com /kim_newman_archive/h/hills_have_eyes_part_2_review.htm

Newton, Steve. "Take Your Seat at the Nightmare Café." *The Bloody Best of Fangoria* #11. July 1992.

Nichols, David B. and Bob Martin. "An Anatomy of Terror." *Fangoria* #10. January 1981.

O'Rawa, Timothy. "An Interview with a (Wes) Craven." *Slaughterhouse* #2. 1989.

Osborne, Robert. "On Location." *The Hollywood Reporter.* January 2, 1981.

Parker, Donna. "Hammer Time for Donners, WB." *The Hollywood Reporter.* July 26, 1993.

Palmer, Randy. "The Screams of Summer." *Fangoria* #168. November 1997.

Parfitt, Orlando. "Craven's Elm Street Nightmare." IGN.com. June 9, 2009.

Parisi, Paula. "Showtime Opens a Drive-In." *The Hollywood Reporter.* May 14, 1993.

Pearce, Jane and Saul Newton. *The Conditions of Human Growth.* Citadel, 1963.

Peitzman, Louis. "How *New Nightmare* Changed the Horror Genre." Buzzfeed.com. October 15, 2014.

Persons, Dan. "*A Vampire in Brooklyn.*" *Cinefantastique* Vol. 27, No. 2. November 1995.

Pond, Steve. "Dateline Hollywood." *The Washington Post.* August 29, 1985.

Portman, Jamie. "The Reality Behind the Reality." *Ottawa Citizen.* February 4, 2000.

Portman, Jamie. "Stormy Shoot for *Scream 4.*" *Calgary Herald.* April 14, 2011.

Power, Tom. (Host.) *The Q Interview.* "Episode #26: Neve Campbell." February 2, 2022. Podcast.

Price, James. "The Andalusian Smile: Reflections on Luis Buñuel." *Evergreen Review*, No. 4o. April 1966.

Prigge, Steven. *Movie Moguls Speak: Interviews with Top Film Producers.* McFarland, 2004.

Prokopy, Steven. "Wes Craven Talks to Capone." Aintitcoolnews.com. March 1, 2009.

Rahman, Abid and Meena Jang. "Wes Craven Dead: Hollywood Reacts." *The Hollywood Reporter*. August 30, 2015.

Rainer, Tristine. *The New Diary: How to use a journal for self guidance and expanded creativity.* Tarcher, 1978.

Reagan, Ronald. "Proclamation 5500: Youth Suicide Prevention Month, 1986." June 10, 1986.

Reesman, Bryan. "Exclusive! Interview with Horror Mastermind Wes Craven." Knac.com. January 1, 2004.

Reesman, Bryan. "Wes Craven Screams Anew." *Moviemaker Magazine*. April 15, 2011.

Rein, David. (Director.) *Fangoria Frightfest Presents: Screamography.* Episode 1. 2006.

Ressner, Jeffrey. "*Serpent*'s Craven unearths new film, TV prod'n entity." *The Hollywood Reporter*. February 5, 1988.

Rice, Nicholas. "*Scream*'s Matthew Lillard Recalls 'Weeping Uncontrollably for an Hour' at Wes Craven's Memorial." People. com. October 12, 2021.

Richmond, Ray. "Wes Craven Presents: *Don't Look Down*." *Variety*. October 28, 1998.

Riley, Jenelle. "David Arquette Talks 25 Years of *Scream*, That Shocking Scene and What's Next." *Variety*. January 20, 2022.

Roberts, Hilary. "*Flowers in the Attic* provides Wes Craven with a change of direction." *People*. July 20, 1986.

Robins, Wayne. "*Last House on the Left*: Stab Your Way to Fortune." *Creem*. June 1974.

Robb, Brian J. "Living with Nightmares." *Fear #4.* February 1989.

Robb, Brian J. *Screams & Nightmares: The Films of Wes Craven.* Titan, 1998.

Robbins, Jim. "The Haitian Lensing of *Serpent* Provided Its Own Scary Moments." *Variety*. February 10, 1988.

Rome, David. "Wes Craven, Horror Film Godfather." *Cinefantastique*, Vol. 32, No. 6. February 2001.

Rome, David. "Wes Craven Presents *Dracula 2000*." *Cinefantastique*, Vol. 32, No. 6. February 2001.

Rose, Charlie. Interview with Wes Craven. *The Charlie Rose Show*. February 17, 1997. TV.

Rosen, Christopher. "Even Wes Craven Walked Out of *Reservoir Dogs* During the Torture Scene." EW.com. April 29, 2017.

Rubin, Ben. "Cobras and Cults: Wes Craven's Unproduced Twilight Adventure." *Oh, The Horror!: A monthly newsletter featuring Horror Collection updates, Romero news, horror events, and more!* January 20, 2022.

Russo, John. *Scare Tactics.* Dell, 1992.

Sabbott. "IGN for Men Interview: Wes Craven." IGN.com. October 28, 2001.

Saint Charles, Martin. (Director.) *Hollywood's Best Film Directors: Wes Craven.* Prime Entertainment Group, 2011. Video.

Sampson, Edward C., Wesley Hiler, Wesley Craven, et al. "Van Dinh lecture reporting scored." *The Potsdam Courier-Freeman.* February 24, 1966.

Scapperotti, Dan. "*Nightmare on Elm Street*." *Cinefantastique*, Vol. 15, No. 3. July 1985.

Schneider, Michael. "Craven pilots new course for UPN." *Variety*. October 23, 2000.

Schoell, William. *The Nightmare Never Ends: The Official History of Freddy Krueger and the Nightmare on Elm Street Films*. Citadel, 1992.

Schumacher, Michael. *Dharma Lion: A Biography of Allen Ginsberg*. U of Minnesota P, 2016.

Sci-Fi Wire. "Even Famous Film Directors Get the Blues (Studio Shuts Down Wes Craven)." SciFi Wire. September 10, 2003.

See, Carolyn. "*Drowning Ruth* is a morbidly attractive story." *The Washington Post*. August 27, 2000.

Seligson, Tom. "Wes Craven, Who's Made Nightmares Come True." *Twilight Zone*, Vol. 1, No. 11. February 1982.

Shahriari, Sia. "Free University of Potsdam: Purpose, Progress and Program." *The Clarkson Integrator*. October 18, 1966.

Shapiro, Marc. "Brothers in Blood." *Fangoria* #149. January 1996.

Shapiro, Marc. "Craven Images." *Fangoria* #109. January 1992.

Shapiro, Marc. "Craven's Latest." *Fangoria* #70. January 1988.

Shapiro, Marc. "I Survived *The Serpent and the Rainbow*." *Fangoria* #71. February 1988.

Shapiro, Marc. "Is Wes Craven Still Scared?" *Gorezone* #11. January 1990.

Shapiro, Marc. "*The People Under the Stairs*." *Fangoria* #107. October 1991.

Shapiro, Marc. "Scream Goodbye?" *Fangoria* #189. January 2000.

Shapiro, Marc. "Shocker." *Fangoria* #87. October 1989.

Shapiro, Marc. "The *Cursed* is Over?" *Fangoria* #241. March 2005.

Shapiro, Marc. "*Vampire in Brooklyn* is No Laughing Matter." *Fangoria* #148. November 1995.

Shapiro, Marc. "Wake Up to a New Nightmare." *Fangoria* #137. October 1994.

Shapiro, Marc. "Wes Craven's Psycho Analysis." *Fangoria* #138. November 1994.

Sharrett, Christopher. "Fairy Tales for the Apocalypse." *Literature / Film Quarterly* Vol. 13, No. 3. July 1985.

Showers, Ryan C. [Host.] "Episode 27 – 25th Anniversary: Marianne Maddalena." *Scream with Ryan C. Showers*. December 14, 2021. Podcast.

Siegel, Alan. "Your favorite Scary movie: The Oral History of *Scream*." The Ringer.com. December 20, 2021.

Siskel, Gene. "*Friday the 13th*: More bad luck." *The Chicago Tribune*. May 9, 1980.

Siskind, Amy B. *The Sullivan Institute/Fourth Wall Community*. Praeger, 2003.

Sjöman, Vilgot. (Director.) *Ingmar Bergman Makes a Movie*. Sveriges Radio, 1963.

Smith, Michele A.H. "The Big Question." *Johns Hopkins Magazine*, Vol. 53, No. 4. September 2001.

Spelling, Ian. "Black and Fright." *Fangoria* #191. April 2000.

Spelling, Ian. "Joining the *Scream* Team." *Fangoria* #190. March 2000.

Spelling, Ian. "Wes Craven Screams Again." *Fangoria* #171. April 1998.

Sragow, Michael. "The Liberation of Wes Craven—at Johns Hopkins." *The Baltimore Sun*. April 13, 2011.

Stack, Tim. "*Scream 4*: What plot twists didn't make it into the final film?" *Entertainment Weekly*. April 17, 2011.

Stack, Tim. "*Scream 4* Writer Kevin Williamson discusses his 'massive fight' with Bob Weinstein." *Entertainment Weekly*. April 7, 2011.

Stein, Ruthe. "Taking a Stab at Drama: *Scream* creator Craven directs Streep in truth-based story of courageous teacher." Sfgate.com. October 24, 1999.

Strachan, Harry. *Reflections on a Half Century: Class of 1963 (Post-Reunion Edition June 2013)*. Self-published, 2014.

Stratford, Jennifer Juniper. "Wes Craven: One Last Scream." *The Front*. November 4, 2015.

Strickler, Jeff. "Horror master transformed: Craven appears as humanities prof." *Minneapolis Star Tribune*. December 22, 1996.

Sutherland, Amy. "Wes Craven." *The Boston Globe*. October 12, 2013.

Swires, Steve. "John Carpenter's *Prince of Darkness*." *Fangoria* #69. December 1987.

Szebin, Fred. "*Serpent and the Rainbow*." *Cinefantastique* Vol. 18, No. 2. March 1988.

Szulkin, David A. "The Hills Were Alive." *Fangoria* #132. May 1994.

Szulkin, David A. "*Last House* Mates." *Fangoria* #200. March 2001.

Szulkin, David A. *Wes Craven's Last House on the Left: The Making of a Cult Classic*. FAB, 2000.

Taylor, Sally. "Interview [with Wes Craven]." Consenses.org. Undated, c. 2014.

Taylor, Tom. *The Big Deal: Hollywood's Million Dollar Spec Script Market*. Harper, 1999.

Teitelbaum, Sheldon. "*Flowers in the Attic*." *Cinefantastique* Vol. 18, No. 1. December 1987.

Teitelbaum, Sheldon. "Jeffrey Bloom on Directing *Flowers in the Attic*." *Cinefantastique* Vol. 18, No. 4. May 1988.

Thomas, Kevin. "Another Craven Film Soaked in Blood." *Los Angeles Times*. November 10, 1984.

Thomas, Kevin. "What's Under the Stairs is Not for Children." *Los Angeles Times*. November 4, 1991.

THR Staff. "Hollywood's 20 Masters of Horror: The Twisted Talents Raising the Most Hell." *The Hollywood Reporter*. October 9, 2013.

THR Staff. "*Scream* Writer Kevin Williamson Pens Tribute to Wes Craven: He Gave Me 'a Master Class in Building Tension.'" *The Hollywood Reporter*. September 2, 2015.

Tobias, Scott. "Interview: Wes Craven." *The A.V. Club*. March 11, 2009.

Tongeren, Phil van and Roel Haanen. "I Will Make the Picture." 2006. *The Flashback Files*. https://www.flashbackfiles.com/roger-corman-interview-2

Topel, Fred. "Robert Englund Talks *Nightmare on Elm Street*, El Rey Marathon, and Wes Craven Legacy." Denofgeek.com. February 11, 2016.

Tripoli, Steve. "*Halloween 2* Slayer Given Death Sentence." *Los Angeles Times*. December 15, 1984.

Turan, Kenneth and Stephen F. Zito. Sinema: *American Pornographic Films and the People Who Make Them*. Praeger, 1974.

Turek, Ryan. "Event: The *Last House on the Left* Q&A." ComingSoon.net. February 19, 2009.

Turman, Lawrence. *So You Want to Be a Producer*. Crown, 2005.

Uslan, Michael. *The Boy Who Loved Batman: A Memoir*. Chronicle, 2011.

Vahanian, Gabriel. *The Death of God: The Culture of Our Post-Christian Era*. George Braziller, 1961.

Variety Staff. "*The Devil in Miss Jones*." *Variety*. February 21, 1973.

Variety Staff. "Marvel characters holding attraction for filmmakers." *Variety*. December 8, 1992.

Vincent, Mal. "Wes Craven Not What You'd Think." *The Virginian-Pilot*. October 30, 1995.

Wagner, Bruce. "On Wes Craven." *Writers on Directors*. Ed. Susan Gray. Watson-Guptill, 1999.

Watson, Ron. "Interview [with Wes Craven] Los Angeles, 2002." Unpublished. Quoted with permission.

Wayne, Phil. "Film Review: *Fireworks Woman*." *The Boston Phoenix*. September 16, 1975.

Weeks, Lewis E. Jr., et al. "To: President Johnson, Senators Javits and Kennedy, Congressman McEwen." *The Clarkson Integrator*. April 11, 1967.

Weinstein, Bob. "Was *Scream* comedy? Horror? The one thing the head of Dimension Films knew is he wanted Craven to direct it." *The Hollywood Reporter*. September 11, 2015.

Welch, Jon. "Two Coffee Houses in Potsdam." *The Clarkson Integrator*. March 14, 1967.

Werts, Diane. "Where Dread is the Blue-Plate Special." *Newsday*. February 27, 1992.

West, Ashley. "Harry Reems and the Ghosts of Memphis." *The Rialto Report*. August 23, 2013. https://www.therialtoreport. com/2013/08/23/harry-reems/

Westerby, Mark. "I Sing the Body Electric." *Fear* #16. April 1990.

Wheaton College. *Bulletin of Wheaton College, Vol. 35, No. 4. Catalog Number 1958-1959*. April 1958.

Wiater, Stanley. (Director.) *Dark Dreamers Vol. 1*. Smash Vision, 2009. DVD.

Wiater, Stanley. *Dark Visions: Conversations with the Masters of the Horror Film*. Avon, 1992.

Wiater, Stanley. "Wade Davis: Explorer of Unseen Worlds." *Rod Serling's The Twilight Zone Magazine* Vol. 8, No. 3. August 1988.

Williams, Tony. "Wes Craven: An Interview." *Journal of Popular Film & Television*. October 1, 1980.

Williamson, Kevin. "Introduction." *Scream: The Screenplay*. Miramax, 1997.

Williamson, Kyle. "*Nightmare on Elm Street* Actor and Artist Panel—JJHC 2019." Fandomspotlite.com. October 13, 2009.

Wilmington, Michael. "Shocks and Yocks." *Los Angeles Times*. July 27, 1986.

Wilmington, Michael. "This *Nightmare* a New High in the Fine Art of Film Horror." *Orlando Sentinel*. October 14, 1994.

Wood, Robin. "Disreputable Genre." 1972. *Robin Wood on the Horror Film: Collected Essays and Reviews*. Ed. Barry Keith Grant. Wayne State UP, 2018.

Wood, Robin. *Hollywood from Vietnam to Reagan... and Beyond*. Columbia UP, 2003.

Wood, Robin. "An Introduction to the Horror Film." 1978. *Robin Wood on the Horror Film: Collected Essays and Reviews*. Ed. Barry Keith Grant. Wayne State UP, 2018.

Wood, Robin. "Return of the Repressed." 1976. *Robin Wood on the Horror Film: Collected Essays and Reviews*. Ed. Barry Keith Grant. Wayne State UP, 2018.

Wooley, John. *Wes Craven: The Man of Your Nightmares*. Wiley, 2011.

Ziehm, Howard. *Take Your Shame and Shove It: My Wild Journey Through the Mysterious Sexual Cosmos*. Self-published, 2015.

Zimmerman, Samuel. "Do You *Scream 4* More?" *Fangoria* #302. April 2011.

Zinoman, Jason. "Killer Instincts." *Vanity Fair*, Vol. 50, Iss. 3. March 2008.

Zinoman, Jason. *Shock Value: How a Few Eccentric Outsiders Gave Us Nightmares, Conquered Hollywood, and Invented Modern Horror*. Penguin, 2011.

APPENDIX I:
Prose and Poetry by Wes Craven

"Watch Those Black Cats!!" [by Wesley Craven]. *The Collinwood Spotlight*. April 13, 1956.*

"Red Feather Worthiness Confirmed by Reporter." *The Collinwood Spotlight*. September 28, 1956.*

"High-Stepping Majorettes Add Color, Sparkle to Grid Games" *The Collinwood Spotlight*. October 12, 1956.*

"Press Club Shocked at WRU." *The Collinwood Spotlight*. October 12, 1956.*

"Seven Top Candidates Compete for Major Offices." *The Collinwood Spotlight*. December 7, 1956.*

"Craven's Ravin's" (I). *The Collinwood Spotlight*. February 15, 1957.*

"Craven's Ravin's" (II). *The Collinwood Spotlight*. March 8, 1957.*

"Craven's Ravin's" (III). *The Collinwood Spotlight*. March 29, 1957.*

"Dramatics Class to Stage Comedy Tonight." *The Collinwood Spotlight*. March 29, 1957.*

"Craven's Ravin's" (IV). *The Collinwood Spotlight*. May 10, 1957.*

"Craven's Ravin's" (V). *The Collinwood Spotlight*. June 7, 1957.*

"Craven's Ravin's" (VI). *The Collinwood Spotlight*. September 27, 1957.*

"Craven's Ravin's" (VII). *The Collinwood Spotlight*. October 11, 1957.*

"Craven's Ravin's" (VIII). *The Collinwood Spotlight*. November 3, 1957.*

"Craven's Ravin's" (IX). *The Collinwood Spotlight*. November 22, 1957.*

"Craven's Ravin's" (X). *The Collinwood Spotlight*. December 13, 1957.*

"Craven's Ravin's" (XI). *The Collinwood Spotlight.* January 17, 1958.*

"Song for a Winter's Night." Unpublished, undated [from a letter to Caroline Craven, written on Wheaton College stationary].

"Skid Row Nocturne" [by W.E. Craven]. *Kodon* Vol. 15, No. 1. Fall 1960.**

"Coffee Break #2" [by W.E. Craven]. Unpublished, undated. [Poet's Corner]

"I saw a herd of deer go by" [by W.E. Craven]. Unpublished, undated. [Poet's Corner]

"In the Garden of Armageddon" [by W.E. Craven]. Unpublished, undated. [Poet's Corner]

"Leaves of Crabgrass" [by W.E. Craven]. Unpublished, undated. [Poet's Corner]

"Metamorphosis" [by W.E. Craven]. Unpublished, undated. [Poet's Corner]

"Nightlight" [by W.E. Craven]. Unpublished, undated. [Poet's Corner]

"A Note on New York" [by W.E. Craven]. Unpublished, undated. [Poet's Corner]

"Stupe Booth Meditations" [by W.E. Craven]. Unpublished, undated. [Poet's Corner]

"Three Poems on Memory All for the Price of One" [by W.E. Craven]. Early draft. Unpublished, undated. [Poet's Corner]

"Written while reading Kerouac, Huxley, And Scruton, listening to Brubeck, Bartok, Ahmad Jamal, and thinking about my indigestion" [by W.E. Craven]. Unpublished, undated. [Poet's Corner]

"Three Poems on Memory… All for the Price of One" [by W.E. Craven]. *Kodon* Vol. 15, No. 3. Spring 1961.**

"Vespers [Soft voiced stars stand lightly]" [by W.E. Craven]. *Kodon* Vol. 15, No. 4. Summer 1961.**

"A Birth" [Anonymous]. *Kodon* Vol. 16, No. 1. Fall 1961.**

"Onward, Christian Soldiers" [by Wesley Earl Craven]. *Kodon* Vol. 16, No. 1. Fall 1961.**

"Vespers [Evening…]" [by Wesley Earl Craven]. *Westways* Vol. 53, No. 11. November 1961.

"The Day Harry Won." *Kodon* Vol. 17, No. 1 [Vol. 16, No. 2]. Winter [1961/62].**

The 1962 Tower [Wes Craven credited as literary editor]. Wheaton College, Spring 1962.**

To the Woman Who Came to My Office and Wept" [by Wesley Earl Craven]. *Kodon* Vol. 17, No. 2. Winter 1962.

"The Weapon." *Kodon* Vol. 16, No. 3. Spring 1962.**

"Three Poems on Memory... All for the Price of One." *Kodon* Vol. 16, No. 3. Spring 1962.**

"The Weapon." *Kodon* Vol. 16, No. 3. Spring 1962.**

"Death Mask: Three-Quarter View." *Kodon* Vol. 16, No. 4. Summer 1962.**

"See and Tell" [by Wesley Earl Craven]. *Kodon* Vol. 16, No. 4. Summer 1962.**

"A Warning from the Editor." *Kodon* Vol. 17, No. 1. Fall 1962.**

"Program Notes" [by Thomas Sparrow]. *Kodon* Vol. 17, No. 1. Fall 1962.**

"*Kodon* Answers Its Self-Styled Critics" [by Wesley Craven]. *The Wheaton Record*. November 29, 1962.**

To the Woman Who Came to My Office and Wept" [by Wesley Earl Craven]. *Kodon* Vol. 17, No. 2. Winter 1962.**

"Craven Renews Pen Career with Letter Urging Reforms" [by Wesley Earl Craven]. *The Wheaton Record*. March 7, 1963.**

"Resurrection Notes." *The Wheaton Record*. April 11, 1963.

Noah's Ark: The Journals of a Madman [by Wesley Earl Craven]. Unpublished. Spring 1964. [Johns Hopkins University thesis]

"The Doctor." Unpublished, undated [c. June 1964]. Note: *The Doctor: a one-act play* by Wes Craven was copyrighted through Library of Congress on June 26, 1990.

"The Life and Times of Sidney Smerdly." [fragments of a novel] Unpublished, c. 1964-1965.

"The Man Who Wrote Upon the Walls." [short story] Unpublished, c. 1964-1965.

"Van Dinh lecture reporting scored" [co-signed by Wesley Craven]. *The Potsdam Courier-Freeman*. February 24, 1966.

"To President Johnson, Senators Javits and Kennedy, Congressman McEwen [co-signed by Wesley Earl Craven]." *The Integrator*. April 11, 1967.

Jefferson Airplane I. [Co-written with Judi Culbertson and Patti Bard] Unpublished, undated [c. 1967 – 1969].

"The Bogg Report." Unpublished, undated [c. 1968].

"Oracle." [letter to the editor, responding to a Frank Zappa article] *LIFE*. July 19, 1968.

"Tattler." [Co-written with Michael Arthur Betts.] *The Horror Show*. Spring 1987.

"MPAA: The Horror in My Life." *Films in Review*. Sept/Oct. 1996.

"Introduction." *Scream: A Screenplay* by Kevin Williamson. Hyperion, 1997.

Fountain Society. Simon & Schuster, 1999.

"The Night I Met Freddy." *CosmoGirl*. October 2004.

"Introduction [to *Containment* by Eric Red]." Scary Tales, September 2005.

"An Apology from Wes Craven." Foreword to *How to Survive a Horror Movie: All the Kills to Dodge the Kills* by Seth Grahame-Smith. Quirk, 2007.

"Introduction." *Hollywood Monster: A Walk Down Elm Street with the Man of Your Dreams* by Robert Englund with Alan Goldsher. Pocket, 2009.

"Wes Craven: 10 Movies That Shook Me Up." *Entertainment Weekly*. October 22, 2009.

"Foreword." *Night of the Living Dead: Behind the Scenes of the Most Terrifying Zombie Movie Ever* by Joe Kane. Citadel, 2010.

"Retirement: Scarier Than Freddy Krueger." *The New York Times*. February 16, 2013.

"Foreword." *Never Sleep Again: The Elm Street Legacy* by Thommy Hutson. Red Rover, 2014.

"The Man Who Vanished." Written for Sally Taylor's *Consenses* Curriculum, c. 2014.

"Wes Craven's The Birds: Part 1." *The Vineyard Gazette*. April 1, 2014.

"Wes Craven's The Birds: Part 2." *The Vineyard Gazette*. May 1, 2014.

"Wes Craven's The Birds: Part 3." *The Vineyard Gazette*. July 1, 2014.

"Wes Craven's The Birds: Part 4." *The Vineyard Gazette*. August 1, 2014.

"Wes Craven's The Birds: Part 5." *The Vineyard Gazette*. September 1, 2014.

Coming of Rage #1. [Co-written with Steve Niles.] Liquid Comics, October 2014.

Coming of Rage #2. [Co-written with Steve Niles.] Liquid Comics, October 2014.

Coming of Rage #3. [Co-written with Steve Niles.] Liquid Comics, October 2014.

"Guest Post by Writer/Director Wes Craven." *Kindle Daily Post*. Amazon.com. October 28, 2014.

"Wes Craven's The Birds: Part 6." *The Vineyard Gazette*. November 1, 2014.

"Wes Craven's The Birds: Part 7." *The Vineyard Gazette*. November 10, 2014.

"Wes Craven Remembers Christopher Lee: 'A Man of Infinite Class and Talent.'" *The Hollywood Reporter*. June 17, 2015.

"Wes Craven's The Birds: Part 8." *The Vineyard Gazette*. June 18, 2015.

Coming of Rage #4. [Co-written with Steve Niles.] Liquid Comics, January 2016.

Coming of Rage #5. [Co-written with Steve Niles.] Liquid Comics, February 2016.

APPENDIX II:
Screenplays Attributed to Wes Craven
(and where to find them)

Last House on the Left (1972 film)
> *Sex Crime of the Century*, First Draft, 1971, 61 pages – Horror Scripts and
> Ephemera Collection, UPitt
> *Night of Vengeance*, Filmscript [shooting script], 1971, 159 pages – Horror
> Scripts and Ephemera Collection, UPitt

The Fireworks Woman (1975 film)
> *The Fireworks Man* [co-credited to Roger Murphy], 1974, 61 pages – Harry
> Ransom Center, UT Austin (Norman Mailer Papers)

Hansel and Gretel (unproduced)
> 1976, 92 pages

The Hills Have Eyes (1977 film)
> *Blood Relations: The Sun Wars*, [July 6] 1976, 89 pages – circulates online
> *Blood Relations: The Sun Wars*, Unknown Draft [c. 1976], 131 pages –
> Margaret Herrick Library, AMPAS (Core Collection)
> *Blood Relations*, Draft #4, 1976, 122 pages – Horror Scripts and Ephemera
> Collection, UPitt
> Unknown Draft, 1976 – Louis B. Mayer Library, AFI

Deep in the Heart (a.k.a. *The Last Battle*, unproduced)
> 2nd draft, 1977, 157 pages – Library of Congress copyright record
> 1st Draft, January 31, 1983, 157 pages

Marimba (unproduced)
> Third Draft, 1980, 131 pages

Swamp Thing (1982 film)
> First Draft, 1980, 113 pages
> Second Draft, 1980, 103 pages
> January 1, 1981 Draft – Charles E. Young Research Library, UCLA
> Third Draft, Undated, 115 pages – Writer's Guild Foundation Shavelson
> Webb Library, WGA / circulates among collectors

Deadly Blessing (1982 film, co-written with Glenn M. Benest and Matthew Barr)
> May 29, 1979 draft, 123 pages [Director's Polish] – Charles E. Young
> Research Library, UCLA / Margaret Herrick Library, AMPAS
> (Core Collection) / circulates among collectors
> November 11, 1980 draft – Charles E. Young Research Library, UCLA
> 1981 draft, 104 pages – Cinematic Arts Library, USC

A Nightmare on Elm Street (1984 film)
>First Draft, Fourth Revision, c. Dec. 1, 1981
>Third Draft, August 27, 1982, 134 pages
>Draft 4, 106 pages, 1984
>Fourth Draft, April 10, 1984 with revisions through May 8, 1984, 106 pages
>>[shooting script] – Charles E. Young Research Library, UCLA /
>>Louis B. Mayer Library, AFI / Horror Scripts and Ephemera
>>Collection, UPitt / Margaret Herrick Library, AMPAS (Core
>>Collection) / circulates among collectors

The Innocents (unproduced, based on an original script by Christopher Mankiewicz)
>First Draft Rewrite Outline of a screenplay by Chris Mankiewicz and Wes
>>Craven, July 7, 1983, 78 pages
>Undated [c. 1983] draft by Wes Craven, Based on an Original Script by
>>Christopher Mankiewicz, 106 pages – Margaret Herrick Library,
>>AMPAS (Unproduced Scripts Collection)

I Was a Teenage Bombshell (unproduced, based on a story by Randy Rovins and Chuck Minskoff)
>First Draft, 1983, 135 pages – Horror Scripts and Ephemera Collection, UPitt

The Hills Have Eyes Part 2 (1984 film)
>*The Hills Have Eyes Part II: The Night of Jupiter*, First Draft, April 11, 1983,
>>103 pages – Horror Scripts and Ephemera Collection, UPitt
>*The Revenge of Jupiter: The Hills Have Eyes Part II*, Draft Two, July 29,
>>1983, 112 pages – Horror Scripts and Ephemera Collection, UPitt /
>>Louis B. Mayer Library, AFI / Margaret Herrick Library, AMPAS
>>(Core Collection)
>*The Reaper: The Hills Have Eyes Part II*, Draft Three, August 31, 1983,
>>102 pages – Charles E. Young Research Library, UCLA / Horror
>>Scripts and Ephemera Collection, UPitt

Twilight Adventure (a.k.a. *The Fallen*, unproduced, co-written with Veda Nayak)
>Revised August 1984, 108 pages – Horror Scripts and Ephemera Collection,
>UPitt / circulates online

Invitation to Hell (1984 TV movie)
>Feb. 15, 1984 draft by Richard Rothstein [uncredited rewrite by Wes Craven]
>– Louis B. Mayer Library, AFI

Flowers in the Attic (unproduced, based on the novel by V.C. Andrews)
>Second Draft, March 28, 1985 draft, 117 pages – circulates online

Roger Corman's Frankenstein (unproduced)
>Second Draft, October 28, 1985, 100 pages – circulates online

A Nightmare on Elm Street III: Dream Warriors (1987 film, co-written with Bruce Wagner)
First Draft, June 16, 1986, 117 pages – Louis B. Mayer Library, AFI /
Writers Guild Foundation Shavelson-Webb Library, WGA /
circulates online
Second Draft, July 7, 1986 – Frances Howard Goldwyn Hollywood Regional
Branch, LAPL
Rev. 9/24/86 thru Oct. 6, 1986, Revised by Chuck Russell and Frank
Darabont, 106 pages – Margaret Herrick Library, AMPAS (Core
Collection) / circulates online
Revised by Chuck Russell and Frank Darabont, December 15, 1986 – Louis
B. Mayer Library, AFI
Unknown Draft, Revised by Chuck Russell and Frank Darabont, 1986 –
Cinematic Arts Library, USC

Serpent and the Rainbow (1988 film)
Revised Draft by Richard Maxwell, Story by Adam Rodman and Richard
Maxwell, from the book by Wade Davis [uncredited director's
polish], 109 pages, February 2, 1987 – William H. Hannon
Library, Loyola Marymount University (Film and Television
Screenplay Collection)

Shocker (1989 film)
Alive Project #1, Fourth Draft, September 28, 1988, 95 pages + 7-page alt.
ending – Writers Guild Foundation Shavelson-Webb Library, WGA
/ circulates online
Shocker: No More Mister Nice Guy, Fifth Draft, November 21, 1988, 98
pages – Louis B. Mayer Library, AFI
Shocker: No More Mister Nice Guy, Unknown Draft, 1988 – Cinematic Arts
Library, USC
Revised 11/21/88 thru 3/28/89, 5th Draft, 103 pages – Margaret Herrick
Library, AMPAS (Core Collection)

Night Visions (1990 TV movie, co-written with Thomas Baum)
Chameleon Blue, First Draft, March 12, 1990, 115 pages – Louis B. Mayer
Library, AFI / circulates online

The People Under the Stairs (1991 film)
December 3, 1990, 114 pages
Universal Project #2, Second Draft, February 4, 1991, 101 pages – Charles
E. Young Research Library, UCLA / Writers Guild Foundation
Shavelson-Webb Library, WGA / circulates online
Revised 2/25/91 thru 4/22/91, 1991, 101 pages – California Institute of the
Arts Library

Shades of Gray (unproduced, co-written with Thomas Baum)
Third Draft, May 31, 1994, 117 pages

Laurel Canyon (unproduced TV pilot, story by Wes Craven and Ellen Herman, teleplay by Ellen Herman)
> 2/17/1993, 62 pages – Horror Scripts and Ephemera Collection, UPitt / Writers Guild Foundation Shavelson-Webb Library, WGA

Wes Craven's New Nightmare (1993 film)
> *A Nightmare on Elm Street 7*, First Draft, July 9, 1993
> *A Nightmare on Elm Street 7: Freddy Unbound*, Third Draft, October 1, 1993, 100 pages – Writers Guild Foundation Shavelson-Webb Library, WGA / circulates online
> *A Nightmare on Elm Street 7: The Ascension*, Third Draft, October 1, 1993 revised through January 5, 1994, 100 pages – Margaret Herrick Library, AMPAS (Core Collection)
> *Wes Craven's New Nightmare*, Unknown Draft, 1993 – Louis B. Mayer Library, AFI

Vampire in Brooklyn (1995 film)
> Director's Polish, August 1, 1994 – Louis B. Mayer Library, AFI
> Shooting Script, October 3, 1994 revised through October 13, 1994 by Wes Craven, Michael Lucker, Charles Murphy and Christopher Parker, 117 pages – Margaret Herrick Library, AMPAS (Core Collection)

Pulse (unproduced pilot script)
> Undated [c. 2001-2002], Story by Wes Craven, Mark Kruger & Julie Plec, Written by Mark Kruger, 60 pages

Pulse (2006 film based on the Japanese film *Kairo* by Kiyoshi Kurosawa)
> Revised Draft, January 5, 2005, Revisions by Ray Wright, 113 pages – Shavelson-Webb Library, WGA / circulates online
> Revised Draft, February 3, 2005, Revisions by Ray Wright, 117 pages – Louis B. Mayer Library, AFI
> Revised Draft, February 23, 2005, Revisions by Ray Wright and Stephen Susco, 112 pages – circulates online
> Revised Draft, June 13, 2005, 103 pages – Margaret Herrick Library, AMPAS (Core Collection)

The Hills Have Eyes II (2007 film, co-written with Jonathan Craven)
> Working 1st draft, May 29, 2006 revised thru June 13, 2006, 104 pages – Margaret Herrick Library, AMPAS (Core Collection)
> June 16, 2006 draft, 97 pages – circulates online

My Soul to Take (2010 film)
> *25/8*, March 4, 2008 revised thru December 22, 2008 + reshoot pages dated July 27, 2009, 140 pages – Margaret Herrick Library, AMPAS (CoreCollection)
> *25-8 (Working Title: Bug)*, Undated, 112 pages – circulates online

APPENDIX III:
Wes Craven's Favorites

As told to *Entertainment Weekly* around Halloween 2009:
Nosferatu (1922), dir. F.W. Murnau
Frankenstein (1931), dir. James Whale
Beauty and the Beast (1946), dir. Jean Cocteau
The War of the Worlds (1953), dir. Byron Haskin
The Bad Seed (1956), dir. Mervyn LeRoy
Psycho (1960), dir. Alfred Hitchcock
The Virgin Spring (1960), dir. Ingmar Bergman
Repulsion (1965), dir. Roman Polanski
Blow-Up (1966), dir. Michelangelo Antonioni
Don't Look Now (1973), dir. Nicolas Roeg

As told to *The Morning Call* (Allentown, PA) around Halloween 1989:
Repulsion (1965), dir. Roman Polanski
The Exorcist (1973), dir. William Friedkin
The Texas Chainsaw Massacre (1974), dir. Tobe Hooper
Rabid (1977), dir. David Cronenberg
The Brood (1979), dir. David Cronenberg
Big Top Pee Wee (1988), dir. Randal Kleiser

As told to *The Hollywood Reporter* in January 1981:
Psycho (1960), dir. Alfred Hitchcock
Repulsion (1965), dir. Roman Polanski
The Texas Chainsaw Massacre (1974), dir. Tobe Hooper
Eraserhead (1977), dir. David Lynch

In 1992, Wes also named his favorite films for *Sight & Sound* magazine:
Beauty and the Beast (1946), dir. Jean Cocteau
Red River (1948), dir. Howard Hawks
The Treasure of Sierra Madre (1948), dir. John Huston
Forbidden Games (1952), dir. René Clément
Psycho (1960), dir. Alfred Hitchcock
Dr. Strangelove (1964), dir. Stanley Kubrick
Repulsion (1965), dir. Roman Polanski
El Topo (1970), dir. Alejandro Jodorowsky
Network (1976), dir. Sidney Lumet
The Tenant (1976), dir. Roman Polanski

In a 2007 essay for *Variety*, he named three films that meant a lot to him:
Red River (1948), dir. Howard Hawks
Amarcord (1973), dir. Federico Fellini
Being John Malkovich (1999), dir. Spike Jonze

Most Influential Books and Authors

As told to Kevin Kelly, author of *Books That Shaped Successful People*, in 1991:
The Stranger by Albert Camus
Don Quixote by Miguel de Cervantes
Invisible Man by Ralph Ellison
Civilization and Its Discontents by Sigmund Freud
Catch-22 by Joseph Heller
Dubliners by James Joyce
The Castle by Franz Kafka
The Battle for the Mind: A Physiology of Conversion and Brainwashing by William Sargent
The Magic Christian by Terry Southern
Candide by Voltaire

In a 2007 essay for *Variety*, he named three books that meant a lot to him:
Crime and Punishment by Dostoevsky, *Ornithology* by Frank B. Gill, and *Candide* by Voltaire

In an interview with Joe Mynhardt published in 2015, he also named the following books and authors as inspirations: Samuel Beckett, Bertolt Brecht, Roald Dahl's *Kiss Kiss*, Charles Dickens, Fyodor Dostoevsky, Ernest Hemingway, Jack Kerouac, Ken Kesey, Stephen King, Norman Mailer, Thomas Mann, Edgar Allan Poe, and Terry Southern.

Favorite Music

In a private letter to an old friend, written in the summer of 1985, Wes summed up his eclectic taste in music by naming a few favorites: Mozart, Laurie Johnson, The Bobs, John Coltrane, and Donald Fagan (of Steely Dan).

In 1991, he made the following mix tape paying tribute to his recently departed dog (Punch):
Keith Jarrett – "Köln, January 25, 1975, Pt. 1"
Cannonball Adderley – "Mercy, Mercy, Mercy"
Chick Corea, Gary Burton – "Brasilia"
Herbie Hancock – "The Peacocks"
Bob Kindler – "Grace"
Ennio Morricone – "Romanza quartiere"

Stan Getz – "Her"
Johann Sebastian Bach, Andrés Segovia – "Violin Partita No. 2 in D Minor"
Samuel Barber, Leonard Slatkin, St. Louis Symphony – "Adagio for Strings"
Linda Rondstadt, Aaron Neville – "Goodbye, My Friend"

In a 2007 essay for *Variety*, he named three songs that meant a lot to him:
James Brown – "I'll Go Crazy"
The Dixie Chicks – "Not Ready to Make Nice"
Billie Holiday – "Strange Fruit"

In a 2011 interview on BET.com, he named Miles Davis's *Kind of Blue* as a favorite album.

Joe's 2023 Mix Tape for Wes:
Béla Bartók, Andrew Rangell – "Romanian Folk Dances, Sz 56: III. Pe-Loc (Andante)"
Les Paul, Mary Ford – "St. Louis Blues"
Dave Brubeck – "Unsquare Dance"
The Cascades – "Rhythm of the Rain"
The Kingston Trio – "The Wanderer"
Joan Baez – "House of the Rising Sun"
Wes Montgomery Trio – "'Round Midnight"
John Cage – "Dream"
Procol Harum – "Quite Rightly So"
Blood, Sweat & Tears – "Spinning Wheel"
Jefferson Airplane – "White Rabbit"
The Mothers of Invention – "Who Are the Brain Police?"
Simon & Garfunkel – "Old Friends / Bookends"
The Beatles – "I Am the Walrus"
The Doors – "Horse Latitudes"
Little Anthony & The Imperials – "Goin' Out of My Head"
Harry Chapin – "Taxi"
Leon Russell – "Tight Rope"
Miles Davis – "Flamenco Sketches"
Grateful Dead – "Truckin'"

About Joseph Maddrey

Joseph Maddrey is the author of more than a dozen books, including *Nightmares in Red, White and Blue: The Evolution of the American Horror Film* (2004); *Not Bad for a Human*, the official biography of film actor Lance Henriksen (2011); *Simply Eliot*, a biography of poet T.S. Eliot (2018); two volumes of *Adapting Stephen King* (2021-2022), and the graphic novel *To Hell You Ride* (2013). He has written or produced over 100 hours of documentary television, including episodes of Discovery Channel's *A Haunting*, History Channel's *Ancient Aliens*, Oxygen's *Snapped*, and TVOne's *Payback*.

If you enjoyed this book,
consider other titles from

HARKER PRESS
PUBLISHER OF SCARY GOOD BOOKS

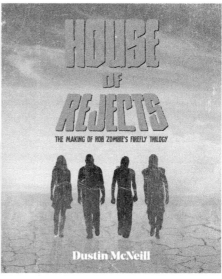

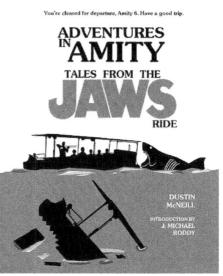

Printed in Great Britain
by Amazon